# HISTORY

OF THE

# FORMATION OF THE CONSTITUTION

OF THE

# UNITED STATES OF AMERICA.

BY
GEORGE BANCROFT.

NEW YORK:
D. APPLETON AND COMPANY.

Copyright, 1882, 1884,
By GEORGE BANCROFT,

# CONTENTS.

## THE FORMATION OF THE AMERICAN CONSTITUTION.

### IN FIVE BOOKS.

#### I.—THE CONFEDERATION.

#### CHAPTER I.

##### A RETROSPECT. MOVEMENTS TOWARD UNION.
##### 1643–1781.

|  | PAGE |
|---|---|
| Progress of the world by mastery over the forces of nature | 5 |
| By a better knowledge of the nature of justice | 6 |
| The laws of morals may be proved by inductions from experience | 7 |
| First American union. Concert of the colonies in action, 1684 | 7 |
| Consolidation of colonies attempted by an absolute king | 7 |
| Effect of the revolution of 1688. Plan of union of William Penn | 8 |
| Of Lord Stairs. Of Franklin in 1754. Of Lord Halifax | 8 |
| Plan of unity through the British parliament. First American congress | 9 |
| The elder Pitt and colonial liberty | 9 |
| The American congress of 1774 | 10 |
| Independence and a continental convention and charter | 10 |
| Question at issue between Great Britain and the colonies | 10 |
| The confederation imperfect from jealousy of central power | 10 |
| Rutledge proposes a constituent congress | 11 |
| New England convention at Boston | 11 |
| Measures of New York of September 1780 | 11 |
| Effort of Hamilton. Thomas Paine and a continental convention | 12 |
| Greene's opinion | 12 |
| Convention of New York and New England at Hartford | 13 |
| Reception of its proceedings in congress | 13 |
| New Jersey and the federal republic | 14 |
| Cession of western lands by New York and Virginia | 14 |
| The confederation adopted | 15 |
| Washington appeals to the statesmen of Virginia | 16 |
| His emphatic letter for a stronger government | 18 |
| His instructions to Custis and to Jones | 18 |

## CONTENTS.

|  | PAGE |
|---|---|
| Madison's report of March 1781 | 19 |
| Madison receives a copy of Washington's letter | 20 |
| Reports of Luzerne. Pamphlet by William Barton | 20 |
| Report of the grand committee of congress | 21 |
| Appeals of Hamilton through the press | 21 |
| The committee of three on the confederation and their report | 22 |
| Coercion impossible. Washington desires a new constitution | 23 |

## CHAPTER II.

### THE STRUGGLE FOR REVENUE.

### 1781–1782.

|  |  |
|---|---|
| Schuyler proposes the union of New England and New York | 24 |
| Congress establishes departments. The minister of war. Of finance | 25 |
| Hamilton on a national debt and a national bank | 25 |
| Robert Morris and a national bank | 26 |
| Congress and a national bank | 27 |
| New Jersey demands for congress the power to regulate commerce | 27 |
| Congress asks power to levy an impost. Protection of American industries | 27 |
| The answers of the states | 27 |
| How Morris started the bank | 28 |
| Hamilton on regulating trade | 29 |
| A receiver of the United States revenue | 30 |
| Schuyler in the New York legislature | 30 |
| New York sanctions a federal convention | 31 |
| Hamilton elected to congress. Morris entreats a loan from France | 31 |
| Embarkation of the French troops | 31 |
| What befell their officers | 32 |
| Pennsylvania and the public debt. Rhode Island refuses the impost | 33 |
| Hamilton's reply to Rhode Island. Richard Henry Lee divides Virginia | 34 |
| Congress by its judicial powers reconciles states | 35 |

## CHAPTER III.

### AMERICA AND GREAT BRITAIN.

### 1782–1783.

|  |  |
|---|---|
| Peace between America and Great Britain | 36 |
| Moderation of Vergennes and Shelburne | 37 |
| Cessation of hostilities | 37 |
| The king of England invites a cordial understanding with France | 38 |
| Commercial relations between America and England | 38 |
| Fox refuses an invitation to join the ministry | 38 |
| Coalition of Lord North and Fox | 39 |
| Debate in the peers. Shelburne's defence | 40 |
| The ministry tottering. Pitt retires with dignity | 41 |
| Shelburne's modification of the navigation act | 42 |
| Liberal opinion of Burke | 43 |

## CONTENTS.

|  | PAGE |
|---|---|
| Ministry of Fox and the duke of Portland. The king against the ministry | 44 |
| Fox and the navigation act | 45 |
| The unfair offers of Fox to America. Jay and the slave-trade | 46 |
| The American commissioners offer mutual unconditional free trade | 47 |
| Debate in the house of lords | 47 |
| England excludes American shipping from the British West Indies | 48 |
| Renounces the right to purchase American-built ships | 48 |
| Creates a national spirit in America | 49 |
| Believes American union impossible | 50 |
| Lord Sheffield on American commerce | 50 |
| The king sure that America could establish no stable government | 51 |
| Regret that the treaty of peace had been made with the collective states | 51 |
| The fur-traders induce Lord North to retain the interior American posts. Pitt | 52 |
| Fox and reform. The new colonial system of Great Britain | 53 |

### CHAPTER IV.

#### AMERICA AND CONTINENTAL EUROPE.

#### 1783.

| Sweden. Prussia | 54 |
|---|---|
| Joseph II. and Belgium | 55 |
| Denmark. The free city of Hamburg. Portugal. Russia | 56 |
| Holland. Spain | 57 |
| France | 58 |

### CHAPTER V.

#### A CALL ON THE ARMY TO INTERPOSE.

#### January–March 1783.

| The army at Newburg. Its appeal to congress | 59 |
|---|---|
| Financial scheme of Morris and the grand committee of congress | 60 |
| Interview of the grand committee with the deputies of the army | 61 |
| Disinterested conduct of Hamilton | 61 |
| Plan of Morris to coerce congress into bolder measures | 61 |
| The debt to the army and half pay | 62 |
| Debate on revenue | 63 |
| Madison speaks | 64 |
| Methods of general revenue | 65 |
| Pamphlet of Pelatiah Webster | 66 |
| The army to force the grant of new powers to the government | 66 |
| Hamilton to Washington. Gouverneur Morris to Greene | 67 |
| Opinions of Knox and Washington | 67 |
| The news of peace | 68 |
| Rutledge proposes a preference of military creditors | 68 |
| Mercer and Arthur Lee combat Madison | 69 |
| Robert Morris publishes his letter of resignation | 69 |

## CONTENTS.

### CHAPTER VI.

#### THE AMERICAN ARMY AND ITS CHIEF.
#### March 1783.

|  | PAGE |
|---|---|
| Washington's meditations. His appeal to the governor of Virginia | 70 |
| Conduct of Gates. His plan of action. Armstrong's anonymous address | 71 |
| Washington's reply in general orders | 72 |
| Meeting of officers of the army. Washington's address to them | 73 |
| Their resolutions | 74 |
| Result of the meeting. What congress did for the army. News of peace | 75 |
| Washington's zeal for establishing a permanent union | 76 |
| Proclamation of congress | 77 |

### CHAPTER VII.

#### DISBANDING THE ARMY.
#### March–July 1783.

| The rightful claims of the army | 78 |
|---|---|
| Madison proposes a plan for revenue | 79 |
| Debt and resources of the United States. Slaves rated as five to three | 79 |
| Hamilton wishes to propose a federal convention | 79 |
| The financial report adopted. The appeal of congress to the states | 80 |
| Committee on the New York resolutions in favor of a general convention | 80 |
| Rufus Putnam plans colonizing Ohio | 81 |
| Timothy Pickering advises the exclusion of slavery | 81 |
| The ordinance of Bland | 81 |
| Discharging the army. Society of the Cincinnati | 82 |
| How the army was disbanded and how it was paid | 82 |
| Washington's legacy to the people | 83 |
| The opportunity of the citizens of America | 84 |
| The necessity of a supreme power | 85 |
| The choice between union or anarchy followed by arbitrary power | 85 |
| Washington wished reform through a convention of the people | 86 |

### II.—ON THE WAY TO A FEDERAL CONVENTION. 1783-1787.

### CHAPTER I.

#### HOW THE LAND RECEIVED THE LEGACY OF WASHINGTON.
#### June–December 1783.

| The universal love of union. Inter-citizenship | 89 |
|---|---|
| How Washington's legacy was received in Connecticut | 90 |
| In Delaware. In Pennsylvania | 91 |
| In South Carolina | 92 |

## CONTENTS.

|   | PAGE |
|---|---|
| In New York. In Massachusetts | 93 |
| In Virginia | 95 |
| In Maryland. In congress. Riot in Philadelphia | 97 |
| Congress adjourns to Princeton | 97 |
| Rivalry for the site of the federal government | 97 |
| Coalition in favor of its present site | 98 |
| Hamilton on the defects of the confederation | 99 |
| Ellsworth on national existence | 99 |
| Forebodings of Hamilton. He retires from congress | 100 |
| Connecticut delays its adhesion to a federal convention | 100 |
| Forced emigration of royalists | 101 |
| Washington examines the inland water communications of New York | 101 |
| Haldimand refuses to surrender the interior posts | 102 |
| Congress votes Washington a statue. It receives him publicly | 102 |
| Follows his counsels on the army and navy | 103 |
| On interior trade. On the state of Ohio | 103 |
| On doing honor to Kosciuszko | 104 |
| An envoy from the Dutch republic | 104 |
| Madison forced to retire by the rule of rotation | 105 |
| Washington calls on his old soldiers to promote union | 105 |
| The city of New York restored | 106 |
| The officers of the army bid farewell to Washington | 106 |
| His journey through New Jersey. Through Philadelphia | 107 |
| He resigns his commission | 108 |
| He returns to Mount Vernon | 109 |

## CHAPTER II.

### VIRGINIA STATESMEN LEAD TOWARD A BETTER UNION.

### 1784.

|   |   |
|---|---|
| Four motives to union | 110 |
| Congress declines to lead the way. England compels union | 111 |
| The views of Virginia | 111 |
| Jefferson describes the United States as one nation | 112 |
| Congress vote them to be one nation | 113 |
| Jefferson's plan for international commerce. Accepted by congress | 113 |
| Jefferson and Washington on commerce with the West | 114 |
| Honors decreed to Washington by Virginia | 114 |
| Washington pleads with Virginia statesmen for a national constitution | 115 |
| The great West to form an empire of republics | 115 |
| Jefferson's ordinance | 116 |
| Against slavery in the West. How it was lost | 117 |
| Jefferson's life-long opinion on slavery | 118 |
| His ordinance for disposing of the public lands | 118 |
| The mint and American coinage. The cost of the war | 119 |
| Holland and John Adams. Generosity of France. Jefferson's financial plan | 120 |
| Patrick Henry disposed to increase the power of congress | 121 |

## CONTENTS.

|  | PAGE |
|---|---|
| National measures of Virginia | 121 |
| Jefferson enforces union | 122 |
| The committee of states. Retirement of Robert Morris | 123 |
| Lee and Madison on a federal convention | 124 |
| France sees the tendency of the confederation to dissolution | 124 |

## CHAPTER III.

### THE WEST.

### 1784–1785.

|  |  |
|---|---|
| Washington's tour to the West | 125 |
| His scheme of internal navigation. His report to Governor Harrison | 126 |
| Lafayette in the United States | 127 |
| Washington negotiates between Virginia and Maryland. He refuses gifts | 128 |
| Virginia appoints commissioners to treat with Maryland | 129 |
| The fifth congress and Richard Henry Lee as its president | 129 |
| Samuel Adams for a firm government | 130 |
| The politics of New York corrupted by its custom-house | 130 |
| Washington's western policy | 130 |
| He brings it before congress. William Grayson | 131 |
| Pickering against slavery in the West | 132 |
| King revives Jefferson's antislavery clause | 132 |
| The proposal committed. King's report | 133 |
| Grayson favors the prohibition of slavery | 134 |
| His ordinance for the disposal of western lands | 134 |
| Can congress levy armed men? | 135 |

## CHAPTER IV.

### THE REGULATION OF COMMERCE. THE FIFTH CONGRESS.

### 1784–1785.

|  |  |
|---|---|
| Proposed reform of the confederacy by less than a unanimous vote | 136 |
| Tract by Noah Webster | 136 |
| Excessive importations of British goods. The consequent distress | 137 |
| Remedies proposed in New York | 138 |
| Pennsylvania proposes a protective system | 138 |
| Movements in Boston noted by Grayson | 139 |
| Boston demands more powers for congress and a protective tariff | 139 |
| Bowdoin recommends a federal convention | 140 |
| Instructions to the Massachusetts delegates | 140 |
| Movements in New Hampshire and Rhode Island. In Pennsylvania | 141 |
| John Adams applauds a navigation act. James Monroe | 141 |
| His compromise proposal for a revenue. His report | 142 |
| His procrastination | 143 |
| Is puzzled by Adam Smith on the Wealth of Nations | 144 |
| The extreme South afraid of a navigation act | 144 |

## CONTENTS.

|  | PAGE |
|---|---|
| The objections of Richard Henry Lee | 144 |
| Monroe wishes his measure delayed. Congress regrets Madison | 145 |
| The Massachusetts delegates disobey their instructions | 146 |
| Their reasons. Bowdoin's reply | 146 |
| The effect | 147 |
| The American commissioners for treaties meet with a rebuff from England | 147 |
| John Adams and King George | 148 |
| England will not treat except on the condition of a preference | 148 |
| Adams proposes retaliation. Interview of Adams with Pitt | 149 |
| The United States agree with France for a perfect reciprocity | 152 |
| France reduces the duty on American fish-oil. Treaty with Prussia | 152 |
| Spain reserved. Noble spirit of South Carolina. Treaty with Morocco | 153 |
| A new constitution cannot spring from congress | 153 |

## CHAPTER V.

### OBSTACLES TO UNION REMOVED OR QUIETED.

#### 1783–1787.

| | |
|---|---|
| State of religion in the colonies | 154 |
| Virginia disestablishes the church | 155 |
| Hawley and the inquisition into faith by the temporal power | 155 |
| Decline of the Anglican church in Virginia | 156 |
| Does religion need compulsory support? Opinions of the Presbyterians | 156 |
| Of the Baptists. Patrick Henry proposes a legal support for Christianity | 156 |
| Madison opposes. Opinion of Washington | 157 |
| Of the Baptists. Of the convention of the Presbyterian church | 158 |
| Jefferson's bill for religious freedom adopted. Other states follow | 158 |
| The statute in French and Italian | 159 |
| The Protestant Episcopal church of the United States | 159 |
| The Methodists. Their missionaries in America | 160 |
| Their superintendents. Their liturgy | 161 |
| Their first general conference | 162 |
| The superintendent defined to be a bishop. The Methodists and slavery | 163 |
| Rapid increase of the Methodists. Roman Catholics in the United States | 164 |
| Adjustment of claims to land by Massachusetts, Connecticut, New York | 165 |
| By South Carolina, Virginia. Enlargement of Pennsylvania | 165 |
| New York yields to temptation. Slavery and freedom never reconciled | 166 |

## CHAPTER VI.

### STATE LAWS IMPAIRING THE OBLIGATION OF CONTRACTS PROVE THE NEED OF AN OVERRULING UNION.

#### Before May 1787.

| | |
|---|---|
| Paper money in the American states | 167 |
| Laws of Connecticut. Of Massachusetts | 168 |
| Of New Hampshire. Rhode Island | 169 |

# CONTENTS.

|  | PAGE |
|---|---|
| The court and the legislature of Rhode Island in conflict | 169 |
| The laws of New York. Of New Jersey | 170 |
| Of Pennsylvania | 171 |
| Of Delaware. Of Maryland. Of Georgia. Of South Carolina | 172 |
| Of North Carolina. Of Virginia | 173 |
| Inflexibility of Washington | 174 |
| Public opinion on paper money | 175 |
| Opinions of Madison and Roger Sherman | 176 |

## CHAPTER VII.
### CONGRESS CONFESSES ITS HELPLESSNESS.
### 1783–1786.

|  | |
|---|---|
| Washington in private life. The visit of Houdon | 177 |
| Invitations to France by its king and queen | 177 |
| Situation and value of Mount Vernon. The house and grounds | 178 |
| The lands, negroes, and produce | 178 |
| Washington embarrassed for income. A gradual abolitionist | 179 |
| His love of hunting. He arranges his papers | 180 |
| His perfect amiability. His exemplary life | 180 |
| His religion. His hatred of war | 181 |
| His sympathy for the Irish and the Greeks | 182 |
| His enthusiasm at the beginning of the French revolution | 182 |
| He enjoins moderation on Lafayette. In politics an impartial American | 182 |
| The commissioners of Maryland and Virginia meet at Mount Vernon | 182 |
| The results. States divided on granting power over trade to congress | 183 |
| Opinion of Madison | 183 |
| Of Washington. Hesitation of Virginia | 184 |
| Maryland suggests a politico-commercial commission | 184 |
| The wisdom of Madison. Calling a convention at Annapolis | 185 |
| The sixth congress | 185 |
| More strength to the confederacy, or an end to the union | 186 |
| Plan for a federal convention | 187 |
| Strife between New Jersey and New York. Congress interposes | 187 |
| New Jersey leads the way to a general convention | 188 |
| What was written by Monroe | 188 |
| By Grayson. The views of South Carolina | 189 |
| Monroe opposes a general convention | 189 |
| Grayson's proposal. Proposal of Charles Pinckney | 190 |
| His committee offer seven new articles of confederation | 191 |
| Congress rests its hopes on the system of April 1783 | 192 |
| Discussions in New York city | 192 |
| New York retains the collecting of the revenue | 193 |
| Pennsylvania recedes from the revenue plan of congress | 193 |
| Does not heed a delegation from congress | 193 |
| Congress expostulates with the governor of New York | 193 |
| Clinton will not yield. Congress fails | 193 |
| Why it could not but fail | 194 |

# CONTENTS.

## CHAPTER VIII.

### VIRGINIA INVITES DEPUTIES OF THE SEVERAL LEGISLATURES OF THE STATES TO MEET IN CONVENTION.

### September 1786 to May 1787.

|  | PAGE |
|---|---|
| The convention at Annapolis | 195 |
| Only five states appear. Their extreme caution in their report | 196 |
| They fix the time and place of a federal convention | 196 |
| King prevents the recommendation of the measure by congress | 196 |
| Clinton condemns the commissioners from New York | 196 |
| King before the legislature of Massachusetts | 196 |
| Followed by Nathan Dane | 197 |
| Massachusetts declines the suggestions from Annapolis | 197 |
| Madison and Virginia. The assembly unanimous. Its declaratory preamble | 197 |
| Virginia selects its delegates. Decision of New Jersey | 198 |
| Of Pennsylvania. North Carolina and Delaware | 199 |
| The conciliatory movement of King in congress. It succeeds | 199 |
| The decision of New York. The insurrection in Massachusetts | 200 |
| Its legislature accepts the invitation from Annapolis | 201 |
| So do South Carolina and Georgia. Connecticut. New Hampshire | 201 |
| Expectation of the British ministry | 202 |
| Madison prepares a complete plan of a constitution. Jefferson's advice | 202 |
| Conciliates Randolph, governor of Virginia | 202 |
| Principles that governed Madison | 202 |
| The preparation of Washington for the convention | 203 |

## III.—THE FEDERAL CONVENTION.

## CHAPTER I.

### THE CONSTITUTION IN OUTLINE.

### 14 May to 13 June 1787.

| | |
|---|---|
| Events overruled by justice. General desire for a closer union | 207 |
| Character of the elections to the federal convention | 207 |
| Journey to Philadelphia | 207 |
| Arrival of Washington. Opening of the federal convention | 208 |
| The Virginia members prepare a finished plan | 208 |
| Washington declares for a new constitution | 208 |
| Position of Edmund Randolph | 208 |
| His station and character | 209 |
| Virginia unites under the lead of Madison | 209 |
| Shall the convention vote by states? Arrival of delegates | 210 |
| Their jarring opinions. Washington's appeal to them | 210 |
| The convention organized | 211 |

## CONTENTS.

|  | PAGE |
|---|---|
| Limited power of the delegates from Delaware | 211 |
| Position of Rhode Island. Character of the delegates | 211 |
| Votes of individuals not to be recorded. Randolph opens the convention | 212 |
| He proposes an outline of a constitution | 212 |
| Proposal of Virginia to found representation on free inhabitants | 214 |
| Charles Pinckney presents a plan. Debates in committee | 215 |
| Butler supports the Virginia plan. Government must act on individuals | 215 |
| Sherman not yet ready | 215 |
| Debate on equality of suffrage. Delaware interposes | 216 |
| The legislature to be of two branches | 216 |
| One branch to be directly chosen by the people | 216 |
| Extent of the federal legislative powers | 217 |
| The right to negative any state law denied. Coercion of states | 218 |
| The national executive. The mode of its election and its powers | 219 |
| Shall it be of one or more? Sherman for its subordination to the legislature | 219 |
| Shall there be unity in the executive? Shall it be chosen by the people? | 220 |
| Its period of service | 220 |
| How to be chosen. How to be removed | 221 |
| Speech of Dickinson for a vote by states in one branch of the legislature | 221 |
| Randolph proposes an executive of three members | 222 |
| Opinions on an executive council. The executive to be single | 222 |
| The veto power | 222 |
| The judiciary | 223 |
| Appointment of judges | 224 |
| Shall the house of representatives be chosen by the states? | 224 |
| Or by the people? | 224 |
| How both branches are to be chosen. Hamilton's opinion | 225 |
| How to choose the senate | 226 |
| Are the states in danger? The equality of the small states defended | 227 |
| Franklin interposes as a peacemaker | 227 |
| Connecticut the umpire between the small states and the large ones | 228 |
| The large states prevail | 228 |
| The requirement of an oath | 229 |
| Term of office and qualifications of representatives | 229 |
| Of senators. The work of the committee ended | 230 |

## CHAPTER II.

### NEW JERSEY CLAIMS AN EQUAL REPRESENTATION OF THE STATES.

#### From the Fifteenth to the Nineteenth of June 1787.

|  |  |
|---|---|
| The small states dissatisfied. The plan of Connecticut | 231 |
| New Jersey resists the large states | 232 |
| The plan of New Jersey | 233 |
| Debate on the extent of the powers of the convention | 233 |
| Paterson pleads for the equality of the states in one supreme council | 234 |
| Debate on the sovereignty of a single body | 234 |
| Speech and plan of Hamilton | 235 |

## CONTENTS. xiii

|  | PAGE |
|---|---|
| How his plan was received | 237 |
| The Virginia plan reported to the house | 238 |

## CHAPTER III.

### THE CONNECTICUT COMPROMISE.

### From the Nineteenth of June to the Second of July 1787.

| | |
|---|---|
| The states and the nation. Independence declared unitedly | 239 |
| Connecticut takes the lead | 239 |
| Character of Roger Sherman | 240 |
| Of Johnson. Of Ellsworth | 241 |
| Federal and national. Speech of Mason for two branches | 242 |
| Sherman for two branches | 243 |
| The convention decides for two branches | 244 |
| Wilson speaks for the general government and the state governments | 244 |
| Ellsworth would graft a general government on the state governments | 245 |
| The mode of choosing and term of office of the senators | 245 |
| The decision. Fierce contest between the smaller states and the large ones | 246 |
| Franklin proposes prayer | 247 |
| The debate continues | 248 |
| Suffrage in the first branch proportioned to population | 249 |
| Ellsworth would have the vote in the senate by states | 249 |
| Speech of Baldwin. Wilson refuses to yield | 250 |
| So does Madison. Persistence of Ellsworth | 251 |
| He is supported by North Carolina | 252 |
| The convention equally divided | 253 |
| Appointment of a grand committee to report a compromise | 253 |

## CHAPTER IV.

### THE ADJUSTMENT OF REPRESENTATION.

### From the Third to the Twenty-third of July 1787.

| | |
|---|---|
| Franklin's compromise | 255 |
| Morris claims representation for property | 256 |
| The ratio of representation referred to a committee | 256 |
| Report of the committee | 257 |
| Appointment of a committee of one from each state | 257 |
| Madison's proposal of compromise. Report of the new committee | 258 |
| Approved by all except South Carolina and Georgia | 259 |
| Yates and Lansing desert their post | 259 |
| The southern states have a majority in the convention | 260 |
| Abolition of slavery in the North | 260 |
| Movement against the slave-trade. Two classes of slave states | 261 |
| Jealousy of the speedy preponderance of western states | 262 |
| The equal rights of the western states maintained | 263 |
| Strife on the representation for slaves | 264 |
| A triple set of parties prevent a decision. Rash proposal of Morris | 265 |

## CONTENTS.

|  | PAGE |
|---|---|
| Taxation and representation | 265 |
| Slaves to be counted as three fifths in representation | 266 |
| Morris fears injury to commerce from the influence of western states | 267 |
| Representation in the second branch proportioned to numbers | 267 |
| Effect of the decision on the political power of the South | 268 |
| The senate to vote by states | 269 |

### CHAPTER V.

#### THE OUTLINE OF THE CONSTITUTION COMPLETED AND REFERRED.

#### From the Seventeenth to the Twenty-seventh of July 1787.

| | |
|---|---|
| The distribution of powers between the general government and the states | 270 |
| Relation of federal legislation to that of the states | 270 |
| Property qualification as a condition of holding office | 271 |
| Qualification of the electors left to the states | 272 |
| Extent of the jurisdiction of federal tribunals | 272 |
| How the new constitution was to be ratified | 273 |
| Committee of five ordered to report the resolutions of the convention in the form of a constitution | 274 |
| Character of Rutledge | 274 |
| Industry of the committee | 275 |
| Anxiety of the country | 276 |

### CHAPTER VI.

#### THE COLONIAL SYSTEM OF THE UNITED STATES.

#### From January 1786 to July 1787.

| | |
|---|---|
| The ordinance of 1787. Treaty with the Shawnees | 277 |
| Monroe's journey to the West | 277 |
| Report of a grand committee on the western territory | 278 |
| Monroe's plan for a north-western ordinance | 279 |
| Monroe and restrictions on slavery | 279 |
| Certain waters and carrying places declared free. The Connecticut reserve | 279 |
| The proposed five states in the North-west | 280 |
| Jealousy of the western states. Kaskaskias | 280 |
| Urgent need of a territorial government. Progress of the bill | 281 |
| Rufus Putnam's plan for colonizing the West. His appeal to Washington | 282 |
| Parsons visits the West | 283 |
| Congress quiets the Indian title to a great part of Ohio | 283 |
| Formation of the Ohio company | 284 |
| Parsons presents its memorial to congress. Effect of the memorial | 285 |
| Power of the South | 285 |
| Cutler before congress. Carrington's report | 286 |
| Richard Henry Lee on a new committee of seven | 286 |
| Ordinance for governing the territory of the United States. Its clauses | 287 |
| Clause on contracts | 288 |
| Grayson and slavery. Nathan Dane and King | 289 |

## CONTENTS. xix

|   | PAGE |
|---|---|
| Long debates upon it | 382 |
| Reception of the resolution of congress. A convention called | 383 |
| Lee and Wilson in Pennsylvania | 383 |
| Prompt meeting of the Pennsylvania convention | 384 |
| Speech of Wilson in favor of the constitution | 384 |
| Opposed by Smilie. And by Whitehill | 386 |
| On the want of a bill of rights | 387 |
| Speech of Findley | 388 |
| The constitution in the Delaware legislature | 389 |
| The Delaware convention ratifies the constitution | 389 |
| Pennsylvania ratifies the constitution | 390 |
| Act of the legislature of New Jersey | 391 |
| The New Jersey convention ratifies the constitution | 391 |
| The legislature of Georgia | 392 |
| Georgia unanimously ratifies the constitution | 392 |

## CHAPTER III.

### THE CONSTITUTION IN CONNECTICUT AND MASSACHUSETTS.

### From 26 September 1787 to 6 February 1788.

| | |
|---|---|
| Letter of Sherman and Ellsworth to the governor of Connecticut | 393 |
| The Connecticut convention. Speeches of Ellsworth and Johnson | 394 |
| James Wadsworth and answers to him | 394 |
| Wise conduct of Hancock | 395 |
| Massachusetts calls a convention | 395 |
| Condition of the state. The elections | 396 |
| Samuel Adams. Opening of the convention | 397 |
| Elbridge Gerry. Conduct of Samuel Adams | 398 |
| Objections to the constitution. Property qualifications | 398 |
| Representation of slaves. On a religious test | 399 |
| Period of office for senators. King explains the constitution | 399 |
| Dawes argues for protective duties | 399 |
| The convention wavering | 400 |
| It follows Washington's mode of avoiding a second convention | 401 |
| Objections made and answered | 401 |
| The slave-trade. Hancock proposes resolutions | 402 |
| Supported by Samuel Adams | 403 |
| Amendments referred to a committee | 404 |
| The committee report its approval of the constitution | 404 |
| Objections on the score of the slave-trade | 404 |
| And for the want of a bill of rights | 405 |
| Stillman speaks for the constitution | 405 |
| In what words Hancock proposed the question | 405 |
| The vote. Acquiescence of the opposition | 406 |
| Madison adopts the policy of Massachusetts | 406 |
| Opinions of Jefferson | 406 |
| Of John Adams | 408 |

## CONTENTS.

### CHAPTER IV.

THE CONSTITUTION IN NEW HAMPSHIRE, MARYLAND, AND SOUTH CAROLINA.

#### From February to the Twenty-third of May 1788.

|  | PAGE |
|---|---|
| The constitution in New Hampshire | 409 |
| Its convention adjourns. The assembly of Maryland calls a convention | 410 |
| The cabals of Virginia. Influence of Washington | 410 |
| The election of a convention in Maryland | 410 |
| Advice of Washington. The convention of Maryland at Annapolis | 411 |
| Conduct of Chase. Of Paca | 412 |
| Conduct of enemies and friends to the federal government | 412 |
| The constitution ratified. No amendments proposed | 413 |
| Maryland will have no separate confederacy. Hopefulness of Washington | 413 |
| The constitution in South Carolina. Attitude of its assembly | 414 |
| Debate between Lowndes and Pinckney | 415 |
| Why there was no bill of rights | 418 |
| Speech of Rutledge. Call of a convention. The convention organized | 419 |
| The constitution ratified. Joy of Gadsden. Effect on New Hampshire | 420 |

### CHAPTER V.

THE CONSTITUTION IN VIRGINIA AND IN NEW HAMPSHIRE.

#### From May 1785 to the Twenty-fifth of June 1788.

| Jay's negotiation with Gardoqui | 421 |
|---|---|
| Alarm of the southern states | 422 |
| Danger of a separation of the southern states | 422 |
| Failure of the negotiation. Washington | 423 |
| And Jefferson. Randolph will support the constitution | 424 |
| Effect of the example of Massachusetts on Virginia | 425 |
| The opposition in the Virginia convention. Madison | 425 |
| And Pendleton. Mason. Patrick Henry leads the opposition | 426 |
| Is replied to by Pendleton and Madison | 427 |
| Praise of the British constitution | 427 |
| Madison compares the British and American constitutions | 428 |
| Henry speaks against the judiciary system. Marshall defends it | 429 |
| The debtor planters. Henry on a separate confederacy | 430 |
| Mason and Madison on the slave-trade | 431 |
| And Tyler. Henry fears emancipation by the general government | 432 |
| Noble speech of Randolph. Slavery condemned by Johnson | 432 |
| Navigation of the Mississippi | 433 |
| Contest between the North and the South | 433 |
| The power to regulate commerce. The prohibition of paper money | 434 |
| Quieting language of Henry | 435 |
| The convention refuses a conditional ratification | 436 |
| The ratification. Its form. Acquiescence of the opposition | 436 |
| New Hampshire ratifies before Virginia | 437 |

## CONTENTS.

*V.—THE FEDERAL GOVERNMENT. JUNE 1787.*

### CHAPTER I.

#### THE CONSTITUTION.

#### 1787.

|  | PAGE |
|---|---|
| The American constitution. Its forerunners | 441 |
| Its place in the world's history. Individuality the character of Americans | 442 |
| Why the English language maintained itself | 442 |
| The constitution in harmony with individuality | 443 |
| Freedom of the individual in religion | 443 |
| Slavery an anomaly | 444 |
| Tripartite division of the powers of government | 445 |
| Tripartite division of the power of legislation | 446 |
| How the constitution is to be amended | 447 |
| The United States a continental republic | 447 |
| A federal republic with complete powers of government | 448 |
| Powers of the states not by grace, but of right | 448 |
| Sovereignty of the law. Who are the people of the United States? | 449 |
| Their power. New states to be admitted on equal terms | 450 |
| Necessity of revolution provided against | 450 |
| Extending influence of the federal republic | 450 |
| The philosophy of the people | 451 |

### CHAPTER II.

#### THE LINGERING STATES.

#### From 1787 to the Second of August 1788.

|  | |
|---|---|
| The Federalist and its authors | 452 |
| Hamilton and a revenue tariff | 453 |
| Unreasonableness of New York. Organization of the federal republicans | 454 |
| Clinton recommends the encouragement of manufactures | 455 |
| New York legislature orders a state convention. The electors | 455 |
| The meeting of the convention deferred till June | 455 |
| Division of parties in New York | 455 |
| Meeting of the convention. Livingston opens the debate | 456 |
| Speeches of Lansing, Smith, and Hamilton | 456 |
| News from New Hampshire. Success in New York depends on Virginia | 457 |
| Hamilton declares his opinions. Clinton replies | 457 |
| News received of the ratification by Virginia | 458 |
| May New York ratify conditionally? | 458 |
| Debate between Smith and Hamilton. Lansing holds out | 459 |
| Madison condemns a conditional ratification | 459 |
| The opposition in New York give way | 460 |
| But ask for a second federal convention. Joy of New York city | 460 |
| Convention of North Carolina | 460 |

Is divided by parties . . . . . . . . . . . 461
Amendments proposed. The decision postponed . . . . . . 462
Conduct of Rhode Island . . . . . . . . . . 462

## CHAPTER III.

### THE FEDERAL GOVERNMENT OF THE UNITED STATES.

#### From 1788 to the Fifth of May 1789.

Relations of America to Europe . . . . . . . . . 463
Encroachments of England in Maine and in the West . . . . 463
John Adams returns home. Adams and Jefferson . . . . 464
Moderation of the Pennsylvania minority. Albert Gallatin . . . 465
The Virginia assembly demands a second federal convention . . 465
Lee and Grayson elected senators . . . . . . . . 465
Connecticut refuses a second convention. And Massachusetts . . 466
And Pennsylvania. Dilatoriness of congress . . . . . 466
Measures for commencing proceedings under the constitution . . 466
Federal elections in New York . . . . . . . . 466
In Virginia. In South Carolina . . . . . . . . 467
Party divisions. Debates in congress on protection . . . . 468
Washington sees danger to the union from the South . . . . 469
His resolution on leaving Mount Vernon . . . . . . 469
His reception at Alexandria. At Baltimore. In Delaware . . . 470
At Philadelphia. At Trenton. In New York . . . . . 470
His inauguration. His address to the two houses . . . . 471
Public prayers in the church. Description of Washington . . . 472
Address to him from the senate. From the representatives . . . 472
State of Europe at the time . . . . . . . . . 472
And of America . . . . . . . . . . . 474

# HISTORY

OF THE

## FORMATION OF THE CONSTITUTION

OF THE

## UNITED STATES OF AMERICA.

*IN FIVE BOOKS.*

I.—THE CONFEDERATION.

II.—ON THE WAY TO A FEDERAL CONVENTION.

III.—THE FEDERAL CONVENTION.

IV.—THE PEOPLE OF THE STATES IN JUDGMENT ON THE CONSTITUTION.

V.—THE FEDERAL GOVERNMENT.

# THE FORMATION OF THE CONSTITUTION

## OF THE UNITED STATES OF AMERICA

*IN FIVE BOOKS.*

### BOOK FIRST.

### THE CONFEDERATION.

### To June 1783.

# CHAPTER I.

A RETROSPECT. EARLY MOVEMENTS TOWARD UNION.

## 1643–1781.

THE order of time brings us to the most cheering act in the political history of mankind, when thirteen republics, of which at least three reached from the sea to the Mississippi, formed themselves into one federal commonwealth. There was no revolt against the past, but a persistent and healthy progress. The sublime achievement was the work of a people led by statesmen of earnestness, perseverance, and public spirit, instructed by the widest experience in the forms of representative government, and warmed by that mutual love which proceeds from ancient connection, harmonious effort in perils, and common aspirations.

Scarcely one who wished me good speed when I first essayed to trace the history of America remains to greet me with a welcome as I near the goal. Deeply grateful as I am for the friends who rise up to gladden my old age, their encouragement must renew my grief for those who have gone before me.

While so much is changed in the living objects of personal respect and affection, infinitely greater are the transformations in the condition of the world. Power has come to dwell with every people, from the Arctic sea to the Mediterranean, from Portugal to the borders of Russia. From end to end of the United States, the slave has become a freeman; and the various forms of bondage have disappeared from European Christendom. Abounding harvests of scientific discovery have been garnered by numberless inquisitive minds, and the wildest forces of nature have been taught to become the docile helpmates of man. The application of steam to the purposes of travel on land and on water, the employment of a spark of light as the carrier of thought across continents and beneath oceans, have made of all the inhabitants of the earth one society. A journey round the world has become the pastime of a holiday vacation. The morning newspaper gathers up and brings us the noteworthy events of the last four-and-twenty hours in every quarter of the globe. All states are beginning to form parts of one system. The "new nations," which Shakespeare's prophetic eye saw rising on our eastern shore, dwell securely along two oceans, midway between their kin of Great Britain on the one side and the world's oldest surviving empire on the other.

More than two thousand years ago it was truly said that the nature of justice can be more easily discerned in a state than in one man.* It may now be studied in the collective states of all the continents. The ignorance and prejudices that come from isolation are worn away in the conflict of the forms of culture. We learn to think the thought, to hope the hope of mankind. Former times spoke of the dawn of civilization in some one land; we live in the morning of the world. Day by day the men who guide public affairs are arraigned before the judgment-seat of the race. A government which adopts a merely selfish policy is pronounced to be the foe of the human family. The statesman who founds and builds up the well-being of his country on justice has all the nations for a cloud of witnesses, and, as one of our own poets † has said, "The linkéd hemispheres attest his deed." He thrills the world with joy; and man becomes of a nobler spirit as he learns to gauge his opinions and his acts by a scale commensurate with his nature.

History carries forward the study of ethics by following the footsteps of states from the earliest times of which there is a record. The individual who undertakes to capture truth by solitary thought loses his way in the mazes of speculation, or involves himself in mystic visions, so that the arms which

---

\* Plato in the Republic, Book ii. Bekker, III., i., 78.
† Emerson: The Adirondacks, 248.

he extends to embrace what are but formless shadows return empty to his own breast. To find moral truth, he must study man in action. The laws of which reason is conscious can be tested best by experience; and inductions will be the more sure, the larger the experience from which they are drawn. However great may be the number of those who persuade themselves that there is in man nothing superior to himself, history interposes with evidence that tyranny and wrong lead inevitably to decay; that freedom and right, however hard may be the struggle, always prove resistless. Through this assurance ancient nations learn to renew their youth; the rising generation is incited to take a generous part in the grand drama of time; and old age, staying itself upon sweet Hope as its companion and cherisher,* not bating a jot of courage, nor seeing cause to argue against the hand or the will of a higher power, stands waiting in the tranquil conviction that the path of humanity is still fresh with the dews of morning, that the Redeemer of the nations liveth.

The colonies, which became one federal republic, were founded by rival powers. That difference of origin and the consequent antagonism of interest were the motives to the first American union. In 1643 three New England colonies joined in a short-lived "confederacy" for mutual protection, especially against the Dutch; each member reserving its peculiar jurisdiction and government, and an equal vote in the general council.

Common danger gave the next impulse to collective action. Rivers, which were the convenient war-paths of the natives, flowed in every direction from the land of the Five Nations; against whom, in 1684, measures of defence, extending from North Carolina to the northern boundary of New England, were concerted. Later, in 1751, South Carolina joined northern colonies in a treaty with the same tribes.

On the side of England, James II., using the simple method of the prerogative of an absolute king, began the suppression of colonial legislatures, and the consolidation of colonies under

* γλυκεῖά οἱ καρδίαν ἀτάλλοισα γηροτρόφος συναορεῖ ἐλπίς. Pindar in Plato, Republic, Book i. Bekker, III., i., 10.

the rule of one governor. After the English revolution of 1688 had gained consistency, the responsible government which it established would gladly have devised one uniform system of colonial administration; and in 1696 the newly created board of trade, of which John Locke was a member, suggested the appointment of a captain-general of all the forces on the continent of North America, with such power as could be exercised through the prerogative of a constitutional king.

In 1697 William Penn appeared before the board and advised an annual "congress" of two delegates from each one of the American provinces, to determine by plurality of voices the ways and means for supporting their union, providing for their safety, and regulating their commerce.

In 1721, to ensure the needed co-operation of the colonies in the rivalry of England with France for North American territory, the plan attributed to Lord Stairs provided for a lord-lieutenant or captain-general over them all; and for a general council to which each provincial assembly should send two of its members, electing one of the two in alternate years. The lord-lieutenant of the king, in conjunction with the general council on behalf of the colonies, was then to allot the quotas of men and money which the several assemblies were to raise by laws of their own. All these projects slumbered among heaps of neglected papers.

On the final struggle between England and France, the zeal of the colonists surpassed that of the mother country. A union, proposed by Franklin in 1754, would have preserved the domestic institutions of the several colonies. For the affairs of the whole, a governor-general was to be appointed from England, and a legislature, in which the representation would have borne some proportion to population, was to be chosen triennially by the colonies. This plan, which foreshadowed the present constitution of the Dominion of Canada and the federation which with hope and applause was lately offered by rival ministries to South Africa, was at that day rejected by the British government with abhorrence and disdain.

The English administration confined itself next to methods for obtaining a colonial revenue. For this end Lord Halifax, in 1754, advised that the commander-in-chief, attended by one commissioner from each colony, whose election should be subject to one negative of the king by the royal council and another by the royal governor, should adjust the quotas of each colony, which were then to be enforced by the authority of parliament. This plan was suppressed by impending war.

Great Britain having, with the lavish aid of her colonies, driven France from Canada, needed them no more as allies in war. From 1762 to 1765 the problem was how to create a grand system of empire. James Otis, of Boston, would have had all kingdoms and all outlying possessions of the crown wrought into the flesh and blood and membership of one organization; but this advice, which would have required home governments for every kingdom and for every colony, and, for general affairs, one imperial parliament representing the whole, found no favor.

In those days of aristocratic rule, the forming of a grand plan of union was assigned by the Bedford faction to George Grenville, a statesman bred to the law, the impersonation of idolatry of the protective system as the source of British prosperity, and of faith in the omnipotence of the British parliament as the groundwork of British liberty. He sought to unite the thirteen colonies in their home administration by the prerogative; in their home legislation by a royal veto of acts of their own legislatures; in the establishment of their general revenue and the regulation of their commerce by acts of the British parliament.

And now came into the view of the world the rare aptitude of the colonies for concert and organization. James Otis, in the general court of Massachusetts, spoke the word for an American congress, and in 1765 nine of the thirteen met at New York: the British parliament aimed at consolidating their administration without their own consent, and did but force them to unite in the denial of its power.

The truest and greatest Englishman of that century breasted the heaving wave and by his own force stayed it, but only for the moment. An aristocratic house of commons, piqued and vexed at its own concession, imposed a tax on the colonies in the least hateful form that it could devise; and in 1773 the sound of tea-chests, falling into Boston harbor, startled the nations with the news of a united and resistant America.

In 1774 the British parliament thought proper to punish Boston and attempt coercion by arms; "delegates of the inhabitants" of twelve American colonies in a continental congress acted as one in a petition to the king.

The petition was not received. Six months before the declaration of independence, Thomas Paine, in "Common Sense," had written and published to the world : "Nothing but a continental form of government can keep the peace of the continent.* Let a CONTINENTAL CONFERENCE be held,† to frame a CONTINENTAL CHARTER, drawing the line of business and jurisdiction between members of congress and members of assembly, always remembering that our strength and happiness are continental, not provincial.‡ The bodies chosen conformably to said charter shall be the legislators and governors of this continent.# We have every opportunity and every encouragement to form the noblest, purest constitution on the face of the earth." ‖ The continental convention which was to frame the constitution for the union was to represent both the colonies and the people of each colony; its members were to be chosen, two by congress from the delegation of each colony, two by the legislature of each colony out of its own body, and five directly by the people.△

Great Britain offered its transatlantic dominions no unity but under a parliament in which they were not represented; the people of thirteen colonies by special instructions to their delegates in congress, on the fourth of July 1776, declared themselves to be states, independent and united, and began the search for a fitting constitution.

In their first formative effort they missed the plain road of English and American experience. They had rightly been jealous of extending the supremacy of England, because it was a government outside of themselves; they now applied that jealousy to one another, forgetting that the general power

---

* Common Sense: original edition of 8 January 1776, p. 51.
† Ibid., 55.          ‡ Ibid., 56.          # Ibid., 56.
‖ Appendix, annexed to second edition of Common Sense, 14 February 1776.
△ Common Sense, original edition, 55.

would be in their own hands. Joseph Hawley of Massachusetts had, in November 1775, advised annual parliaments of two houses; the committee for framing the confederation, misled partly by the rooted distrust for which the motive had ceased, and partly by erudition which studied Hellenic councils and leagues as well as later confederacies, took for its pattern the constitution of the United Provinces, with one house and no central power of final decision. These evils were nearly fatal to the United Provinces themselves, although every one of them could be reached by a messenger within a day's journey; and here was a continent of states which could not be consulted without the loss of many months, and would ever tend to anarchy from the want of agreement in their separate deliberations.

Hopeless of a good result from the deliberations of congress on a confederation, Edward Rutledge, in August 1776, in a letter to Robert R. Livingston, avowed his readiness to "propose that the states should appoint a special congress, to be composed of new members, for this purpose." *

The necessities of the war called into being, north of the Potomac, successive conventions of a cluster of states. In August 1780, a convention of the New England states at Boston declared for a more solid and permanent union with one supreme head, and "a congress competent for the government of all those common and national affairs which do not nor can come within the jurisdiction of the particular states." At the same time it issued an invitation for a convention of the New England states, New York, and "others that shall think proper to join them," † to meet at Hartford.

The legislature of New York approved the measure.‡ "Our embarrassments in the prosecution of the war," such was the message of Governor George Clinton on the fourth of September, at the opening of the session, "are chiefly to be attributed to a defect of power in those who ought to exercise a supreme jurisdiction; for, while congress only recommends and the different states deliberate upon the propriety of the

---

\* Rutledge to Livingston, August 1776. MS.
† Hough's Convention of New England States at Boston, 50, 52.
‡ Duane to Washington, 19 September 1780. Letters to Washington, iii., 92.

recommendation, we cannot expect a union of force or council." The senate answered in the words of Philip Schuyler: "We perceive the defects of the present system, and the necessity of a supreme and coercive power in the government of these states; and are persuaded that, unless congress are authorized to direct uncontrollably the operations of war and enabled to enforce a compliance with their requisitions, the common force can never be properly united." *

Meantime Alexander Hamilton in swiftness of thought outran all that was possible. Early in September, in a private letter to James Duane, then a member of congress, he took up the proposal, which, nearly five years before, Thomas Paine had made known, and advised that a convention of all the states should meet on the first of the following November, with full authority to conclude finally and set in motion a "vigorous" general confederation.† His ardor would have surprised the people into greater happiness without giving them an opportunity to view and reject his project.‡

Before the end of the year the author of "Common Sense" himself, publishing in Philadelphia a tract asserting the right of the United States to the vacant western territory, closed his argument for the "Public Good" with these words: "I take the opportunity of renewing a hint which I formerly threw out in the pamphlet 'Common Sense,' and which the several states will, sooner or later, see the convenience, if not the necessity, of adopting; which is, that of electing a continental convention, for the purpose of forming a continental constitution, defining and describing the powers of congress. To have them marked out legally will give additional energy to the whole, and a new confidence to the several parts." #

"Call a convention of the states, and establish a congress upon a constitutional footing," wrote Greene, after taking command of the southern army, to a member of congress. ‖

On the eleventh of November able representatives from

---

* Hough's Convention, 63–65.
† Hamilton to Duane, 3 September 1780. Hamilton, i., 157.
‡ Compare McHenry to Hamilton. Hamilton, i., 411.
# Thomas Paine's Public Good. Original edition, 38.
‖ Johnson's Life of Greene, ii., 446.

each of the four New England states and New York—John T. Gilman of New Hampshire, Thomas Cushing, Azor Orne, and George Partridge of Massachusetts, William Bradford of Rhode Island, Eliphalet Dyer and William Williams of Connecticut, John Sloss Hobart and Egbert Benson of New York —assembled at Hartford.* The lead in the convention was taken by the delegates from New York, Hobart, a judge of its supreme court, and Benson, its attorney-general.† At their instance it was proposed, as a foundation for a safe system of finance, to provide by taxes or duties a certain and inalienable revenue, to discharge the interest on any funded part of the public debt, and on future loans. As it had proved impossible to get at the valuation of lands, congress should be empowered to apportion taxes on the states according to their number of inhabitants, black as well as white. They then prepared a circular letter to all the states, in which they said: "Our embarrassments arise from a defect in the present government of the United States. All government supposes the power of coercion; this power, however, never did exist in the general government of the continent, or has never been exercised. Under these circumstances, the resources and force of the country can never be properly united and drawn forth. The states individually considered, while they endeavor to retain too much of their independence, may finally lose the whole. By the expulsion of the enemy we may be emancipated from the tyranny of Great Britain; we shall, however, be without a solid hope of peace and freedom unless we are properly cemented among ourselves."

The proceedings of this convention were sent to every state in the union, to Washington, and to congress. ‡ They were read in congress on the twelfth of December 1780; and were

---

* The names of all the delegates are given in Papers of the Old Congress, xxxiii., 391, MS.

† That New York took the lead appears from comparison of the message of Clinton in September and the circular letter of the convention; and from the public tribute of Hamilton to the New York delegates in the presence of Hobart. Hamilton, ii., 360.

‡ Papers of the Old Congress, xxxiii., 391, containing copies of the credentials of the commissioners, the resolutions of the convention, and its letters to the several states, to congress, and to Washington. MS.

referred to a committee of five, on which were John Witherspoon and James Madison,* the master and his pupil. In the same days Pennsylvania instructed its delegates in congress that imposts on trade were absolutely necessary; and, in order to prevent any state from taking advantage of a neighbor, congress should recommend to the several states in union a system of imposts.† Before the end of 1780 the legislative council and general assembly of New Jersey, while they insisted "that the rights of every state in the union should be strictly maintained," declared that "congress represent the federal republic." ‡ Thus early was that name applied to the United States. Both branches of the legislature of New York, which at that time was "as well disposed a state as any in the union," # approved the proceedings of the convention as promoting the interest of the continent. ‖

With the year 1781, when the ministry of Great Britain believed themselves in possession of the three southernmost states and were cheering Cornwallis to complete his glory by the conquest of Virginia; when congress was confessedly without the means to recover the city of New York; when a large contingent from France was at Newport, serious efforts for the creation of a federal republic began, and never ceased until it was established. The people of New York, from motives of the highest patriotism, had already ceded its claims to western lands. The territory north-west of the Ohio, which Virginia had conquered, was on the second of January △ surrendered to the United States of America. For this renunciation one state and one state only had made delay. On the twenty-ninth, congress received the news so long anxiously waited for, that Maryland by a resolution of both branches of her legislature had acceded to the confederation, seven members only in the house voting in the negative. Duane, who had been taught by Washington that "greater powers to congress were indispensably necessary to the well-being and good government

* Endorsement by Charles Thomson, secretary of congress. MS.
† Journals of Assembly, 564.
‡ Representation and Remonstrance, printed in Mulford's New Jersey, 469, 470.     # Washington to Jefferson, 1 August 1786. Sparks, ix., 186.
‖ Journals of Assembly, 91, 93.
△ Journal of Virginia House of Delegates, 79.

of public affairs," * instantly addressed him : " Let us devote this day to joy and congratulation, since by the accomplishment of our federal union we are become a nation. In a political view it is of more real importance than a victory over all our enemies. We shall not fail of taking advantage of the favorable temper of the states and recommending for ratification such additional articles as will give vigor and authority to government." † The enthusiasm of the moment could not hide the truth, that without amendments the new system would struggle vainly for life. Washington answered: " Our affairs will not put on a different aspect unless congress is vested with, or will assume, greater powers than they exert at present." ‡

To John Sullivan of New Hampshire, another member of congress, Washington wrote : " I never expect to see a happy termination of the war, nor great national concerns well conducted in peace, till there is something more than a recommendatory power in congress. The last words, therefore, of my letter and the first wish of my heart concur in favor of it." #

The legislature of Maryland swiftly transformed its resolution into an act. The delegates having full authority, in the presence of congress, on the first day of March, subscribed the articles of confederation, and its complete, formal, and final ratification by all the United States was announced to the public ; to the executives of the several states ; to the American ministers in Europe, and through them to the courts at which they resided ; to the minister plenipotentiary of France in America ; to the commander-in-chief, and through him to the army.‖ Clinton communicated " the important event " to the legislature of New York, adding : " This great national compact establishes our union." ᐃ But the completion of the confederation was the instant revelation of its insufficiency, and the summons to the people of America to form a better constitution.

* Washington to James Duane, 26 December 1780. MS.
† James Duane to Washington, 29 January 1781.
‡ Washington to Duane, 19 February 1781.
# Washington to Sullivan, 4 February 1781. Sparks, vii., 402.
‖ Journals of Congress, iii., 581, 582, 591.
ᐃ Journal of New York Assembly, for 19 March 1781.

Washington rejoiced that Virginia had relinquished her claim to the land south of the great lakes and north-west of the Ohio, which, he said, "for fertility of soil, pleasantness of climate, and other natural advantages, is equal to any known tract of country of the same extent in the universe." * He was pleased that Maryland had acceded to the confederation; but he saw no ground to rest satisfied.

On taking command of the army in Massachusetts in 1775, he at once discriminated between the proper functions of individual colonies and "that power and weight which ought of right to belong only to the whole;" † and he applied to Richard Henry Lee, then in congress, for aid in establishing the distinction. In the following years he steadily counselled the formation of one continental army. As a faithful laborer in the cause, as a man injuring his private estate without the smallest personal advantage, as one who wished the prosperity of America most devoutly, he in the last days of 1778 had pleaded with the statesmen of Virginia for that which to him was more than life. He called on Benjamin Harrison, then speaker of the house of delegates, on Mason, Wythe, Jefferson, Nicholas, Pendleton, and Nelson, "not to be satisfied with places in their own state while the common interests of America were mouldering and sinking into irretrievable ruin, but to attend to the momentous concerns of an empire." ‡ "Till the great national interest is fixed upon a solid basis," so he wrote, in March 1779, to George Mason, "I lament the fatal policy of the states of employing their ablest men at home. How useless to put in fine order the smallest parts of a clock unless the great spring which is to set the whole in motion is well attended to! Let this voice call forth you, Jefferson, and others to save their country." # But now, with deeper emotion, he turns to his own state as he had done in the gloomy winter of 1778. He has no consolation but in the hope of a good federal government. His growing desire has the character of the forces of nature, which from the opening year increase in power till the earth is renewed.

---

\* Washington to Sullivan, 4 February 1781. Sparks, vii., 400.
† Washington to Richard H. Lee, 29 August 1775. Sparks, iii., 68, 69.
‡ Sparks, vi., 150.   # See above, v., 298, 319.

A constant, close observer of what was done by Virginia, he held in mind that on the twenty-fourth day of December 1779, on occasion of some unwise proceedings of congress, she had resolved "that the legislature of this commonwealth are greatly alarmed at the assumption of power lately exercised by congress. While the right of recommending measures to each state by congress is admitted, we contend for that of judging of their utility and expediency, and of course either to approve or reject. Making any state answerable for not agreeing to any of its recommendations would establish a dangerous precedent against the authority of the legislature and the sovereignty of the separate states." *

This interposition of the Virginia legislature so haunted Washington's mind that he felt himself more particularly impelled to address with freedom men of whose abilities and judgments he wished to avail himself. He thoroughly understood the obstinacy and strength of opinion which he must encounter and overcome. His native state, reaching to the Mississippi and dividing the South from the North, held, from its geographical place, its numbers, and the influence of its statesmen, a power of obstructing union such as belonged to no other state. He must persuade it to renounce some share of its individual sovereignty and forego " the liberty to reject or alter any act of congress which in a full representation of states has been solemnly debated and decided on," † or there is no hope of consolidating the union. His position was one of extreme delicacy; for he was at the head of the army which could alone be employed to enforce the requisitions of congress. He therefore selected, as the Virginians to whom he could safely address himself, the three great civilians whom that commonwealth had appointed to codify its laws and adapt them to the new state of society consequent on independence, Jefferson, its governor, Pendleton, the president of its court of appeals, and Wythe, its spotless chancellor. ‡

---

\* Journal of House of Delegates of Virginia, for 24 December 1779, 108.

† Washington to James Duane, 26 December 1780.

‡ Washington to Jefferson, Pendleton, and Wythe, Madison Papers, 83, Gilpin's edition. The date of the letter is not given. It was written soon after the accession of Maryland to the confederation; probably in February, before the middle of the month, which was the time fixed for his departure from New Windsor

"The alliance of the states," he said, " is now complete. If the powers granted to the respective body of the states are inadequate, the defects should be considered and remedied. Danger may spring from delay; good will result from a timely application of a remedy. The present temper of the states is friendly to the establishment of a lasting union; the moment should be improved; if suffered to pass away it may never return, and, after gloriously and successfully contending against the usurpations of Britain, we may fall a prey to our own follies and disputes." He argued for the power of compelling the states to comply with the requisitions for men and money agreeably to their respective quotas; adding: " It would give me concern should it be thought of me that I am desirous of enlarging the powers of congress unnecessarily; I declare to God, my only aim is the general good." And he promised to make his views known to others besides the three.

His stepson, John Parke Custis, who was just entering into public life, he thus instructed: " The fear of giving sufficient powers to congress is futile. Under its present constitution, each assembly will be annihilated, and we must once more return to the government of Great Britain, and be made to kiss the rod preparing for our correction. A nominal head, which at present is but another name for congress, will no longer do. That honorable body, after hearing the interests and views of the several states fairly discussed and explained by their respective representatives, must dictate, and not merely recommend." *

To another Virginian, Joseph Jones of King George county, whom he regarded with sincere affection and perfect trust, he wrote: " Without a controlling power in congress it will be impossible to carry on the war; and we shall speedily be

---

for Newport. The dates of the letters of 1781, informing him of the accession of Maryland, were, from Duane, 29 January, MS.; from Sullivan, 29 January, MS.; from Matthews, 30 January. Letters to Washington, iii., 218. Washington's answer to Sullivan is 4 February, Sparks, vii., 402; to Matthews, 14 February. " The confederation being now closed will, I trust, enable congress to speak decisively in their requisitions," etc. MS. On the evening of the fourteenth, Washington was preparing to leave for Newport; an unexpected letter from Rochambeau detained him in camp till the second of March. Sparks, vii., 446, note.

* Washington to John Parke Custis, 28 February 1781. Sparks, vii., 440–444

thirteen distinct states, each pursuing its local interests, till they are annihilated in a general crash. The fable of the bunch of sticks may well be applied to us." * In a like strain he addressed other trusty correspondents and friends. † His wants as commander-in-chief did not confine his attention to the progress of the war; he aimed at nothing less than an enduring government for all times of war and peace.

As soon as the new form of union was proclaimed, congress saw its want of real authority, and sought a way to remedy the defect. A report by Madison, from a committee,‡ was completed on the twelfth and read in congress on the sixteenth of March; and this was its reasoning: " The articles of confederation, which declare that every state shall abide by the determinations of congress, imply a general power vested in congress to enforce them and carry them into effect. The United States in congress assembled, being desirous as far as possible to cement and invigorate the federal union, recommend to the legislature of every state to give authority to employ the force of the United States as well by sea as by land to compel the states to fulfil their federal engagements." #

Madison enclosed to Jefferson a copy of his report, and, on account of the delicacy and importance of the subject, expressed a wish for his judgment on it before it should undergo the final decision of congress. No direct reply from him is preserved, ‖ but Joseph Jones, who, after a visit to Richmond,

* Washington to Joseph Jones, 24 March 1781. MS.
† Compare his letters to R. R. Livingston of New York, 31 January 1781—Sparks, vii., 391; to John Sullivan of New Hampshire, 4 February 1781—Sparks, vii., 401, 402; to John Matthews of South Carolina, 14 February 1781, MS.; to James Duane of New York, 19 February 1781, MS.; to Philip Schuyler of New York, 20 February 1781, MS.; to John Parke Custis of Virginia, 28 February 1781—Sparks, vii., 442; to William Gordon, in Massachusetts, 9 March 1781—Sparks, vii., 448; to Joseph Jones of King George, Virginia, 24 March 1781, MS.; to John Armstrong of Pennsylvania, 26 March 1781—Sparks, vii., 403.
‡ Reports of committees on increasing the powers of congress, p. 19. MS.
# Madison Papers, Gilpin's edition, 88–90. Reports of committees, 20, 22. MS. Madison was a member of the committee to which were referred the papers from the Hartford convention of November 1780. That committee, on the sixteenth of February 1781, made a report, which was referred back to it. Whether Madison's report of the twelfth of March proceeded from that committee, the imperfect record does not show.
‖ None of the letters of Jefferson to Madison of this year have been preserved.

was again in Philadelphia about the middle of May, gave to Madison a copy of the letter of Washington to Jefferson and his two associates.* There were no chances that the proposal of Madison would be approved by any one state, yet on the second of May it was referred to a grand committee; that is, to a committee of one from each state.† On the eighteenth the Chevalier de la Luzerne, then the French minister in America, sent this dispatch to Vergennes: "There is a feeling to reform the constitution of congress; but the articles of confederation, defective as they are, cost a year and a half of labor and of debates; a change will not encounter less difficulty, and it appears to me there is more room for desire than for hope." ‡

Even while he was writing, the movement for reform received a new impulse. In a pamphlet dated the twenty-fourth, and dedicated to the congress of the United States of America and to the assembly of the state of Pennsylvania, William Barton # insisted that congress should "not be left with the mere shadow of sovereign authority, without the right of exacting obedience to their ordinances, and destitute of the means of executing their resolves." To remedy this evil he did not look to congress itself, but "indicated the necessity of their calling a continental convention, for the express purpose of ascertaining, defining, enlarging, and limiting the duties and powers of their constitution." ‖ This is the third time that the suggestion of a general constituent convention was brought before the country by the press of Philadelphia.

* Madison Papers, Gilpin's edition, 81.
† Reports of committees on increasing the powers of congress, 22. MS.
‡ Luzerne to Vergennes, 18 May 1781. MS.
# Not by Pelatiah Webster, as stated by Madison. Madison Papers, Gilpin's edition, 706; Elliot's stereotyped reprint, 117. First: at a later period, Webster collected his pamphlets in a volume, and this one is not among them; a disclaimer which, under the circumstances, is conclusive. The style of this pamphlet of 1781 is totally unlike the style of Pelatiah Webster. Through my friend F. D. Stone of Philadelphia I have seen the bill for printing the pamphlet; it was made out against William Barton and paid by him. Further: Barton from time to time wrote pamphlets, of which, on a careful comparison, the style, language, and forms of expression are found to correspond to this pamphlet published in 1781. Without doubt it was written by William Barton.

‖ Observations on the Nature and Use of Paper Credit, etc., Philadelphia, 1781, 37. The preface of the pamphlet is dated 24 May 1781.

The grand committee of thirteen delayed their report till the twentieth of July, and then only expressed a wish to give congress power in time of war to lay an embargo at least for sixty days, and to appoint receivers of the money of the United States as soon as collected by state officers. By their advice the business was then referred to a committee of three.*

Day seemed to break when, on the twentieth of July, Edmund Randolph, who had just brought from Virginia the news of its disposition to strengthen the general government, Oliver Ellsworth of Connecticut, and James M. Varnum of Rhode Island, three of the ablest lawyers in their states, were selected to "prepare an exposition of the confederation, to devise a plan for its complete execution, and to present supplemental articles." †

In support of the proceedings of congress, Hamilton, during July and August, published a series of papers which he called "The Continentalist." "There is hardly a man," said he, "who will not acknowledge the confederation unequal to a vigorous prosecution of the war, or to the preservation of the union in peace. The federal government, too weak at first, will continually grow weaker." ‡ "Already some of the states have evaded or refused the demands of congress; the currency is depreciated; public credit is at the lowest ebb; our army deficient in numbers and unprovided with everything; the enemy making an alarming progress in the southern states; Cornwallis still formidable to Virginia. As in explanation of our embarrassments nothing can be alleged to the disaffection of the people, we must have recourse to impolicy and mismanagement in their rulers. We ought, therefore, not only to strain every nerve to render the present campaign as decisive as possible, but we ought, without delay, to enlarge the powers of congress. Every plan of which this is not the foundation will be illusory. The separate exertions of the states will never suffice. Nothing but a well-proportioned exertion of the resources for the whole, under the direction of a common

---

* Report of the grand committee. MS.
† Report of the committee of three.
‡ Continentalist. Reprinted in J. C. Hamilton's edition of the Federalist, cxl., cxli., cxlv., cxlvi., cxlvii., cxlviii.

council with power sufficient to give efficacy to their resolutions, can preserve us from being a conquered people now, or can make us a happy one hereafter."

The committee of three, Randolph, Ellsworth, and Varnum, made their report on the twenty-second of August. They declined to prepare an exposition of the confederation, because such a comment would be voluminous if co-extensive with the subject; and, in the enumeration of powers, omissions would become an argument against their existence. With professional exactness they explained in twenty-one cases the "manner" in which "the confederation required execution." As to delinquent states, they advised, " That—as America became a confederate republic to crush the present and future foes of her independence; as of this republic a general council is a necessary organ; and as, without the extension of its power, war may receive a fatal inclination and peace be exposed to daily convulsions—it be resolved to recommend to the several states to authorize the United States in congress assembled to lay embargoes and prescribe rules for impressing property in time of war; to appoint collectors of taxes required by congress; to admit new states with the consent of any dismembered state; to establish a consular system without reference to the states individually; to distrain the property of a state delinquent in its assigned proportion of men and money; and to vary the rules of suffrage in congress so as to decide the most important questions by the agreement of two thirds of the United States." *

It was further proposed to make a representation to the several states of the necessity for these supplemental powers, and of pursuing in their development one uniform plan.

At the time when this report was made the country was rousing its energies for a final campaign. New England with its militia assisted to man the lines near New York; the commander-in-chief with his army had gone to meet Cornwallis in Virginia; and Greene was recovering the three southernmost states. Few persons in that moment of suspense cared to read the political essays of Hamilton, and he hastened to take part in the war under the command of Lafayette. The hurry of

* Reports on increasing the powers of congress.

crowded hours left no opportunity for deliberation on the reform of the constitution. Moreover, the committee of three, while they recognised the duty of obedience on the part of the states to the requisitions of congress, knew no way to force men into the ranks of the army, or distrain the property of a state. There could be no coercion; for every state was a delinquent. Had it been otherwise, the coercion of a state by force of arms is civil war, and, from the weakness of the confederacy and the strength of organization of each separate state, the attempt at coercion would have been disunion.

Yet it was necessary for the public mind to pass through this process of reasoning. The conviction that the confederacy could propose no remedy for its weakness but the impracticable one of the coercion of sovereign states compelled the search for a really efficient and more humane form of government. Meantime the report of Randolph, Ellsworth, and Varnum, which was the result of the deliberations of nearly eight months, fell to the ground. We shall not have to wait long for a word from Washington; and, when he next speaks, he will propose "A NEW CONSTITUTION."

## CHAPTER II.

### THE STRUGGLE FOR REVENUE.

#### 1781–1782.

SCHUYLER had been led by his own experience to perceive the necessity for the states to surrender some part of their sovereignty, and "adopt another system of government." On the twenty-first of January 1781 he moved in the senate of New York to request the eastern states to join in an early convention, which should form a perpetual league of incorporation, subservient, however, to the common interest of all the states; invite others to accede to it; erect Vermont into a state; devise a fund for the redemption of the common debts; substitute a permanent and uniform system for temporary expedients; and invest the confederacy with powers of coercion.*

"We stand ready on our part to confer adequate powers on congress," was the message of both houses to that body in a letter of the fifth of February, written in the name of the state by their joint committee, on which were Schuyler and Benson. †

Washington had been taught by his earliest observation as general, and had often declared the indispensable necessity of more responsibility and permanency in the executive bodies. ‡ The convention at Boston of August 1780 had recommended

---

\* Schuyler to Washington, 21 January 1781. Letters to Washington, iii., 213.
† Letter from the state of New York to congress, 5 February 1781. Papers of Old Congress, lxvii., 344. MS. A copy of the letter was sent to Washington by Clinton, 14 February 1781. Letters to Washington, xlvi., 172. MS.
‡ Washington to Duane, 26 December 1780.

"a permanent system for the several departments." * Hamilton "was among the first who were convinced that their administration by single men was essential to the proper management of affairs." † On the tenth of January 1781, congress initiated a reform by establishing a department of foreign affairs; ‡ but more than eight months elapsed before it was filled by Robert R. Livingston.

There was the most pressing need of a minister of war. After tedious rivalries and delays, Benjamin Lincoln was elected; but he did not enter upon the office till near the end of November, when the attempt of Great Britain to subjugate America had ceased.

For the treasury, John Sullivan suggested to Washington the name of Hamilton. # How far Hamilton had made a study of finance, Washington did not know; but he said: "Few of his age have a more general knowledge, and no one is more firmly engaged in the cause, or exceeds him in probity and sterling virtue." ‖ In February the choice fell on Robert Morris, and unanimously, except that Massachusetts abstained from the ballot, ᐃ Samuel Adams preferring the old system of committees.◊

While Morris delayed his acceptance, Hamilton, who had been the first to present his name for the place, opened a correspondence with him. "A national debt," he wrote, "if it is not excessive, will be a national blessing, a powerful cement of union, a necessity for keeping up taxation, and a spur to industry." ‡ He recommended a national bank, with a capital of ten or fifteen millions of dollars, to be paid two sixths in specie, one sixth in bills or securities on good European funds, and three sixths in good landed security. It was to be erected into a legal corporation for thirty years, during which no

---

* Hough's edition of Convention at Boston, 3–9 August 1780, 51.
† Hamilton to Robert Morris, 30 April 1781; Hamilton, i., 223; to Duane, 3 September 1780. Ibid., i., 154.
‡ Journals of Congress, iii., 564.
# Sullivan to Washington, 29 January 1781. MS.
‖ Washington to Sullivan, 4 February 1781. Sparks, vii., 399.
ᐃ Journals of Congress, iii., 580.
◊ Luzerne to Vergennes, 25 March 1781. Partly printed in Sparks, vii., 400.
‡ Hamilton, i., 257.

other bank, public or private, was to be permitted. Its capital and deposits were to be exempt from taxation, and the United States, collectively and particularly, and conjointly with the private proprietors, were to become responsible for all its transactions. Its sources of profit were to be the sole right of issuing a currency for the United States equal in amount to the whole capital of the bank; loans at a rate not exceeding eight per cent; discount of bills of exchange; contracts with the French government for the supply of its fleets and armies in America, with the United States for the supply of their army; dealings in real estates, especially, with its large capital, buying at favorable opportunities the real estates of men who, having rendered themselves odious, would be obliged to leave the country. Another source of immense gain, contingently even of one hundred per cent, was to be a contract with the United States for taking up all their paper emissions. Incidentally, Hamilton expressed his "wish to see a convention of all the states, with full power to alter and amend, finally and irrevocably, the present futile and senseless confederation." *

This communication led to the closest relations between Hamilton and Robert Morris; but, vehement as was the character of the older man, his schemes fell far short of the daring suggestions of his young counsellor. On the fourteenth of May, Morris was installed as the superintendent of finance, and three days later he laid before congress his plan for a national bank. † Its capital was to be four hundred thousand dollars in gold and silver, with power of increase at discretion; its notes were to form the currency of the country, and be receivable as specie for duties and taxes by every state and by the United States. Authority to constitute the company a legal body not being granted by the articles of confederation, Morris submitted that congress should apply to the states for the power of incorporating a bank and prohibiting all other banks. ‡

On the twenty-sixth, congress, without waiting to hear the

* Hamilton, i., 223–257.
† Journals of Congress, iii., 624; Diplomatic Correspondence, vii., 444–449.
‡ R. Morris to congress, 17 May 1781. Diplomatic Correspondence, xi., 364.

voices of the states, resolved that the bank should be incorporated so soon as the subscription should be filled and officers chosen. This vote was carried by New Hampshire, New Jersey, and the five southernmost states, Massachusetts being in the negative, Pennsylvania divided, and Madison alone of the four members from Virginia opposing it as not within the powers of the confederation.

From the want of a valuation of private lands and buildings, congress had not even the right to apportion requisitions. The five states which met at Hartford had suggested for the United States an impost as a source of revenue. New Jersey and North Carolina suffered from the legislation of the neighboring states, which were the natural channels of a part of their foreign trade: on the third of February 1781, Witherspoon and Burke, their representatives in congress, reviving an amendment to the articles of confederation proposed by New Jersey in 1778,* moved to vest in the United States the power of regulating commerce according to "the common interest," and, under restrictions calculated to soothe state jealousies, the exclusive right of laying duties upon imported articles. This motion, which was a memorable step toward union, failed of success;† and on the same day congress contented itself with asking of the states, as an "indispensable necessity," the power to levy a duty of five per cent ad valorem on all imports, with no permanent exemptions except of wool cards and cotton cards, and wire for making them. This first scheme of duties on foreign commerce sought to foster American industry by the free admission of materials necessary to the manufacturer.

The letter of the fifth of February from the state of New York was met on its way by the vote of congress of the third. In March, New York granted the duties, to "be collected in such manner and by such officers as congress should direct." ‡ Connecticut had acted a month earlier at a special session called by Governor Trumbull, but had limited its grant to the end of the third year after the war.# New Hampshire fol-

* Journals of Congress, ii., 604.          † Ibid., iii., 573.
‡ Papers of Old Congress, lxxv.
# Journals of Congress, iii., 594, 600. Papers of Old Congress, lxxv. MS.
VOL. VI.—4

lowed in the first week of April.* Massachusetts delayed its consent till the next year, and then reserved to itself the appointment of the collectors.

Outside of the five states which met at Hartford, the first to agree to the new demand were Pennsylvania and New Jersey.† The general assembly of Virginia, which was to have met in Richmond on the seventh of May, was chased by the enemy to Charlottesville, where it elected Benjamin Harrison its speaker, and where John Taylor of Caroline,‡ according to order, presented a bill to enable the United States to levy the needed duty. Fleeing beyond the mountains, they completed the act at Staunton. The grant, of which Harrison had been the great promoter,# was restricted neither as to time nor as to form.‖ Early in September, North Carolina adopted the measure;△ Delaware in November; South Carolina in February 1782; and Maryland in its following April session. The consent of Georgia was confidently expected.

After the surrender of Cornwallis, the legislature of New York once more declared the readiness of their state to comply with any measures to render the union of the United States more intimate, and to contribute their proportion of well-established funds.◊ This alacrity Clinton, on the twenty-fourth of November, reported to congress as the highest "evidence of a sincere disposition in the state to promote the common interest."‡

Meantime the subscriptions to the bank languished, and Morris thought fit to apply to John Jay for money from the court of Madrid for its benefit, saying: "I am determined that the bank shall be well supported until it can support itself, and then it will support us."‡ But there was no ray of hope

---

* Papers of Old Congress, lxxiv., 9. MS.
† Dallas's Laws of Pennsylvania, i., 890. The act was of 5 April 1781. Journals of Congress, iii., 632. The act of New Jersey was passed 2 June 1781. Wilson's Acts of New Jersey, 191.
‡ Journal of House of Delegates, 30 May 1781.
# Harrison to Washington 31 March 1783.
‖ Papers of Old Congress, lxxv., 359. Hening's Statutes at Large, x., 409.
△ Papers of Old Congress, lxxvi., 91. Journals of Congress, iii., 674.
◊ Papers of Old Congress, lxvii., 438. MS.
‡ Ibid., 443.     ‡ Morris to Jay, 13 July 1781. Dip. Cor., vii., 440.

from that quarter. Though so late as October 1781 the subscription amounted to no more than seventy thousand dollars,* he was yet able to prevail with congress, on the thirty-first day of December, to incorporate the bank "forever" by the name of the Bank of North America; but it was not to exercise powers in any one of the United States repugnant to the laws or constitution of that state.† But for this restriction Madison would have seen in the ordinance "a precedent of usurpation."‡

The bank still wanted capital. During the autumn of 1781 a remittance in specie of nearly five hundred thousand dollars had been received from the king of France, and brought to Philadelphia. In January 1782, Morris, with no clear warrant, subscribed all of this sum that remained in the treasury, being about two hundred and fifty-four thousand dollars, to the stock of the bank,# which was thus nursed into life by the public moneys. In return, it did very little, and could do very little, for the United States. Its legal establishment was supported by a charter from the state of Massachusetts, in March 1782; by an act of recognition from Pennsylvania in March, and a charter on the first of April; and ten days later by a charter from New York. The final proviso of the New York charter was, "that nothing in this act contained shall be construed to imply any right or power in the United States in congress assembled to create bodies politic, or grant letters of incorporation in any case whatsoever."∥ The acts of Pennsylvania were repealed in 1785. Delaware gave a charter in 1786.

The confederacy promised itself a solid foundation for a system of finance from a duty on imports. Through the press, Hamilton now pleads for vesting congress with full power of regulating trade; and he contrasts the "prospect of a number of petty states, jarring, jealous, and perverse, fluctuating and unhappy at home, weak by their dissensions in the eyes of other nations," with the "noble and magnificent perspective of a great federal republic."

* Life of Morris, 81.
† Ordinance to incorporate, etc. Journals of Congress, iii., 706, 707.
‡ Gilpin, 105.
# From the narrative of Robert Morris in Life of Morris, 90.
∥ Jones & Varick's edition of Laws of New York, 1789, 77.

It is the glory of New York that its legislature was the first to impart the sanction of a state to the great conception of a federal convention to frame a constitution for the United States. On the report of a committee of which Madison was the head, congress, in May 1782, took into consideration the desperate condition of the finances of the country, and divided between four of its members the office of explaining the common danger to every state.* At the request of the delegation which repaired to the North, Clinton convened an extra session of the senate and assembly of New York at Poughkeepsie, where, in July, they received from the committee of congress a full communication † " on the necessity of providing for a vigorous prosecution of the war."

The legislature had been in session for a week when Hamilton, who for a few months filled the office of United States receiver of revenue for his state, repaired to Poughkeepsie " to second the views " of his superior. In obedience to instructions, he strongly represented " the necessity of solid arrangements of finance; " but he went to the work " without very sanguine expectations," for he believed that, " whatever momentary effort the legislature might make, very little would be done till the entire change of the present system ; " and, before this could be effected, " mountains of prejudice and particular interest were to be levelled." ‡

On the nineteenth, three days after his arrival, on the motion of Schuyler, his father-in-law, who was ever constant in support of a national system, the senate resolved itself into "a committee of the whole on the state of the nation." From its deliberations on two successive days a series of resolutions proceeded, which, as all agree, Hamilton drafted, and which, after they had been considered by paragraphs, were unanimously adopted by the senate. The house concurred in them without amendment and with equal unanimity. These resolutions as they went forth from the legislature find in the public experience " the strongest reason to apprehend from a continuance of the present constitution of the continental government a subversion of public credit," and a danger " to the safety and

---

\* Journals of Congress, 22 May and 15 and 18 July 1782.
† Clinton's message of 11 July 1782.     ‡ Hamilton, i., 286, 288

independence of the states." They repeat the words of the Hartford convention and of Clinton, that the radical source of the public embarrassments had been the want of sufficient power in congress, particularly the power of providing for itself a revenue, which could not be obtained by partial deliberations of the separate states. For these reasons the legislature of New York invite congress for the common welfare "to recommend and each state to adopt the measure of assembling a general convention of the states specially authorized to revise and amend the confederation, reserving a right to the respective legislatures to ratify their determinations." * These resolutions the governor of New York was requested to transmit to congress and to the executive of every state.

The legislature held a conference with Hamilton, as the receiver of revenue, but without permanent results; and it included him "pretty unanimously" in its appointment of delegates to congress for the ensuing year. On the fourth of August the resolutions for a federal convention were communicated by Clinton without a word of remark to the congress then in session. There, on the fifteenth, they were referred to a grand committee; but there is no evidence that that congress proceeded to its election.

In his distress for money, Morris solicited a new French loan of twenty millions of livres. The demand was excessive: the king, however, consented to a loan of six millions for the year 1783, of which Franklin immediately received one tenth part. "You will take care," so Vergennes wrote to Luzerne, "not to leave them any hope that the king can make them further advances or guarantee for them new loans from others;" and he complained that the United States did not give sufficient proofs of their readiness to create the means for meeting their debts.†

On the twenty-fourth of December the French auxiliary forces in the United States, except one regiment which soon followed, embarked at Boston for the West Indies. The affections, the gratitude, the sympathy, the hopes of America followed the French officers as they left her shores. What

* MS. copy of the Journals of the Senate and Assembly of New York for the session of July 1782. † Vergennes to Luzerne, 21 December 1782.

boundless services they had rendered in the establishment of her independence! What creative ideas they were to carry home! How did they in later wars defy death in all climes, from San Domingo to Moscow and to the Nile, always ready to bleed for their beautiful land, often yielding up their lives for liberty! Rochambeau, who was received with special honor by Louis XVI., through a happy accident escaped the perils of the revolution, and lived to be more than fourscore years of age. Viomenil, his second in command, was mortally wounded while defending his king in the palace of the Tuileries. De Grasse died before a new war broke out. For more than fifty years Lafayette—in the states general, in convention, in legislative assemblies, at the head of armies, in exile, in cruel and illegal imprisonment, in retirement, in his renewed public life, the emancipator of slaves, the apostle of free labor, the dearest guest of America—remained to his latest hour the true and the ever hopeful representative of loyalty to the cause of liberty. The Viscount de Noailles, who so gladly assisted to build in America the home of human freedom for comers from all nations, was destined to make the motion which in one night swept from his own country feudal privilege and personal servitude. The young Count Henri de Saint-Simon, who during his four campaigns in America mused on the neverending succession of sorrows for the many, devoted himself to the reform of society, government, and industry. Dumas survived long enough to take part in the revolution of July 1830. Charles Lameth, in the states general and constituent assembly, proved one of the wisest and ablest of the popular party, truly loving liberty and hating all excesses in its name. Alexander Lameth, acting with the third estate in the states general, proposed the abolition of all privileges, the enfranchisement of every slave, and freedom of the press; he shared the captivity of Lafayette in Olmütz, and to the end of his life was a defender of constitutional rights. Custine of Metz, whose brilliant services in the United States had won for him very high promotion, represented in the states general the nobility of Lorraine, and insisted on a declaration of the rights of man. Of the Marquis de Chastellux Washington said: "Never have I parted with a man to whom my soul clave more sincerely." * His philanthropic zeal for "the greatest good of the greatest number" was interrupted only by an early death.

Let it not be forgotten that Sécondat, a grandson of the great Montesquieu, obtained promotion for good service in America. Nor may an Amercan fail to name the young Prince de Broglie, though he arrived too late to take part in any battle. In the midday of life, just before he was wantonly sent to the guillotine, he said to his child, then nine years old, afterward the self-sacrificing minister, who kept faith with the United States at the cost of popularity and place: "My son, they may strive to draw you away from the side of liberty, by saying to you that it took the life of your father; never believe them, and remain true to its noble cause."

At the time when the strength which came from the presence of a wealthy and generous ally was departing, the ground was shaking beneath the feet of congress. Pennsylvania, the great central state, in two memorials offered to congress the dilemma, either to satisfy its creditors in that state, or to suffer them to be paid by the state itself out of its contributions to the general revenue. The first was impossible; the second would dissolve the union. Yet it was with extreme difficulty that Rutledge, Madison, and Hamilton, a committee from congress, prevailed upon the assembly of Pennsylvania to desist for the time from appropriating funds raised for the confederation. †

The system for revenue by duties on importations seemed now to await only the assent of Rhode Island. That commonwealth in 1781 gave a wavering answer; and then instructed its delegates in congress to uphold state sovereignty and independence. On the first of November 1782 its assembly unanimously rejected the measure for three reasons: the impost would bear hardest on the most commercial states, particularly upon Rhode Island; officers unknown to the constitution would be introduced; a revenue for the expenditure of which congress is not to be accountable to the states would

---

\* Sparks, viii., 367.

† Gilpin, 199, 216, 224, 488; Journals of Congress, 4 December 1782; Minutes of Assembly of Pennsylvania for 1782, pp. 663, 675, 733.

render that body independent of its constituents, and would be repugnant to the liberty of the United States.*

The necessity of the consent of every one of the thirteen states to any amendment of the confederacy gave to Rhode Island a control over the destinies of America. Against its obstinacy the confederation was helpless. The reply to its communication, drafted by Hamilton, declared, first: that the duty would prove a charge not on the importing state, but on the consumer; next, that no government can exist without a right of appointing officers for those purposes which proceed from and centre in itself, though the power may not be expressly known to the constitution; lastly, the impost is a measure of necessity, "and, if not within the letter, is within the spirit of the confederation." †

The growing discontent of the army, the clamor of public creditors, the enormous deficit in the revenue, were invincible arguments for a plan which promised relief. Congress having no resource except persuasion, three of its members would have borne its letter to Rhode Island but for intelligence from Virginia.‡

In the legislature of that state, Richard Henry Lee, waiting till the business of the session was nearly over and the house very thin,# proposed to the assembly to withdraw its assent to the federal impost; and the repeal was carried in the house on the sixth, in the senate on the seventh of December, ‖ without a negative. The reasons for the act, as recited in its preamble, were: "The permitting any power other than the general assembly of this commonwealth to levy duties or taxes upon the citizens of this state within the same is injurious to its sovereignty, may prove destructive of the rights and liberty of the people, and, so far as congress may exercise the same, is contravening the spirit of the confederation." ▲

Far-sighted members of congress prognosticated the most pernicious effects on the character, interests, and duration of

---

\* Records of Rhode Island, ix., 487, 612, 682, 683, 684.
† Journals of Congress, iv., 200. ‡ Gilpin, 488, 238; Elliot, 17.
# Governor B. Harrison to Washington, 31 March 1783.
‖ Papers of Old Congress, vol. lxv. Journals of House of Delegates, 55–58.
▲ Hening, xi., 171.

the confederacy. The broad line of party division was clearly drawn. The contest was between the existing league of states and a republic of united states; between "state sovereignty "* and a "consolidated union;" † between "state politics and continental politics;" ‡ between the fear of "the centripetal" and the fear of "the centrifugal force" in the system.# Virginia made itself the battle-ground on which for the next six years the warring opinions were to meet. During all that time Washington and Madison led the striving for a more perfect union; Richard Henry Lee, at present sustained by the legislature of Virginia, was the persistent champion of separatism and the sovereignty of each state.

How beneficent was the authority of the union appeared at this time from a shining example. To quell the wild strife which had grown out of the claim of Connecticut to lands within the charter boundary of Pennsylvania, five commissioners appointed by congress opened their court at Trenton. "The case was well argued by learned counsel on both sides," and, after a session of more than six weeks, the court pronounced ‖ their unanimous opinion, that the jurisdiction and pre-emption of the lands in controversy did of right belong to the state of Pennsylvania. The judgment was approved by congress; and the parties in the litigation gave the example of submission to this first settlement of a controversy between states by the decree of a court established by the United States.

\* William Gordon to A. Lee. Lee's Life of Arthur Lee, ii., 291.
† Lafayette in Diplomatic Correspondence, x., 41.
‡ Hamilton, i., 356.
# Speech of Wilson, 28 January 1783, in Gilpin, 290; Elliot, 34. The same figure was used by Hamilton to Washington, 24 March 1783. Hamilton, i., 348.
‖ Journals of Congress, 30 December 1782.

## CHAPTER III.

### AMERICA AND GREAT BRITAIN.

### 1782–1783.

The king of France heard from Vergennes, with surprise and resentment, that the American deputies had signed their treaty of peace;* Marie Antoinette was conciliated by the assurance that "they had obtained for their constituents the most advantageous conditions." "The English buy the peace rather than make it," wrote Vergennes to his subaltern in London; their "concessions as to boundaries, the fisheries, and the loyalists, exceed everything that I had thought possible." † "The treaty with America," answered Rayneval, "appears to me like a dream." ‡ Kaunitz # and his emperor ‖ mocked at its articles.

King George of England was mastered by a consuming grief for the loss of America, and knew no ease of mind by day or by night. When, on the fifth of December, in his speech at the opening of parliament, he came to read that he had offered to declare the colonies of America free and independent states, his manner was constrained △ and his voice fell. To wound him least, Shelburne in the house of lords, confining himself to the language of the speech from the throne,

---

\* Count Mercy's report from Paris, 6 December 1782. MS. from Vienna archives. † Vergennes to Rayneval, 4 December 1782. MS.
‡ Rayneval to Vergennes, 12 December 1782. MS.
# Kaunitz's note of 22 December 1782, written on the emperor's copy of the speech of the king of England at the opening of parliament. MS.
‖ Autograph memorandum of Joseph. MS. Joseph II. und Leopold von Toscana. Ihr Briefwechsel von 1781 bis 1790, i., 146.
△ Rayneval to Vergennes, 12 December 1782. MS.

represented the offer of independence to America as contingent on peace with France. To a question from Fox on the following night in the other house, Pitt, with unfaltering courage, answered that the recognition was unqualified and irrevocable.

During the Christmas holidays the negotiations for a general peace were pursued with equal diligence and moderation by Vergennes and Shelburne; and France made sacrifices of its own to induce Spain to forego the recovery of Gibraltar and assent to terms which in all other respects were most generous. The Netherlands, though their definitive peace was delayed, agreed in the suspension of arms. Franklin shrewdly and truly observed that it would be better for the nations then possessing the West India islands to let them govern themselves as neutral powers, open to the commerce of all, the profits of the present monopolies being by no means equivalent to the expense of maintaining them;* but the old system was preserved. Conquests were restored, and England felt it to be no wound to her dignity to give back an unimportant island which she had wrested from the house of Bourbon in a former war. The East Indian allies of France, of whom the foremost was Tippoo Saib, the son and successor of Hyder Ali, were invited to join in the peace. France recovered St. Pierre and Miquelon and her old share in the fisheries of Newfoundland; Spain retained Minorca, and, what was of the greatest moment for the United States, both the Floridas, which she certainly would find a burden. Treaties of commerce between Great Britain and each of the two Bourbon kingdoms were to be made within two years.

When, on the twentieth of January, these preliminaries were signed by the respective plenipotentiaries, John Adams and Benjamin Franklin, on the summons of Vergennes, were present, and in the name of the United States acceded to the declaration of the cessation of hostilities. The provisional treaty between Great Britain and the United States was held to take effect from that day.

"At last," wrote Vergennes to Rayneval, as soon as the meeting was over, "we are about to breathe under the shadow of peace. Let us take care to make it a solid one; may the

* Diplomatic Correspondence, iv., 69.

name of war be forgotten forever." * In a letter to Shelburne on that same day he expressed the confident hope that all ancient distrust would be removed; and Shelburne replied: "The liberal spirit and good faith which have governed our negotiations leave no room to fear for the future either distrust or jealousy." † King George dwelt with Rayneval on the cordial understanding which he desired to establish with Louis XVI. "I wish," said he, "never again to have a war with France; we have had a first division of Poland; there must not be a second." ‡

So came the peace which recognised the right of a commonwealth of Europeans outside of Europe, occupying a continental territory within the temperate zone; remote from foreign interference; needing no standing armies; with every augury of a rapid growth; and sure of exercising the most quickening and widest influence on political ideas, " to assume an equal station among the powers of the earth."

The restoration of intercourse with America pressed for instant consideration. Burke was of opinion that the navigation act should be completely revised; Shelburne and his colleagues, aware that no paltry regulation would now succeed, were indefatigable in digesting a great and extensive system of trade, and sought, by the emancipation of commerce, to bring about with the Americans a family friendship more beneficial to England than their former dependence.# To promote this end, on the evening of the eleventh of February, William Pitt, with the permission of the king, repaired to Charles James Fox and invited him to join the ministry of Shelburne. The only good course for Fox was to take the hand which the young statesman offered; but he put aside the overture with coldness, if not with disdain, choosing a desperate alliance with those whose conduct he had pretended to detest, and whose principles it was in later years his redeeming glory to have opposed.

* Vergennes to Rayneval, 20 January 1783. MS.
† Vergennes to Shelburne, 20 January 1783; Shelburne to Vergennes, 24 January 1783. Lansdowne House MSS.
‡ Rayneval to Vergennes, 24 and 28 January 1783. MS.
# Price in Lee's Life of Arthur Lee, ii., 349.

Pending the negotiations with France and Spain, Fox and Lord North remained quiet, from the desire to throw the undivided responsibility for the peace on Lord Shelburne; but when on the seventeenth of February, in a house of four hundred and fifty members, the treaties with the United States and with both branches of the Bourbons were laid before parliament, and an address of approval, promising a liberal revision of commercial law, was moved, the long-pent-up passions raged without restraint. No sooner had William Wilberforce, with grace and good feeling, seconded the motion and in the warmest language assured to the loyal refugees compensation for their losses, than Lord John Cavendish, the nearest friend of Fox, condemned the peace, though supporting its conditions. Lord North then pronounced against it a most elaborate, uncandid, and factious invective. He would have deprived the United States of access to the upper lakes; he would have retained for Canada the country north and northwest of the Ohio; and, bad as is a possession which gives no advantage but powers of annoyance, he would have kept east Florida as well as the Bahamas, so as to compel the ships of America, in passing through the Florida channel, to run the gauntlet between British posts. He would have had no peace without the reinstatement of the loyalists, nor without securing independence to the savage allies of Great Britain. He enumerated one by one the posts in the West which by the treaty fell to America, dwelt on the cost of their construction and on their importance to the fur-trade, and foreshadowed the policy of delaying their surrender. He not only censured the grant to the Americans of a right to fish on the coast of Nova Scotia, but spoke as if they derived from Great Britain the right to fish on the banks in the sea which are the exclusive property of no one. At the side of Lord North stood Edmund Burke, with hotter zeal as a partisan, though with better intentions toward America. Pitt answered every objection to the treaty; but, after a debate of twelve hours, the ministry on the division found themselves in a minority of sixteen.

On the same evening, to a larger number of peers than had met in their house since the accession of George III., Carlisle, the unsuccessful commissioner of 1778, Keppel, the inglorious admiral, and Stormont, the late headstrong ambassador at Paris, eager to become once more a secretary of state, Lord George Germain, now known as Lord Sackville, Wedderburn, now Lord Loughborough and coveting the office of lord chancellor, poured forth criminations of a treaty for which the necessity was due to their own incapacity. In perfect understanding with Fox and Lord North, they complained that the ministers had given up the banks of the Ohio, "the paradise of America," had surrendered the fur-trade, had broken faith with the Indians, had been false to the loyalists. Thurlow ably defended every article of the treaty that had been impeached, and then asked: "Is there any individual in this house who dares to avow that his wish is for war?" The interest of the debate centred in Shelburne, and the house gave him the closest attention as he spoke: "Noble lords who made a lavish use of these Indians have taken great pains to show their immense value, but those who abhorred their violence will think the ministry have done wisely." Naming a British agent who had been detested for wanton cruelty, he continued: "The descendants of William Penn will manage them better than all the Stuarts, with all the trumpery and jobs that we could contrive.

"With regard to the loyalists, I have but one answer to give the house. It is the answer I gave my own bleeding heart. A part must be wounded that the whole empire may not perish. If better terms could have been had, think you, my lords, that I would not have embraced them? If it had been possible to put aside the bitter cup which the adversities of this country presented to me, you know I would have done it.

"The fur-trade is not given up; it is only divided, and divided for our benefit. Its best resources lie to the northward. Monopolies, some way or other, are ever justly punished. They forbid rivalry, and rivalry is the very essence of the well-being of trade. This seems to be the era of protestantism in trade. All Europe appears enlightened and eager to throw off the vile shackles of oppressive, ignorant, unmanly monopoly. It is always unwise; but, if there is any nation under heaven who ought to be the first to reject monopoly, it is the English. Situated as we are between the Old World and the New, and between southern and northern Europe, all that we ought to covet is equality and free-trade. With more industry, with more enterprise, with more capital than any trading nation upon earth, it ought to be our constant cry, Let every market be open; let us meet our rivals fairly and ask no more, telling the Americans that we desire to live with them in communion of benefits and in sincerity of friendship." *

At near half-past four in the morning the majority of the lords for the ministry was only thirteen.

On the twenty-first, resolutions censuring them were offered in the house of commons. In the former debate, Fox had excused the change in his relations to Lord North by the plea that his friendships were perpetual, his enmities placable; keeping out of sight that political principles may not be sacrificed to personal reconciliations, he now proclaimed and justified their coalition. "Their coalition," replied Pitt, "originated rather in an inclination to force the earl of Shelburne from the treasury than in any real conviction that ministers deserve censure for the concessions they have made. † Whatever appears dishonorable or inadequate in the peace on your table is strictly chargeable to the noble lord in the blue ribbon," Lord North, " whose profusion of the public money, whose notorious temerity and obstinacy in prosecuting the war which originated in his pernicious and oppressive policy, and whose utter incapacity to fill the station he occupied, rendered peace of any description indispensable to the preservation of the state. The triumph of party shall never induce me to call the abandonment of former principles a forgetting of ancient prejudices, or to pass an amnesty upon measures which have brought my country almost to the verge of ruin. I will never engage in political enmities without a public cause; I will never forego such enmities without the public approbation. High situation and great influence I am solicitous to possess, whenever they can be acquired with dignity. I relinquish them the moment any duty to my country, my character, or my friends, renders such a sacrifice indispensable. I look

* Almon's Parliamentary Register, xxviii., 67, 68. † Ibid., xxvi., 347.

to the independent part of the house and to the public at large for that acquittal from blame to which my innocence entitles me. My earliest impressions were in favor of the noblest and most disinterested modes of serving the public. These impressions I will cherish as a legacy infinitely more valuable than the greatest inheritance. You may take from me the privileges and emoluments of place, but you cannot, you shall not, take from me those habitual regards for the prosperity of Great Britain which constitute the honor, the happiness, the pride of my life. With this consolation, the loss of power and the loss of fortune, though I affect not to despise, I hope I shall soon be able to forget. I praise Fortune when constant; if she strikes her swift wing, I resign her gifts and seek upright, unportioned poverty." *

The eloquence of Pitt, his wise conduct, and the purity of his morals, gained him the confidence to which Fox vainly aspired.†

A majority of seventeen appearing against Shelburne, he resigned on the twenty-fourth; and by his advice the king on the same day offered to Pitt, though not yet twenty-four years old, the treasury, with power to form an administration and with every assurance of support. But the young statesman, obeying alike the dictates of prudence and the custom of the British constitution, would not accept office without a majority in the house of commons; and on the twenty-seventh, finding that such a majority could not be obtained but by the aid, or at least the neutrality, of Lord North, he refused the splendid offer, unalterably firm alike against the entreaties and the reproaches of the king. This moderation in a young man, panting with ambition and conscious of his powers, added new lustre to his fame.

While the imperfect agreement between the members of the coalition delayed the formation of a ministry, on the third of March, Pitt, as chancellor of the exchequer, presented a bill framed after the liberal principles of Shelburne. ‡ Its preamble, which rightly described the Americans as aliens, declared

---

* Almon, xxvi., 341, 352; Life of Romilly, i., 205.
† Moustier to Vergennes, 1 March 1783. MS.
‡ Fox in Moustier to Vergennes, 11 April 1783, MS.; Price in Life of A. Lee. ii., 349.

"it highly expedient that the intercourse between Great Britain and the United States should be established on the most enlarged principles of reciprocal benefit;" and, as a consequence, not only were the ports of Great Britain to be opened to them on the same terms as to other sovereign states, but, alone of the foreign world, their ships and vessels, laden with the produce or manufactures of their own country, might as of old enter all British ports in America, paying no other duties than those imposed on British vessels.

On the seventh Eden objected, saying: "The bill will introduce a total revolution in our commercial system. Reciprocity with the United States is nearly impracticable, from their provincial constitutions. The plan is utterly improper, for it completely repeals the navigation act. The American states lie so contiguous to our West Indian islands, they will supply them with provisions to the ruin of the provision trade with Ireland. We shall lose the carrying trade, for the Americans are to be permitted under this bill to bring West Indian commodities to Europe. The Americans on their return from our ports may export our manufacturing tools, and, our artificers emigrating at the same time, we shall see our manufactures transplanted to America. Nothing more should be done than to repeal the prohibitory acts and vest the king in council with powers for six months to suspend such laws as stand in the way of an amicable intercourse."

Pitt agreed that "the bill was most complicated in its nature and most extensive in its consequences," [*] and, giving it but faint support, he solicited the assistance and the information of every one present to mould it, so that it might prove most useful at home and most acceptable in America. "While there is an immense extent of unoccupied territory to attract the inhabitants to agriculture," said Edmund Burke, "they will not be able to rival us in manufactures. Do not treat them as aliens. Let all prohibitory acts be repealed, and leave the Americans in every respect as they were before in point of trade." The clause authorizing direct intercourse between the United States and the British West India islands was allowed to remain in the report to the house.[†]

[*] Almon, xxvi., 439.     [†] Almon, xxvi., 503.

Before the bill was discussed again, the coalition, after long delays caused by almost fatal dissensions among themselves, had been installed. In pursuit of an ascendency in the cabinet, Lord North plumed himself on having ever been a consistent whig; believing that "the appearance of power was all that a king of England could have;" * and insisting that during all his ministry " he had never attributed to the crown any other prerogative than it was acknowledged to possess by every sound whig and by all those authors who had written on the side of liberty." † But he betrayed his friends by contenting himself with a subordinate office in a cabinet in which there would always be a majority against him, and, while Fox seized on the lead, the nominal chieftainship was left to the duke of Portland, who had neither capacity for business, nor activity, nor power as a speaker, nor knowledge of liberal principles.

The necessity of accepting a ministry so composed drove the king to the verge of madness. He sorrowed over "the most profligate age;" "the most unnatural coalition;" ‡ and he was heard to use "strong expressions of personal abhorrence of Lord North, whom he charged with treachery and ingratitude of the blackest nature." # "Wait till you see the end," ‖ said the king to the representative of France at the next levee; and Fox knew that the chances in the game were against him, as he called to mind that he had sought in vain the support of Pitt; had defied the king; and had joined himself to colleagues whom he had taught liberal Englishmen to despise, and whom he himself could not trust.

In the slowly advancing changes of the British constitution, the old whig party, as first conceived by Shaftesbury and Locke to resist the democratic revolution in England on the one side, and the claim of arbitrary sovereignty by the Stuarts on the other, was near its end. The time was coming for the people to share in power. For the rest of his life, Fox battled for the reform of the house of commons, so that it became the rallying cry of the liberal party in England. A ministry di-

---

* Russell's Memorials of Charles James Fox, ii., 38. † Almon, xxvi., 355.
‡ The king to Shelburne, 22 February 1783. MS. # Memorials of Fox, ii., 249.
‖ Moustier to Vergennes, 3 April 1783. MS.

vided within itself by irreconcilable opinions, detested by the king, confronted by a strong and watchful and cautious opposition, was forced to follow the line of precedents. The settlement of the commercial relations to be established with the United States had belonged to the treasury; it was at once brought by Fox within his department, although, from his ignorance of political economy, he could have neither firm convictions nor a consistent policy. He was not, indeed, without glimpses of the benefit of liberty in trade. To him it was a problem how far the act of navigation had ever been useful, and what ought to be its fate;* but the bill in which the late ministry had begun to apply the principle of free commerce with America he utterly condemned, "not," as he said, "from animosity toward Shelburne, but because great injury often came from reducing commercial theories to practice." More over, the house of commons would insist on much deliberation and very much inquiry before it would sacrifice the navigation act to the circumstances of the present crisis.†

In judging his conduct, it must be considered that the changes in the opinion of a people come from the slow evolution of thought in the public mind. One of the poets of England, in the flush of youth, had prophesied:

"The time shall come when, free as seas or wind,
Unbounded Thames shall flow for all mankind,
Whole nations enter with each swelling tide,
And seas but join the regions they divide."

More than half a century must pass away before the prophecy will come true by the efforts of statesmen, who, had they lived in the time of Fox, might have shared his indecision.

The coalition cabinet at its first meeting agreed to yield no part of the navigation act, ‡ and, as a matter of policy, to put off the bill before parliament relating to commerce with America "till some progress should be made in a negotiation with the American commissioners at Paris." Thither without delay Fox sent, as minister on the part of Great Britain, David Hartley, a friend of Franklin and a well-wisher to the United States.

---

* Moustier to Vergennes, 11 April 1783. MS.
† Fox to Hartley, 10 June 1783. MS.
‡ Fox to the king, Memorials of Fox, ii., 122.

The avowed liberal opinions of Hartley raising distrust, Lord Sheffield, a supporter of the ministry, and, on trade with America, the master authority of that day for parliament, immediately sounded an alarm. "Let the ministers know," said he on the fifteenth, in the house of lords, "the country is as tenacious of the principle of the navigation act as of the principle of Magna Charta. They must not allow America to take British colonial produce to ports in Europe. They must reserve to our remaining dominions the exclusive trade to the West India islands; otherwise, the only use of them will be lost. If we permit any state to trade with our islands or to carry into this country any produce but its own, we desert the navigation act and sacrifice the marine of England. The peace is in comparison a trifling object." * But there was no need of fear lest Fox should yield too much. In his instructions to Hartley, he was for taking the lion's share, as Vergennes truly said.† He proposed that the manufactures of the thirteen states should as a matter of course be excluded from Great Britain, but that British manufactures should be admitted everywhere in the United States. While America was dependent, parliament had taxed importations of its produce, but British ships and manufactures entered the colonies free of duty. "The true object of the treaty in this business," so Fox enforced his plan, "is the mutual admission of ships and merchandise free from any new duty or imposition;" ‡ that is, the Americans on their side should leave the British navigation act in full force and renounce all right to establish an act of navigation of their own; should continue to pay duties in the British ports on their own produce; and receive in their own ports British produce and manufactures duty free. One subject appealed successfully to the generous side of his nature. To the earnest wish of Jay that British ships should have no right under the convention to carry into the states any slaves from any part of the world, it being the intention of the United States entirely to prohibit their importation,# Fox answered promptly: "If that be their policy, it never can be

---

\* Almon, xxvi., 615.      † Works of John Adams, iii., 380.
‡ Fox to Hartley, 10 April 1783. MS.
\# June 1783. Diplomatic Correspondence, x., 154.

competent to us to dispute with them their own regulations." *
In like spirit, to formal complaints that Carleton, "in the face
of the treaty, persisted in sending off negroes by hundreds,"
Fox made answer: "To have restored negroes whom we invited, seduced if you will, under a promise of liberty, to the
tyranny and possibly to the vengeance of their former masters,
would have been such an act as scarce any orders from his
employers (and no such orders exist) could have induced a
man of honor to execute." †

The dignity and interests of the republic were safe, for
they were confided to Adams, Franklin, and Jay. In America
there existed as yet no system of restrictions; and congress
had not power to protect shipping or establish a custom-house.
The states as dependencies had been so severely and so wantonly cramped by British navigation acts, and for more than a
century had so steadily resisted them, that the desire of absolute freedom of commerce had become a part of their nature.
The American commissioners were very much pleased with
the trade-bill of Pitt, and with the principles expressed in its
preamble; the debates upon it in parliament awakened their
distrust. They were ready for any event, having but the one
simple and invariable policy of reciprocity. Their choice and
their offer was mutual unconditional free trade; but, however
narrow might be the limits which England should impose, they
were resolved to insist on like for like. ‡ The British commissioner was himself in favor of the largest liberty for commerce,
but he was reproved by Fox for transmitting a proposition not
authorized by his instructions.

A debate in the house of lords on the sixth of May revealed
the rapidity with which the conviction was spreading that
America had no power to adopt measures of defensive legislation. There were many who considered the United States as
having no government at all, and there were some who looked
for the early dissolution of the governments even of the separate states. Lord Walsingham, accordingly, proposed that the
law for admitting American ships should apply not merely to
the ships of the United States, but to ships belonging to any

---

\* Fox to Hartley, 10 June 1783. MS.     † Fox to Hartley, 9 August 1783.
‡ Hartley to Fox, 20 May 1783. MS.

one of the states and to any ship or vessel belonging to any of the inhabitants thereof. He was supported by Thurlow, who said: "I have read an account which stated the government of America to be totally unsettled, and that each province seemed intent on establishing a distinct, independent, sovereign state. If this is really the case, the amendment will be highly necessary and proper." * The amendment was dropped; and the bill under discussion, in its final shape, repealed prohibitory acts made during the war, removed the formalities which attended the admission of ships from the colonies during their state of dependency, and for a limited time left the power of regulating commerce with America to the king in council.

Immediately the proclamation of an order in council of the second of July confined the trade between the American states and the British West India islands to British-built ships owned and navigated "by British subjects." "Undoubtedly," wrote the king, "the Americans cannot expect nor ever will receive any favor from me."† To an American, Fox said: "For myself, I have no objection to opening the West India trade to the Americans, but there are many parties to please."‡

The blow fell heavily on America, and compelled a readjustment of its industry. Ships had been its great manufacture for exportation. For nicety of workmanship, the palm was awarded to Philadelphia, but nowhere could they be built so cheaply as at Boston. More than one third of the tonnage employed in British commerce before the war was of American construction. Britain renounced this resource. The continent and West India islands had prospered by the convenient interchange of their produce; the trade between nearest and friendliest neighbors was forbidden, till England should find out that she was waging war against a higher power than the United States; that her adversary was nature itself. Her statesmen confounded the "navigation act" and "the marine of Britain;" # the one the offspring of selfishness, the other the sublime display of the creative power of a free people.

* Almon, xxviii., 180, 181.
† Correspondence of George III. with Lord North, ii., 442.
‡ Diplomatic Correspondence, 1783-1787, ii., 513; Fox to Hartley, 10 June 1783. MS. # Sheffield's Commerce of the American States, preface, 10.

Such was the issue between the ancient nation which falsely and foolishly and mischievously believed that its superiority in commerce was due to artificial legislation, and a young people which solicited free trade. Yet thrice blessed was this assertion of monopoly by an ignorant parliament, for it went forth as a summons to the commercial and the manufacturing interests of the American states and to the self-respect and patriotism of their citizens to speak an efficient government into being.

Full of faith in the rising power of America, Jay, on the seventeenth of July, wrote to Gouverneur Morris: "The present ministry are duped by an opinion of our not having union and energy sufficient to retaliate their restrictions. No time is to be lost in raising and maintaining a national spirit in America. Power to govern the confederacy as to all general purposes should be granted and exercised. In a word, everthing conducive to union and constitutional energy should be cultivated, cherished, and protected." * Two days later he wrote to William Livingston of New Jersey: "A continental, national spirit should pervade our country, and congress should be enabled, by a grant of the necessary powers, to regulate the commerce and general concerns of the confederacy." On the same day, meeting Hartley, the British envoy, Jay said to him: "The British ministry will find us like a globe—not to be overset. They wish to be the only carriers between their islands and other countries; and though they are apprized of our right to regulate our trade as we please, yet I suspect they flatter themselves that the different states possess too little of a national or continental spirit ever to agree in any one national system. I think they will find themselves mistaken." "The British ministers," so Gouverneur Morris in due time replied to Jay, "are deceived, for their conduct itself will give congress a power to retaliate their restrictions.† This country has never yet been known in Europe, least of all to England, because they constantly view it through a medium of prejudice or of faction. True it is that the general government wants energy, and equally true it is that this want

---

* Jay to G. Morris, 17 July 1783. Sparks's Life of G. Morris, i., 258.
† Gouverneur Morris to Jay, 24 September 1783. Sparks's G. Morris, i., 259.

will eventually be supplied. Do not ask the British to take off their foolish restrictions; the present regulation does us more political good than commercial mischief." *

On the side of those in England who were willing to accept the doctrines of free trade, Josiah Tucker, the dean of Gloucester, remarked: "As to the future grandeur of America, and its being a rising empire, under one head, whether republican or monarchical, it is one of the idlest and most visionary notions that ever was conceived even by writers of romance. The mutual antipathies and clashing interests of the Americans, their difference of governments, habitudes, and manners, indicate that they will have no centre of union and no common interest. They never can be united into one compact empire under any species of government whatever; a disunited people till the end of time, suspicious and distrustful of each other, they will be divided and subdivided into little commonwealths or principalities, according to natural boundaries, by great bays of the sea, and by vast rivers, lakes, and ridges of mountains." †

The principle of trade adopted by the coalition ministry Sheffield set forth with authority in a pamphlet, which was accepted as an oracle. "There should be no treaty with the American states because they will not place England on a better footing than France and Holland, and equal rights will be enjoyed of course without a treaty. The nominal subjects of congress in the distant and boundless regions of the valley of the Mississippi will speedily imitate and multiply the examples of independence. It will not be an easy matter to bring the American states to act as a nation; they are not to be feared as such by us. The confederation does not enable congress to form more than general treaties; when treaties become necessary, they must be made with the states separately. Each state has reserved every power relative to imposts, exports, prohibitions, duties, etc., to itself. ‡ If the American states choose to send consuls, receive them and send a consul to each state. Each state will soon enter into all necessary

---

* Gouverneur Morris to Jay, 10 January 1784. Ibid., 266, 267.
† Dean Tucker's Cui Bono, 1781, 117–119.
‡ Sheffield's Commerce of the American States, 183, 190, 191, 198–200.

regulations with the consul, and this is the whole that is necessary.* The American states will not have a very free trade in the Mediterranean, if the Barbary states know their interests. That the Barbary states are advantageous to the maritime powers is certain; if they were suppressed, little states would have much more of the carrying trade. The armed neutrality would be as hurtful to the great maritime powers as the Barbary states are useful." †

In London it was a maxim among the merchants that, if there were no Algiers, it would be worth England's while to build one. ‡

Already the navigation act was looked to as a protection to English commerce, because it would require at least three fourths of the crews of American ships to be Americans; and they pretended that during the war three fourths of the crews of the American privateers were Europeans.# The exclusion of European seamen from service in the American marine was made a part of British policy from the first establishment of the peace.

In August, Laurens, by the advice of his associates, came over to England to inquire whether a minister from the United States of America would be properly received. "Most undoubtedly," answered Fox, and Laurens left England in that belief. ‖ But the king, when his pleasure was taken, said: " I certainly can never express its being agreeable to me; and, indeed, I should think it wisest for both parties to have only agents who can settle any matters of commerce. That revolted state certainly for years cannot establish a stable government." ᐃ The plan at court was to divide the United States, and for that end to receive only consuls from each one of the separate states and not a minister for the whole. ◊

British statesmen had begun to regret that any treaty whatever had been made with the United States collectively; they would have granted independence and peace, but without

---
\* Sheffield's Commerce of the United States, 277.   † Ibid., 204, 205, note.
‡ Franklin in Diplomatic Correspondence, iv., 149.
# Sheffield's Commerce of the American States, 205, note.
‖ Diplomatic Correspondence, ii., 510–515.
ᐃ King to Fox, 7 August 1783; Memorials of Fox, ii., 141.
◊ Adhémar to Vergennes, 7 August 1783. MS.

further stipulations of any kind, so that all other questions might have been left at loose ends. Even Fox was disinclined to impart any new life to the provisional articles agreed upon by the ministry which he supplanted. He repeatedly avowed the opinion that "a definitive treaty with the United States was perfectly superfluous." * The American commissioners became uneasy; but Vergennes pledged himself not to proceed without them,† and Fox readily yielded. On the third of September, when the minister of France and the ambassadors of Great Britain and Spain concluded their conventions at Versailles, the American provisional articles, shaped into a definitive treaty, were signed by Hartley for Great Britain; by Adams, Franklin, and Jay for the United States of America.

The coalition ministry did not last long enough to exchange ratifications. To save the enormous expense of maintaining the British army in New York, Fox hastened its departure; but while "the speedy and complete evacuation of all the territories of the United States" ‡ was authoritatively promised to the American commissioners at Paris in the name of the king, Lord North, acting on the petition of merchants interested in the Canada trade,# withheld orders for the evacuation of the western and north-western interior posts, although by the treaty they were as much an integral part of the United States as Albany or Boston; and this policy, like that relating to commerce, was continued by the ministry that succeeded him.

We may not turn away from England without relating that Pitt for the second time proposed in the house of commons, though in vain, a change in the representation, by introducing one hundred new members from the counties and from the metropolis. Universal suffrage he condemned, and the privilege of the owners of rotten boroughs to name members of parliament had for him the sanctity of private property, to

---

* Fox to duke of Manchester, 9 August 1783. Same to same, 4 August 1783. MS. Same to Hartley 4 August 1783. MS.

† Hartley to Fox, 31 July 1783. MS.

‡ Fox to Hartley, 10 June 1783. MS. Compare Fox to Hartley, 15 May 1783. MS.

# Regulations proposed by the merchants interested in the trade to the province of Quebec, 1783. MS.

be taken away only after compensation. "Mankind," said Fox, "are made for themselves, not for others. The best government is that in which the people have the greatest share. The present motion will not go far enough; but, as it is an amendment, I give it my hearty support."

An early and a most beneficent result of the American revolution was a reform of the British colonial system. Taxation of colonies by the parliament of Great Britain, treatment of them as worthless except as drudges for the enrichment of the ruling kingdom, plans of governing them on the maxims of a Hillsborough or a Thurlow,* came to an end. It grew to be the rule to give them content by the establishment of liberal constitutions.

* Sheffield's Commerce of the American States, 175-180.

## CHAPTER IV.

### AMERICA AND CONTINENTAL EUROPE.

### 1783.

THE governments of continental Europe vied with each other in welcoming the new republic to its place among the powers of the world. In May 1782, as soon as it was known at Stockholm that the negotiations for peace were begun, the adventurous king of Sweden sent messages of his desire, through Franklin above all others, to enter into a treaty with the United States. Franklin promptly accepted the invitation. The ambassador of Gustavus at Paris remarked: "I hope it will be remembered that Sweden was the first power in Europe which, without being solicited, offered its friendship to the United States." * Exactly five months before the definitive peace between the United States and Great Britain was signed, the treaty with Sweden was concluded. Each party was put on the footing of the most favored nations. Free ships were to make passengers free as well as goods. Liberty of commerce was to extend to all kinds of merchandise. The number of contraband articles was carefully limited. In case of a maritime war in which both the contracting parties should remain neutral, their ships of war were to protect and assist each other's vessels. The treaty was ratified and proclaimed in the United States before the definitive treaty with Great Britain had arrived.†

The successful termination of the war aroused in Prussia hope for the new birth of Europe, that, by the teachings of America, despotism might be struck down, and the caste of

---

\* Franklin's Works, ix., 342.      † Journals of Congress, iv., 241.

hereditary nobility give place to republican equality. These aspirations were suffered to be printed at Berlin.*

The great Frederick had, late in 1782, declared to the British minister at his court, half in earnest and half cajoling, that " he was persuaded the American union could not long subsist under its present form. The great extent of country would alone be a sufficient obstacle, since a republican government had never been known to exist for any length of time where the territory was not limited and concentred. It would not be more absurd to propose the establishment of a democracy to govern the whole country from Brest to Riga. No inference could be drawn from the states of Venice, Holland, and Switzerland, of which the situation and circumstances were perfectly different from those of the colonies." † He did not know the power of the representative system, nor could he foresee that by the wise use of it the fourth of his successors would evoke the German state from the eclipse of centuries, to shine with replenished light as the empire of a people. For the moment he kept close watch of the progress of the convention with Sweden, and, so soon as it was signed, directed his minister in France to make overtures to Franklin, which were most gladly received. ‡

Full seven months before the peace a member of the government at Brussels intimated to William Lee, a former commissioner of congress at the court of Vienna, that Joseph II., who at that time harbored the hope of restoring to Belgian commerce its rights by opening the Scheldt and so preparing the way for a direct trade with America, was disposed to enter into a treaty with the United States.# Soon after the preliminaries of peace between France and Great Britain had been signed, the emperor let it be insinuated to Franklin that he would be well received at Vienna as the minister of a sovereign power. ‖ In the following year an agent was sent from Bel-

* Die Freiheit Amerika's. Ode vom Herrn Pr. J. E. H. Berlinische Monatsschrift, April 1783, 386. See J. Scherr's Kultur und Sittengeschichte, 508, 619.

† Sir John Stepney to secretary of state, 22 October 1782. MS.

‡ Goltz to Frederick, 3 March, 28 April, 30 June 1783. MSS.

# William Lee to secretary of foreign affairs, 31 March 1782, Diplomatic Correspondence, ii., 360.

‖ Letter to Franklin from Vienna, 8 April 1783, Franklin's Works, ix., 501.

gium to the United States. The Belgians produced in unsurpassed excellence manufactures which America needed; but they were not enterprising enough to establish houses in America, or to grant its merchants the extended credits which were offered in England.* The subject gained less and less attention, for the emperor was compelled, in violation of natural rights, to suffer the Scheldt to be closed.

On the twenty-second of February 1783, Rosencrone, minister of foreign affairs in Denmark, communicated to Franklin "the satisfaction with which the king's ministry had learned the glorious issue of the war for the United States of America," and their desire to form connections of friendship and commerce. "To overtures for a treaty like that between congress and the states general," he added, "we should eagerly and frankly reply." But a question of indemnity for violations of neutrality by Denmark during the war impeded the negotiation.

Before the end of March the burgomaster and senate of the imperial free city of Hamburg, seeing "European powers courting in rivalry the friendship of" the new state, and impressed with "the illustrious event" of the acknowledged independence of America as "the wonder of that age and of remotest ages to come," deputed one of their citizens to bear to congress their letter, offering free trade between the two republics.

In midsummer, 1783, Portugal made overtures to treat with Franklin, but did not persist in them.

Russia was at that time too much engrossed by affairs in the East to take thought for opening new channels of commerce with the West; and the United States, recalling their minister, declined to make advances. But the two nations, without any mutual stipulations, had rendered each other the most precious services. Catherine had scornfully refused to lend troops to George III., rejected his entreaties for an alliance, and by the armed neutrality insulated his kingdom; the United States, by giving full employment to the maritime powers, had made for the empress the opportunity of annexing to her dominions the plains of Kuban and the Crimea.

* Correspondence of the Austrian agent, Baron de Beelen Bertholff. MS.

Of the chief commercial nations of Europe, Holland entertained for America the most friendly sentiments, invited her trade, and readily granted to her congress all the credit which it had any right to expect.

The independence of the United States gave umbrage to the Spanish court. Galvez, the minister of the colonies, was fiercely and persistently hostile to the extent of the United States in the South-west. Florida Blanca himself wished for amicable rectifications of the boundary; but, on the remonstrances of Lafayette, he, in the presence of the ambassador of France, pledged his word of honor to accept the boundary as laid down in the Anglo-American treaty, and authorized Lafayette to bind him with congress to that pledge. The Spanish statesmen feared the loss of their own colonies, and the success of the American revolution excited new and never-ceasing alarm. They could have wished that North America might disappear from the face of the earth; but they tried to reconcile themselves to living in good harmony with the United States. The Mississippi was the great source of anxiety.

Spain thought it not for her interest that the American states should consolidate their union. She had dreaded the neighborhood of English colonies to her own; she dreaded still more to border all the way from the Atlantic to the fountains of the Mississippi on a republic whose colossal growth was distinctly foreseen. Besides this, the suppression of a rebellion in South America had just cost more than a hundred thousand lives; and the difficulty of governing distant and boundless regions was so great that Aranda, the far-sighted statesman who had signed the treaty of peace, in his official dispatches to Florida Blanca, set forth the opinion that Portugal would be worth more to Spain than all the American main-land. Of the islands he never depreciated the value; but he clearly perceived how precarious was the hold of Spain on her continental possessions; and he left on record the advice, which he may never have had an opportunity to offer personally to his king, that Spain should transform all the vice-royalties in America into secundo-genitures, retaining in direct dependence only Cuba and Porto Rico.*

* Ferro del Rio, iii., 460, 407, note. Muriel, vi, 45–54. Revista Española de

Even Vergennes, while he believed that the attachment of America to the alliance would be safest if the confederation could keep itself alive, held it best for France that the United States should fail to attain the political consistency of which he saw that they were susceptible; and he remained a tranquil spectator of their efforts for a better constitution. Lafayette not only watched over the interests of America in Europe, but to the president of congress and to the secretary for foreign affairs he sent messages imploring American patriots to strengthen the federal union.

Ambos Mundos, for May 1855, written by Ferro del Rio. In his letter on exchanging for Portugal the Spanish possessions in America, Aranda writes, "exceptuando las islas." The train of thought is the same.

## CHAPTER V.

A CALL ON THE ARMY TO INTERPOSE.

JANUARY–MARCH 1783.

IN the fall of 1782 the main army was moved for winter quarters to the wooded hills in the rear of Newburg. No part of the community had undergone equal hardships or borne injustice with equal patriotism. In the leisure of the camp they brooded over their wrongs and their chances of redress, and at the close of the year the officers sent to Philadelphia as their committee Major-General Macdougall and Colonels Ogden and Brooks, who, in their address of the sixth of January 1783, used these words:

"To the United States in congress assembled: We, the officers of the army of the United States, in behalf of ourselves and our brethren the soldiers, beg leave freely to state to the supreme power, our head and sovereign, the great distress under which we labor. Our embarrassments thicken so fast that many of us are unable to go farther. Shadows have been offered to us, while the substance has been gleaned by others. The citizens murmur at the greatness of their taxes, and no part reaches the army. We have borne all that men can bear. Our property is expended; our private resources are at an end. We therefore beg that a supply of money may be forwarded to the army as soon as possible.

"The uneasiness of the soldiers for want of pay is great and dangerous; further experiments on their patience may have fatal effects. There is a balance due for retained rations, forage, and arrearages on the score of clothing. Whenever there has been a real want of means, defect in system, or neglect in execution, we have invariably been the sufferers by hunger and nakedness, and by languishing in a hospital. We beg leave to urge an immediate adjustment of all dues.

"We see with chagrin the odious point of view in which the citizens of too many of the states endeavor to place the men entitled to half-pay. For the honor of human nature we hope that there are none so hardened in the sin of ingratitude as to deny the justice of the reward. To prevent altercations, we are willing to commute the half-pay pledged for full-pay for a certain number of years, or for a sum in gross. And in this we pray that the disabled officers and soldiers, with the widows and orphans of those who have expended, or may expend, their lives in the service of their country, may be fully comprehended.

"General dissatisfaction is gaining ground in the army, from evils and injuries which, in the course of seven long years, have made their condition in many instances wretched. They therefore entreat that congress, to convince the army and the world that the independence of America shall not be placed on the ruin of any particular class of her citizens, will point out a mode for immediate redress."

The grand committee to whom the memorial was referred held a conference with the superintendent of finance. He declared peremptorily that it was impossible, in the present state of the finances, to make any payment to the army, and that it would be imprudent to give assurances with regard to future pay until funds that could be relied upon should be established. Not only had he no money in hand, but he had overdrawn his account in Europe to the amount of three and a half millions of livres. He therefore asked a decision on the expediency of staking the public credit on further drafts to be met by the contingent proceeds of a loan from the Dutch and by the friendship of France. On the tenth of January, congress, under an injunction of secrecy, authorized the superintendent to draw bills on the credit of applications for loans in Europe. Dyer of Connecticut alone opposed the measure as unwarranted and dishonorable, but allowed the resolution to be entered as unanimous.*

* Gilpin, 248–252, 299; Elliot, 21, 22, 38; Secret Journals of Congress, i., 253.

In an interview with the grand committee on the evening of the thirteenth,* the deputies from the army explained that, without an immediate payment of some part of the overdue pay, the discontent alike of officers and soldiers could not be soothed; that a mutiny might ensue; and that it would be hard to punish soldiers for a breach of engagements to the public which the public itself had already flagrantly broken. "The army," said Macdougall, "is verging to that state which, we are told, will make a wise man mad." It was a source of irritation that the members of the legislatures never adjourned till they had paid themselves fully, that all on the civil lists of the United States regularly received their salaries, and that all on the military lists were as regularly left unpaid. †

The deputies animadverted with surprise and even indignation on the repugnance of some of the states to establish a federal revenue for discharging federal engagements, while the affluence of the people indicated adequate resources. Speaking with peculiar emphasis and making a strong impression by his manner, General Macdougall declared "that the most intelligent part of the army were deeply touched by the debility of the federal government and the unwillingness of the states to invigorate it; in case of its dissolution, the benefits expected from the revolution would be greatly impaired; and the contests which might ensue among the states would be sure to embroil their respective officers."

Hamilton had for himself renounced the half-pay. The grand committee, in their report which he drafted, advised some payment to the army as soon as possible; for the rest, they were to have no priority over other creditors; all were to wait alike for the funding of the whole debt of the United States by general revenues. The officers were to have the option of preserving their claim to half-pay as it then stood, or accepting a commutation. ‡

"A great majority of the members of congress," avowed Robert Morris, "will not adopt the necessary measures because they are afraid of offending their states;" and he un-

---
\* Gilpin, 256, 257; Elliot, 23.
† Gilpin, 256–258; Elliot, 23, 24; Washington to J. Jones, Sparks, viii., 370.
‡ Hamilton, i., 274; Gilpin, 276, 277; Elliot, 29, 30.

dertook to drive them to decisive action. Accordingly, on the twenty-fourth, the day on which the report was taken up, he sent to them his resignation of office in these words: "The funding the public debts on solid revenues, I fear, will never be made. If before the end of May effectual measures to make permanent provision for the public debts of every kind are not taken, congress will be pleased to appoint some other man to be the superintendent of their finances: I will never be the minister of injustice." The design of Robert Morris required the immediate publication of his letter, that, by uniting the army with all other creditors, congress and the states might be coerced into an efficient system; but congress reasoned that this authoritative statement of the financial ruin of the country would encourage the enemy, annihilate foreign and domestic credit, and provoke the army to mutiny. They therefore placed the communication under the injunction of secrecy.*

Resuming the consideration of the report of their grand committee on the memorial from the army, they referred a present payment to the discretion of the superintendent of finance; and, on the fifth of February, he issued a warrant, out of which the officers received one month's pay in notes and the private soldiers one month's pay in weekly instalments of half a dollar. †

The annual amount of the half-pay promised to the officers for life was nearly five hundred thousand dollars. The validity of the engagement was questioned. The grant was disliked by the common soldiers; it found no favor in the legislature of Massachusetts; the delegates of Connecticut and Rhode Island were instructed to oppose it altogether. To avoid defeat, this article was laid over till there should be a fuller representation. ‡ Delegates from the states in which the domestic debt was chiefly held hoped for efficient co-operation from the army. Pennsylvania was the largest creditor; Massachusetts ranked next; South Carolina, Georgia, and

---

* Diplomatic Correspondence, xii., 325–328.  Gilpin, 274, 275; Elliot, 29.

† Report of the deputies in Sparks, viii., 552. The amount of this one month's pay was 253,232.86 dollars. Old account-books in Treasury department. Wastebook D, Ledger B. MS. ‡ Gilpin, 281, 321; Elliot, 31, 45.

Delaware were the lowest; Virginia was but the ninth, holding less than New Hampshire and not half so much as Rhode Island. The zeal for the equal support of all classes of public creditors culminated in those states whose citizens originally owned nearly four times as much as those of all the six southern states, and by transfers were constantly acquiring more.*

Adopting unanimously a resolution which Hamilton had prepared, congress pledged itself to consider immediately the most likely mode of obtaining revenues adequate to the funding of the whole debt of the United States.† Encouraged by this seeming heartiness, Wilson of Pennsylvania, on the twenty-seventh, proposed "the establishment of general funds to be collected by congress." ‡ To the dismay of the friends of a general revenue, Theodorick Bland of Virginia interposed and officially presented the act of his state repealing the grant of the impost, and a resolution of both its houses declaring its present inability to pay more than fifty thousand pounds Virginia currency toward the demands of congress for 1782.#

The debate, nevertheless, went on. Gorham of Massachusetts suggested polls and commerce as most proper objects of taxation. Hamilton, discussing the subject in a comprehensive manner, spoke for permanent sources of revenue which should extend uniformly throughout the United States, and be collected by the authority of congress. Dyer strongly disliked the appointment of collectors by congress; the states would never consent to it. Ramsay of South Carolina supported Gorham and Hamilton. Again Bland placed himself in the way, saying: "The states are so averse to a general revenue in the hands of congress that, even if it were proper, it is unattainable." He therefore advised congress to pursue the rule of the confederation and ground requisitions on an actual valuation of houses and lands in the several states.

At this stage of the discussion, an efficient reply could be made only by one who was of Virginia. To Randolph, then in Richmond, Madison had already written: "Virginia could never have cut off the impost at a more unlucky crisis than

---

\* Gilpin, 364, note; Elliot, 60. † Gilpin, 277, 280; Elliot, 30, 31.
‡ Gilpin, 282, 285; Elliot, 32.
# Resolution of 28 December 1782, in Journal of the Delegates, 80, 90.

when she is protesting her inability to comply with the continental requisitions. Congress cannot abandon the plan as long as there is a spark of hope. Nay, other plans on a like principle must be added. Justice, gratitude, our reputation abroad and our tranquillity at home, require provision for a debt of not less than fifty millions of dollars; and this provision will not be adequately met by separate acts of the states. If there are not revenue laws which operate at the same time through all the states, and are exempt from the control of each, mutual jealousies will assuredly defraud both our foreign and domestic creditors of their just claims." *

Madison, on the twenty-eighth, presented a milder form of the resolution for a general revenue. Arthur Lee lost no time in confronting his colleague : " The states will never consent to a uniform tax, because it will be unequal; is repugnant to the articles of confederation ; and, by placing the purse in the same hands with the sword, subverts the fundamental principles of liberty." Wilson explained : The articles of confederation have expressly provided for amendments ; there is more of a centrifugal than centripetal force in the states; the funding of a common debt would invigorate the union. Ellsworth despaired of a continental revenue ; condemned periodical requisitions from congress as inadequate; and inclined to the trial of permanent state funds. In reply, Hamilton showed that state funds would meet with even greater obstacles than a general revenue ; but he lost the sympathy of the house by adding that the influence of federal collectors would assist in giving energy to the federal government. Rutledge thought that the prejudices of the people were opposed to a general tax, and seemed disinclined to it himself. Williamson was of opinion that continental funds, though desirable, were unattainable.

"The idea," said Madison, "of erecting our national independence on the ruins of public faith and national honor must be horrid to every mind which retains either honesty or pride. Is a continental revenue indispensably necessary for doing complete justice to the public creditors ? This is the question.

---

* Madison to Randolph, 22 January 1783, in Gilpin, 111. The date is erroneously given as of 1782.

"A punctual compliance by thirteen independent governments with periodical demands of money from congress can never be reckoned upon with certainty. The articles of confederation authorize congress to borrow money. To borrow money, permanent and certain provision is necessary; and, as this cannot be made in any other way, a general revenue is within the spirit of the confederation. Congress are already invested by the states with constitutional authority over the purse as well as the sword. A general revenue would only give this authority a more certain and equal efficacy.

"The necessity and reasonableness of a general revenue have been gaining ground among the states. I am aware that one exception ought to be made. The state of Virginia, as appears by an act yesterday laid before congress, has withdrawn its assent once given to the scheme. This circumstance cannot but embarrass a representative of that state advocating it; one, too, whose principles are extremely unfavorable to a disregard of the sense of constituents. But, though the delegates who compose congress more immediately represent and are amenable to the states from which they come, yet they owe a fidelity to the collective interests of the whole. The part I take is the more fully justified to my own mind by my thorough persuasion that, with the same knowledge of public affairs which my station commands, the legislature of Virginia would not have repealed the law in favor of the impost, and would even now rescind the repeal."

On the following day the proposition of Wilson and Madison, with slight amendments, passed the committee of the whole without opposition. On the twelfth of February it was adopted in congress by seven states in the affirmative, and without the negative of any state.

For methods of revenue, the choice of Madison was an impost, a poll-tax which should rate blacks somewhat lower than whites, and a moderate land-tax. To these Wilson wished to add a duty on salt and an excise on wine, imported spirits, and coffee. Hamilton, who held the attempt at a land-tax to be futile and impossible, suggested a house- and window-tax. Wolcott of Connecticut thought requisitions should be in proportion to the population of each state; but was willing to include in the enumeration those only of the blacks who were within sixteen and sixty years of age.*

Just at this time Pelatiah Webster, a graduate of Yale college, in a dissertation published at Philadelphia, † proposed for the legislature of the United States a congress of two houses which should have ample authority for making laws " of general necessity and utility," and enforcing them as well on individuals as on states. He further suggested not only heads of executive departments, but judges of law and chancery. The tract was reprinted in Hartford, and called forth a reply.

Plans of closer union offered only a remote solution of the difficulties under which the confederation was sinking. How the united demand of all public creditors could wrest immediately from congress and the states the grant of a general revenue and power for its collection employed the thoughts of Robert Morris and his friends. On Christmas eve 1781, Gouverneur Morris, the assistant financier, had written to Greene: " I have no expectation that the government will acquire force; and no hope that our union can subsist, except in the form of an absolute monarchy, and this does not seem to consist with the taste and temper of the people." To Jay, in January 1783, ‡ he wrote: " The army have swords in their hands. Good will arise from the situation to which we are hastening; much of convulsion will probably ensue, yet it must terminate in giving to government that power without which government is but a name."

Hamilton held it as certain that the army had secretly determined not to lay down their arms until due provision and a satisfactory prospect should be afforded on the subject of their pay; that the commander-in-chief was already become extremely unpopular among all ranks from his known dislike to every unlawful proceeding; but, as from his virtue, his patriotism, and firmness, he would sooner suffer himself to be cut in pieces than yield to disloyal plans, Hamilton wished him

---

* Gilpin, 300, 304–306, 331; Elliot, 38–40, 48.

† A Dissertation on the Political Union and Constitution of the thirteen United States of North America, dated 16 February 1783. In Pelatiah Webster's Political Essays, 228.   ‡ Sparks's G. Morris, i., 240, 249.

to be the "conductor of the army in their plans for redress," to the exclusion of a leader like Horatio Gates.*

With these convictions and with exceeding caution, he, on the seventh of February, addressed himself directly to Washington in a letter, of which Brooks, on his return to the camp, was the bearer. "We," so he wrote of congress, "are a body not governed by reason or foresight, but by circumstances. It appears to be a prevailing opinion in the army that, if they once lay down their arms, they part with the means of obtaining justice. Their claims, urged with moderation but with firmness, may operate on those weak minds which are influenced by their apprehensions more than by their judgments, so as to produce a concurrence in the measures which the exigencies of affairs demand. To restore public credit is the object of all men of sense; in this the influence of the army, properly directed, may co-operate." And he invited Washington to make use of General Knox, † to whom Gouverneur Morris wrote on the same day and by the same channel.

To ensure the concerted action of the southern army, Gouverneur Morris wrote privately to Greene: "The main army will not easily forego their expectations. Their murmurs, though not loud, are deep. If the army, in common with all other public creditors, insist on the grant of general, permanent funds for liquidating all the public debts, there can be little doubt that such revenues will be obtained, and will afford to every order of public creditors a solid security. With the due exception of miracles, there is no probability that the states will ever make such grants unless the army be united and determined in the pursuit of it, and unless they be firmly supported by and as firmly support the other creditors. That this may happen must be the entire wish of every intelligently just man and of every real friend to our glorious revolution." ‡

The letter of Gouverneur Morris to Knox, which was in reality a communication through Knox to Washington, cannot be found. It evidently expressed the opinion that the army might be made to co-operate in bringing about a closer union

---

* Gilpin, 350, 351; Elliot, 55.
† Hamilton to Washington, 7 February 1783. Hamilton, i., 327.
‡ G. Morris to Greene, 15 February 1783. Sparks's G. Morris, i., 250.

of the states and a stronger government. The answer of Knox expresses the advice of Washington: "The army are good patriots, and would forward everything that would tend to produce union and a permanent general constitution; but they are yet to be taught how their influence is to effect this matter. A 'hoop to the barrel' is their favorite toast. America will have fought and bled to little purpose if the powers of government shall be insufficient to preserve the peace, and this must be the case without general funds. As the present constitution is so defective, why do not you great men call the people together and tell them so—that is, to have a convention of the states to form a better constitution? This appears to us, who have a superficial view only, to be the most efficacious remedy." *

On the thirteenth of February the speech of the king of Great Britain, at the opening of parliament in December, was received. His announcement of provisional articles of peace with the United States produced great joy; yet that joy was clouded by apprehensions from the impossibility of meeting the just claims of the army.

Congress was brought no nearer to decisive action. Hamilton proposed that the doors of congress should be thrown wide open whenever the finances were under discussion, though the proposal, had it been accepted, would have filled the galleries with holders of certificates of the public debt. †

On the other side, John Rutledge again and again moved that the proceeds of the impost should be appropriated exclusively to the army, but was supported only by his own state. Ruffled by his indifference to the civil creditors, Wilson had one day answered with warmth: "Pennsylvania will take her own measures without regard to those of congress, and she ought to do so. She is willing to sink or swim according to the common fate; but she will not suffer herself, with a millstone of six millions of the continental debt, to go to the bottom alone."

The weakness of the friends of a general revenue appeared from their consenting to leave to the several states the ap-

* Knox to G. Morris, 21 February 1783, in Sparks's G. Morris, i., 256.
† Gilpin, 336, 341; Elliot, 50, 52.

pointment of the collectors of taxes, and to limit the grant of the impost to twenty-five years.*

Once more Mercer and Arthur Lee renewed their war upon Madison, who in reply made a convincing plea for the necessity of a permanent general revenue. "The purse," repeated Arthur Lee, " ought never to be put in the same hand with the sword. I will be explicit; I would rather see congress a rope of sand than a rod of iron. Virginia ought not to concur in granting to congress a permanent revenue." "If the federal compact is such as has been represented," said Mercer, "I will immediately withdraw from congress, and do everything in my power to destroy its existence." Chafed by these expressions, Gorham of Massachusetts cried out: "The sooner this is known the better, that some of the states may form other confederacies adequate to their safety." †

The assiduous labors of congress for two months had failed to devise the means for restoring public credit. In February some of its members thought the time had arrived when order and credit could come, if the army would support its demands by its strength. Robert Morris extorted from congress a removal of the injunction of secrecy on his letter of resignation, and forthwith sent it not only to Washington but to the public press, through which it immediately reached the army.

* Gilpin, 314, 347, 348; Elliot, 43, 54.   † Gilpin, 357, 511; Elliot, 57.

## CHAPTER VI.

### THE AMERICAN ARMY AND ITS CHIEF.

### MARCH 1783.

THE commander-in-chief suppressed the wish to visit Mount Vernon during the winter, for the army at Newburg was more unquiet than at any former period.* The Massachusetts line formed more than half of it, and so many of the remainder were from other eastern states that he could describe them all as New England men.† He had made the delicate state of affairs "the object of many contemplative hours," and he was aware of the prevailing sentiment that the prospect of compensation for past services would terminate with the war. ‡

Now that peace was at hand, his first act was by a letter to Harrison, then governor of Virginia, to entreat his own state to enter upon a movement toward a real union. "From the observations I have made in the course of this war—and my intercourse with the states in their united as well as separate capacities has afforded ample opportunities of judging—I am decided in my opinion," such were his words, "that, if the powers of congress are not enlarged and made competent to all general purposes, the blood which has been spilt, the expense that has been incurred, and the distresses which have been felt, will avail nothing; and that the band which holds us together, already too weak, will soon be broken; when anar-

* Sparks, viii., 355, 369.
† Gorham in Gilpin, 315. Elliot, 43. Washington to Joseph Jones. Sparks, viii., 383; and compare Sparks, viii., 456.
‡ Washington to Hamilton, 4 March 1783. Sparks, viii., 389, 390.

chy and confusion will prevail.* I shall make no apology for the freedom of these sentiments; they proceed from an honest heart; they will at least prove the sincerity of my friendship, as they are altogether undisguised." The governor received this letter as a public appeal, and placed it among the archives of Virginia.

Before the officers had taken into consideration the cautious report of their committee to congress, Colonel Walter Stewart, an inspector of troops, coming back from Philadelphia, presented himself at the quarters of Gates as "a kind of agent from the friends of the army in congress;" † and rumors were immediately circulated through the camp that it was universally expected the army would not disband until they had obtained justice; that the public creditors looked up to them for aid, and, if necessary, would even join them in the field; that some members of congress wished the measure might take effect, in order to compel the public, particularly the delinquent states, to do justice. ‡

A plan of action was in the utmost secrecy devised by Gates and those around him. To touch with ability the several chords of feeling which lay slumbering in the army, his aide-de-camp, Major John Armstrong, was selected to draft an address. This was copied, and Colonel Barber, the assistant adjutant-general of the division of Gates, taking care not to be tracked, put it in circulation through the line of every state,# with a notice for a meeting of the general and field officers on the next day, to consider what measures should be adopted to obtain that redress of grievances which they seemed to have solicited in vain. ||

"My friends!" so ran the anonymous appeal, "after seven long years your suffering courage has conducted the United States of America through a doubtful and a bloody war; and

* Washington to Harrison, 4 March 1783. Maxwell's Virginia Historical Register, vi., 36, 37.
† Gates to Armstrong, 22 June 1783. I follow a manuscript copy received from J. K. Armstrong. The letter has been printed in United States Magazine, i., 40.
‡ Washington to Joseph Jones, 12 March 1783. Sparks, viii., 393, 394. Washington to Hamilton, 12 March 1783. Hamilton, i., 343.
# Gates to Armstrong, 22 June, 1783. || Journal of Congress, iv., 208.

peace returns to bless—whom? A country willing to redress your wrongs, cherish your worth, and reward your services? Or is it rather a country that tramples upon your rights, disdains your cries, and insults your distresses? Have you not lately, in the meek language of humble petitioners, begged from the justice of congress what you could no longer expect from their favor? How have you been answered? Let the letter which you are called to consider to-morrow make reply!

"If this be your treatment while the swords you wear are necessary for the defence of America, what have you to expect when those very swords, the instruments and companions of your glory, shall be taken from your sides, and no mark of military distinction left but your wants, infirmities, and scars? If you have sense enough to discover and spirit to oppose tyranny, whatever garb it may assume, awake to your situation. If the present moment be lost, your threats hereafter will be as empty as your entreaties now. Appeal from the justice to the fears of government; and suspect the man"—here Washington was pointed at—"who would advise to longer forbearance." *

A copy of the address reached Washington on Tuesday, the eleventh, and the meeting was to take place in the evening of that very day. Resolutions dictated by passion and tending to anarchy, if once adopted, could never be effaced, and might bring ruin on the army and the nation. There was need of instant action, "to arrest the feet that stood wavering on a precipice." † To change ill-considered menaces into a legal presentment of grievances, the commander, in general orders, disapproved the anonymous and irregular invitation to a meeting, and at the same time requested all the highest officers and a representation of the rest to assemble at twelve o'clock on the next Saturday to hear the report of the committee which they had sent to congress. "After mature deliberation, they will devise what further measures ought to be adopted to attain the just and important object in view. The senior officer in rank present will preside and report the result of their deliberations to the commander-in-chief." Gates quailed, and the

\* Journal of Congress, iv., 208.
† Washington to Hamilton, 12 March 1783. Hamilton, i., 344.

gathering for that evening was given up; but under his eye Armstrong prepared a second anonymous address, which, while it professed to consider the general orders of Washington "as giving stability to their resolves," recommended "suspicion" as their "sentinel." During the week, Washington employed himself, with Knox and others whom he could trust, in preparing methods to avert every fatal consequence.

At noon on the fifteenth the officers assembled, with Gates in the chair. They were surprised to find that the commander-in-chief was with them. Every eye was fixed on him; and all were mute, awaiting his words.*

After an apology to his "brother officers" for his presence, he read his analysis of the anonymous addresses. Their author he praised for his rhetorical skill, but denied the rectitude of his heart, and denounced his scheme as fit to proceed from no one but a British emissary. He thus continued:

"As I was among the first who embarked in the cause of our common country; as I have never left your side one moment, but when called from you on public duty; as I have been the constant companion and witness of your distresses, it can scarcely be supposed that I am indifferent to your interests." He proceeded to demonstrate that any attempt to compel an instant compliance with their demands would certainly remove to a still greater distance the attainment of their ends. They must place their reliance on the plighted faith of their country and the purity of the intentions of congress to render them ample justice, though its deliberations, from the difficulty of reconciling different interests, might be slow.

"For myself," he said, "so far as may be done consistently with the great duty I owe my country and those powers we are bound to respect, you may command my services to the utmost extent of my abilities.

"While I give you these assurances, let me entreat you, gentlemen, on your part, not to take any measures which, in the calm light of reason, will lessen the dignity and sully the glory you have hitherto maintained. Let me conjure you in the name of our common country, as you value your own sacred honor, as you respect the rights of humanity, and as you regard

* Shaw to Rev. John Eliot, 27 April 1783.

the military and national character of America, to express your utmost horror and detestation of the man who wickedly attempts to open the floodgates of civil discord and deluge our rising empire in blood.

"By thus determining and thus acting, you will pursue the plain and direct road to the attainment of your wishes; you will give one more proof of unexampled patriotism and patient virtue, rising superior to the pressure of the most complicated sufferings; and you will afford occasion for posterity to say: 'Had this day been wanting, the world had never seen the last stage of perfection to which human nature is capable of attaining.'"

On concluding his address, the general, in further proof of the good disposition of congress, began to read parts of a letter from a member of that body; but, after getting through a single paragraph, he paused, and asked leave of his audience to put on spectacles, which he had so lately received * that he had never yet worn them in public,† saying: "I have grown gray in your service, and now find myself growing blind." These unaffected words touched every heart. The letter, which was from Joseph Jones of King George county in Virginia, set forth the embarrassments of congress and their resolve that the army should at all events be justly dealt with. Washington then withdrew.

Officers, who a few hours before had yielded themselves to the anonymous addresses, veered about, and would now follow no counsellor but their own commander. The assembly unanimously thanked him for his communications and assured him of their affection, "with the greatest sincerity of which the human heart is capable." Then, after a reference to Knox, Brooks, and Howard as their committee, they resolved unanimously: "At the commencement of the present war, the officers of the American army engaged in the service of their country from the purest love and attachment to the rights and liberties of human nature, which motives still exist in the high-

---

* From Rittenhouse. Washington to Rittenhouse, 16 February 1783; Memoirs of Rittenhouse, 299, 300.

† "C'étoit la première fois qu'il les prenoit en publique." Mazzei, Recherches. iv., 122.

est degree; and no circumstances of distress or danger shall induce a conduct that may tend to sully the reputation and glory which they have acquired at the price of their blood and eight years' faithful services." Making no demands and confining their expectations within the most reasonable limits, they declared their unshaken confidence in the justice of congress and their country, and they asked nothing of their chief but to urge congress to a speedy decision upon their late memorial.

Another resolution declared "that the officers of the American army view with abhorrence and reject with disdain the infamous propositions contained in a late anonymous address to them." Gates meekly put the question, and was obliged to report that it was carried unanimously.

No one ever ruled the hearts of his officers like Washington. The army of America had seen him calm and commanding in the rage of battle; patient and persistent under multiplied misfortunes; moderate in victory; but then he had been countenanced by his troops and his friends; here he stood alone, amid injured men of inflamed passions, with swords at their sides, persuaded that forbearance would be their ruin, and, for a fearful moment, looking upon him as their adversary. As he spoke, every cloud was scattered, and the full light of love of country broke forth. Happy for America that she had a patriot army; happy for America and for the world that that army had Washington for its chief!

The official narrative of these events was received in congress on the twenty-second, and, before the day came to an end, nine states concurred in a resolution * commuting the half-pay promised to the officers into a sum equal to five years' full pay, to be discharged by certificates bearing interest at six per cent. Georgia and Rhode Island were not adequately represented; New Hampshire and New Jersey voted in the negative; all the other states irrevocably pledged the United States to redeem their promise made to the officers in the dark hours of their encampment at Valley Forge.

On the next day a ship dispatched from Cadiz by d'Estaing, at the instance of Lafayette, brought authentic news that the American and British commissioners had signed defini-

---

* Bland to Washington, 22 March 1783. MS.

tively a provisional treaty, of which an official copy had been received eleven days before, and that peace with Great Britain had already taken effect. The American boundaries on the northwest exceeded alike the demands and the hopes of congress, and it was already believed that a later generation would make its way to the Pacific ocean.*

The glad tidings drew from Washington tears of joy in that "happiest moment of his life." "All the world is touched by his republican virtues," wrote Luzerne. "It will be in vain for him to wish to hide himself and live as a simple, private man; he will always be the first citizen of the United States." † All the while no one like him had pursued with single-mindedness and perseverance and constant activity the great object of creating a republican government for the continent. To Hamilton he wrote on the last day of March 1783 : "I rejoice most exceedingly that there is an end to our warfare, and that such a field is opening to our view, as will with wisdom to direct the cultivation of it, make us a great, a respectable, and happy people ; but it must be improved by other means than state politics, and unreasonable jealousies and prejudices, or it requires not the second sight to see that we shall be instruments in the hands of our enemies and those European powers who may be jealous of our greatness in union, to dissolve the confederation. But to obtain this, although the way seems extremely plain, is not so easy.

"My wish to see the union of these states established upon liberal and permanent principles, and inclination to contribute my mite in pointing out the defects of the present constitution, are equally great. All my private letters have teemed with these sentiments, and, whenever this topic has been the subject of conversation, I have endeavored to diffuse and enforce them. No man in the United States is or can be more deeply impressed with the necessity of a reform in our present confederation than myself. No man, perhaps, has felt the bad effects of it more sensibly; for to the defects thereof, and want of power in congress, may justly be ascribed the prolongation of the war and consequently the expenses occasioned

* Luzerne to Vergennes, 19 March 1783. MS.
† Luzerne to Vergennes, 29 March 1783.

by it. More than half the perplexities I have experienced in the course of my command, and almost the whole of the difficulties and distress of the army, have had their origin here. But still, the prejudices of some, the designs of others, and the mere machinery of the majority, make address and management necessary to give weight to opinions which are to combat the doctrines of those different classes of men in the field of politics." *

Upon official information from Franklin and Adams, congress on the eleventh of April made proclamation for the cessation of hostilities. In announcing the great event to the army, Washington did especial honor to the men who had enlisted for the war, and added: "Happy, thrice happy shall they be pronounced hereafter who have contributed anything in erecting this stupendous fabric of freedom and empire; who have assisted in protecting the rights of human nature, and establishing an asylum for the poor and oppressed of all nations and religions." † The proclamation of congress that war was at an end was published to the army on the nineteenth, exactly eight years from the day when the embattled farmers of Concord "fired the shot heard round the world."

* Sparks's Washington, viii., 409, 410, 411. Washington to Hamilton, 31 March 1783. † Sparks, viii., 568.

## CHAPTER VII.

### DISBANDING THE ARMY.

### MARCH–JULY 1783.

WASHINGTON presented the rightful claims of the "patriot army"* with a warmth and energy which never but this once appear in his communications to congress; and his words gained intenser power from his disinterestedness. To a committee on which were Bland and Hamilton, he enforced, by every consideration of gratitude, justice, honor, and national pride, the "universal" expectations of the army, that, before their disbanding, they should receive pay for at least one month in hand, with an absolute assurance in a short time of pay for two months more. "The financier will take his own measures, but this sum must be procured. The soldier is willing to risk the hard-earned remainder due him for four, five, perhaps six years upon the same basis of security with the general mass of other public creditors." †

"The expectations of the army," answered Hamilton, "are moderation itself." ‡ But, after a week's reflection, Morris, who had already written to congress "our public credit is gone," # replied to the committee that the amount of three months' pay was more than all the receipts from all the states since 1781; that there was no resource but the issue of paper notes in anticipation of revenue. ‖

* Washington to congress, 18 March 1783. Sparks, viii., 396–399.
† Washington to Bland, 4 April 1783.
‡ Hamilton to Washington, 11 April 1783. Letters to Washington, iv., 17.
\# Diplomatic Correspondence, xii., 342.
‖ R. Morris to Hamilton, 14 April 1783. Diplomatic Correspondence, xii., 346.

## DISBANDING THE ARMY.

A sharp admonition from Vergennes to the United States speedily to meet their engagements in France and Holland,* and the representations of Washington, quickened the determination of congress. In preparing the plan for a revenue, Madison was assisted by Jefferson, who passed a large part of the winter in Philadelphia.

The national debt of Great Britain at the beginning of the war with America amounted to one hundred and thirty-six millions of pounds; at the close of it, including deficiencies that were still to be funded, it amounted to twice that sum. The debt of the United States did not much exceed forty-two millions of dollars; the annual interest on that debt was not far from two and a half millions, and to fund it successfully there was need of a yearly revenue of at least that sum. One million was hoped for from specific duties on enumerated imports, and a duty of five per cent on the value of all others. A million and a half dollars more were to be raised by requisitions of congress, apportioned on the states according to population. This more convenient method had hitherto failed from conflicts on the rule for counting slaves. The South had insisted on the ratio of two for one freeman. Williamson of North Carolina said: "I am principled against slavery. I think slaves an incumbrance to society instead of increasing its ability to pay taxes." † To effect an agreement, Madison, seconded by John Rutledge, offered that slaves should be rated as five to three, and this compromise, which then affected taxation only and not representation, was accepted almost with unanimity. ‡

In the beginning of April, Hamilton had declared in congress that he wished to strengthen the federal constitution through a general convention, and should soon, in pursuance of instructions from his constituents, propose a plan for that purpose. # In the mean time, he remained inflexible in the opinion that an attempt to obtain revenue by an application to the several states would be futile, because an agreement could never be arrived at through partial deliberations. The

---
* Luzerne to R. Morris, 15 March 1783. Diplomatic Correspondence, xi., 157, 158.
† Gilpin, 423; Elliot, 79.
‡ Gilpin, 423, 424; Elliot, 79.
# Gilpin, 429, 430; Elliot, 81.

vote on the report of the new financial measure, which he opposed as inadequate, was taken on the eighteenth of April. Georgia alone was absent; eleven states were fully represented; New Hampshire by a single delegate. Hamilton and the two representatives of Rhode Island, alone and for the most opposite reasons, gave their votes in the negative. New York being divided, nine states and a half against one, twenty-five delegates against three, recorded their votes for the adoption of the report.

To the relentless exigencies of the moment the financial proposition of the eighteenth of April offered no relief, nor could it take effect until it should be accepted by every one of the thirteen states. To win this unanimous assent, congress, in the words of Madison, enforced the peculiar nature of their obligations to France, to members of the republic of Holland, and to the army. Moreover, "the citizens of the United States are responsible for the greatest trust ever confided to a political society. If justice, good faith, honor, gratitude, and all the other qualities which ennoble the character of a nation and fulfil the ends of government, be the fruits of our unadulterated forms of republican government, the cause of liberty will acquire a dignity and lustre which it has never yet enjoyed; and an example will be set which cannot but have the most favorable influence on the rights of mankind." New York, North and South Carolina, and Massachusetts were following the example of Virginia, and repealing their revenue acts of former years; when the address went forth, accompanied by the letter of congress to the governor of Rhode Island which Hamilton had drafted, and by various papers showing the amount and the character of the debt of the United States.

Then, on the twenty-eighth, and so far as the records show never till then, congress appointed a committee on the New York resolutions of the preceding July in favor of a general convention. Its choice fell on Ellsworth, Carroll, Wilson, Gorham, Hamilton, Peters, McHenry, Izard, and Duane.*

---

* Madison, on whom we depend for a report of the debates of congress of that period, was absent from Saturday, April the twenty-sixth, to Tuesday, May sixth. So details are wanting. That Clinton's letter and the New York resolutions were committed on the twenty-eighth of April, we know from a MS. memorandum by Charles Thomson.

In October 1780, congress provided for forming new states out of the north-western territory.* A most elaborate report, read in November 1781, recommended that the lands for settlements " should be laid out into townships of about six miles square." † Early in 1783 Rufus Putnam, with other officers and soldiers of the army in New England, engaged heartily in a plan to form a state westward of the Ohio, and Timothy Pickering, who had framed a complete plan for settling lands in Ohio, proposed to them that " the total exclusion of slavery from the state should form an essential and irrevocable part of the constitution." ‡ To " unite the thirteen states in one great political interest," Bland, a man of culture, who had served with credit as a colonel of dragoons, and had been a member of congress from Virginia since 1780, now, on the fifth of June 1783, brought forward an " ordinance " to accept conditionally the cession of Virginia, divide it into districts of two degrees of latitude by three degrees of longitude, and subdivide each district into townships of a fixed number of miles square; each district to be received into the union as a " sovereign " state, so soon as it could count twenty thousand inhabitants. In these embryo states, every one who had enlisted for the war or had served for three years was to receive the bounty lands promised him, and thirty acres more for each dollar due to him from the United States. One tenth part of the soil was to be reserved for " the payment of the civil list of the United States, the erecting of frontier posts, and the founding of seminaries of learning; the surplus to be appropriated to the building and equipping a navy, and to no other purpose whatever." This pioneer ordinance for colonizing the territory north-west of the Ohio was seconded by Hamilton, and referred to a grand committee.#

From the moment when it became officially known that a

* Laws relating to Public Lands, 338; Journals of Congress, iii., 535.
† Endorsement on the original report in the state department is: " Read in congress 3 November 1781."
‡ Pickering's Pickering, i., 546.
# Papers of Old Congress, xxxvi. MS. The ordinance is in the handwriting of Theodorick Bland, and indorsed by Charles Thomson: " Motion of Mr. Bland seconded by Mr. Hamilton. June 5, 1783. Referred to the grand committee of 30 May 1783."

preliminary treaty of peace had been concluded, Robert Morris persistently demanded the immediate discharge of the army.* The city of New York and the interior posts being still in British hands, his importunity was resisted by Gorham and Hamilton, and disapproved by the secretary of foreign affairs; but the public penury overcame all scruples.

As the time drew near for the officers to pass from military service to civil life, they recalled the example of the Roman Cincinnatus, and, adopting his name, formed themselves into "one society of friends," to perpetuate "the spirit of brotherly kindness" and to help officers and their families in their times of need. An immutable attachment to the rights and liberties of human nature was made the law of conduct for members, to whatever nation they might belong; and those who were Americans pledged to each other their "unalterable determination to promote and cherish union between the states."† By one grave error, which called forth from many sides in America and in Europe the severest censure, membership was made hereditary in their eldest male posterity. The commander-in-chief, who had no offspring, refused to separate himself from his faithful associates in the war; but by his influence the society at its first general meeting in May 1784 proposed to its branches in the states to expunge from its constitution the clauses which had excited alarm and just complaint.

The general order of the second day of June published the resolve of congress that the men engaged for the war, with a proper proportion of officers, were immediately to receive furloughs, on the reverse of which was their discharge, to take effect on the definitive treaty of peace. Washington felt the keenest sensibility at their distresses; ‡ but he had exhausted all his influence. The army, for three months' pay, received only notes exactly "like other notes issued from the office of finance." # These were nominally due in six months to the bearer, with six per cent interest till paid. Their value in the

---

* Diary of Morris in Dip. Cor., xii., 367, note.   † Sparks, ix., 23, note.
‡ Washington to Heath, 6 June 1783. Sparks, viii., 435.
# Washington to Bland, 4 April 1783; Journals of Congress, for July 9 and following days, iv., 237, 238; Morris to congress, 18 July 1783, Dip. Cor., xii., 376, 380–386 and 387–389, and other letters.

market was two shillings or two and sixpence for twenty shillings.* The veterans were enthusiasts for liberty, and therefore, with the consciousness of having done their duty to their native land and to mankind, they, in perfect good order, bearing with them their arms as memorials of their service, retired to their homes "without a settlement of their accounts, and without a farthing of money in their pockets." †

The events of the last four months called into full action the powers and emotions of Washington. "State politics," said he, "interfere too much with the more liberal and extensive plan of government which wisdom and foresight would dictate. The honor, power, and true interest of this country must be measured by a continental scale. To form a new constitution that will give consistency, stability, and dignity to the union and sufficient powers to the great council of the nation for general purposes, is a duty incumbent upon every man who wishes well to his country." ‡

Lifted above himself, and borne on by the energy of his belief, he in June addressed the whole people through a last circular to the governor of every state,# for he was persuaded that immediate and extreme danger overhung the life of the union. "With this conviction of the importance of the present crisis," such are his words, "silence in me would be a crime; I will therefore speak without disguise the language of freedom and of sincerity. Those who differ from me in political sentiment may remark that I am stepping out of the proper line of my duty; but the rectitude of my own heart, the part I have hitherto acted, experience acquired by long and close attention to the business of that country in whose service I have spent the prime of my life and whose happiness will always constitute my own, the ardent desire I feel of enjoying in private life, after all the toils of war, the benefits of a wise and liberal government, will sooner or later convince my countrymen that this address is the result of the purest intention."

* Pelatiah Webster's Political Essays, 310; compare 272.
† Washington to Congress, 7 and 24 June 1783. Sparks, viii., 438, 456.
‡ Washington to Lafayette, 5 April 1783. Sparks, viii., 412.
# Sparks, viii., 439. The date of the circular varies with the time of its successive emission to the several states.

Thoughtful for the defence of the republic, the retiring commander-in-chief recommended "a proper peace establishment," and an absolutely uniform organization of the "militia of the union" throughout "the continent." He pleaded for complete justice to all classes of public creditors. He entreated the legislature of each state to pension its disabled non-commissioned officers and privates. He enforced the duty of the states, without "hesitating a single moment," to give their sanction to the act of congress establishing a revenue for the United States, for the only alternative was a national bankruptcy. "Honesty," he said, "will be found on every experiment to be the best and only true policy. In what part of the continent shall we find any man or body of men who would not blush to propose measures purposely calculated to rob the soldier of his stipend, and the public creditor of his due?"

He then proceeded to pronounce solemn judgment, and to summon the people of America to fulfil their duty to Providence and to their fellow-men. "If a spirit of disunion, or obstinacy and perverseness, should in any of the states attempt to frustrate all the happy effects that might be expected to flow from the union, that state which puts itself in opposition to the aggregate wisdom of the continent will alone be responsible for all the consequences.*

"The citizens of America, the sole lords and proprietors of a vast tract of continent, are now acknowledged to be possessed of absolute freedom and independency. Here Heaven has crowned all its other blessings by giving a fairer opportunity for political happiness than any other nation has ever been favored with. The rights of mankind are better understood and more clearly defined than at any former period. The collected wisdom acquired through a long succession of years is laid open for our use in the establishment of our forms of government. The free cultivation of letters, the unbounded extension of commerce, the progressive refinement of manners, the growing liberality of sentiment, and, above all, the pure and benign light of revelation, have had a meliorating influence on mankind. At this auspicious period, the United States came into existence as a nation.

* Sparks, viii., 446, 447.

"Happiness is ours if we seize the occasion and make it our own. This is the moment to give such a tone to our federal government as will enable it to answer the ends of its institution. According to the system of policy the states shall adopt at this moment, it is to be decided whether the revolution must ultimately be considered as a blessing or a curse; a blessing or a curse, not to the present age alone, for with our fate will the destiny of unborn millions be involved.

"Essential to the existence of the United States is the friendly disposition which will forget local prejudices and policies, make mutual concessions to the general prosperity, and, in some instances, sacrifice individual advantages to the interest of the community. Liberty is the basis of the glorious fabric of our independency and national character, and whoever would dare to sap the foundation, or overturn the structure, under whatever specious pretext he may attempt it, will merit the bitterest execration and the severest punishment which can be inflicted by his injured country.

"It is indispensable to the happiness of the individual states that there should be lodged somewhere a supreme power to regulate and govern the general concerns of the confederated republic, without which the union cannot be of long duration,* and everything must very rapidly tend to anarchy and confusion. Whatever measures have a tendency to dissolve the union, or to violate or lessen the sovereign authority, ought to be considered as hostile to the liberty and independence of America. It is only in our united character that we are known as an empire, that our independence is acknowledged, that our power can be regarded, or our credit supported among foreign nations. The treaties of the European powers with the United States of America will have no validity on a dissolution of the union. We shall be left nearly in a state of nature; or we may find by our own unhappy experience that there is a natural and necessary progression from the extreme of anarchy to the extreme of tyranny, and that arbitrary power is most easily established on the ruins of liberty abused to licentiousness."

This circular letter of Washington the governors of the

---
* Sparks, viii., 444.

states, according to his request, communicated to their respective legislatures. In this way it was borne to every home in the United States, and he entreated the people to receive it as "his legacy" on his retirement to private life.

He avoided the appearance of dictating to congress how the constitution should be formed; but, while he was careful to declare himself "no advocate for their having to do with the particular policy of any state further than it concerns the union at large," he had no reserve in avowing his "wish to see energy given to the federal constitution by a convention of the people." *

The newspapers of the day, as they carried the letter of Washington into every home, caught up the theme, and demanded a revision of the constitution, "not by congress, but by a continental convention, authorized for the purpose." †

* Washington to Dr. William Gordon, 8 July 1783.
† Among them: Philadelphia, 3 July 1783; Maryland Gazette, 11 July; Virginia Gazette, 19 July.

# THE FORMATION OF THE CONSTITUTION

OF THE

# UNITED STATES OF AMERICA.

*IN FIVE BOOKS.*

BOOK SECOND.

ON THE WAY TO A FEDERAL CONVENTION.

1783–1787.

## CHAPTER I.

#### HOW THE LAND RECEIVED THE LEGACY OF WASHINGTON.

#### JUNE–DECEMBER 1783.

ALL movements conspired to form for the thirteen states a constitution, sooner than they dared to hope and "better than they knew." "The love of union and the resistance to the claims of Great Britain were the inseparable inmates of the same bosom. Brave men from different states, risking life and everything valuable in a common cause, believed by all to be most precious, were confirmed in the habit of considering America as their country and congress as their government." * Acting as one, they had attained independence. Moreover, it was their fixed belief that they had waged battle not for themselves alone, but for the hopes and the rights of mankind; and this faith overleapt the limits of separate commonwealths with the force of a religious conviction. For eighteen years the states had watched together over their liberties; for eight they had borne arms together to preserve them; for more than two they had been confederates under a compact to remain united forever.

The federation excelled every one that had preceded it. Inter-citizenship and mutual equality of rights between all its members gave to it a new character and an enduring unity. The Hebrew commonwealth was intensely exclusive, both by descent and from religion; every Greek republic grew out of families and tribes; the word nation originally implied a common ancestry. All mediæval republics, like the Roman municipalities, rested on privilege. The principle of inter-citi-

* Marshall in Van Santvoord's Chief Justices of the United States, 314, 315.

zenship infused itself neither into the constitution of the old German empire, nor of Switzerland, nor of Holland. Even when the American people took up arms against Great Britain, congress defined only the membership * of each colony; the articles of confederation first brought in the rule that any one might at will transfer his membership from one state to another. Of old a family, a sept, a clan, a tribe, a nation, a race, owed its unity to consanguinity. Inter-citizenship now took the place of consanguinity; the Americans became not only one people, but one nation. They had framed a union of several states in one confederacy, fortified and bound in with a further union of the inhabitants of every one of them by a mutual and reciprocally perfect naturalization.† This inter-citizenship, though only in its third year, has been so ratified by national affections, by the national acquisition of independence, by national treaties, by national interests, by national history, that the people possessing it cannot but take one step more, and from an indwelling necessity form above the states a common constitution for the whole.

It was to a nation which had not as yet a self-existent government, and which needed and felt the need of one, that Washington's legacy went forth. The love which was everywhere cherished for him, in itself had become a bond of union. "They are compelled to await the result of his letter," reported Luzerne; ‡ "they hope more from the weight of a single citizen than from the authority of the sovereign body." Jonathan Trumbull, the venerable governor of Connecticut, in his prompt reply extolled "this last address which exhibited the foundation principles" of "an indissoluble union of the states under one federal head." # When in the next autumn this faithful war governor, after more than fifty years of service, bade farewell to public life, imitating Washington, he set forth to the legislature of Connecticut, and through them to its people, that the grant to the federal constitution of powers clearly defined, ascertained, and understood, and sufficient

---

\* Journals of Congress, i., 365.
† Bacon's speech for general naturalization, Spedding's Bacon's Letters and Life, iii., 319.    ‡ Luzerne to Vergennes, 4 August 1783.
\# Jonathan Trumbull to Washington, 10 June 1783.

for all the great purposes of union, could alone lead from the danger of anarchy to national happiness and glory. *

In June the general assembly of Delaware complied with all parts of the recommendation of congress, coupling the impost with the state's quota of the federal requisition.† To Washington, Nicholas Van Dyke, the governor, on receiving the circular, reported this proof of their zeal for establishing the credit of the union, adding: "The state which declines a similar conduct must be blind to the united interest with which that of the individual states is inseparably connected." ‡

Pennsylvania, linking together the North and the South, never hesitated; then and ever after, it made the reasoning and the hopefulness of Washington its own. At a festival in Philadelphia, held near the middle of July, with Dickinson, the president of the state, in the chair, the leading toast was: " New strength to the union;" and, when " Honor and immortality to the principles in Washington's circular letter " was proposed, the company rose twice and manifested their approbation by nine huzzas.

A month later, Dickinson and the council of Pennsylvania sent to the general assembly the valedictory of the commander-in-chief, quoting and enforcing his words, saying: "We most earnestly recommend that the confederation be strengthened and improved. To advance the dignity of the union is the best way to advance the interest of each state. A federal supremacy, with a competent national revenue, to govern firmly general and relative concerns," can alone " ensure the respect, tranquillity, and safety, that are naturally attached to an extensive and well-established empire. All the authorities before mentioned may be vested in a federal council, not only without the least danger to liberty, but liberty will be thereby better secured." # The house on the twenty-fifth, joining together the impost and the quota of the state, unanimously ordered the grant of them both,‖ and at a later session thanked Washington specially for his final "circular letter, the inestimable legacy bequeathed to his country."

---

\* Stuart's Trumbull, 604–608. † Papers of Old Congress, lxxv. MS.
‡ Nicholas Van Dyke to Washington, 2 July 1783.
# Colonial Records, xiii., 648, 649. ‖ Papers of Old Congress, lxxv. MS.

In March, during a session of the legislature of South Carolina, Greene, who had received the suggestions of Gouverneur Morris, addressed a letter to the state through Guerard, the governor, representing the sufferings and mutinous temper of the army, and the need of a revenue for congress, and saying: " Independence can only prove a blessing under congressional influence. More is to be dreaded from the members of congress exercising too little than too much power. The financier says his department is on the brink of ruin. To the northward, to the southward, the eyes of the army are turned upon the states, whose measures will determine their conduct. They will not be satisfied with general promises; nothing short of permanent and certain revenue will keep them subject to authority."

" No dictation by a Cromwell! " cried impatient members who could scarcely wait to hear the conclusion of the letter. To mark independence of congress and resistance to the requisitions of "its swordsmen," South Carolina revoked its grant to the United States of power to levy a five per cent duty on imports.* Greene consoled himself with the thought that "he had done his duty, and would await events;" but he was made wiser by the rebuff. While he perceived that without more effectual support the power of congress must expire, he saw that the movement of soldiers without civil authority is pregnant with danger, and would naturally fall under the " direction of the Clodiuses and Catilines in America." † The appeal of congress in April exercised little counteracting influence; but, when the circular of Washington arrived, the force and affection with which it was written produced an alteration of sentiment in more than one quarter of the members. " Washington was admired before; now he was little less than adored." ‡ The continental impost act was adopted, though not without a clause reserving the collection of the duties to the officers of the state, and appropriating them to the payment of the federal quota of South Carolina.#

* Johnson's Life of Greene, ii., 387, 388.
† Greene to G. Morris, 3 April 1783. Sparks' Life of G. Morris, i., 251, 252.
‡ Greene to Washington, 8 August 1783. Letters to Washington, iv., 38.
# Statute No. 1,190, passed 13 August 1783, in Statutes at Large of South Carolina, iv., 570.

In October, Clinton, the governor of New York, responded to Washington: "Unless the powers of the national council are enlarged, and that body better supported than at present, all its measures will discover such feebleness and want of energy as will stain us with disgrace and expose us to the worst of evils." * And in the following January, holding up to the legislature the last circular of the commander-in-chief, he charged them to "be attentive to every measure which has a tendency to cement the union and to give to the national councils that energy which may be necessary for the general welfare." †

The circular reached Massachusetts just when the legislature was complaining of the half-pay and of excessively large salaries to civil officers. The senate and the house dispatched a most affectionate joint address to Washington, attributing to the guidance of an all-wise Providence his selection as commander-in-chief, adding: "While patriots shall not cease to applaud your sacred attachment to the rights of citizens, your military virtue and achievements will make the brightest pages in the history of mankind." ‡ To congress the legislature gave assurances that "it could not without horror entertain the most distant idea of the dissolution of the union;" though "the extraordinary grants of congress to civil and military officers had produced in the commonwealth effects of a threatening aspect." # John Hancock, the popular governor, commending Washington's circular, looked to him as the statesman "of wisdom and experience," teaching them how to improve to the happiest purposes the advantages gained by arms.

As president of the senate, Samuel Adams officially signed the remonstrance of Massachusetts against half-pay; as a citizen, he frankly and boldly, in his own state and in Connecticut, defended the advice of Washington: "In resisting encroachments on our rights, an army became necessary. Congress were and ought to be the sole judge of the means of supporting that army; they had an undoubted right in the very nature of their appointment to make the grant of half

---

* Clinton to Washington, 14 October 1783.   Letters to Washington, iv., 48.
† Speech to the legislature, 21 January 1784.
‡ Boston Gazette, 22 August 1783.         # Journals of Congress, iv., 275.

pay; and, as it was made in behalf of the United States, each state is bound in justice to comply with it, even though it should seem to them to have been an ill-judged measure. States as well as individual persons are equally bound to fulfil their engagements, and it is one part of the description given to us in the sacred scriptures of an honest man, that, though 'he sweareth to his own hurt, he changeth not.'" *

In like spirit congress replied to the protest against half-pay. "The measure was the result of a deliberate judgment framed on a general view of the interests of the union, and pledged the national faith to carry it into effect. If a state every way so important as Massachusetts should withhold her solid support to constitutional measures of the confederacy, the result must be a dissolution of the union; and then she must hold herself as alone responsible for the anarchy and domestic confusion that may succeed." †

At the opening of the autumn session, Hancock, recalling the attention of the legislature to the words of Washington, said: "How to strengthen and improve this union, so as to render it more completely adequate, demands the immediate attention of these states. Our very existence as a free nation is suspended upon it." ‡

On the ninth of October he cited to the general court extracts of letters from John Adams confirming the sentiments of Washington. Near forty towns in the state had instructed their representatives against granting the impost recommended by congress. And yet it was carried in the house by seventy-two against sixty-five; a proviso that it should not be used to discharge half-pay or its commutation was rejected by a majority of ten; and the bill passed the senate almost unanimously.# Some of the towns still murmured, but Boston in

---

* Samuel Adams to a friend in Connecticut. Boston, 25 September 1783. Same to Noah Webster, 30 April 1784. MS.

† Journals of Congress, iv., 277, 278. Congress, on which Washington was then in attendance, would surely have consulted him on the half-pay of which he was the author. The original papers prove that the congressional reply to Massachusetts was prepared after much consultation, and here and there show traces of his mind. ‡ Salem Gazette of 2 October 1783.

# Samuel Cooper to Franklin, 16 October 1783. Works of Franklin, x., 25. Salem Gazette, 30 October 1783.

town-meeting answered: "The commutation is wisely blended with the national debt. With respect to the impost, if we ever mean to be a nation, we must give power to congress, and funds, too."

But Washington's letter achieved its greatest victory in his own state. Mercer had said in congress that, sooner than reinstate the impost, he would "crawl to Richmond on his bare knees." * The legislature, which was in session when the communication from congress arrived, ordered a bill to grant the impost. Jefferson was hoping that Henry would speak for the grant, but he remained mute in his place.† Richard Henry Lee and Thurston spoke of congress as "lusting for power." The extent of the implied powers which Hamilton had asserted in the letter of congress to Rhode Island was "reprobated as alarming and of dangerous tendency;"‡ and on the eleventh of June the proposition of congress was pronounced to be inadmissible, because the revenue-officers were not to be amenable to the commonwealth; because the power of collecting a revenue by penal laws could not be delegated without danger; and because the moneys to be raised from citizens of Virginia were to go into the general treasury. So the proposition of congress was left without any support. Virginia, to discharge her continental debt, preferred to establish a custom-house of her own, appropriating its income to congress for five-and-twenty years, and making good the deficiency by taxes on land, negroes, and polls. "The state," said Arthur Lee, "is resolved not to suffer the exercise of any foreign power or influence within it." # But, when the words of Washington were read, the house gave leave to the advocates for a continental impost to provide for it by a bill which was to have its first reading at the opening of the next session.

These events did but render Richard Henry Lee more obdurate. Placing himself directly in the way of Washington and Madison, he wrote to a friend at the North: "The late

---

\* Madison to Randolph, 18 February 1783. Gilpin, 506.

† Jefferson to Madison, 7 May, 1 June, 17 June 1783.

‡ Joseph Jones of King George to Madison, 14 June 1783, MS.; in part in Rives's Madison, i., 436.

\# Arthur Lee to Theodorick Bland, 13 June 1783. Bland Papers, ii., 110.

address of congress to the states on the impost I think a too early and too strong attempt to overleap those fences established by the confederation to secure the liberties of the respective states. Give the purse to an aristocratic assembly, the sword will follow, and liberty become an empty name. As for increasing the power of congress, I would answer as the discerning men of old, with the change of a word only: 'Nolumus leges confederationis mutari—we forbid change in the laws of the confederation.'" * But, in the time afforded for reflection, Washington's valedictory letter, which Jefferson describes as "deservedly applauded by the world," † gained more and more power; at the adjourned session, the legislature of Virginia, with absolute unanimity, reversed its decision and granted by law the continental impost. ‡ "Everything will come right at last," said Washington, as he heard the gladdening news.#

"Never," said George Mason, "have I heard one single man deny the necessity and propriety of the union. No object can be lost when the mind of every man in the country is strongly attached to it." ‖ "I do not believe," witnesses Jefferson, "there has ever been a moment when a single whig in any one state would not have shuddered at the very idea of a separation of their state from the confederacy." △ A proposition had been made in June to revoke the release to the United States of the territory north-west of the river Ohio. Patrick Henry was for bounding the state reasonably enough, but, instead of ceding the parts lopped off, he was for forming them into small republics ◊ under the direction of Virginia. Nevertheless, the legislature, guided by the sincerity and perseverance of Joseph Jones of King George county, conformed to the wishes of congress, and, on the nineteenth and twentieth of December, cheerfully amended and confirmed their former cession. ‡

The last legislature to address Washington in his public

---

\* R. H. Lee to William Whipple, 1 July 1783. † Jefferson's Works, ix., 266.
‡ Hening, xi., 313. # Sparks, ix., 5.
‖ George Mason in the Virginia Convention, 11 June 1788.
△ Jefferson, ix., 251. ◊ Jefferson to Madison, 17 June 1783
‡ Journals of House of Delegates, 71, 79.

character was Maryland, and they said : "By your letter you have taught us how to value, preserve, and improve that liberty which your services under the smiles of Providence have secured. If the powers given to congress by the confederation should be found incompetent to the purposes of the union, our constituents will readily consent to enlarge them."*

On the part of congress, its president, Elias Boudinot of New Jersey, transmitted to the ministers of America in Europe the circular letter of Washington as the most perfect evidence of "his inimitable character." †

Before the end of June, raw recruits of the Pennsylvania line, in the barracks at Philadelphia, many of them foreign born, joined by others from Lancaster,‡ "soldiers of a day, who could have very few hardships to complain of," # with some returning veterans whom they forced into their ranks, ‖ encouraged by no officer of note, ᐃ surrounding congress ◊ and the council of Pennsylvania, mutinously presented to them demands for pay. Congress insisted with the state authorities that the militia should be called out to restore order, and, the request being refused, ‡ it adjourned to Princeton. On the rumor that the commander-in-chief was sending troops to quell the mutiny, the insurgents, about three hundred in number, made their submission to the president of the state. ⟡

The incident hastened the selection of a place for the permanent residence of congress. The articles of confederation left congress free to meet where it would. With the knowledge of the treaty of peace, the idea naturally arose of a federal town, and for its site there were many competitors. Of the thirteen states which at that time fringed the Atlantic, the central point was in Maryland or Virginia. In March 1783, New York tendered Kingston; in May, Maryland urged the choice of Annapolis; in June, New Jersey offered a district below the falls of the Delaware. Virginia, having George-

---

\* Address of the Maryland legislature, 22 December 1783. MS.
† Diplomatic Correspondence, 1783–1789, i., 14.
‡ Ibid., i., 9.     # Sparks, viii., 455.
‖ Diplomatic Correspondence, 1783–1789, i., 10, 22, 23; Hamilton, i., 387.
ᐃ Diplomatic Correspondence, ii., 514; i., 37, 50.
◊ Gilpin, 548; Colonial Records, xiii., 655.     ‡ Hamilton, ii., 276.
⟡ Diplomatic Correspondence, i., 12.

town for its object,* invited Maryland to join in a cession of equal portions of territory lying together on the Potomac; leaving congress to fix its residence on either side.†

During the summer, congress appointed a committee to consider what jurisdiction it should exercise in its abiding-place. Madison took counsel with Randolph, and especially with Jefferson;‡ and in September the committee of which he was a member reported that the state ceding the territory must give up all jurisdiction over it; the inhabitants were to be assured of a government of laws made by representatives of their own election.# In October, congress took up the question of its permanent residence. ‖ Gerry struggled hard for the district on the Potomac; but, by the vote of Delaware and all the northern states, "a place on the Delaware near the falls" was selected. Within a few days the fear of an overpowering influence of the middle states led to what was called "the happy coalition;" on the seventeenth Gerry insisted that the alternate residence of congress in two places would secure the mutual confidence and affections of the states and preserve the federal balance of power. After a debate of several days, New England, with Maryland, Virginia, and the two Carolinas, decided that congress should reside for equal periods on the Delaware and near the lower falls of the Potomac. Till buildings for its use should be erected, it was to meet alternately in Annapolis and Trenton.△ To carry out the engagement, a committee, of which James Monroe was a member, made an excursion from Annapolis in the following May to view the country round Georgetown; and they reported in favor of the position on which the city of Washington now stands. ◊

The farewell circular letter of Washington addressed to all his countrymen had attracted the attention of congress, and in particular of Hamilton, who roused himself from his own

---

\* Madison to Randolph, 13 October 1783. Gilpin, 578.
† Journals of the Virginia House of Delegates, 28 June 1783, p. 97.
‡ Madison to Jefferson, 20 September 1783. Gilpin, 573.
# Gilpin, 559, 571–575.
‖ Madison to Randolph, 13 October 1783. Gilpin, 576.
△ Higginson to Bland, January 1784. Bland Papers, ii., 113, 114. Compare Boudinot to R. R. Livingston, 23 October 1783.
◊ Monroe to Jefferson, 20 May and 25 May 1784.

desponding mood when he saw the great chieftain go forth alone to combat "the epidemic phrenzy" * of the supreme sovereignty of the separate states. During the time of disturbances in the army, "could force have availed, he had almost wished to see it employed." † Knowing nothing beforehand of Washington's intention to address the people, he had favored some combined action of congress and the general to compel the states forthwith to choose between national anarchy and a consolidated union.‡ No sooner had congress established itself in Princeton # than the youthful statesman drafted a most elaborate and comprehensive series of resolutions embodying in clear and definite language the defects in the confederation as a form of federal government; and closing with an earnest recommendation to the several states to appoint a convention to meet at a fixed time and place, with full powers to revise the confederation, and adopt and propose such alterations as to them should appear necessary; to be finally approved or rejected by the states respectively.

But in the congress of that day he found little disposition to second an immediate effort for a new constitution. Of the committee elected on the twenty-eighth of April, which counted among its members the great names of Ellsworth, Wilson, and Hamilton, Wilson and two others had gone home; Ellsworth followed in the first half of July, but not till he had announced to the governor of Connecticut: "It will soon be of very little consequence where congress go, if they are not made respectable as well as responsible; which can never be done without giving them a power to perform engagements as well as make them. There must be a revenue somehow established that can be relied on and applied for national purposes, independent of the will of a single state, or it will be impossible to support national faith, or national existence. The powers of congress must be adequate to the purposes of their constitution. It is possible there may be abuses and misapplications; still it is better to hazard something than to hazard

---

* Hamilton, i., 403.  † Ibid., i., 352.  ‡ Ibid., i., 402.
# Hamilton's endorsement on his own paper is: "Resolutions intended to be submitted to congress at Princeton in 1783, but abandoned for want of support." MS.

all." * Nearly at the same moment Hamilton wrote to Greene : "There is so little disposition, either in or out of congress, to give solidity to our national system, that there is no motive to a man to lose his time in the public service who has no other view than to promote its welfare. Experience must convince us that our present establishments are utopian before we shall be ready to part with them for better." To Jay his words were: "It is to be hoped that, when prejudice and folly have run themselves out of breath, we may return to reason and correct our errors." † Confirmed in "his ill forebodings as to the future system of the country," ‡ "he abandoned his resolutions for the want of support."

In congress, which he left near the end of July, three months before the period for which he was chosen expired, we know through an ardent friend that "his homilies were recollected with pleasure;" that his extreme zeal made impressions in favor of his integrity, honor, and republican principles; that he had displayed various knowledge, had been sometimes intemperate and sometimes, though rarely, visionary; that cautious statesmen thought, if he could pursue an object with as much cold perseverance as he could defend it with ardor and argument, he would prove irresistible.# From the goodness of his heart, his pride, and his sense of duty, he gave up "future views of public life," ‖ to toil for the support of his wife and children in a profession of which to him the labors were alike engrossing and irksome.△ In four successive years, with few to heed him, he had written and spoken for a constituent federal convention. His last official word to Clinton was: "Strengthen the confederation." ◊

On the second of September, more than a month after Hamilton had withdrawn, the remnant of the committee of the twenty-eighth of April, increased by Samuel Huntington, of Connecticut, reported that "until the effect of the resolu-

---

\* Ellsworth, infra, 324.          † Johnson, ii., 442.   Jay's Jay, ii., 123.

‡ Hamilton, i., 352.

# McHenry to Hamilton, 22 October 1783.   Hamilton, i., 411.

‖ Hamilton to Clinton, 14 May 1783.   Hamilton, i., 368.

△ That Hamilton disliked the labors of a lawyer, I received from Eliphalet Nott.

◊ Hamilton to Clinton, 3 October 1783.   Hamilton, i., 407.

tion of congress, of April last, relating to revenue, should be known, it would be proper to postpone the further consideration of the concurrent resolutions of the senate and assembly of New York." * In this way the first proposition by a state for reforming the government through a federal convention was put to sleep.

All this while the British commander was preparing for the evacuation of New York. The malignant cruelty of royalists, especially in New York and South Carolina, who prompted and loved to execute the ruthless orders of Germain, aroused against them, as had been foretold, a just indignation, which unhappily extended to thousands of families in the United States who had taken no part in the excesses. Toward these Washington and Adams, Jay and Hamilton, and Jefferson who was especially called "their protector and support," † and many of the best counselled forbearance and forgiveness. Motives of policy urged their absorption into the population of the union now that the sovereign to whom they had continued their allegiance had given them their release. But a dread of their political influence prevailed, and before the end of 1783 thousands of loyalists, families of superior culture, like the original planters of Massachusetts, were driven to seek homes in the wilds of Nova Scotia. ‡ In this way the United States out of their own children built up on their border a colony of rivals in navigation and the fishery whose loyalty to the British crown was sanctified by misfortunes. Nor did the British parliament hesitate for a moment to compensate all refugees for the confiscation of their property, and, when the amount was ascertained, it voted them from the British treasury as an indemnity very nearly fifteen and a half millions of dollars.#

The American army being nearly disbanded, Washington, on the eighteenth of July, with Governor Clinton as his companion, made an excursion into the interior, during which he personally examined the lines of water communication between branches of the Hudson and the Saint Lawrence, the lakes and the Susquehanna. By these observations, he comprehended

---

* Report of Peters, McHenry, Izard, Duane, and S. Huntingdon, of 2 September 1783. † Luzerne to Rayneval, of 18 June 1784. MS.
‡ Haliburton's Nova Scotia, i., 263. # Sabine's Loyalists, 111.

more clearly "the immense extent and importance of the inland navigation of the United States. I shall not rest contented," said he, "till I have explored the western country and traversed great part of those lines which give bounds to a new empire." *

He wished at that time to visit the Niagara; but over the fort on the American side of that river the British flag still waved. Thrice Washington had invited the attention of congress to the western posts; and he was now instructed to demand them. He accordingly accredited Steuben to Haldimand, the British commander-in-chief in Canada, with power to receive them. At Sorel, on the eighth of August, Steuben explained his mission to Haldimand, who answered that he had not received any orders for making the least arrangements for the evacuation of a single post; and without positive orders he would not evacuate one inch of ground. † Nor would he permit Steuben to communicate with the inhabitants of any place occupied by the British.

On the seventh of August, just as Washington had returned from his northern tour, congress, ten states being present, unanimously voted him a statue of bronze, to be executed by the best artist of Europe. ‡ On the marble pedestal were to be represented, in low relief, the evacuation of Boston, the capture of Hessians at Trenton, the victory at Princeton, the action at Monmouth, and the surrender of Cornwallis at Yorktown. "The statue," wrote Luzerne, "is the only mark of public gratitude which Washington can accept, and the only one which the government in its poverty can offer." #

But a greater honor awaited him. At the request of congress, he removed his quarters to the neighborhood of Princeton; and on the twenty-sixth, in a public audience, Boudinot, the president, said to him: "In other nations many have deserved and received the thanks of the public; but to you, sir, peculiar praise is due; your services have been essential in

---

\* Washington to Chastellux, 12 October 1783. Sparks, viii., 489.
† Baron Steuben to Washington, 23 August 1783. Letters to Washington, iv., 41, 42.
‡ Journals of Congress, iv., 251. It still remains to give effect to the vote.
# Luzerne to Vergennes, 25 August 1783. MS.

acquiring and establishing the freedom and independence of your country. It still needs your services in forming arrangements for the time of peace." A committee was charged to receive his assistance in preparing and directing the necessary plans.*

The choice of Washington for a counsellor proved the sincerity of congress in favor of union, and a series of national measures was inaugurated. For a peace establishment, he matured a system which was capable of a gradual development. He would have a regular and standing force of twenty-six hundred and thirty-one men, to be employed chiefly in garrisoning the frontier posts. Light troops he specially recommended as suited to the genius of the people. The people in all the states were to be organized and trained in arms as one grand national militia. He proposed a military academy like the Prussian schools, of which he had learned the character from Steuben. Vacancies in the class of officers were to be filled from its graduates; but promotions were not to depend on seniority alone. For the materials essential to war, there were to be not only national arsenals but national manufactories. The protection of foreign commerce would require a navy. All branches in the service were to look exclusively to congress for their orders and their pay. A penniless treasury, which congress knew not how to fill, made the scheme for the moment an ideal one.

To regulate intercourse with the tribes of Indians, Washington laid down the outlines of a system. Outside of the limits of the states no purchase of their lands was to be made, but by the United States as "the sovereign power." All traders with them were to be under strict control. He penetrated the sinister design of the British government to hold the western posts, and recommended friendly attention to the French and other settlers at Detroit and elsewhere in the western territory. Looking to "the formation of new states," he sketched the boundaries of Ohio and of Michigan, and, on his advice,† congress in October resolved on appointing a committee to re-

---

\* Journals of Congress, iv., 256.

† Washington to Duane, 7 September 1783. Sparks, viii., 477. Secret Journals of Congress, i., 255–260.

port a plan of a temporary government for the western territory whose inhabitants were one day to be received into the union under republican constitutions of their own choice. Here the greatness of the intention was not impaired by the public penury, for the work was to be executed by the emigrants themselves. In anticipation of an acceptable cession of the north-western lands by all the claimant states, officers and soldiers who had a right to bounty lands began to gain the West by way of the lakes or across the mountains.* This was the movement toward union which nothing could repress or weaken. Especially Maryland insisted that "the sovereignty over the western territory was vested in the United States as one undivided and independent nation." †

Among his latest official acts, Washington interceded with congress on behalf of Kosciuszko, pleading for him "his merit and services from the concurrent testimony of all who knew him;" and congress accordingly granted the Polish exile who was to become dear to many nations the brevet commission of brigadier-general. ‡

The last days of this congress were cheered by the arrival of Van Berckel as envoy from the Dutch republic, the first minister accredited to America since the peace.♯ An escort was sent out to meet him, and on the thirty-first of October, in a public audience, congress gave him a national welcome.

On the first of November the third congress under the confederation came together for the last time. It made persistent attempts to invigorate the union; declared the inviolable sanctity of the national debt; asked of the states a general revenue; prepared for planting new states in the continental domain; and extended diplomatic relations. Its demand of powers of government did not reach far enough, but it kept alive the desire of reform. It appointed a day of public thanksgiving, that "all the people might assemble to give praise to their Supreme Benefactor for the freedom, sovereignty, and independence of

---

* Journals of Congress, iv., 294–296.
† Journals of Congress, iv., 265. In the original MS. the word "one" is twice underscored.
‡ Washington to Congress, 2 October 1783. Sparks, viii., 487.
♯ Van Berckel to the states general, 3 November 1783. MS.

the United States;" and, as the day came, the pulpit echoed the prayer: "May all the states be one." *

The principle of rotation drove Madison from the national councils. He was unmarried and above care; and, until he should again be eligible to congress, he devoted himself to the study of federal government and to public service in the legislature of his own state, where with strong convictions and unselfish patriotism he wrought with single-mindedness to bring about an efficient form of republican government. He was calm, wakeful, and cautious, pursuing with patience his one great object, never missing an opportunity to advance it, caring not overmuch for conspicuousness or fame, and ever ready to efface himself if he could but accomplish his design.

On Sunday, the second of November, the day before the discharge of all persons enlisted for the war, the commander-in-chief addressed the armies of the United States, however widely their members might be dispersed. Mingling affectionate thanks with praise, he described their unparalleled perseverance for eight long years as little short of a standing miracle, and for their solace bade them call to recollection the astonishing events in which they had taken part, the enlarged prospects of happiness which they had assisted to open for the human race. He encouraged them as citizens to renew their old occupations; and, to those hardy soldiers who were fond of domestic enjoyment and personal independence, he pointed to the fertile regions beyond the Alleghanies as the most happy asylum. In the moment of parting, he held up as an example to the country the harmony which had prevailed in the camp, where men from different parts of the continent and of the most violent local prejudices instantly became but one patriotic band of brothers. "Although the general," these are the words of his last order, "has so frequently given it as his opinion in the most public and explicit manner, that, unless the principles of the federal government were properly supported, and the powers of the union increased, the honor, dignity, and justice of the nation would be lost forever, yet he cannot help leaving it as his last injunction to every officer and every soldier to add

* John Murray's thanksgiving sermon, Tyranny's grove destroyed, p. 71.

his best endeavors toward effecting these great purposes."*
Washington sent forth every one of his fellow-soldiers as an apostle of union under a new constitution.

Almost all the Germans who had been prisoners preferred to abide in the United States, where they soon became useful citizens. The remnant of the British army had crossed to Staten Island and Long Island for embarkation, when, on the twenty-fifth of November, Washington and the governor and other officers of the state and city of New York were met at the Bowery by Knox and citizens, and in orderly procession made their glad progress into the heart of the town. Rejoicings followed. The emblem chosen to introduce the evening display of fireworks was a dove descending with the olive-branch.

For their farewell to Washington, the officers of the army, on the fourth of December, met at a public-house near the Battery, and were soon joined by their commander. The thoughts of the eight years which they had passed together, their common distresses, their victories, and now their parting from the public service, the future of themselves and of their country, came thronging to every mind. No relation of friendship is stronger or more tender than that between men who have shared together the perils of war in a noble and upright cause. The officers could attest that the courage which is the most perfect and the most rare, the courage which determines the man, without the least hesitation, to hold his life of less account than the success of the cause for which he contends, was the habit of Washington. Pledging them in a glass of wine, he thus addressed them: "With a heart full of love and gratitude, I now take leave of you. May your latter days be as prosperous and happy as your former ones have been glorious. I shall be obliged to you if each of you will come and take me by the hand." With tears on his cheeks, he grasped the hand of Knox, who stood nearest, and embraced him. In the same manner he took leave of every officer. Followed by the company in a silent procession, he passed through a corps of light infantry to the ferry at Whitehall. Entering

* Farewell address to the armies of the United States. Rocky Hill, near Princeton, 2 November 1783. Sparks, viii., 495.

his barge, he waved his hat to them; with the same silence they returned that last voiceless farewell, and the boat pushed across the Hudson. A father parting from his children could not excite more regret nor draw more tears.*

On his way through New Jersey the chief was received with the tenderest respect and affection by all classes of men. The roads were covered with people who came from all quarters to see him, to get near to him, to speak to him. Alone and ready to lay down in the hands of congress the command which had been confided to him, he appeared even greater than when he was at the head of the armies of the United States. The inhabitants of Philadelphia knew that he was drawing near, and, without other notice, an innumerable crowd placed themselves along the road where he was to pass. Women, aged men, left their houses to see him. Children passed among the horses to touch his garments. Acclamations of joy and gratitude accompanied him in all the streets. Never was homage more spontaneous or more pure. The general enjoyed the scene, and owned himself by this moment repaid for eight years of toils and wants and tribulations.†

At Philadelphia he put into the hands of the comptroller his accounts to the thirteenth of December 1783, all written with minute exactness by his own hand, and accompanied by vouchers conveniently arranged. Every debit against him was credited; but, as he had not always made an entry of moneys of his own expended in the public service, he was, and chose to remain, a considerable loser. To the last he refused all compensation and all indemnity, though his resources had been greatly diminished by the war.

On the twenty-third of December, at noon, congress in Annapolis received the commander-in-chief. Its members, when seated, wore their hats, as a sign that they represented the sovereignty of the union. Places were assigned to the governor, council, and legislature of Maryland, to general officers, and to the representative of France. Spectators filled the gallery and crowded upon the floor. Hope gladdened all as they forecast the coming greatness of their land.

* Luzerne to Vergennes, 13 December 1783. MS.
† Ibid.

VOL. VI.—9

Rising with dignity, Washington spoke of the rectitude of the common cause; the support of congress; of his countrymen; of Providence; and he commended the interests of "our dearest country to the care of Almighty God." Then saying that he had finished the work assigned him to do, he bade an affectionate farewell to the august body under whose orders he had so long acted, resigned with satisfaction the commission which he had accepted with diffidence, and took leave of public life. His emotion was so great that, as he advanced and delivered up his commission, he seemed unable to have uttered more.

The hand that wrote the declaration of independence prepared the words which, in the name of congress, its president, turning pale from excess of feeling, then addressed to Washington, who stood, filling and commanding every eye:

"Sir: The United States in congress assembled receive with emotions too affecting for utterance the solemn resignation of the authorities under which you have led their troops with success through a perilous and a doubtful war. Called upon by your country to defend its invaded rights, you accepted the sacred charge before it had formed alliances, and whilst it was without funds or a government to support you. You have conducted the great military contest with wisdom and fortitude, invariably regarding the rights of the civil power through all disasters and changes. You have persevered till these United States, aided by a magnanimous king and nation, have been enabled under a just Providence to close the war in freedom, safety, and independence. Having taught a lesson useful to those who inflict and to those who feel oppression, with the blessings of your fellow-citizens, you retire from the great theatre of action; but the glory of your virtues will continue to animate remotest ages. We join you in commending the interests of our dearest country to the protection of Almighty God, beseeching him to dispose the hearts and minds of its citizens to improve the opportunity afforded them of becoming a happy and respectable nation."

No more pleasing words could have reached Washington than those which pledged congress to the reform of the national government. The allusion to the alliance with France was right, for otherwise the achievement of independence would seem to have been attributed to the United States alone. But France and England were now at peace; and after their reconciliation Washington, the happiest of warriors, as he ungirded the sword, would not recall that they had been at war.

The business of the day being over, Washington set out for Mount Vernon, and on Christmas eve, after an absence of nearly nine years, he crossed the threshold of his own home; but not to find rest there, for the doom of greatness was upon him.

## CHAPTER II.

VIRGINIA STATESMEN LEAD TOWARD A BETTER UNION.

### 1784.

OF many causes promoting union, four above others exercised a steady and commanding influence. The new republic as one nation must have power to regulate its foreign commerce; to colonize its large domain; to provide an adequate revenue; and to establish justice in domestic trade by prohibiting the separate states from impairing the obligation of contracts. Each of these four causes was of vital importance; but the necessity for regulating commerce gave the immediate impulse to a more perfect constitution. Happily, the British order in council of the second of July 1783 restricted to British subjects and ships the carrying of American produce from American ports to any British West India island, and the carrying of the produce of those islands to any port in America. "This proclamation," wrote John Adams to Secretary Livingston, "is issued in full confidence that the United States cannot agree to act as one nation. They will soon see the necessity of measures to counteract their enemies. If there is not sufficient authority to draw together the minds, affections, and forces of the states in their common foreign concerns, we shall be the sport of transatlantic politicians, who hate liberty and every country that enjoys it." *

Letters of Adams and one of like tenor from Franklin having been fully considered, congress, on the twenty-ninth of September 1783, agreed that the United States could become respectable only by more energy in government; but, as usual,

* Diplomatic Correspondence, vii., 81, 100.

they only referred " the important subject under deliberation " to a special committee,* which, having Arthur Lee for one of its members, in due time reported that " as the several states are sovereign and independent, and possess the power of acting as may to them seem best, congress will not attempt to point out the path. The mode for joint efforts will suggest itself to the good sense of America." †

The states could not successfully defend themselves against the policy of Great Britain by separate legislation, because it was not the interest of any one of them to exclude British vessels from their harbors unless the like measure should be adopted by every other; and a union of thirteen distinct powers would encounter the very difficulty which had so often proved insuperable. But, while every increase of the power of congress in domestic affairs roused jealousies between the states, the selfish design of a foreign government to repress their industry drew them together against a common adversary.

The complete cession of the North-west and the grant of the desired impost were the offerings of Virginia to the general welfare. ‡ Simultaneously her legislature, on the fourth of December, took cognizance of the aggressions on equal commerce. The Virginians owned not much shipping, and had no special interest in the West India trade; but the British prohibitory policy offended their pride and their sense of honor, and, as in the war they had looked upon "union as the rock of their political salvation," so they again " rang the bell " to call the other states to council. They complained of " a disposition in Great Britain to gain partial advantages, injurious to the rights of free commerce and repugnant to the principles of reciprocal interest and convenience which form the only permanent foundation of friendly intercourse;" and on the ninth unanimously consented to empower congress to adopt the most effectual mode of counteracting restrictions on American navigation so long as they should be continued.# The

---

* Secret Journals of Congress, iii., 398–400.
† Reports of committees on increasing the powers of congress, p. 95. MS.
‡ Joseph Jones to Jefferson, 21 and 29 December 1783.
# Journal of House of Delegates, 50; Hening, xi., 313.

governor, by direction, communicated the act to the executive authority of the other states, requesting their immediate adoption of similar measures;"* and he sent to the delegates of his own state in congress a report of what had been done. This is the first in the series of measures through which Virginia marshalled the United States on their way to a better union.

In the fourth congress Jefferson carried forward the work of Madison with alacrity. The two cherished for each other the closest and the most honorable friendship, agreeing in efforts to bind the states more closely in all that related to the common welfare. In their copious correspondence they opened their minds to each other with frankness and independence.

The delegates of Rhode Island insisted that the counteraction of the British navigation acts must be intrusted to each separate state; but they stood alone, Roger Sherman voting against them, and so dividing Connecticut. Then the proposal of the committee of which Jefferson was a member and of which all but Gerry were from the South, that congress, with the assent of nine states, might exercise prohibitory powers over foreign commerce for the term of fifteen years, was adopted without opposition.†

Keeping in mind that, while the articles of confederation did not directly confer on congress the regulation of commerce by enactments, they granted the amplest authority to frame commercial treaties, Jefferson prepared a plan for intercourse with powers of Europe from Britain to the Ottoman Porte, and with the Barbary states. His draft of instructions ‡ described "the United States as one nation upon the principles of the federal constitution." # In a document of the preceding congress mention had been made of "the federal government," and Rhode Island had forthwith moved to substitute the word union, conceding that there was a union of the states, but not a government; but the motion had been supported by

* Journal of House of Delegates for 22 December 1783. Governor Harrison to the governor of Massachusetts, 25 December 1783. MS.
† Journals of Congress, iv., 392, 393.
‡ Jefferson to John Q. Adams, 30 March 1826. Jefferson, vii., 436.
# Secret Journals of Congress, iii., 453.

no other state, and by no individuals outside of Rhode Island except Holten and Arthur Lee. This time Sherman and his colleague, James Wadsworth, placed Connecticut by the side of Rhode Island. They were joined only by Arthur Lee, and congress, on the twenty-sixth of March, adopting the words of Jefferson, by the vote of eight states to two, of nineteen individuals to five, decided that in treaties and all cases arising under them the United States form "one nation." *

On the principles according to which commercial treaties should be framed America was unanimous. In October 1783 congress had proposed the most perfect equality and reciprocity. † Jefferson, while he would accept a system of reciprocity, reported as the choice of America that there should be no navigation laws; no distinction between metropolitan and colonial ports; an equal right for each party to carry its own products in its own ships into all ports of the other and to take away its products, freely if possible, if not, paying no other duties than are paid by the most favored nation. In time of war there should be an abandonment of privateering; the least possible interference with industry on land; the inviolability of fishermen; the strictest limitation of contraband; free commerce between neutrals and belligerents in articles not contraband; no paper blockades; in short, free trade and a humane international code. These instructions congress accepted, and, to give them effect, Adams, Franklin, and Jefferson were, on the seventh of May, commissioned for two years, with the consent of any two of them, to negotiate treaties of ten or fifteen years' duration. ‡

The foreign commercial system of the nation was to be blended with the domestic intercourse of the states. Highways by water and land from Virginia to the West would advance its welfare and strengthen the union. Jefferson opened the subject to Madison,# who, in reply, explained the necessity of a mutual appointment of commissioners by Maryland and Virginia for regulating the navigation of the Potomac. "The

---

* Secret Journals of Congress for 26 March 1784, iii., 452–454.
† Secret Journals of Congress, iii., 412, 413.
‡ Secret Journals of Congress, iii., 484, 485, and 491–499.
# Jefferson to Madison, Annapolis, 20 February 1784.

good humor into which the cession of the back lands must have put Maryland forms an apt crisis for negotiations." *

In March 1784 Jefferson cautiously introduced the subject to Washington,† and then wrote more urgently: "Your future time and wishes are sacred in my eye; but, if the superintendence of this work would be only a dignified amusement to you, what a monument of your retirement would follow that of your public life!" ‡

Washington "was very happy that a man of discernment and liberality like Jefferson thought as he did." More than ten years before he had been a principal mover of a bill for the extension of navigation from tide-water to Will's creek. "To get the business in motion," he writes, "I was obliged to comprehend James river. The plan was in a tolerably good train when I set out for Cambridge in 1775, and would have been in an excellent way had it not met with difficulties in the Maryland assembly. Not a moment ought to be lost in recommencing this business." #

He too, like Madison, advised concert with the men of Maryland. Conforming to their advice, Jefferson conferred with Thomas Stone, then one of the Maryland delegates in congress, and undertook by letters to originate the subject in the legislature of Virginia. ||

Before the end of June the two houses unanimously requested the executive to procure a statue of Washington, to be of the finest marble and best workmanship, with this inscription on its pedestal:

"The general assembly of the commonwealth of Virginia have caused this statue to be erected as a monument of affection and gratitude to George Washington, who, to the endowments of the hero uniting the virtues of the patriot, and exerting both in establishing the liberties of his country, has rendered his name dear to his fellow-citizens, and given the world an immortal example of true glory." ∆

* Madison to Jefferson, 16 March 1784. Madison, i., 74.
† Jefferson to Washington, 6 March 1784.
‡ Jefferson to Washington, 15 March 1784. Letters to W., iv., 62–66.
# Washington to Jefferson, 29 March 1784. Sparks, ix., 31, 32.
|| Jefferson to Madison, 25 April 1784. Partly printed in Rives, i., 550.
∆ Hening, xi., 552.

The vote, emanating from the affections of the people of Virginia, marks his mastery over the heart of his native state. That mastery he always used to promote the formation of a national constitution. He had hardly reached home from the war when he poured out his inmost thoughts to Harrison, the doubting governor of his commonwealth:

"The prospect before us is fair; I believe all things will come right at last; but the disinclination of the states to yield competent powers to congress for the federal government will, if there is not a change in the system, be our downfall as a nation. This is as clear to me as A, B, C. We have arrived at peace and independency to very little purpose, if we cannot conquer our own prejudices. The powers of Europe begin to see this, and our newly acquired friends, the British, are already and professedly acting upon this ground; and wisely too, if we are determined to persevere in our folly. They know that individual opposition to their measures is futile, and boast that we are not sufficiently united as a nation to give a general one. Is not the indignity of this declaration, in the very act of peacemaking and conciliation, sufficient to stimulate us to vest adequate powers in the sovereign of these United States?

"An extension of federal powers would make us one of the most wealthy, happy, respectable and powerful nations that ever inhabited the terrestrial globe. Without them, we shall soon be everything which is the direct reverse. I predict the worst consequences from a half-starved, limping government, always moving upon crutches and tottering at every step." *

The immensity of the ungranted public domain which had passed from the English crown to the American people invited them to establish a continental empire of republics. Lines of communication with the western country implied its colonization. In the war, Jefferson, as a member of the legislature, had promoted the expedition by which Virginia conquered the region north-west of the Ohio; as governor he had taken part in its cession to the United States. The cession had included the demand of a guarantee to Virginia of the remainder of its territory. This the United States had refused, and Virginia receded from the demand. On the first day of March 1784,

---

* Washington to Harrison, 18 January 1784. Sparks, ix., 12 and 13.

Jefferson, in congress, with his colleagues, Hardy, Arthur Lee, and James Monroe, in conformity with full powers from their commonwealth, signed, sealed, and delivered a deed by which, with some reservation of land, they ceded to the United States all claim to the territory north-west of the Ohio. On that same day, before the deed could be recorded and enrolled among the acts of the United States, Jefferson, as chairman of a committee, presented a plan for the temporary government of the western territory from the southern boundary of the United States in the latitude of thirty-one degrees to the Lake of the Woods. It is still preserved in the national archives in his own handwriting, and is as completely his own work as the declaration of independence.

He pressed upon Virginia to establish the meridian of the mouth of the Kanawha as its western boundary, and to cede all beyond to the United States. To Madison he wrote: "For God's sake, push this at the next session of assembly. We hope North Carolina will cede all beyond the same meridian,"[*] his object being to obtain cessions to the United States of all southern territory west of the meridian of the Kanawha.

In dividing all the country north-west of the Ohio into ten states, Jefferson was controlled by an act of congress of 1780 which was incorporated into the cession of Virginia. No land was to be taken up till it should have been purchased from the Indian proprietors and offered for sale by the United States. In each incipient state no property qualification was required either of the electors or the elected; it was enough for them to be free men, resident, and of full age. Under the authority of congress, and following the precedent of any one of the states, the settlers were to establish a temporary government; when they should have increased to twenty thousand, they might institute a permanent government, with a member in congress, having a right to debate but not to vote; and, when they should be equal in number to the inhabitants of the least populous state, their delegates, with the consent of nine states, as required by the confederation, were to be admitted into the congress of the United States on an equal footing.

The ordinance contained five other articles: The new states

[*] Jefferson to Madison, 20 February 1784.

shall remain forever a part of the United States of America; they shall bear the same relation to the confederation as the original states; they shall pay their apportionment of the federal debts; they shall in their governments uphold republican forms; and after the year 1800 of the Christian era there shall be neither slavery nor involuntary servitude in any of them.

At that time slavery prevailed throughout much more than half the lands of Europe. Jefferson, following an impulse from his own mind, designed by his ordinance to establish from end to end of the whole country a north and south line, at which the westward extension of slavery should be stayed by an impassable bound. Of the men held in bondage beyond that line he did not propose the instant emancipation; but slavery was to be rung out with the departing century, so that in all the western territory, whether held in 1784 by Georgia, North Carolina, Virginia, or the United States, the sun of the new century might dawn on no slave.

To make the decree irrevocable, he further proposed that all the articles should form a charter of compact, to be executed in congress under the seal of the United States, and to stand as fundamental constitutions between the thirteen original states and the new states to be erected under the ordinance.

The design of Jefferson marks an era in the history of universal freedom. For the moment more was attempted than could be accomplished. North Carolina, in the following June, made a cession of all her western lands, but soon revoked it; and Virginia did not release Kentucky till it became a state of the union. Moreover, the sixteen years during which slavery was to have a respite might nurse it into such strength that at their end it would be able to defy or reverse the ordinance.

Exactly on the ninth anniversary of the fight at Concord and Lexington, Richard Dobbs Spaight of North Carolina, seconded by Jacob Read of South Carolina, moved "to strike out" the fifth article. The presiding officer, following the rule of the time, put the question: "Shall the words stand?" Seven states, and seven only, were needed to carry the affirmative. Let Jefferson, who did not refrain from describing Spaight as "a young fool," relate what followed. "The clause was lost by an individual vote only. Ten states were present.

The four eastern states, New York, and Pennsylvania were for the clause; Jersey would have been for it, but there were but two members, one of whom was sick in his chambers. South Carolina, Maryland, and ! Virginia ! voted against it. North Carolina was divided, as would have been Virginia, had not one of its delegates been sick in bed." * The absent Virginian was Monroe, who for himself has left no evidence of such an intention, and who was again absent when in the following year the question was revived. For North Carolina, the vote of Spaight was neutralized by Williamson.

Six states against three, sixteen men against seven, proscribed slavery. Jefferson bore witness against it all his life long. Wythe and himself, as commissioners to codify the laws of Virginia, had provided for gradual emancipation. When, in 1785, the legislature refused to consider the proposal, Jefferson wrote: "We must hope that an overruling Providence is preparing the deliverance of these our suffering brethren." † In 1786, narrating the loss of the clause against slavery in the ordinance of 1784, he said: "The voice of a single individual would have prevented this abominable crime; heaven will not always be silent; the friends to the rights of human nature will in the end prevail." ‡

To friends who visited him in the last period of his life he delighted to renew these aspirations of his earlier years.# In a letter written just forty-five days before his death he refers to the ordinance of 1784, saying: "My sentiments have been forty years before the public; although I shall not live to see them consummated, they will not die with me; but, living or dying, they will ever be in my most fervent prayer." ‖

On the twenty-third of April the ordinance for the government of the north-western territory, shorn of its proscription of slavery, was adopted, and remained in force for three years. On the 7th of May, Jefferson reported an ordinance for ascertaining the mode of locating and disposing of the public lands. The continental domain, when purchased of the Indians, was

---

\* Jefferson to Madison, 25 April 1784.
† Jefferson, ix., 279.        ‡ Ibid., 276.
\# Oral communication from William Campbell Preston of South Carolina.
‖ Jefferson to James Heaton, 20 May 1826.

to be divided by the surveyors into townships of ten geographical miles square, the townships into hundreds of one mile square, and with such precautions that the wilderness could be mapped out into ranges of lots so exactly as to preclude uncertainty of title. As to inheritance, the words of the ordinance were: "The lands therein shall pass in descent and dower according to the customs known in the common law by the name of gavelkind." * Upon this ordinance of Jefferson, most thoughtfully prepared and written wholly by his own hand, no final vote was taken.

Congress had already decided to establish a mint. For the American coinage, Robert and Gouverneur Morris proposed the decimal system of computation, with silver as the only metallic money, and the fourteen hundred and fortieth part of a Spanish piece of eight reals, or, as the Americans called it, the dollar, as the unit of the currency. Jefferson chose the dollar, which circulated freely in every part of the American continent, as the money unit for computation; and the subdivision of the dollar into a tenth, a hundredth, and a thousandth part. For coinage, he proposed a gold coin of ten dollars; silver coins of one dollar and of one tenth of a dollar; and copper coins of one hundredth part of a dollar. † This system steadily grew in favor; and, in 1786, was established by congress without a negative vote. ‡

The total cost of the war, from the first blood shed at Lexington to the general orders of Washington in April 1783, proclaiming peace, was reckoned by Jefferson # at one hundred and forty millions of dollars. Congress, before the formation of the confederacy, had emitted paper money to the amount of two hundred millions of dollars, which at the time of its emission might, as he thought, have had the value of thirty-six millions of silver dollars; the value of the masses of paper emitted by the several states at various stages of the war he estimated at thirty-six millions more. This estimate of the values of the paper money rests in part upon conjecture, and

---

\* Papers of Old Congress, xxx., 59. MS.

† Jefferson, i., 54. Notes on the establishment of a money unit and of a coinage for the United States. Ibid., 162–174.

‡ Journals of Congress, iv., 376, for 8 August 1786.     # Jefferson, ix., 260.

the materials for correcting it with accuracy, especially as it regards the issues of the states, are wanting. The remaining cost of the war, or sixty-eight millions of dollars, with the exception of about one and a half million paid on requisition by the several states, existed on the first of January 1784, in the form of debts in Europe to the amount of nearly eight millions of dollars; of debts due to the several classes of domestic creditors; and of debts due to states for advances on the common account. The value of the paper money issued by congress had perished as it passed from hand to hand, and its circulation had ceased.

In preparing the appropriations for the coming year, congress was met at the threshold by an unforeseen difficulty. Bills of Morris on Holland, that were protested for non-acceptance, would amount, with damages on protest for non-acceptance, to six hundred and thirty-six thousand dollars. To save the honor of the country, this sum was demanded of the separate states in a circular letter drawn by Jefferson. But, meantime, John Adams, in Amsterdam, manfully struggled to meet the drafts, and, by combining the allurement of a lottery with that of a very profitable loan, he succeeded.

The court of France, with delicacy and generosity, of its own motion released the United States from the payment of interest on their obligations during the war and for the first period of peace; and they on their part by formal treaty bound themselves to the payment of interest as it should accrue from the beginning of the year 1784.

For that year the sum required for the several branches of the public service was estimated at about four hundred and fifty thousand dollars; for the interest on the foreign debt, nearly four hundred thousand dollars; the balance of interest and the interest on the domestic debt, about six hundred and eighty thousand dollars; the deficit of the last two years, one million; other arrears connected with the debt, nearly one million three hundred thousand dollars: in all, about four millions. This was a greater sum than could be asked for. Instead of making new requisitions, Jefferson credited all federal payments of the states to the requisition of eight millions of dollars in the first year of the confederacy. One half of that requisition was remitted; of the other, three states had paid nothing, the rest had paid less than a million and a half; a balance would remain of nearly two millions seven hundred thousand dollars; and of this balance a requisition was made on each of the states for its just proportion. The apportionment, if collected within the year, would defray the expenses of all the departments of the general government and the interest on the foreign and domestic loans, leaving only some part of domestic arrears to be provided for at a later day. Could this system be carried into effect, the credit of the government would be established.

Madison had acceded to the wishes of his county, that he should be one of its representatives in the legislature, believing that he might there best awaken Virginia to the glory of taking the lead in the rescue of the union and the blessings staked on union from an impending catastrophe.* Jefferson had kept him thoroughly informed of the movement for bringing order into the public finances. At the instigation of Madison, Philip Mazzei, an Italian, then in quest of a consular appointment in Europe,† paid a visit to Patrick Henry, "the great leader who had been violently opposed to every idea of increasing the power of congress." ‡ On his return, Mazzei reported that the present politics of Henry comprehended very friendly views toward the confederacy, and a support of the payment of British debts.#

At Richmond, on the fourteenth of May, before the assembly proceeded to active business, Henry sought a conference with Madison and Jones, and declared to them that "a bold example set by Virginia would have influence on the other states;" "he saw ruin inevitable unless something was done to give congress a compulsory process on delinquent states." This conviction, he said, was his only inducement for coming into the present assembly. It was agreed that Jones and Madison should sketch some plan for giving greater power to the federal government, and Henry promised to sustain it on the floor. A majority of the assembly were new members, composed of young men and officers of the late army, so that

---
\* Gilpin, 693, 694; Elliot, 113.   † Jefferson to Madison, 16 March 1784.
‡ Edward Bancroft to William Frazer, 28 May 1784.
# Madison to Jefferson, 25 April 1784. Madison, i., 78.

new measures were expected. Great hopes were formed of Madison, and those who knew him best were sure that he would not disappoint the most sanguine expectations.*

Virginia passed an act empowering congress, for any term not exceeding fifteen years, to prohibit the importation or exportation of goods to or from that state in vessels belonging to subjects of powers with whom the United States had no commercial treaty.† They consented that the contributions of the state to the general treasury should be in proportion to the population, counting three fifths of the slaves. All apprehension of danger from conceding a revenue to the confederacy seemed to have passed away; and it was agreed that, pending the acceptance of the amendment to the constitution, any apportionment of the requisitions directed by congress for the purpose of discharging the national debt and the expenses of the national government ought to be complied with. It was further resolved that the accounts subsisting between the United States and individual states should be settled, and that then the balance due ought to be enforced, if necessary, by distress on the property of defaulting states or of their citizens. These resolutions passed the legislature without a division.‡ It remained to see what effect the measures of Virginia would have on the other twelve states and on herself.

Experience had proved the impossibility of keeping together a sufficient representation of the states in congress. It began to be thought better to hold but a short and active annual session of the national congress with compulsory attendance of its members, and appoint commissioners of the states to conduct executive business for the rest of the year. This proposition was one of the last which Jefferson assisted to carry through. He had wished to visit Washington before his voyage; but, armed with at least one-and-twenty commissions for himself and his two associates to negotiate treaties with foreign powers, he was obliged to repair to Boston,

---

\* William Short to T. Jefferson, 14 May 1784; Madison to Jefferson, 15 May 1784, Madison, i., 80; Edward Bancroft to William Frazer, 28 May 1784. In the letter of Short to Jefferson, the date is probably an error for May 15. See Madison, i., 80, "last evening."

† Hening, xi., 388.   ‡ Journal of the Committee of the States, p. 7.

where, after "experiencing in the highest degree its hospitality and civilities," * he embarked for France on the fifth of July, full of hope that the attempt to negotiate a treaty of commerce with Great Britain would meet with success. † Before leaving the country he wrote to Madison: "The best effects are produced by sending our young statesmen to congress. Here they see the affairs of the confederacy from a high ground; they learn the importance of the union, and befriend federal measures when they return." ‡

The committee of states came together on the fourth of June. Four states never attended; and, as the assent of nine was required to carry any proposition except adjournment, the absence or the negative of one state stopped all proceedings. A difference occurring on the eleventh of August, the members from three New England states went home; the remaining six states met irregularly till the nineteenth of that month; and then, from inability to do any manner of business, they withdrew. The United States of America were left without any visible representation whatever. The chief benefit from the experiment was to establish in the minds of Americans the necessity of vesting the executive power, not in a body of men, but, as Jefferson phrased it, in a single arbiter.

This was the state of the government when, on the first of November, Robert Morris retired from his office as superintendent of the finances of the United States. He had conciliated the support of the moneyed men at home.# His bank of North America, necessarily of little advantage to the United States, proved highly remunerative to its stockholders; ‖ the bankruptcy of the nation could have been prevented only by the nation itself. Congress passed an act that for the future no person, appointed a commissioner of the treasury of the United States, should be permitted to be engaged, either di-

---

\* Jefferson to Gerry, 2 July 1784. Austin's Life of Gerry, i., 55.
† Information from Edward Bancroft, 26 August 1784.
‡ Jefferson to Madison, 25 April 1784.     # Hamilton, i., 316, 317.
‖ The dividend for the first half year of the bank was four and a half per cent; for the second, four and one fourth; for the third, six and one half; for the fourth, eight; for the fifth, a little more than nine and a half per cent. Official report in Pennsylvania Packet for 6 July 1782; 7 January 1783; 8 July 1783; 5 January 1784; 8 July 1784.

VOL. VI.—10

rectly or indirectly, in any trade or commerce whatsoever.*  Before retiring, Morris announced to the representative of France in America that he could not pay the interest on the Dutch loan of ten million livres for which France was the guarantee, † a default which deeply injured the reputation of the United States in Paris. ‡ He could still less provide for paying the interest for 1784 on the direct debt to France.

The members of the fifth congress arrived so slowly at Trenton that Marbois, who was charged with French affairs, on the twentieth of November reported what at the moment was true: "There is in America no general government, neither congress, nor president, nor head of any one administrative department." # Six days later, while there was still no quorum in congress, Richard Henry Lee, a delegate from Virginia, wrote to Madison: "It is by many here suggested, as a very necessary step for congress to take, the calling on the states to form a convention for the sole purpose of revising the confederation, so far as to enable congress to execute with more energy, effect, and vigor the powers assigned to it than it appears by experience that they can do under the present state of things." In a letter of the same date Mercer said: "There will be a motion made early in the ensuing congress for such a convention." ‖ Madison, who knew the heart of his correspondents, answered Lee firmly and yet warily: "The union of the states is essential to their safety against foreign danger and internal contention; the perpetuity and efficacy of the present system cannot be confided in; the question, therefore, is, in what mode and at what moment the experiment for supplying the defects ought to be made." △

"The American confederation," so thought the French minister at Versailles, "has a strong tendency to dissolution; it is well that on this point we have neither obligations to fulfil nor any interest to care for." ◊

---

* Journals of Congress for 28 May 1784.
† Robert Morris to Marbois, 17 August 1784. Diplomatic Correspondence, xii., 494. ‡ Edward Bancroft to Lord Carmarthen, Paris, 8 December 1784.
# Marbois to Rayneval, 20 November 1784.
‖ J. F. Mercer to Madison, 26 November 1784. △ Gilpin, 707, 708.
◊ To Marbois, Versailles, 14 December 1784.

## CHAPTER III.

### THE WEST.

### 1784–1785.

The desire to hold and to people the great western domain mingled with every effort for imparting greater energy to the union. In that happy region each state saw the means of granting lands to its soldiers of the revolution and a possession of inestimable promise. Washington took up the office of securing the national allegiance of the transmontane woodsmen by improving the channels of communication with the states on the Atlantic. For that purpose, more than to look after lands of his own, he, on the first day of September, began a tour to the westward to make an examination of the portages between the nearest navigable branches of the Potomac and James river on the one side and of the Ohio and the Kanawha on the other. Wherever he came, he sought and closely questioned the men famed for personal observation of the streams and paths on each side of the Alleghanies.

From Fort Cumberland he took the usual road over the mountains to the valley of the Yohogany,* and studied closely the branches of that stream. The country between the Little Kanawha and the branches of the James river being at that moment infested with hostile Indians, he returned through the houseless solitude between affluents of the Cheat river and of

---

* Yohogany is the "phonetical" mode of spelling for yOugHIOgany, as the English wrote the Indian name; the French, discarding the gutturals, wrote Ohio. So at the North-east the French dropped the first two syllables of Passam-Aquoddy, and made of the last three Acadie. The name Belle Rivière is a translation of Allegh-any.

the Potomac. As he traced the way for commerce over that wild region he was compelled to pass a night on a rough mountain-side in a pouring rain, with no companion but a servant and no protection but his cloak; one day he was without food; sometimes he could find no path except the track of buffaloes; and in unceasing showers his ride through the close bushes seemed to him little better than the swimming of rivulets.*

Reaching home after an absence of thirty-three days, he declared himself pleased with the results of his tour. Combining his observations with the reminiscences of his youthful mission to the French in the heart of Ohio, he sketched in his mind a system of internal communication of the Potomac with the Ohio; of an affluent of the Ohio with the Cuyahoga; and so from the site of Cleveland to Detroit, and onward to the Lake of the Woods.

Six days after his return he sent a most able report to Harrison, then governor of Virginia. "We should do our part toward opening the communication for the fur and peltry trade of the lakes," such were his words, "and for the produce of the country, which will be settled faster than any other ever was, or any one would imagine. But there is a political consideration for so doing which is of still greater importance.

"I need not remark to you, sir, that the flanks and rear of the United States are possessed by other powers, and formidable ones too; nor how necessary it is to apply interest to bind all parts of the union together by indissoluble bonds. The western states, I speak now from my own observation, stand as it were upon a pivot; the touch of a feather would turn them any way. They have looked down the Mississippi until the Spaniards threw difficulties in their way. The untoward disposition of the Spaniards on the one hand and the policy of Great Britain on the other to retain as long as possible the posts of Detroit, Niagara, and Oswego, may be improved to the greatest advantage by this state if she would open the avenues to the trade of that country." †

Harrison heartily approved the views of Washington, and laid his letter before the assembly of Virginia, whose members

\* Washington's Journal. MS.
† Washington to Harrison, 10 October 1784. Sparks, ix., 62, 63, 64.

gladly accepted its large views and stood ready to give them legislative support.*

Meantime Lafayette, who was making a tour through the United States and receiving everywhere a grateful and joyous welcome, was expected in Virginia. For the occasion, Washington repaired to Richmond; and there, on the fifteenth of November, the assembly, to mark their reverence and affection, sent Patrick Henry, Madison, and others to assure him that they retained the most lasting impressions of the transcendent services rendered in his late public character, and had proofs that no change of situation could turn his thoughts from the welfare of his country.

Three days later the house, by the same committee, addressed Lafayette, recalling "his cool intrepidity and wise conduct during his command in the campaign of 1781, and, as the wish most suitable to his character, desired that those who might emulate his glory would equally pursue the interests of humanity."

From Richmond Lafayette accompanied Washington to Mount Vernon, and, after a short visit, was attended by his host as far as Annapolis, where he received the congratulations of Maryland. On the thirteenth of December congress, in a public session, took leave of him with every mark of honor. In his answer he repeated the great injunctions of Washington's farewell letter, and, having travelled widely in the country, bore witness to "the prevailing disposition of the people to strengthen the confederation." For America his three "hobbies," as he called them, were the closer federal union, the alliance with France, and the abolition of slavery. He embarked for his native land "fraught with affection to America, and disposed to render it every possible service." † To Washington he announced from Europe that he was about to attempt the relief of the protestants in France. ‡

The conversation of Washington during his stay in Richmond had still further impressed members of the legislature with the magnitude of his designs. Shortly after his de-

---

* Harrison to Washington, 13 November 1784. Sparks, ix., 68.
† Jefferson to Madison, 18 March 1785.
‡ Lafayette to Washington, 11 May 1785.

parture a joint memorial from inhabitants of Maryland and of Virginia, representing the advantages which would flow from establishing under the authority of the two states a company for improving the navigation of the Potomac, was presented to the general assembly of each of them. But the proposed plan had defects, and, moreover, previous communication between the two states could alone secure uniformity of action. It was decided to consult with Maryland, and the negotiation was committed to Washington himself. Leaving Mount Vernon on the fourteenth of December 1784 at a few hours' notice, the general hastened to Annapolis. Amendments of the plan were thoughtfully digested, rapidly carried through both houses, and dispatched to Richmond. There a law of the same tenor was immediately passed * without opposition, " to the mutual satisfaction of both states," and, as Washington hoped, "to the advantage of the union." †

At the same time the two governments made appropriations for opening a road from the highest practicable navigation of the Potomac to that of the river Cheat or Monongahela, and they concurred in an application to Pennsylvania for permission to open another road from Fort Cumberland to the Yohogany. Like measures were initiated by Virginia for connecting James river with some affluent of the Great Kanawha. Moreover, the executive was authorized to appoint commissioners to examine the most convenient course for a canal between Elizabeth river and the waters of the Roanoke, and contingently to make application to the legislature of North Carolina for its concurrence. ‡

Early in 1785 the legislature of Virginia, repeating, in words written by Madison, "their sense of the unexampled merits of George Washington toward his country," vested in him shares in both the companies alike of the Potomac and of James river.# But, conscious of the weight of his counsels, he never suffered his influence to be impaired by any suspicion of interested motives, and, not able to undo an act of the legislature, held the shares, but only as a trustee for the public.

* Hening, x., 510.   † Madison, i., 123, 124. Sparks, ix., 82.
‡ Washington to R. H. Lee, 8 February 1785. Sparks, ix., 91.
# Hening, xi., 525, 526.

Another question between Maryland and Virginia remained for solution. The charter to Lord Baltimore, which Virginia had resisted as a severance of her territory, bounded his jurisdiction by the "further bank" of the Potomac. When both states assumed independence, Virginia welcomed her northern neighbor to the common war for liberty by releasing every claim to its territory, but she reserved the navigation of the border stream. To define with exactness their respective rights on its waters, the Virginia legislature, in June 1784, led the way by naming George Mason, Edmund Randolph, Madison, and Alexander Henderson as their commissioners to frame, "in concert with commissioners of Maryland, liberal, equitable, and mutually advantageous regulations touching the jurisdiction and navigation of the river." * Maryland gladly accepted the invitation, and in the following March the joint commission was to meet at Alexandria, hard by Mount Vernon. In this manner, through the acts and appropriations of the legislature of Virginia, Washington connected the interests and hopes of her people with the largest and noblest conceptions, and to the states alike on her southern and her northern border and to the rising empire in the West, where she would surely meet New York and New England, she gave the weightiest pledges of inviolable attachment to the union. To carry forward these designs, the next step must be taken by congress, which should have met at Trenton on the first day of November 1784, but, from the tardy arrival of its members, was not organized until the thirtieth. It was the rule of congress that its president should be chosen in succession from each one of the different states. Beginning with Virginia, it had proceeded through them all except New Hampshire, Rhode Island, North Carolina, and Georgia. But now the rule, which in itself was a bad one, was broken,† and Richard Henry Lee was elected president. The rule of rotation was never again followed; but this want of fidelity to a custom that had long been respected tended to increase the jealousy of the small states. Before Christmas and before finishing any important business, congress, not finding sufficient accommodations in Trenton, ad-

* Journals of House of Delegates for 28 June 1784.
† Madison, i., 117. Otto to Vergennes, 15 June 1786. MS.

journed to the eleventh of January 1785, and to New York as its abode.

Congress had put at its head the most determined and the most restlessly indefatigable opponent of any change whatever in the articles of confederation. Lee renewed intimate relations with Gerry, the leading member of congress from Massachusetts. He sought to revive his earlier influence in Boston through Samuel Adams. The venerable patriot shared his jealousy of conferring too great powers on a body far removed from its constituents, but had always supported a strict enforcement of the just authority of government, and he replied: "Better it would have been for us to have fallen in our highly famed struggle for our rights than now to become a contemptible nation." *

The harbor at the mouth of the Hudson was at that time the most convenient port of entry for New Jersey and Connecticut, and the State of New York, through its custom-house, levied on their inhabitants as well as on its own an ever increasing revenue by imposts. The collector was a stubborn partisan. The last legislature had elected to the fifth congress Jay, Robert R. Livingston, Egbert Benson, and Lansing, of whom, even after Jay became the minister for foreign affairs, a majority favored the founding of a nation. But the opinions of the president of congress, who was respected as one of the most illustrious statesmen of Virginia, assisted to bring about a revolution in the politics of New York.† On the nineteenth of March 1785 its legislature appointed three "additional delegates" to congress, of whom Haring and Melancton Smith, like Lansing, opposed federal measures; and for the next four years the state of New York obstinately resisted a thorough revision of the constitution. Of the city of New York, the aspirations for a national union could not be repressed.

On the fourteenth of December 1784, soon after the organization of congress, Washington, with a careful discrimination between the office of that body and the functions of the states, urged through its president that congress should have the western waters well explored, their capacities for navigation

---

* S. Adams to R. H. Lee, 23 December 1784.
† Jay to Washington, 27 June 1786. Letters to Washington, iv., 136.

ascertained as far as the communications between Lake Erie and the Wabash, and between Lake Michigan and the Mississippi, and a complete and perfect map made of the country at least as far west as the Miamis, which run into the Ohio and Lake Erie. And he pointed out the Miami village as the place for a very important post for the union. The expense attending such an undertaking could not be great; the advantages would be unbounded. "Nature," he said, "has made such a display of her bounty in those regions that the more the country is explored the more it will rise in estimation. The spirit of emigration is great; people have got impatient; and, though you cannot stop the road, it is yet in your power to mark the way. A little while and you will not be able to do either." *

In the same week in which the legislature of New York reversed its position on national policy, Washington renewed his admonitions to Lee on planting the western territory. "The mission of congress will now be to fix a medium price on these lands and to point out the most advantageous mode of seating them, so that law and good government may be administered, and the union strengthened and supported. Progressive seating is the only means by which this can be effected;" and, resisting the politicians who might wish to balance northern states by southern, he insisted that to mark out but one new state would better advance the public welfare than to mark out ten. †

On the eleventh of March William Grayson took his seat for the first time as a member of congress. He had been educated in England at Oxford, and had resided at the Temple in London. His short career furnishes only glimpses of his character. In 1776 he had been an aide-de-camp to Washington, with whom he kept up affectionate relations; in 1777 he commanded a Virginia regiment and gained honors at Monmouth. His private life appears to have been faultless; his public acts show independence, courage, and a humane and noble nature. In the state legislature of the previous winter he was chairman of the committee to which Washington's re-

* Washington to R. H. Lee, 14 December 1784. Sparks, ix., 80, 81.
† Washington to R. H. Lee, 15 March 1785.

port on the negotiations with Maryland had been referred.* The first evidence of his arrival in New York is a letter of the tenth of March 1785, to his former chief, announcing that Jefferson's ordinance for disposing of western lands, which had had its first reading in May 1784, had been brought once more before congress.

Not Washington alone had reminded congress of its duties to the West. Informed by Gerry of the course of public business, Timothy Pickering, from Philadelphia, addressed most earnest letters to Rufus King. He complained that no reservation of land was made for the support of ministers of the gospel, nor even for schools and academies, and he further wrote: "Congress once made this important declaration, 'that all men are created equal; that they are endowed by their Creator with certain unalienable rights; that among these are life, liberty, and the pursuit of happiness'; and these truths were held to be self-evident. To suffer the continuance of slaves till they can gradually be emancipated, in states already overrun with them, may be pardonable because unavoidable without hazarding greater evils; but to introduce them into countries where none now exist can never be forgiven. For God's sake, then, let one more effort be made to prevent so terrible a calamity! The fundamental constitutions for those states are yet liable to alterations, and this is probably the only time when the evil can certainly be prevented." Nor would Pickering harbor the thought of delay in the exclusion of slavery. "It will be infinitely easier," he said, "to prevent the evil at first than to eradicate it or check it in any future time." †

The sixteenth of March was fixed for the discussion of the affairs of the West. The report that was before congress was Jefferson's scheme for "locating and disposing of land in the western territory;" and it was readily referred to a committee of one from each state, Grayson being the member from Virginia and King from Massachusetts. King, seconded by Ellery of Rhode Island, proposed that a part of the rejected antislavery clause in Jefferson's ordinance for the government of

---

* Journals Virginia House of Delegates, 99.
† Pickering to King, 8 March 1785. Pickering's Pickering, i., 509, 510.

the western territory should be referred to a committee;* all that related to the western territory of the three southern states was omitted; and so, too, was the clause postponing the prohibition of slavery.

On the question for committing this proposition, the four New England states, New York, New Jersey, and Pennsylvania, voted unanimously in the affirmative; Maryland by a majority, McHenry going with the South, John Henry and William Hindman with the North. For Virginia, Grayson voted aye, but was overpowered by Hardy and Richard Henry Lee. The two Carolinas were unanimous for the negative. Houston of Georgia answered no, but being on that day the sole representative of Georgia, his vote was not counted. So the vote stood eight states against three; eighteen members against eight;† and the motion was forthwith committed to King, Howell, and Ellery. ‡

On the sixth of April, King from his committee reported his resolution, which is entirely in his own handwriting,# and which consists of two clauses: it allowed slavery in the Northwest until the first day of the year 1801, but no longer; and it "provided that always, upon the escape of any person into any of the states described in the resolve of congress of the twenty-third day of April 1784, from whom labor or service is lawfully claimed in any one of the thirteen original states, such fugitive might be lawfully reclaimed and carried back to the person claiming his labor or service, this resolve notwithstanding." ‖

* The original motion of Rufus King for the reference, in his handwriting, is preserved in Papers of Old Congress, vol. xxxi.

† Journals of Congress, iv., 481, 482.

‡ It is indorsed in the handwriting of Charles Thomson: "Motion for preventing slavery in new states, 16 March 1785. Referred to Mr. King, Mr. Howell, Mr. Ellery."

# It is to be found in Papers of Old Congress, xxxi., 329, and is indorsed in the handwriting of Rufus King: "Report on Mr. King's motion for the exclusion of slavery in the new states." And it is further indorsed in the handwriting of Charles Thomson: "Mr. King, Mr. Howell, Mr. Ellery. Entered 6 April 1785, read. Thursday, April 14, assigned for consideration."

‖ The printed copy of this report of King is to be found in Papers of Old Congress, xxxi., 331, and is indorsed in the handwriting of Charles Thomson: "To prevent slavery in the new states. Included in substance in the ordinance for a temporary government passed the 13 July 1787."

King reserved his resolution to be brought forward as a separate measure, after the land ordinance should be passed. "I expect," wrote Grayson to Madison, "seven states may be found liberal enough to adopt it;"* but there is no evidence that it was ever again called up in that congress.

On the twelfth of April † the committee for framing an ordinance for the disposal of the western lands made their report. It was written by Grayson, ‡ who formed it out of a conflict of opinions, and took the chief part in conducting it through the house. As an inducement for neighborhoods of the same religious sentiments to confederate for the purpose of purchasing and settling together, it was a land law for a people going forth to take possession of a seemingly endless domain. Its division was to be into townships, with a perpetual reservation of one mile square in every township for the support of religion, and another for education. The house refused its assent to the reservation for the support of religion, as connecting the church with the state; but the reservation for the support of schools received a general welcome. Jefferson had proposed townships of ten miles square; the committee, of seven; but the motion of Grayson, that they should be of six miles square,# was finally accepted. The South, accustomed to the mode of indiscriminate locations and settlements, insisted on the rule which would give the most free scope to the roving emigrant; and, as the bill required the vote of nine states for adoption, and during the debates on the subject more than ten were never present, the eastern people, though "amazingly attached to their own custom of planting by townships," yielded to the compromise that every other township should be sold by sections. ‖ The surveys were to be confined to one state and to five ranges, extending from the Ohio to Lake Erie, and were to be made under the direction of the geographer of the United States. The bounds of

---

* Grayson to Madison, 1 May 1785. The ordinance for the sale of lands required the consent of nine states; the regulative ordinance, of but seven.

† Grayson to Washington, 15 April 1785.

‡ The original report in the handwriting of Grayson is preserved in the Papers of Old Congress, lvi., 451.

# Journals of Congress, iv., 512.     ‖ Grayson to Madison, 1 May 1785.

every parcel that was sold were fixed beyond a question; the mode of registry was simple, convenient, and almost without cost; the form of conveyance most concise and clear. Never was land offered to a poor man at less cost or with a safer title. For one bad provision, which, however, was three years after repealed, the consent of congress was for the moment extorted; the lands, as surveyed, were to be drawn for by lot by the several states in proportion to the requisitions made upon them, and were to be sold publicly within the states. But it was carefully provided that they should be paid for in the obligations of the United States, at the rate of a dollar an acre. To secure the promises made to Virginia, chiefly on behalf of the officers and soldiers who took part in conquering the Northwest from British authority, it was agreed, after a discussion of four days,* to reserve the district between the Little Miami and the Scioto.

The land ordinance of Jefferson, as amended from 1784 to 1788, definitively settled the character of the national land laws, which are still treasured up as one of the most precious heritages from the founders of the republic.

The frontier settlements at the west needed the protection of a military force. In 1784, soon after the exchange of the ratifications of peace, Gerry at Annapolis protested against the right of congress on its own authority to raise standing armies or even a few armed men in time of peace. His conduct was approved by his state, whose delegation was instructed to oppose and protest on all occasions against the exercise of the power. From that time congress had done no more than recommend the states to raise troops. It was now thought necessary to raise seven hundred men to protect the West. The recommendation should have been apportioned among all the states; but congress ventured to call only on Connecticut, New York, New Jersey, and Pennsylvania as the states most conveniently situated to furnish troops who were to be formed into one regiment and for three years guard the north-western frontiers and the public stores.

* Grayson to Madison, 1 May 1785.

## CHAPTER IV.

### THE REGULATION OF COMMERCE. THE FIFTH CONGRESS.

#### 1784–1785.

The legislature of Connecticut in 1783, angry at the grant of half pay to the officers of the army, insisted that the requisitions of congress had no validity until they received the approval of the state. But the vote was only " a fire among the brambles;" and the people at the next election chose a legislature which accepted the general impost on commerce, even though it should be assented to by no more than twelve states.* The Virginia assembly of that year discountenanced the deviation from the rule of unanimity as a dangerous precedent; † but it was adopted by Maryland. ‡

In the following winter Noah Webster of Hartford busied himself in the search for a form of a continental government which should act as efficaciously on its members as a local government. "So long as any individual state has power to defeat the measures of the other twelve, our pretended union," so he expressed the opinion which began to prevail, " is but a name, and our confederation a cobweb. The sovereignty of each state ought not to be abridged in any article relating to its own government; in a matter that equally respects all the states, a majority of the states must decide. We cannot and ought not to divest ourselves of provincial attachments, but we should subordinate them to the general interest of the con-

---

* Monroe to Madison, 14 December 1784.
† Madison to Monroe, 24 December 1784. Madison, i., 114, 115.
‡ Act of Maryland. Session of 1784, 1785. In Pennsylvania Packet of 8 February 1785.

tinent; as a citizen of the American empire, every individual has a national interest far superior to all others." *

The outlays in America of the British in the last year of their occupation of New York, and the previous expenditures for the French army, had supplied the northern states with specie; so that purchasers were found for the bills of Robert Morris on Europe, which were sold at a discount of twenty or even forty per cent.† The prospect of enormous gains tempted American merchants to import in one year more than their exports could pay for in three;‡ while factors of English houses, bringing over British goods on British account, jostled the American merchants in their own streets. Fires which still burn were then lighted. He that will trace the American policy of that day to its cause must look to British restrictions and British protective duties suddenly applied to Americans as aliens.

The people had looked for peace and prosperity to come hand in hand, and, when hostilities ceased, they ran into debt for English goods, never doubting that their wonted industries would yield them the means of payment as of old. But excessive importations at low prices crushed domestic manufactures; trade with the British West Indies was obstructed; neither rice, tobacco, pitch, turpentine, nor ships could be remitted as heretofore. The whale fishery of Massachusetts had brought to its mariners in a year more than eight hundred thousand dollars in specie, the clear gain of perilous labor. The export of their oil was now obstructed by a duty in England of ninety dollars the ton. Importations from England must be paid for chiefly by cash and bills of exchange. The Americans had chosen to be aliens to England; they could not complain of being taxed like aliens, but they awoke to demand powers of retaliation.

The country began to be in earnest as it summoned congress to change its barren discussions for efficient remedies. The ever increasing voice of complaint broke out from the impatient commercial towns of the northern and central states.

* Sketches of American Policy by Noah Webster, pp. 32–38.
† Pelatiah Webster's Essays, Edition 1791, 266, 267, note.
‡ E. Bancroft to W. Frazer, 8 November 1783.

On the eleventh of January 1785, the day on which congress established itself in New York, the artificers, tradesmen, and mechanics of that city, as they gave it a welcome, added these brave words: "We hope our representatives will coincide with the other states in augmenting your power to every exigency of the union." * The New York chamber of commerce in like manner entreated it to make the commerce of the United States one of the first objects of its care, and to counteract the injurious restrictions of foreign nations. † The New York legislature, then in session, imposed a double duty on all goods imported in British bottoms. ‡

On the twenty-second of March 1785 a bill to "protect the manufactures" of Pennsylvania by specific or ad valorem duties on more than seventy articles, among them on manufactures of iron and steel, was read in its assembly for the second time, debated by paragraphs, and then ordered to be printed for public consideration.# The citizens of Philadelphia, recalling the usages of the revolution, on the second of June held a town-meeting; and, after the deliberations of their committee for eighteen days, they declared that relief from the oppressions under which the American trade and manufactures languished could spring only from the grant to congress of full constitutional powers over the commerce of the United States; that foreign manufactures interfering with domestic industry ought to be discouraged by prohibitions or protective duties. They raised a committee to lay their resolutions in the form of a petition before their own assembly, and to correspond with committees appointed elsewhere for similar purposes. On the twentieth of September, after the bill of the Pennsylvania legislature had been nearly six months under consideration by the people, and after it had been amended by an increase of duties, especially on manufactures of iron, and by a discriminating tonnage duty on ships of nations having no treaty of commerce with congress, it became a law ‖ with general acclamation.

* MS. vol. of Remonstrances and Addresses, 343.
† MS. vol. of Remonstrances and Addresses, 351.
‡ Chief Justice Smith's extract of letters from New York. MS.
# Pennsylvania Packet, 13 May 1785.
‖ The Act appears in full in Pennsylvania Packet of 22 September 1785. Van Berckel's report to the States-General, 4 October 1785.

Pennsylvania had been cheered on its way by voices from Boston. On the eighteenth of April the merchants and tradesmen of that town, meeting in Faneuil Hall, established a committee of correspondence with merchants of other towns, bound themselves not to buy British goods of resident British factors, and prayed congress for the needed immediate relief.* Their petition was reserved by congress for consideration when the report of its committee on commerce should be taken up. The movement in Boston penetrated every class of its citizens; its artisans and mechanics joined the merchants and tradesmen in condemning the ruinous excess of British importations. To these proceedings Grayson directed the attention of Madison.†

On the tenth of May the town of Boston elected its representatives to the general court, among them Hancock, whose health had not permitted him to be a candidate for the place of governor. Two years before, Boston, in its mandate to the men of its choice, had, in extreme language, vindicated the absolute sovereignty of the state; the town, no longer wedded to the pride of independence, instructed its representatives in this wise: Peace has not brought back prosperity; foreigners monopolize our commerce; the American carrying trade and the American finances are threatened with annihilation; the government should encourage agriculture, protect manufactures, and establish a public revenue; the confederacy is inadequate to its purposes; congress should be invested with power competent to the wants of the country; the legislature of Massachusetts should request the executive to open a correspondence with the governors of all the states; from national unanimity and national exertion we have derived our freedom; the joint action of the several parts of the union can alone restore happiness and security. ‡

No candidate for the office of governor of Massachusetts having for that year received a majority of the votes of the people, the general court, in May 1785, made choice of James Bowdoin, a veteran statesman who thirty years before had distinguished himself in the legislature by a speech in favor of the union of the colonies. He had led one branch of

* Journals of Congress, iv., 516, 517.   † Grayson to Madison, 1 May 1785.
‡ Boston Town Records. MS.

the government in its resistance to British usurpations; and, when hostilities broke out, he served his native state as president of its supreme executive council till the British were driven from the commonwealth. His long years of public service had established his fame for moderation, courage, consistency, and uprightness. A republican at heart, he had had an important share in framing the constitution of Massachusetts. In his inaugural address he scorned to complain of the restrictive policy of England, saying rather: Britain and other nations have an undoubted right to regulate their trade with us; and the United States have an equal right to regulate ours with them. Congress should be vested with all the powers necessary to preserve the union, manage its general concerns, and promote the common interest. For the commercial intercourse with foreign nations the confederation does not sufficiently provide. "This matter," these were his words, "merits your particular attention; if you think that congress should be vested with ampler powers, and that special delegates should be convened to settle and define them, you will take measures for such a convention, whose agreement, when confirmed by the states, would ascertain those powers."

In reply, the two branches of the legislature jointly pledged "their most earnest endeavor" to establish "the federal government on a firm basis, and to perfect the union;" and on the first day of July the general court united in the following resolve: "The present powers of the congress of the United States, as contained in the articles of confederation, are not fully adequate to the great purposes they were originally designed to effect." *

That the want of adequate powers in the federal government might find a remedy as soon as possible, they sent to the president of congress, through their own delegation, the resolution which they had adopted, with a circular letter to be forwarded by him to the supreme executive of each state; and they further "directed the delegates of the state to take the earliest opportunity of laying them before congress, and making every exertion to carry the object of them into effect." †

\* Massachusetts Resolve, lxxvi., in Resolves, July 1785, 38, 39.
† Massachusetts Resolve, lxxix.

In concert with New Hampshire, and followed by Rhode Island, they passed a navigation act forbidding exports from their harbors in British bottoms, and establishing a discriminating tonnage duty on foreign vessels;* but only as "a temporary expedient, until a well-guarded power to regulate trade shall be intrusted to congress." † Domestic manufactures were protected by more than a fourfold increase of duties; ‡ and "congress was requested to recommend a convention of delegates from all the states to revise the confederation and report how far it may be necessary to alter or enlarge the same, in order to secure and perpetuate the primary objects of the union." #

In August, the council of Pennsylvania and Dickinson, its president, in a message to the general assembly, renewed the recommendation adopted in that state two years before, saying: "We again declare that further authorities ought to be vested in the federal council; may the present dispositions lead to as perfect an establishment as can be devised." ‖

To his friend Bowdoin John Adams wrote: "The Massachusetts has often been wise and able; but she never took a deeper measure than her late navigation act. I hope she will persist in it even though she should be alone." △

The nation looked to congress for relief. In 1776 James Monroe left the college of William and Mary to enter the army; when but nineteen he gained an honorable wound and promotion; and rapidly rose to the rank of colonel. Jefferson in 1781 described him as a Virginian "of abilities, merit, and fortune," and as "his own particular friend." ◊ In 1782 he was of the assembly of Virginia; and was chosen at three-and-twenty a member of the executive council. In 1783 he was elected to the fourth congress, and at Annapolis saw Washing-

* Annual Register, xxvii., 356. Pennsylvania Packet of 18 July 1785 has the Massachusetts act, and of 20 July that of New Hampshire.

† Bowdoin's circular of 28 July, enclosing the act. MS.

‡ Bradford's Massachusetts, ii., 244; Pennsylvania Packet, 19 July 1785.

# Massachusetts Resolves, lxxvi., 1 July 1785. Resolves of the General Court, p 38.

‖ Minutes of Pennsylvania Council, 25 August 1785. Colonial Records, xiv. 523. △ Adams to Governor Bowdoin, 2 September 1785. MS.

◊ Jefferson to Franklin, 5 October 1781.

ton resign his commission. When Jefferson embarked for France, he remained, not the ablest, but the most conspicuous representative of Virginia on the floor of congress. He sought the friendship of nearly every leading statesman of his commonwealth; and every one seemed glad to call him a friend. It was hard to say whether he was addressed with most affection by Jefferson or by John Marshall. His ambition made him jealous of Randolph; the precedence of Madison he acknowledged, yet not so but that he might consent to become his rival. To Richard Henry Lee he turned as to one from whose zeal for liberty he might seek the confirmation of his own.

Everybody in Virginia resented the restrictive policy of England. Monroe, elected to the fifth congress, embarked on the tide of the rising popular feeling. He was willing to invest the confederation with a perpetual grant of power to regulate commerce; but on condition that it should not be exercised without the consent of nine states. He favored a revenue to be derived from imports, provided that the revenue should be collected under the authority and pass into the treasury of the state in which it should accrue.*

He from the first applauded the good temper and propriety of the new congress, the comprehensiveness of mind with which they attended to the public interests, and their inclination to the most general and liberal principles, which seemed to him "really to promise great good to the union." They showed the like good-will for him. On bringing forward the all-important motion on commerce, they readily referred it to himself as the chief of the committee, with four associates, of whom Spaight from North Carolina, and Houston from Georgia, represented the South; King of Massachusetts, and Johnson of Connecticut, the North.

The complaisant committee lent their names to the proposal of Monroe, whose report was read in congress on the twenty-eighth of March.† It was to be accompanied by a

* Monroe to Jefferson, 14 December 1784.

† Sparks, ix., 503, gives the report in its first form; his date, however, is erroneous, from a misunderstanding of a letter of Grayson, in Letters to Washington, iv., 102, 103. The day on which the report was made is not certain; the day

letter to be addressed to the legislatures of the several states explaining and recommending it; and the fifth day of April was assigned for its consideration.

But it was no part of Monroe's plan to press the matter for a decision. "It will be best," so he wrote to Jefferson, "to postpone this for the present; its adoption must depend on the several legislatures. It hath been brought so far without a prejudice against it. If carried farther here, I fear prejudices will take place. It proposes a radical change in the whole system of our government. It can be carried only by thorough investigation and a conviction of every citizen that it is right. The slower it moves on, therefore, in my opinion, the better." *

Jefferson, as he was passing through Boston on his way to France, had shown pleasure at finding "the conviction growing strongly that nothing could preserve the confederacy unless the bond of union, their common council, should be strengthened." † He now made answer to the urgent inquiries of Monroe: "The interests of the states ought to be made joint in every possible instance, in order to cultivate the idea of our being one nation, and to multiply the instances in which the people shall look up to congress as their head." He approved Monroe's report without reservation; but wished it adopted at once, "before the admission of western states." ‡

Months passed away, but still the subject was not called up in congress; and the mind of Monroe as a southern statesman became shaken. The confederation seemed to him at present but little more than an offensive and defensive alliance, and if the right to raise troops at pleasure was denied, merely a defensive one. His report would put the commercial economy of every state entirely and permanently into the hands of the

---

on which it was read was certainly the 28th of March. The report of the committee is in the volume, "Reports of Committees on Increasing the Powers of Congress," p. 125, with a copy in print. The few corrections that have been made in the copy are in the handwriting of Monroe. The State Dept. MS. copy is indorsed: Report of Mr. Monroe, Mr. Spaight, Mr. Houston, Mr. Johnson, Mr. King. See 11 March—to grant congress power of regulating trade. Entered—read 28 March 1785. Tuesday, April 5, assigned.

\* Monroe to Jefferson, New York, 12 April 1785.

† Jefferson to Madison, Boston, 1 July 1784.

‡ Jefferson to Monroe, Paris, 17 June 1785. Jefferson, i., 347.

union; which might then protect the carrying trade, and encourage domestic industry by a tax on foreign industry. He asked himself if the carrying trade would increase the wealth of the South; and he cited "a Mr. Smith on the Wealth of Nations," as having written "that the doctrine of the balance of trade is a chimera." *

The southernmost states began to reason that Maryland had a great commercial port, and, like Delaware, excelled in naval architecture; and these, joining the seven northern states, might vote to themselves the monopoly of the transport of southern products. Besides, Virginia, more than any other state in the union, was opposed to the slave-trade; and Virginia and all north of her might join in its absolute prohibition. The three more southern states were, therefore, unwilling to trust a navigation act to the voice even of ten; and in his report Monroe substituted eleven states for his first proposal of nine.†

At last, on the thirteenth and fourteenth of July, the report was considered in a committee of the whole. It was held that the regulation of trade by the union was desirable, because it would open a way to encourage domestic industry by imposing a tax upon foreign manufactures; because it was needed in order to secure reciprocity in commercial intercourse with foreign nations; because it would counteract external commercial influence by establishing a commercial interest at home; and because it would prepare the way for a navy. These ends could never be obtained unless the states should act in concert, for their separate regulations would impede and defeat each other.

The opponents of the measure left their cause in the hands of Richard Henry Lee, as their only spokesman; and his mature age, courteous manner, skill as an orator and debater, and his rank as president of congress, gave him great authority. He insisted that the new grant of power would endanger public liberty; that it would be made subservient to further attempts to enlarge the authority of the government; that the concentration of the control of commerce would put the country more in the power of other nations; that the interests of

---

\* Monroe to Jefferson, 16 June 1785.  † Monroe to Madison, 26 July 1785.

the North were different from the interests of the South; that the regulation of trade which suited the one would not suit the other; that eight states were interested in the carrying trade, and would combine together to shackle and fetter the five southern states, which, without having shipping of their own, raised the chief staples for exportation; and, finally, that any attempt whatever at a change in the articles of confederation had a tendency to weaken the union.

In these objections Lee was consistent. He pressed upon Madison, with earnest frankness, that power in congress to legislate over the trade of the union would expose the five staple states, from their want of ships and seamen, to a most pernicious and destructive monopoly; that even the purchase, as well as the carrying, of their produce, might be at the mercy of the East and the North; and that the spirit of commerce throughout the world is a spirit of avarice.*

A plan of a navigation act originated with McHenry of Maryland; but it came before congress only as a subject of conversation. Nothing was done with the report of Monroe, who said of it: "The longer it is delayed, the more certain is its passage through the several states ultimately;" † and his committee only asked leave to sit again. "We have nothing pleasing in prospect," wrote Jacob Read to Madison; "and, if in a short time the states do not enable congress to act with vigor and put the power of compulsion into the hand of the union, I think it almost time to give over the form of what I cannot consider as an efficient government. We want, greatly want, the assistance of your abilities and experience in congress; one cannot help drawing comparisons between the language of 1783 and 1785." ‡

From the delegation of Virginia no hope could spring; but the state which exceeded all others in the number of its freemen and in age was second only to the Old Dominion, had directed its delegates to present to congress, and through congress to the states, an invitation to meet in a convention and

---

\* R. H. Lee to Madison, 11 August 1785. Rives, ii., 31, 32. Compare Monroe to Madison, 26 July 1785.

† Monroe to Jefferson, 15 August 1785.

‡ Jacob Read of South Carolina to Madison, 29 August 1785.

revise the confederation. And now Gerry, Holten, and Rufus King saw fit to disobey their instructions, and suppressed the acts and resolves of Massachusetts, writing: "Any alteration of the confederation is premature; the grant of commercial power should be temporary, like the proposed treaties with European powers; and for its adoption should depend on an experience of its beneficial results. Power over commerce, once delegated to the confederation, can never be revoked but by the unanimous consent of the states. To seek a reform through a convention is a violation of the rights of congress, and, as a manifestation of a want of confidence in them, must meet their disapprobation. A further question arises whether the convention should revise the constitution generally or only for express purposes. Each of the states in forming its own, as well as the federal constitution, has adopted republican principles; yet plans have been laid which would have changed our republican government into baleful aristocracies. The same spirit remains in their abettors. The institution of the Cincinnati will have the same tendency. The rotation of members is the best check to corruption. The requirement of the unanimous consent of the legislatures of the states for altering the confederation effectually prevents innovations by intrigue or surprise. The cry for more power in congress comes especially from those whose views are extended to an aristocracy that will afford lucrative employments, civil and military, and require a standing army, pensioners, and placemen. The present confederation is preferable to the risk of general dissensions and animosities." *

Bowdoin replied: "If in the union discordant principles make it hazardous to intrust congress with powers necessary to its well-being, the union cannot long subsist." † Gerry and King rejoined: "The best and surest mode of obtaining an addition to the powers of congress is to make the powers temporary in the first instance. If a convention of the states is necessary, its members should be confined to the revision of

* This paper, and a letter which preceded it of 18 August 1785, I found only as copied into the Letter Book in the office of the Secretary of State of Massachusetts, Letter Book, viii., 204, 205, 210–213.

† Bowdoin to Massachusetts Delegates in Congress, 24 October 1785.

such parts of the confederation as are supposed defective; and not intrusted with a general revision of the articles and the right to report a plan of federal government essentially different from the republican form now administered." *

These letters of Gerry and King met with the concurrence of Samuel Adams,† and had so much weight with the general court as to stay its further action. Nor did the evil end there. All the arguments and insinuations against a new constitution as sure to supersede republican government by a corrupt and wasteful aristocracy, were carried into every village in Massachusetts, as the persistent judgment of their representatives in congress with the assent of the home legislature.

It remained to see if anything could come from negotiations in Europe. A treaty with England was in importance paramount to all others. In 1783 Adams with Jay had crossed the channel to England, but had been received with coldness. The assent of the United States to the definitive treaty of peace was long delayed by the difficulty of assembling in congress nine states for its confirmation. At length, on the twelfth of May 1784, the exchange of ratifications took place at Paris. The way being thus opened, the three American commissioners for negotiating treaties—Franklin, John Adams, and Jefferson—informed the duke of Dorset, then British ambassador at Paris, that they had full powers to negotiate a commercial treaty with Great Britain, and for that end were ready to repair to London. The British government consulted the English merchants trading with North America; and near the end of March of the following year the duke answered: "I have been instructed to learn from you, gentlemen, what is the real nature of the powers with which you are invested; whether you are merely commissioned by congress, or have received separate powers from the separate states. The apparent determination of the respective states to regulate their own separate interests renders it absolutely necessary, toward forming a permanent system of commerce, that my court should be informed how far the commissioners can be duly authorized to enter into

* Gerry and King to Governor Bowdoin, 2 November 1785.

† Adams to Gerry, 19 September 1785, in reply to a letter from Gerry of 5 September.

any engagements with Great Britain, which it may not be in the power of any one of the states to render totally fruitless and ineffectual."

When Franklin, taking with him the love of France,* prepared to sail for America, congress, breaking up their triumviral commission in Europe, appointed Jefferson to be minister to France, John Adams to Great Britain. Adams gave the heartiest welcome to his "old friend and coadjutor," in whom he found undiminished "industry, intelligence, and talents," and, full of courage if not of hope, hastened to London. On the first day of June Lord Carmarthen, the secretary of state, presented him to the king. Delivering his credentials, he in perfect sincerity declared: "I shall esteem myself the happiest of men if I can be instrumental in recommending my country more and more to your Majesty's royal benevolence, and of restoring the old good nature and the old good humor between people who, though separated by an ocean and under different governments, have the same language, a similar religion, and kindred blood."

The king answered with more tremor than the bold republican had shown: "I wish it understood in America that I have done nothing in the late contest but what I thought myself indispensably bound to do by the duty which I owed to my people. I will be very frank with you. I was the last to consent to the separation; but, the separation having been made, I have always said, as I say now, that I would be the first to meet the friendship of the United States as an independent power. The moment I see such sentiments and language as yours prevail, and a disposition to give to this country the preference, that moment I shall say, let the circumstances of language, religion, and blood have their natural and full effect." †

The suggestion of a preference by treaty was out of place. The English had it without a treaty by their skill, the reciprocal confidence of the merchants of the two nations, and the habits of the Americans who were accustomed only to the consumption of British goods. But a change had come over the

\* Rayneval to Franklin, 8 May 1785. Diplomatic Correspondence, ii., 47.
† Diplomatic Correspondence, iv., 200, 201.

spirit of England. Before the end of three years of peace, all respect and regard for America were changed into bitter discontent at its independence, and a disbelief in its capacity to establish a firm government. The national judgment and popular voice, as expressed in pamphlets, newspapers, coffee-houses, the streets, and in both houses of parliament, had grown into an unchangeable determination to maintain against them the navigation acts and protective duties, and neither the administration nor the opposition had a thought of relaxing them. Great Britain was sure of its power of attracting American commerce, and believed that the American states were not, and never could be, united. All this had been so often affirmed by the refugees, and Englishmen had so often repeated them to one another, that to argue against it was like breathing against a trade wind. "I may reason till I die to no purpose,"[*] wrote Adams; "it is unanimity in America which will produce a fair treaty of commerce." Yet he presented to Carmarthen a draft of one, though without hope of success. It rested on principles of freedom and reciprocity, and the principles of the armed neutrality with regard to neutral vessels.

Like Franklin, like Jefferson, like Madison, he was at heart for free trade. "I should be sorry," said he to his friend Jefferson, "to adopt a monopoly, but, driven to the necessity of it, I would not do things by halves."[†] "If monopolies and exclusions are the only arms of defence against monopolies and exclusions, I would venture upon them without fear of offending Dean Tucker or the ghost of Doctor Quesnay." "But means of preserving ourselves can never be secured until congress shall be made supreme in foreign commerce."[‡]

On the twenty-fourth of August, when the adjournment of parliament brought leisure, Adams, then fifty years of age, met the youthful prime minister of Britain. Pitt, as any one may see in his portrait at Kensington, had in his nature far more of his mother than of the great Englishman who was his father. He had pride, but suffered from a feebleness of will which left

---

[*] Adams to Jay, 26 June 1785. Works, viii., 276.
[†] Adams to Jefferson, 7 August 1785. Works, viii., 292.
[‡] Adams to John Jay, 10 August, ibid., 299, 300.

him the prey of inferior men. His own chosen measures were noble ones—peace, commercial relations with France, the improvement of the public finances, the payment of the national debt. In the ministry of Shelburne, he had brought in a bill to promote commerce with America by modifying the navigation act; in his own he abandoned the hopeless attempt.

Reverting to the treaty of commerce which Adams had proposed, Pitt asked: "What are the lowest terms which will content America?" Adams replied that the project he had communicated would secure the friendship of the United States and all the best part of their trade; the public mind of America is balancing between free trade and a navigation act; and the question will be decided now by England; but if the Americans are driven to a navigation act, they will become attached to the system. "The United States," answered Pitt, "are forever become a foreign nation; our navigation act would not answer its end if we should dispense with it toward you." "The end of the navigation act," replied Adams, "was to confine the commerce of the colonies to the mother country; if carried into execution against us, now that we are become independent, instead of confining our trade to Great Britain, it will drive it to other countries." "You allow we have a right to impose on you our navigation act," said Pitt. "Certainly," answered Adams, "and you will allow we have a corresponding right." "You cannot blame Englishmen," said Pitt, "for being attached to their ships and seamen." "Indeed, I do not," answered Adams; "nor can you blame Americans for being attached to theirs." Pitt then asked plainly: "Can you grant by treaty to England advantages which would not become immediately the right of France?" "We cannot," answered Adams; "to the advantage granted to England without a compensation France would be entitled without a compensation; if an equivalent is stipulated for, France, to claim it, must allow us the same equivalent." Pitt then put the question: "What do you think that Great Britain ought to do?" And Adams answered: "This country ought to prescribe to herself no other rule than to receive from America everything she can send as a remittance; in which case America will take as much of British productions as she can pay for."

There were mutual complaints of failure in observing the conditions of the peace. Pitt frankly declared "the carrying off of negroes to be so clearly against the treaty that England must satisfy that demand;" but he took no step toward satisfying it. The British government, yielding to the importunity of merchants, and especially of fur-traders, kept possession of the American posts at the West. This was a continuance of war; but Pitt excused it on the ground that, in Virginia and at least two other states, hindrances still remained in the way of British creditors. Congress was sincere in its efforts to obtain for them relief in the courts of the states; but it wanted power to enforce its requisitions. Moreover, the Virginia legislature, not without a ground of equity, delayed judgment against the Virginia debtors until an offset could be made of the indemnity which Pitt himself had owned to be due to them for property carried away by the British in disregard of the treaty of peace. The holding of the western posts had no connection with this debt and no proportion to it; for the profits of the fur trade, thus secured to Great Britain, in each single year very far exceeded the whole debt of which the collection was postponed.

The end of the interview was, that Pitt enforced the navigation acts of England against America with unmitigated severity. For the western posts, Haldimand, as his last act, had strengthened the garrison at Oswego, and charged his successor to exclude the Americans from the enormously remunerative commerce in furs by restricting transportation on the lakes to British vessels alone.* In February of the next year, the British secretary of state announced that the posts would be retained till justice should be done to British creditors. †

"They mean," wrote Adams, "that Americans should have no ships, nor sailors, to annoy their trade." "Patience will do no good; nothing but reciprocal prohibitions and imposts will have any effect." He counselled the United States as their only resource to confine their exports to their own ships and

---

* Haldimand to St. Leger, November 1784; Sidney to St. Leger, 30 April 1785, and other letters of the like tenor.

† Carmarthen to Adams, 28 February 1786.

encourage their own manufactures, though he foresaw that these measures would so annoy England as in a few years to bring on the danger of war. *

The French government could not be induced to change its commercial system for the sake of pleasing the United States; it granted free ports; but the Americans wanted not places of deposit for their staples, but an open market. On one point only did Vergennes bestow anxious attention. He feared the United States might grant favors to England; and, at the request of France, congress, when preparing to treat with the nations of Europe, gave assurance that it would "place no people on more advantageous ground than the subjects of his most Christian Majesty." Through the French envoy in America, Vergennes answered: "This declaration, founded on the treaty of the sixth of February 1778, is very agreeable to the king; and you can assure congress that the United States shall constantly experience a perfect reciprocity in France." †

Jefferson, as minister, obtained a great reduction of the duty on American oil manufactured from fish; ‡ but he was compelled to hear thrice over complaints that the trade of the United States had not learned the way to France; and thrice over that the French government could not depend on engagements taken with the United States. Complaints, too, were made of the navigation acts of Massachusetts and New Hampshire, not without hints at retaliation.

While some of the states of Europe forgot their early zeal to form commercial relations with the United States, the convention for ten years with Frederic of Prussia, to whose dispatch, intelligence, and decision Adams bore witness, was completed in May 1785, and in the following May was unanimously ratified by congress. Free vessels made free goods. Arms, ammunition, and military stores were taken out of the class of contraband. In case of war between these two parties, merchant vessels were still to pass unmolested. Privateering was pronounced a form of piracy. Citizens of the one country

* Adams to Jay, 30 August and 15 October 1785. Works, viii., 313 and 321.
† Diplomatic Correspondence, ii., 33, 34, 36.
‡ Ibid., ii., 491, 492.

domiciled in the other were to enjoy freedom of conscience and worship, and, in case of war between the two parties, might still continue their respective employments.

Spain had anxieties with respect to its future relations with America, and thought proper to accredit an agent to congress; but neither with Spain, nor with France, nor with England was there the least hope of forming liberal commercial relations. American diplomacy had failed; the attempt of the fifth congress to take charge of commerce had failed; the movement for a federal convention, which was desired by the mercantile class throughout the union, had failed; but encouragement came from South Carolina. William Moultrie, its governor, gave support to Bowdoin of Massachusetts, saying: "The existence of this state with every other as a nation depends on the strength of the union. Cemented together in one common interest, they are invincible; divided, they must fall a sacrifice to internal dissensions and foreign usurpations." * The heart of American statesmen beat high with hope and resolution. "It is my first wish," wrote Jay, the American secretary for foreign affairs, in 1785, "to see the United States assume and merit the character of ONE GREAT NATION." † " It has ever been my hobby-horse," wrote John Adams early in 1786, while minister of the United States in England, "to see rising in America an empire of liberty, and a prospect of two or three hundred millions of freemen, without one noble or one king among them." ‡

The confederation framed a treaty with the emperor of Morocco; it was not rich enough to buy immunity for its ships from the corsair powers of Barbary.

Through congress no hope for the regeneration of the union could be cherished. Before we look for the light that may rise outside of that body, it will be well to narrate what real or seeming obstacles to union were removed or quieted, and what motives compelling the forming of a new constitution sprung from the impairment of the obligation of contracts by the states.

* Moultrie to Bowdoin, 10 September 1785.
† Life of John Jay by his son, i., 190.
‡ The Life and Works of John Adams, ix., 546.

## CHAPTER V.

### OBSTACLES TO UNION REMOVED OR QUIETED.

### 1783–1787.

THE early confederacy of New England, though all its colonies were non-conformists, refused fellowship to Rhode Island on account of its variance in dissent. Virginia and Maryland were settled in connection with the church of England, which at the period of the revolution was still the established church of them both. In the constitution of the Carolinas the philosopher Locke introduced a clause for the disfranchisement of the atheist, not considering that the power in the magistrate to inflict a penalty on atheism implied the power which doomed Socrates to drink poison and filled the catacombs of Rome with the graves of martyrs. On the other hand, the Baptists, nurslings of adversity, driven by persecution to find resources within their own souls, when they came to found a state in America, rested it on the truth that the spirit and the mind are not subordinate to the temporal power. For the great central state, the people called Quakers in like manner affirmed the right to spiritual and intellectual liberty, and denied to the magistrate all control over the support of religion. To form a perfect political union it was necessary, in all that relates to religion, that state should not be in conflict with state, and that every citizen, in the exercise of his rights of intercitizenship, should be at his ease in any state in which he might sojourn or abide. In a republican country of wide extent, ideas rule legislation; and the history of reform is the history of thought, gaining strength as it passes from mind to mind, till it finds a place in a statute. We have now to see how it came to pass that the oldest state in the union, first in territory and in numbers, and, from its origin, the upholder of an established church, renounced the support of religious worship by law, and established the largest liberty of conscience.

The legislature of Virginia, within a half year after the declaration of independence, while it presented for public consideration the idea of a general assessment for the support of the Christian religion,* exempted dissenters from contributions to the established church. In 1779 this exemption was extended to churchmen, so that the church was disestablished. But the law for religious freedom, which Jefferson prepared as a part of the revised code, was submitted to the deliberate reflection of the people before the vote should be taken for its adoption.

The Massachusetts constitution of 1780 compelled every member of its legislature on taking his seat to subscribe a declaration that he believed the Christian religion. This regulation Joseph Hawley, who had been elected to the first senate of Massachusetts, in a letter to that body, sternly condemned. A member of the Congregational church of Northampton, severe in his morality, and of unquestioned orthodoxy, he called to mind that the founders of Massachusetts while church membership was their condition for granting the privilege of an elector, never suffered a profession of the Christian religion to be made before a temporal court. Moreover, he held the new requirement to be against common right and the natural franchises of every member of the commonwealth.† In this way, from the heart of rigid Calvinism a protest was heard against any right in the temporal power to demand or to receive a profession of faith in the Christian religion. The church member was subject to no supervision but of those with whom he had entered into covenant. The temporal power might punish the evil deed, but not punish or even search after the thought of the mind.

The inherent perverseness of a religious establishment, of which a king residing in another part of the world and enforcing hostile political interests was the head, showed itself in

* Hening, ix., 165. Jefferson's Autobiography.
† Joseph Hawley to Massachusetts Senate, 28 October 1780.
VOL. VI.—12

Virginia. The majority of the legislators were still churchmen; but gradually a decided majority of the people had become dissenters, of whom the foremost were Baptists and Presbyterians. When the struggle for independence was ended, of ninety-one clergymen of the Anglican church in Virginia, twenty-eight only remained. One fourth of the parishes had become extinct.

Churchmen began to fear the enfeeblement of religion from its want of compulsory support and from the excesses of fanaticism among dissenters. These last had made their way, not only without aid from the state, but under the burden of supporting a church which was not their own. The church which had leaned on the state was alone in a decline. The system of an impartial support by the state of all branches of Christians was revived by members of "the Protestant Episcopal church," as it now began to be called. Their petitions, favored by Patrick Henry, Harrison, then governor, Pendleton, the chancellor, Richard Henry Lee, and many others of the foremost men, alleged a decay of public morals; and the remedy asked for was a general assessment, analogous to the clause in the constitution of Massachusetts which enjoined upon its towns "the maintenance of public Protestant teachers of piety, religion, and morality." *

The Presbyterians at first were divided. Their clergy, even while they held that human legislation should concern human affairs alone, that conscience and religious worship lie beyond its reach, accepted the measure, provided it should respect every human belief, even "of the Mussulman and the Gentoo." The Presbyterian laity, accustomed to support their own ministry, chose rather to continue to do so. Of the Baptists, alike ministers and people rejected any alliance with the state.

Early in the autumnal session of the legislature of 1785, Patrick Henry proposed a resolution for a legal provision for the teachers of the Christian religion. In the absence of Jefferson, the opponents of the measure were led by Madison, whom Witherspoon had imbued with theological lore. The assessment bill, he said, exceeds the functions of civil authority.

* Massachusetts Declaration of Rights, Article III. of 1780

The question has been stated as if it were, is religion necessary? The true question is, are establishments necessary for religion? And the answer is, they corrupt religion. The difficulty of providing for the support of religion is the result of the war, to be remedied by voluntary association for religious purposes. In the event of a statute for the support of the Christian religion, are the courts of law to decide what is Christianity? and, as a consequence, to decide what is orthodoxy and what is heresy? The enforced support of the Christian religion dishonors Christianity. Yet, in spite of all the opposition that could be mustered, leave to bring in the bill was granted by forty-seven votes against thirty-two.* The bill, when reported, prescribed a general assessment on all taxable property for the support of teachers of the Christian religion. Each person, as he paid his tax, was to say to which society he dedicated it; in case he refused to do so, his payment was to be applied toward the maintenance of a county school. On the third reading the bill received a check, and was ordered by a small majority to be printed and distributed for the consideration of the people. Thus the people of Virginia had before them for their choice the bill of the revised code for establishing religious freedom, and the plan of desponding churchmen for supporting religion by a general assessment.

All the state, from the sea to the mountains and beyond them, was alive with the discussion. Madison, in a remonstrance addressed to the legislature, imbodied all that could be said against the compulsory maintenance of Christianity and in behalf of religious freedom as a natural right, the glory of Christianity itself, the surest method of supporting religion, and the only way to produce moderation and harmony among its several sects. George Mason, who was an enthusiast for entire freedom, asked of Washington his opinion, and received for answer that "no man's sentiments were more opposed to any kind of restraint upon religious principles." While he was not among those who were so much alarmed at the thought of making people of the denominations of Christians pay toward the support of that denomination which they professed,

* Madison to Jefferson, 9 January 1785. Madison, i., 130.

provided Jews, Mahometans, and others who were not Christians, might obtain proper relief, his advice was given in these words: "As the matter now stands, I wish an assessment had never been agitated; and, as it has gone so far, that the bill could die an easy death." *

The general committee of the Baptists unanimously appointed a delegate to remonstrate with the general assembly against the assessment, and they resolved that no human laws ought to be established for that purpose; that every free person ought to be free in matters of religion. † The general convention of the Presbyterian church prayed the legislature expressly that the bill concerning religious freedom might be passed into a law as the best safeguard then attainable for their religious rights. ‡

When the legislature of Virginia assembled, no one was willing to bring forward the assessment bill, and it was never heard of more. Out of one hundred and seventeen articles of the revised code which were then reported, Madison selected for immediate consideration the one which related to religious freedom. The people of Virginia had held it under deliberation for six years; in December 1785 it passed the house by a vote of nearly four to one. Attempts in the senate for amendment produced only insignificant changes in the preamble, and on the sixteenth of January 1786 Virginia placed among its statutes the very words of the original draft by Jefferson with the hope that they would endure forever: "No man shall be compelled to frequent or support any religious worship, place, or ministry whatsoever, nor shall suffer on account of his religious opinions or belief; opinion in matters of religion shall in no wise diminish, enlarge, or affect civil capacities. The rights hereby asserted are of the natural rights of mankind." #

"Thus," says Madison, "in Virginia was extinguished forever the ambitious hope of making laws for the human mind." The principle on which religious liberty was settled in Virginia prevailed at once in Maryland. In every other American

* Washington to George Mason, 3 October 1785. Sparks, ix., 137.
† Semple's History of the Baptists, etc., 71; Foote's Sketches of Virginia, 344. ‡ Madison, i., 213. # Hening, xii., 86.

state oppressive statutes concerning religion fell into disuse and were gradually repealed. Survivals may still be found, as in nature we in this day meet with survivals of an earlier geological period. It had been foreseen that "the happy consequences of the grand experiment on the advantages which accompany tolerance and liberty would not be limited to America." * The statute of Virginia, translated into French and into Italian, was widely circulated through Europe. A part of the work of "the noble army of martyrs" was done.

During the colonial period the Anglican establishment was feared, because its head was an external temporal power engaged in the suppression of colonial liberties, and was favored by the officers of that power even to the disregard of justice. National independence and religious freedom dispelled the last remnant of jealousy. The American branch at first thought it possible to perfect their organization by themselves; but they soon preferred as their starting-point a final fraternal act of the church of England. No part of the country, no sect, no person showed a disposition to thwart them in their purpose; and no one complained of the unofficial agency of Jay, the American minister of foreign affairs at home, and of John Adams, the American minister in London, in aid of their desire, which required the consent of the British parliament and a consecration by the Anglican hierarchy. Their wish having been fulfilled in the form to which all of them gave assent and which many of them regarded as indispensable, the Protestant Episcopal church of the United States moved onward with a life of its own to the position which it could never have gained but by independence. For America no bishop was to be chosen at the dictation of a temporal power to electors under the penalty of high treason for disobedience; no advowson of church livings could be tolerated; no room was left for simony; no tenure of a ministry as a life estate was endured where a sufficient reason required a change; the laity was not represented by the highest officer of state and the legislature, but stood for itself; no alteration of prayer, or creed, or government could be introduced by the temporal chief, or by that chief and the legislature. The rule of the church proceeded

* Luzerne to Rayneval, 6 November 1784.

from its own living power representing all its members. The Protestant Episcopal congregations in the several United States of America, including the clergy of Connecticut who at first went a way of their own, soon fell into the custom of meeting in convention as one church, and gave a new bond to union. Since the year 1785 they have never asked of any American government a share in any general assessment, and have grown into greatness by self-reliance.

The acknowledged independence of the United States called suddenly into a like independence a new and self-created rival Episcopal church, destined to spread its branches far and wide over the land with astonishing rapidity. Out of a society of devout and studious scholars in the University of Oxford, within less than sixty years, grew the society of Methodists. As some of the little republics of ancient time selected one man as their law-giver, as all men on board a ship trust implicitly to one commander during the period of the voyage, so the Methodist connection in its beginning left to John Wesley to rule them as he would. Its oldest society in the states was at New York, and of the year 1766. In 1772 Wesley appointed, as his "general assistant" in America,* Francis Asbury, a missionary from England, a man from the people, who had "much wisdom and meekness; and under all this, though hardly to be perceived, much command and authority." †

Wesley never yielded to the temptation to found a separate church within British dominions, and during the war of American independence used his influence to keep the societies which he governed from renouncing their old allegiance. But no sooner had the people of the United States been recognised as a nation by the king of England himself, and the movement to found an American episcopacy had begun, than he burst the bonds that in England held him from schism, and resolved to get the start of the English hierarchy. In October 1783, in a general epistle, he peremptorily directed his American brethren to receive "Francis Asbury as the general assistant." ‡

For nearly forty years Wesley had been persuaded that the apostolical succession is a "fable"; that "bishops and presby-

* Asbury's Journal, 10 October 1772. † Coke's Journal, 16.
‡ Wesley to the brethren in America, 3 October 1783.

ters are the same order, and have the same right to ordain." He looked upon himself to be as much a bishop "as any man in Europe," though he never allowed any one to call him by that name. In his service for the Methodists he substituted the word elders for priests, and superintendents for bishops. He, therefore, did not scruple, on the second day of September 1784, himself, in his own private room at Bristol, in England, assisted by Coke and another English presbyter, to ordain two persons as ministers, and then he, with the assistance of other ministers ordained by himself, equal at least in number to the requisition of the canon, did, "by the imposition of his hands and prayer, set apart Thomas Coke, a presbyter of the church of England, as a superintendent, and, under his hand and seal, recommended him to whom it might concern as a fit person to preside over the flock of Christ." It is Coke himself who writes of Wesley: "He did, indeed, solemnly invest me, as far as he had a right so to do, with episcopal authority." * Eight days later, in a general epistle, he thus addressed Thomas Coke, Francis Asbury, and the brethren in North America: "By a very uncommon train of providences, provinces in North America are erected into independent states. The English government has no authority over them, either civil or ecclesiastical. Bishops and presbyters are the same order, and consequently of the same right to ordain. In America there are no bishops who have a legal jurisdiction. Here, therefore, my scruples are at an end. I have accordingly appointed Dr. Coke and Mr. Francis Asbury to be joint superintendents over our brethren in North America. I cannot see a more rational and scriptural way of feeding and guiding those poor sheep in the wilderness. As our American brethren are now totally disentangled both from the state and from the English hierarchy, we dare not entangle them again either with the one or the other. They are now at full liberty simply to follow the Scriptures and the primitive church, and we judge it best that they should stand fast in that liberty wherewith God has so strangely made them free."

Nor did Wesley neglect to frame from the Anglican Book of Common Prayer a revised liturgy for the new church,

* Coke to Bishop White, 24 April 1791, in White's Memoirs, 424.

and a creed from which the article on predestination was left out.

On the eighteenth of September, about two months before the nonjuring bishops of Scotland consecrated a bishop for Connecticut, Coke, the first Methodist "superintendent" for America, was on the water, emulous of the glory of Francis Xavier. "Oh, for a soul like his!" he cried. "I seem to want the wings of an eagle or the voice of a trumpet, that I may proclaim the gospel through the east and the west, and the north and the south." Arriving in New York, he explained to the preacher stationed at that place the new regulation, and received for answer: "Mr. Wesley has determined the point; and therefore it is not to be investigated, but complied with." *

Coke journeyed at once toward Baltimore, where Asbury had his station. At Dover, in Delaware, " he met with Freeborn Garretson, an excellent young man, all meekness and love, and yet all activity." On Sunday, the fourteenth of November, the day on which a bishop for Connecticut was consecrated at Aberdeen, he preached in a chapel in the midst of a forest to a noble congregation. After the service, a plain, robust man came up to him in the pulpit and kissed him. He was not deceived when he thought it could be no other than Francis Asbury, who had collected there a considerable number of preachers in council. The plan of Wesley pleased them all. At the instance of Asbury it was resolved to hold a general conference; and "they sent off Freeborn Garretson like an arrow from north to south, directing him to dispatch messengers right and left and gather all the preachers together at Baltimore on Christmas eve." †

Thence Coke moved onward, baptizing adults and infants, preaching sometimes in a church, though it would not hold half the persons who wished to hear; sometimes at the door of a cottage when the church-door was locked against him. ‡

On Christmas eve, at Baltimore, began the great conference which organized the Methodists of America as a separate fold in the one "flock of Christ." Of the eighty-one American preachers, nearly sixty were present, most of them young. Here Coke

* Coke's First Journal, 7, 13.    † Coke's Journal, 16.    ‡ Ibid., 27.

## CHAPTER VI.

STATE LAWS IMPAIRING THE OBLIGATION OF CONTRACTS PROVE THE NEED OF AN OVERRULING UNION.

### Before May 1787.

A BRILLIANT artist has painted Fortune as a beautiful woman enthroned on a globe, which for the moment is at rest, but is ready to roll at the slightest touch. A country whose people are marked by inventive genius, industry, and skill, whose immense domain is exuberantly fertile, whose abounding products the rest of the world cannot dispense with, may hold her fast, and seat her immovably on a pedestal of four square sides.

The thirteen American states had a larger experience of the baleful consequences of paper money than all the world besides. As each of them had a legislation of its own, the laws were as variant as they were inconvenient and unjust. The shilling had differing rates from its sterling value to an eighth of a dollar. The confusion in computing the worth of the currency of one state in that of another was hopelessly increased by the laws, which discriminated between different kinds of paper issued by the same state; so that a volume could hardly hold the tables of the reciprocal rates of exchange. Moreover, any man loaning money or making a contract in his own state or in another, was liable at any time to loss by some fitful act of separate legislation. The necessity of providing effectually for the security of private rights and the steady dispensation of justice, more, perhaps, than anything else, brought about the new constitution.*

\* Gilpin, 804 ; Elliot, 162.

No sooner had the cry of the martyrs of Lexington reached Connecticut than its legislature put forth paper money for war expenses, and continued to do so till October 1777. These were not made legal tender in private transactions,* and there were no other issues till 1780.

In October of that year the legislature of the state, once for all, interposed itself between the creditor and debtor. It discriminated between contracts that were rightly to be paid in gold and silver and contracts understood to be made in paper currency, whether of the continent or of the state. A pay-table for settling the progressive rate of depreciation was constructed; and, to avoid the injustice which might come from a strict application of the laws, it gave to the court authority through referees, or, if either party refused a reference, by itself, to take all circumstances into consideration, and to determine the case according to the rules of equity.†

In this wise the relations between debtor and creditor in Connecticut were settled summarily and finally, and no room left for rankling discontent. The first of the New England states to issue paper money on the sudden call to arms was the first to return to the use of coin. The wide-spread movements of 1786 for the issue of paper money never prevailed within its borders. Its people, as they were frugal, industrious, and honest, dwelt together in peace, while other states were rent by faction.

Massachusetts, after the downfall of the continental paper, returned to the sole use of gold and silver in contracts; but its statesmen had before them a most difficult task, for the people had been tempted by the low prices of foreign goods to run into debt, and their resources, from the interruption of their sale of ships and fish-oil in England, of fish and lumber in the British West Indies, and from the ruin of home manufacturers by the cheapness of foreign goods, were exhausted. While it established its scale of depreciation, it did not, like Connecticut, order an impartial and definitive settlement between the creditor and debtor, but dallied with danger. In July 1782 it allowed, for one year, judgments to be satisfied

---

* Bronson's Connecticut Currency, 137.
† Laws of Connecticut, ed. 1786, 49, 50.

by the tender of neat cattle or other enumerated articles at an appraisement; but the creditor had only to wait till the year should expire. Repeated temporary stay-laws gave no real relief; they flattered and deceived the hope of the debtor, exasperating alike him and his creditor.* But when, in May 1786, a petition was presented from towns in Bristol county for an emission of paper money, out of one hundred and eighteen members in the house of representatives, it received only nineteen votes, and only thirty-five out of one hundred and twenty-four supported the plan of making real and personal estate a tender on an appraisement in discharge of an execution.

In like manner New Hampshire, after the peace, shunned the emission of paper money. Its people suffered less than Massachusetts, because they were far less in debt.

Alone of the New England states, Rhode Island, after the peace, resumed the attempt to legislate value into paper. The question had divided the electors of the state into political parties; the farmers in the villages were arrayed against the merchants and traders of the larger towns; and in May 1786, after a hard contest, the party in favor of paper money, with John Collins for governor, came into power.

In all haste the legislature authorized the issue of one hundred thousand pounds to be loaned out to any man of Rhode Island at four per cent for seven years, after which one seventh was to be repaid annually. These bills were made a legal tender except for debts due to charitable corporations. A large part of the debt of the state was paid in them.

To escape the very heavy fine for refusing to sell goods for paper as the full equivalent of specie,† the merchants of Newport closed their shops. The act speedily provoked litigation. In September a complaint was made against a butcher for refusing to receive paper at par in payment for meat. The case was tried before a full bench of the five judges. Varnum in an elaborate argument set forth the unconstitutionality of the law and its danger as a precedent. Goodwin answered that it conflicted with nothing in the charter, which was the fundamental law of Rhode Island. Judge Howell the next

* Minot's Insurrection of Massachusetts, 14.
† Compare Otto to Vergennes, 6 August 1786.

morning, delivering the unanimous opinion of the court, declared the acts unconstitutional and void, and dismissed the case as not within the jurisdiction of the court. At the decision, one universal shout of joy rang through the court-house. The assembly of Rhode Island summoned the judges to assign the reasons for their judgment. Three of the five obeyed the summons. At the next session of the legislature Howell, with two associates, defended the opinion of the bench and denied the accountability of the supreme judiciary to the general assembly. The assembly resolved that no satisfactory reasons had been rendered by the bench for its judgment, and discharged them from further attendance.

New York successfully extricated itself from the confusion of continental and state paper money; but in April of the fatal year 1786 its legislature, after long debates, made remarkable by the remonstrances of Duer, voted to emit two hundred thousand pounds in bills of credit. The money so emitted was receivable for duties, and was made a legal tender in all suits.*

In the council of revision strong but not successful objections were raised. Livingston,† the chancellor, set forth that a scarcity of money can be remedied only by industry and economy, not by laws that foster idleness and dissipation; that the bill, under the appearance of relief, would add to the distress of the debtor; that it at the same instant solicited and destroyed credit; that it would cause the taxes and debts of the state to the United States to be paid in paper. Hobart, one of the justices, reported that it would prove an unwarrantable interference in private contracts, and to this objection Livingston gave his adhesion. Morris, the chief justice, objected to receiving the bills in the custom-house treasury as money, and held that the enactment would be working iniquity by the aid of law; but a veto was not agreed upon. ‡

Livingston, the governor of New Jersey, communicating to its legislature, in May 1783, the tidings of peace, said: "Let us show ourselves worthy of freedom by an inflexible attachment

---

\* Jones and Varick's New York Laws, ed. 1789, 283.
† Street's Council of Revision of the State of New York, 409.
‡ Street's Council of Revision of the State of New York, 412, 415.

to public faith and national honor; let us establish our character as a sovereign state * on the only durable basis of impartial and universal justice." The legislature responded to his words by authorizing the United States to levy the duty on commerce which had been required, and by making a provision for raising ninety thousand pounds by taxation for the exigencies of the year. In settling debts it gave legal power to the court and jury to decide the case to the best of their knowledge, agreeably to equity and good conscience.† But in the following December it returned to paper money, and sanctioned the issue of more than thirty-one thousand pounds ‡ to supply the quota of the state for the year.

In the conflict, the arguments against paper money were stated so fully and so strongly, that later writers on political economy have added nothing to the practical wisdom of the thoughtful men of that day; and yet in 1786 a bill for the emission of one hundred thousand pounds marched in triumph through its assembly, which sat with closed doors. The money was a tender; if it was refused, the debt was suspended for twelve years. In the mean time the act of limitation continued in force, and in effect destroyed it. In the council the bill was lost by eight voices to five.# In consequence of this check, the effigy of Livingston, the aged governor, was drawn up to the stake near Elizabethtown, but not consigned to the flames from reverence for the first magistrate of the commonwealth; that of a member of the council was burned. In May the governor and council thought proper to yield, and the bill for paper money became a law. A law for paying debts in lands or chattels was repealed within eight months of its enactment.

The opulent state of Pennsylvania by a series of laws emerged from the paper currency of the war. But, in December 1784, debts contracted before 1777 were made payable in three annual instalments. ‖ In 1785 one hundred and fifty

---

\* Mulford's New Jersey, 473.

† Act of June 1783. Paterson's Laws of New Jersey, ed. 1800, 50.

‡ Wilson's Laws of New Jersey, ed. 1784, 363.

# Grayson to Madison, 22 March 1786. Otto to Vergennes, 17 March 1786.

‖ Dallas's Laws of Pennsylvania, ii., 236.

thousand pounds were issued in bills of credit, to be received as gold and silver in payments to the state;* and fifty thousand pounds were emitted in bills of credit on loan.† The bank of the United States refusing to receive these bills as of equal value with its own, its act of incorporation by the state was repealed.

In February 1785 Delaware called in all its outstanding bills of credit, whether emitted before or since the declaration of independence, with orders for redeeming them at the rate of one pound for seventy-five. After six months they would cease to be redeemable.‡

Maryland, in its June session of 1780, emitted thirty thousand pounds sterling to be a legal tender for all debts and contracts. In the same session it was enacted that all contracts expressed in writing to be in specie were to be paid in specie. In 1782 it enacted a stay-law extending to January 1784, and during that time the debtor might make a tender of slaves, or land, or almost anything that land produced; but the great attempt in 1786 to renew paper money, though pursued with the utmost violence and passion, and carried in the assembly, was successfully held in check by the senate.

Georgia, in August 1782, stayed execution for two years from and after the passing of the act. In February 1785 its bills of credit were ordered to be redeemed in specie certificates, at the rate of one thousand for one. This having been done, in August of the next year fifty thousand pounds were emitted in bills of credit, which were secured "by the guaranteed honor and faith" of the state, and by a mortgage on a vast and most fertile tract of public land.#

South Carolina attracted special attention. In February 1782 that state repealed its laws making paper money a legal tender. Twenty days later the commencement of suits was suspended till ten days after the sitting of the next general assembly.‖ The new legislature, in March 1783, established,

* Dallas's Laws of Pennsylvania, ii., 257.
† Ibid., 294.
‡ Laws of Delaware, ed. 1797, 801.
# Watkins's Digest of the Laws of Georgia, 314, 315.
‖ Statutes at Large of South Carolina, iv., 513.

as in other states, a table of depreciation, so that debts might be discharged according to their real value at the time of the original contract.* On the twenty-sixth day of March 1784 came the great ordinance for the payment of debts in four annual instalments, beginning on the first day of January 1786; † but before the arrival of the first epoch a law of October 1785, which soon became known as the "barren land law," authorized the debtor to tender to the plaintiff such part of his property, real or personal, as he should think proper, even though it were the very poorest of his estate, and the creditor must accept it at three fourths of its appraised value. Simultaneously with this act South Carolina issued one hundred thousand pounds in bills of credit, to be loaned at seven per cent. The period for the instalments was renewed and prolonged. ‡

During the war, North Carolina made lavish use of paper money. In April 1783, after the return of peace, it still, under various pretences, put into circulation one hundred thousand pounds—the pound in that state being equal to two and one half Spanish milled dollars; and in the same session, but after much debate, suits were suspended for twelve months. The town of Edenton, using the words of James Iredell, instructed their representatives and senator in these words: "We earnestly entreat, for the sake of our officers and soldiers, as well as our own and that of the public at large, that no more paper money under any circumstances may be made, and that, as far as possible, the present emission may be redeemed and burned.# But the protest availed nothing. In November 1785, one hundred thousand pounds paper currency were again ordered to be emitted, and to be a lawful tender in all payments whatever. So, while the confederation was gasping for life, the finances of North Carolina, both public and private, were threatened with ruin by an irredeemable currency.

The redemption of the country from the blight of paper money depended largely on Virginia. The greatest state in the union, resisting the British governor and forces at the outbreak of the revolution, conquering the North-west, the chief reliance of the army of Greene at the South, the scene of

* Statutes at Large of South Carolina, iv., 563. ‡ Ibid., 710–712.
† Ibid., 640, 641. # Life of Iredell, ii., 46, 63.

the war in its last active year, Virginia far exceeded any other state in its emission of millions in paper money. After the victory at Yorktown, it ceased to vote new paper money. The old was declared to be no longer receivable, except for the taxes of the year, and it was made redeemable in loan office certificates at the rate of one thousand for one.* In retaliation for the most wanton destruction of property, British debts were not recoverable in the courts. For others it constructed a scale of depreciation in the settlement of contracts made in the six years following the first of January 1777. It had stay-laws. For a short time it allowed executions to be satisfied by the tender of tobacco, flour, and hemp at a price to be settled every month by county courts.† For a year or two lands and negroes might be tendered on judgments, but every contract made since the first of January 1782 ‡ was to be discharged in the manner specified by the contract. So Virginia returned to the use of coin. But in 1785 rumors went abroad that the assembly was resolved to issue a paper currency. George Mason, then in private life, scoffed at solemnly pledging the public credit which had so often been disregarded, and declared that, though they might pass a law to issue paper money, twenty laws would not make the people receive it.# At the end of the session Madison could write to Jefferson ‖ that, though the desire of paper money had discovered itself, "no overt attempt was made!"

It became known that Meriwether Smith and others, aided by an unfavorable balance of trade and the burden of heavy taxation, would at the next session move for a paper medium. Aware of the danger, Washington insisted that George Mason should be a candidate for the assembly; and his election proved a counterpoise to the popular cry. Again, quoting from his own circular of June 1783, that "honesty will be found, on every experiment, the best policy," he encouraged Bland to firmness. The subject of paper money was introduced in October 1786 by petitions from two counties, was faintly supported by "a few obscure patrons," was resisted as an encour-

---

* Hening, x., 456. † Hening, xi., 75, 76. ‡ Ibid., 176–180.
\# George Mason to Washington, 9 November 1785.
‖ Works of Madison, i., 218.

agement to "fraud in states against each other," and "as a disgrace to republican governments in the eyes of mankind;" then, by eighty-five against seventeen, it was voted to be "unjust, impolitic, destructive of public and private confidence, and of that virtue which is the basis of republican government." The words show the mind and hand of Madison.

There was need of a new bill on the district courts, but it was clogged with the proposal for the payment of private debts in three annual instalments. Madison held that "no legislative principle could vindicate such an interposition of the law in private contracts," and the bill was lost, though but by one vote.* The taxes of the year were allowed to be paid in tobacco as "a commutable." "These, and such like things," such was the unbending criticism of Washington, "are extremely hurtful, and may be reckoned among the principal sources of the evils and the corruption of the present day; and this, too, without accomplishing the object in view, for, if we mean to be honest, debts and taxes must be paid with the substance and not the shadow." †

Excusing the legislature, Madison answered: "The original object was paper money; petitions for graduated certificates succeeded; next came instalments, and lastly a project for making property a tender for debts at four fifths of its value; all these have been happily got rid of by very large majorities." ‡

The mind of the country bent itself with all its energy to root out the evils of paper money, and establish among the states one common rule by which the obligation of contracts might be preserved unimpaired. No remedy would avail that did not reach them all. They found that for the scarcity of money there were but two remedies: frugality to diminish the need of it, and increased industry to produce more of it. They found that paper money drives specie away; that every new issue hastens its disappearance, destroying credit and creating a famine of money; that every penalty for the refusal to accept paper money at par lowers its worth, and that the heavier the penalty the more sure is the decline. They saw the death-blow that is given to credit, when confidence, which must be

* Madison, i., 239, 252, 253, 255, 260, 265, 267.
† Washington to Madison. MS.     ‡ Madison, i., 267, 268.

voluntary, is commanded by force. They saw that the use of paper money robs industry, frugality, and honesty of their natural rights in behalf of spendthrifts and adventurers.* Grayson held that paper money with a tender annexed to it is in conflict with that degree of security to property which is fundamental in every state in the union. † He further thought that "congress should have the power of preventing states from cheating one another, as well as their own citizens, by means of paper money." ‡

Madison classified the evils to be remedied under the four heads of depreciated paper as a legal tender, of property substituted for money in payment of debts, of laws for paying debts by instalments, and "of the occlusion of the courts of justice." To root out the dishonest system effectually, he held it necessary to give the general government not only the right to regulate coin as in the confederation, but to prevent interference with state, inter-state, and foreign contracts by separate legislation of any state. The evil was everywhere the subject of reprobation; the citizens of Massachusetts, as we learn from one of its historians,# complained of "retrospective laws;" Pelatiah Webster of Philadelphia set forth that "these acts alter the value of contracts," ‖ and William Paterson of New Jersey, one of the best writers of that day on the subject, pointed out that "the legislature should leave the parties to the law under which they contracted."

For resisting reform, Rhode Island and North Carolina were likely to be the foremost; for demanding it, and for persisting in the demand, Connecticut had the most hopeful record. Among the statesmen to whom the country might look in the emergency, no one had been more conspicuous or more efficient than Madison; but Roger Sherman had all the while been a member of the superior court of his own state, and so by near observation under great responsibility had thoroughly studied every aspect of the obligation of contracts.

---

\* Compare the writings and opinions of William Paterson, R. R. Livingston, R. H. Lee, Madison, and others, written or uttered in the years immediately preceding 1787.

† Grayson to Madison, 22 March 1786.   ‡ Same to same, 28 May 1786.
# Minot's Insurrection, 15.   ‖ Webster's Essays, 129, 138.

## CHAPTER VII.

### CONGRESS CONFESSES ITS HELPLESSNESS.

#### 1783–1786.

"At length," so wrote Washington to Lafayette in 1783, "I am become a private citizen on the banks of the Potomac, solacing myself with tranquil enjoyments, retiring within myself, able to tread the paths of private life with heartfelt satisfaction, envious of none, determined to be pleased with all; and, this being the order for my march, I will move gently down the stream of life till I sleep with my fathers." The French minister, Luzerne, who visited Washington a few weeks after his return to private life, "found him attired in a plain gray suit like a Virginia farmer." "To secure the happiness of those around him appeared to be his chief occupation." * His country with one voice acknowledged that but for him its war of revolution must have failed. His glory pervaded the world, and the proofs of it followed him to his retirement.

Houdon, the great French sculptor of his day, moved more by enthusiasm for him than by the expected compensation for making his statue, came over with his assistants to Mount Vernon to take a mould of his person, to study his countenance, to watch his step as he walked over his fields, his attitude as he paused; and so he has preserved for posterity the features and the form of Washington.

Marie Antoinette added words of her own to those of the king of France, who invited him to visit them. Luzerne pressed the invitation as the heartfelt desire of the French

* Luzerne to Rayneval, 12 April 1784.

people. "Come to France," wrote Rochambeau, speaking the wish of all the French officers who had served in America; "come, and, in a country which honors you, be assured of a reception without example, after a revolution which has not its like in history." But his presence was needed at home to retrieve his affairs from the confusion consequent on his long service in the war, during which he not only refused all pay, but subscribed what he could to the public loans. Of these the amount of the principal had been reduced, and the interest, proportionately reduced, was paid in paper almost worthless. Moreover, persons indebted to him had seized their opportunity to pay him in depreciated continental bills.

His estate, than which "no one in United America" seemed to him "more pleasantly situated," consisted of over nine thousand acres, for the most part of a grayish clay soil, lying on the south bank of the Potomac, and having, on the east and west, rivulets which rose and fell with the tides, and which, like the main stream, abounded in fish. He would gladly have found a tenant for two thirds of it at an annual rent of three thousand dollars; but was obliged to retain the management of the whole.

His unpretending mansion, with rooms of low ceilings, and neither many nor large, was well placed on a high bank of the river. For beautifying the grounds around it, he would ride in the fine season into the forests and select great numbers of well-shaped trees and shrubs, elms and live-oaks, the pines and the hemlock, holly-trees and magnolias, the red-bud, the thorn, and many others, and would transplant them in the proper season. His orchard he filled with the best cherries and pears and apples.

At the end of a year and a half he had not been able "to rescue his private concerns from the disorder into which they had been thrown by the war," though success in the effort "was become absolutely necessary for his support." * After he had been at home for two seasons, his inventory showed of horses one hundred and thirty, of cattle three hundred and thirty-six, of sheep two hundred and eighty-three; the hogs were untold, but on one winter's day a hundred and twenty-

* Washington to Humphreys. Sparks, ix., 113.

eight were killed, weighing more than seventeen thousand pounds. His "negroes," in February 1786, numbered two hundred and sixteen.* No one of them was willing to leave him for another master. As it was his fixed rule never either to buy or to sell a slave, they had the institution of marriage and secure relations of family. The sick were provided with the best medical attendance; children, the infirm, and the aged were well cared for. Washington was but the director of his community of black people in their labor, mainly for their own subsistence. For the market they produced scarcely anything but "a little wheat;" and after a season of drought even their own support had to be eked out from other resources; so that, with all his method and good judgment, he, like Madison of a later day, and in accord with common experience in Virginia, found that where negroes continued on the same land and they and all their increase were maintained upon it, their owner would gradually become more and more embarrassed or impoverished. As to bounty lands received for service in the seven years' war and his other domains beyond the Alleghany, he "found distant property in lands more pregnant of perplexities than profit." His income, uncertain in its amount, was not sufficient to meet his unavoidable expenses, and he became more straitened for money than he had ever been since his boyhood; so that he was even obliged to delay paying the annual bill of his physician, to put off the tax-gatherer once and again, and, what was harder, to defer his charities; for, while it was his habit to conceal his gifts, he loved to give, and to give liberally.

Toward the runaway slave Washington was severe. He wished that the northern states would permit men of the South to travel in them with their attendants, though they might be slaves; and he earnestly disapproved of the interposition of the philanthropist between the slave and his holder; but, while expressing these opinions, he took care to write, most emphatically, that no one more desired universal emancipation than himself. He pressed his conviction upon the leading politicians in Virginia that the gradual abolition of slavery "certainly might, and assuredly ought to, be effected;

* From entries in Washington's unpublished Diary.

and that, too, by legislative authority." * When Coke and Asbury, the first superintendents of the Methodists, asked him to aid their petition to the Virginia legislature for an act of universal emancipation, he told them frankly that "he was of their sentiments, and, should this petition be taken into consideration, he would signify it to the assembly in a letter." † Finding that the legislature of the state would not entertain a motion to do away with slavery, he sought to devise practicable plans for emancipating his own negroes and providing for himself and them; not succeeding, he secured their enfranchisement by his will. ‡

The hardships of the camp had worn upon his constitution, and he was persuaded that he would not live to great age.# The price of health to him from day to day was to pass much of the time in the open air, especially on horseback. Receiving from Europe gifts of the best fox-hounds, he would join in the chase, sometimes came in first, but delighted most in a good run when every one was present at the death.

It was his earliest care at Mount Vernon to arrange his papers relating to the war for the use of the historian. Being asked to write his commentaries, he answered: "If I had talents for it, the consciousness of a defective education, and a certainty of a want of time, unfit me for such an undertaking." ‖

Every one agreed that Washington's "character was perfectly amiable." In his retirement he so practiced all the virtues of private life that the synod of the Presbyterians held him up to the world as the example of purity. To use the words of one who knew him well, "The breath of slander never breathed upon him in his life nor upon his ashes." He was generous to the extent of his means and beyond them. Young

---

\* Sparks, ix., 163, 164.  † Coke's First Journal, 45.

‡ Washington could emancipate his own slaves, but not those of his wife's estate; and the two classes were linked together by marriage and family ties. To this difficulty in the way of emancipating his own negroes, Madison directed my attention. The idea has prevailed that Washington married a woman of fortune. Her first husband dying, left his affairs in an embarrassed condition, and they certainly remained so in the hands of his executor or agent for nearly thirty years, and probably longer.

# Sparks, ix., 78.  ‖ Sparks, ix., 113.

persons who came under his control or his guardianship he taught method in their expenses, and above all he inculcated on them the duty of husbanding their means so as to be always able and ready to give.

Washington was from his heart truly and deeply religious. His convictions became more intense from the influence of the great events of his life on his character. As he looked back upon the thick-set dangers through which he had steered, we know from himself that he could not but feel that he had been sustained by "the all-powerful guide and dispenser of human things."* Of the Protestant Episcopal Church, he belonged decidedly to the party of moderation, and "had no desire to open a correspondence with the newly ordained bishop" of Connecticut.† Not a metaphysician nor an analyzer of creeds, his religious faith came from his experience in action. No man more thoroughly believed in the overruling Providence of a just and almighty power; and as a chemist knows that the leaf for its greenness and beauty and health needs the help of an effluence from beyond this planet, so Washington beheld in the movements of nations a marshalling intelligence which is above them all, and which gives order and unity to the universe.

Like almost every great warrior, he hated war, and wished to see that plague to mankind banished from the earth. ‡ "I never expect to draw my sword again," he said in 1785 to one of the French officers who had served in America. "I can scarcely conceive the cause that would induce me to do it. My first wish is to see the whole world in peace, and its inhabitants one band of brothers striving who should contribute most to the happiness of mankind." # "As a citizen of the great republic of humanity," such are his words, "I indulge the idea that the period is not remote when the benefits of free commerce will succeed the devastations and horrors of war." ‖ He loved to contemplate human nature in the state of progressive amelioration.△ His faith in Providence led him to found that hope on the belief that justice has a strength of its

---

* Sparks, ix., 21, 22.
† Diary for Monday, 10 October 1785.
‡ Sparks, ix., 112, 113.
# Ibid., 138, 139.
‖ Ibid., 193, 194.
△ Ibid., 306.

own which will by degrees command respect as the rule for all nations.

He wished success to every people that were struggling for better days. Afflicted by the abject penury of the mass of the Irish,* he gave them his sympathies. A hope dawned of renewed national life for the Greeks. He could scarcely conceive that the Turks would be permitted to hold any of their possessions in Europe.†

He welcomed with enthusiasm the approach of the French revolution, and at an early day pointed out the danger that menaced the king and his only avenue of safety; saying: "His Most Christian Majesty speaks and acts in a style not very pleasing to republican ears or to republican forms, nor to the temper of his own subjects at this day. Liberty, when it begins to take root, is a plant of rapid growth; the checks he endeavors to give it, however warranted by ancient usage, will more than probably kindle a flame which may not be easily extinguished, though it may be smothered for awhile by the armies at his command and the nobility in his interest. When a people are oppressed with taxes, and have cause to believe that there has been a misapplication of the money, they ill brook the language of despotism." ‡

To Lafayette, whose desire to signalize himself he well understood, he said: "Great moderation should be used on both sides; I caution you against running into extremes and prejudicing your cause." #

In foreign affairs Washington inclined neither to France nor to England; his system of politics was impartially American. At home he was devoted to no state, to no party. His mind, though he was of Virginia, was free from any bias, northern or southern, the allegiance of his heart being given to United America.

At Mount Vernon, on the twenty-eighth of March 1785, the joint commissioners of the two states divided by the Potomac, George Mason and Alexander Henderson of Virginia, Daniel of St. Thomas Jenifer, Thomas Stone, and Samuel Chase of Maryland, met under the auspices of Washington. As his near neighbor, intimate friend, and old political asso-

* Sparks, ix., 398.     † Ibid., 360.     ‡ Ibid., 332.     # Ibid., 381.

ciate, Mason submitted to his influence and entered with zeal and a strong sense of duty into the movements that led to union.

The commissioners prepared the terms of a compact between the two states for the jurisdiction over the waters of the Chesapeake bay and the rivers that were common to both states; and, conforming to the wishes of Washington, they requested Pennsylvania to grant the free use of the branches of the Ohio within its limits, for establishing the connection between that river and the Potomac.*

The primary object of their commission being fulfilled, they took up matters of general policy, and recommended to the two states a uniformity of duties on imports, a uniformity of commercial regulations, and a uniformity of currency.† George Mason was charged with the report of their doings to the legislature of his state.

When the assembly of Virginia came together, congress and the country were rent by the question of investing congress with an adequate power over trade. The eastern and middle states were zealous for the measure; the southern were divided; Pennsylvania had established duties of its own, with the avowed object of encouraging domestic manufactures; South Carolina was deliberating on the distresses of her commerce. In the assembly of Virginia, in which there was a great conflict of opinion, Madison ‡ spoke for the grant of power as fraught with no danger to the liberties of the states, and as needful in order to conduct the foreign relations, to arrest contention between the states, to prevent enactments of one state to the injury of another, to establish a system intelligible to foreigners trading with the United States, to counteract the evident design of Great Britain to weaken the confederacy, and to preserve the federal constitution, which, like all other institutions, could not remain long after it should cease to be useful. The dissolution of the union would be the signal for standing armies in the several states, burdensome and perpetual taxes, clashing systems of foreign politics, and an appeal to the sword in every petty squabble. Washington

---

\* Pennsylvania Archives, 511. † Rives's Madison, ii., 58.
‡ Notes of Madison's speech in Madison, i., 201, 202.

being invited to offer suggestions,* answered: "The proposition is self-evident. We are either a united people or we are not so. If the former, let us in all matters of general concern act as a nation which has a national character to support." †
"If the states individually attempt to regulate commerce, an abortion or a many-headed monster would be the issue. If we consider ourselves or wish to be considered by others as a united people, why not adopt the measures which are characteristic of it, and support the honor and dignity of one? If we are afraid to trust one another under qualified powers, there is an end of the union." ‡

The house was disposed to confide to congress a power over trade; but, by the stratagem of the adversaries of the resolutions, the duration of the grant was limited to thirteen years. This limitation, which was reported on the last day of November, took from the movement all its value. "It is better," so wrote Madison to Washington, "to trust to further experience, and even distress, for an adequate remedy than to try a temporary measure which may stand in the way of a permanent one. The difficulty now found in obtaining a unanimous concurrence of the states in any measure must increase with every increase of their numbers." #

All was at a stand, when suddenly a ray of light was thrown upon the assembly by Maryland. On the fifth of December the adhesion of that state to the compact relating to the jurisdiction of the waters of Chesapeake bay and the Potomac was laid before Virginia, which without delay enacted a corresponding law of equal liberality and precision. ‖ The desire of Maryland was likewise announced to invite the concurrence of Delaware and Pennsylvania in a plan for a canal between the Chesapeake and the Delaware; "and if that is done," said Madison, "Delaware and Pennsylvania will wish the same compliment paid to their neighbors." But the immediate measure of Maryland was communicated in a letter from its legislature to the legislature of Virginia, proposing that com-

* David Stuart to Washington, 16 November 1785.
† Sparks, ix., 145, 146.          ‡ Washington to Stuart, 30 November 1785.
# In Elliot, i.. 114, the resolutions as reported on the 30th November are published as Madison's; but they found in Madison their strongest opponent. Madison, i., 205, 206, and compare 203.        ‖ Hening, xii., 50, 55.

missioners from all the states should be invited to meet and regulate the restrictions on commerce for the whole.* Madison instantly saw the advantage of "a politico-commercial commission" for the continent.

Tyler, the late speaker of the house, " wished congress to have the" entire "regulation of trade." In concert with him, a resolution was drafted by Madison for the appointment of commissioners from Virginia and all the other states to digest a report for the requisite augmentation of the powers of congress over trade, their report to be of no force until it should be unanimously ratified by the several states. Madison kept in reserve. Tyler, who, having never served in the federal council, was free from every suspicion of inclining to grant it too much power, presented the resolution. It was suffered to lie on the table till the last day in the session; then, on the twenty-first of January 1786, it went through both branches of the legislature by a large majority. Among the commissioners who were chosen, Madison was the first selection on the part of the house. The commissioners named the first Monday of September for the day of their meeting, and Annapolis as the place, on account of its remoteness from the influences of congress and the centres of trade. The invitations to the states were made through the executive of Virginia.

On the twenty-second Madison wrote to Monroe: "The expedient is better than nothing; and, as a recommendation of additional powers to congress is within the purview of the commission, it may possibly lead to better consequences than at first occur." †

The sixth congress could not be organized until the twenty-third of November 1785, when, seven states being present, David Ramsay of South Carolina was elected president. For the half of December not states enough were present to do business. So soon as there was a permanent quorum, it was agreed that the confederation had its vices, and the question of policy was: Shall these vices be corrected gradually through congress, or at once and completely through a convention? Just seventeen days after Virginia had invited the states to a

* Stuart to Washington, 18 December 1785. † Madison, i., 222.

common consultation at Annapolis, Charles Pinckney of South Carolina, in a motion of very great length, ascribed the extension of the commerce and the security of the liberties of the states to the joint efforts of the whole: "They have, therefore," he insisted, "wisely determined to make the welfare of the union their first object, reflecting that in all federal regulations something must be yielded to aid the whole, and that those who expect support must be ready to afford it."* The motion, after being under discussion for two days, was referred to a committee of five. On the fifteenth, King, Pinckney, Kean, Monroe, and Pettit, representatives of South Carolina and the three great states, reported: "The requisitions of congress, for eight years past, have been so irregular in their operation, so uncertain in their collection, and so evidently unproductive, that a reliance on them in future as a source from whence moneys are to be drawn to discharge the engagements of the confederacy would be not less dishonorable to the understandings of those who entertain such confidence than dangerous to the welfare and peace of the union. The committee are, therefore, seriously impressed with the indispensable obligation that congress are under of representing to the immediate and impartial consideration of the several states the utter impossibility of maintaining and preserving the faith of the federal government by temporary requisitions on the states, and the consequent necessity of an early and complete accession of all the states to the revenue system of the eighteenth of April 1783." "After the most solemn deliberation, and under the fullest conviction that the public embarrassments are such as above represented, and that they are daily increasing, the committee are of opinion that it has become the duty of congress to declare most explicitly that the crisis has arrived when the people of these United States, by whose will and for whose benefit the federal government was instituted, must decide whether they will support their rank as a nation by maintaining the public faith at home and abroad; or whether, for want of a timely exertion in establishing a general revenue and thereby giving strength to the confederacy, they will hazard not only the existence of the union, but of those great and in-

* Journals of Congress, iv., 617.

valuable privileges for which they have so arduously and so honorably contended." *

Thus congress put itself on trial before the country, and the result of the year was to decide on their competency to be the guardians of the union and the upholders of its good faith. They must either exercise negation of self and invite the states to call a general convention, or they must themselves present to the country for its approval an amended constitution, or they must find out how to make their own powers under the confederation work efficiently. Should they fail in all the three, they will have given an irreversible verdict against themselves. The course of events relating to the welfare of the whole was watched by the country more carefully than ever before. Far and wide a general convention was become the subject of thought; and "a plan for it was forming, though it was as yet immature." †

New Jersey, which had all along vainly sought the protection of the general government against the taxation of her people by a local duty levied on all their importations from abroad for their own consumption through the port of New York, at last kindled with a sense of her wrongs, and in a resentful mood, on the twentieth of October voted by a very large majority that she would pay no part of the last requisition of congress until all the states should have accepted the measure of an impost for the benefit of the general treasury. Alarmed at this movement, congress deputed Charles Pinckney, Gorham, and Grayson to represent to the legislature of New Jersey the fatal consequences that must inevitably result to that state and to the union from their refusal to comply with the requisition of the last congress. Grayson looked upon their vote as little else than a declaration of independence. Again Pinckney of South Carolina took the lead, and, in an address to the New Jersey legislature of the thirteenth of March, this was part of his language: "When these states united, convinced of the inability of each to support a separate system and that their protection and existence depended on their union, policy as well as prudence dictated the necessity of forming one general and efficient

---

\* Journals of Congress, iv., 619, 620.
† Jay to Washington, 16 March 1786.

government, which, while it protected and secured the whole, left to the several states those rights of internal sovereignty which it was not necessary to delegate and which could be exercised without injury to the federal authority. If New Jersey conceives herself oppressed under the present confederation, let her, through her delegates in congress, state to them the oppression she complains of, and urge the calling of a general convention of the states for the purpose of increasing the powers of the federal government and rendering it more adequate for the ends for which it was instituted; in this constitutional mode of application there can be no doubt of her meeting with all the support and attention she can wish. I have long been of opinion that it is the only true and radical remedy for our public defects, and shall with pleasure assent to and support any measure of that kind which may be introduced while I continue a member of that body." *

Pleased with the idea of a general convention, New Jersey recalled its vote, accepted within a week the invitation of Virginia to a convention at Annapolis, elected its commissioners, and empowered them " to consider how far a uniform system in their commercial regulations and OTHER IMPORTANT MATTERS might be necessary to the common interest and permanent harmony of the several states; and to report such an act on the subject as, when ratified by them, would enable the United States in congress assembled effectually to provide for the exigencies of the union." †

"If it should be determined that the reform of the confederation is to be made by a convention," so wrote Monroe at this time to Madison, "the powers of the Virginia commissioners who are to go to Annapolis are inadequate." ‡ Explaining why more extended powers had not been given, Madison answered: "The assembly would have revolted against a plenipotentiary commission to their deputies for the convention; the option lay between doing what was done and doing nothing." #

* Carey's Museum, ii., 155.   Otto to Vergennes, 17 March 1786.   Report of Bertholff, the Austrian agent. † Elliot, i., 117, 118.

‡ This letter from Monroe, of a date previous to 19 March 1786, is missing. Its contents are known only from the citation of it by Madison.

# Madison to Monroe, 19 March 1786.   Madison, i., 228, 229.

"There have been serious thoughts in the minds of members of congress," wrote Grayson to Madison, "to recommend to the states the meeting of a general convention to consider of an alteration of the confederation, and there is a motion to that effect under consideration. I have not made up my mind whether it is not 'better to bear the ills we have than fly to others we know not of.' I am, however, in no doubt about the weakness of the federal government. If it remains much longer in its present state of imbecility, we shall be one of the most contemptible nations on the face of the earth." *

The subject lingered in congress till the third of May. Then South Carolina for a third time raised her voice, and Charles Pinckney moved that a grand committee be appointed on the affairs of the nation. "It is necessary," he said, "to inform the states of our condition. Congress must be invested with greater powers, or the federal government must fall. It is, therefore, necessary for congress either to appoint a convention for that purpose, or by requisition to call on the states for such powers as are necessary to enable it to administer the federal government." Among some of the defects in the confederation which he enumerated were, the want of powers for regulating commerce, for raising troops, and for executing those powers that were given. Monroe replied: "Congress has full power to raise troops, and has a right to compel compliance with every requisition which does not go beyond the powers with which it is invested by the confederation. All the states but New York have invested congress with commercial powers, and New York is at this time framing an act on the subject. I, therefore, see no occasion for a convention." The discussion was continued at great length, and the matter referred to a committee of the whole.† But the discussion brought congress no nearer to the recommendation of a general convention; its self-love refused to surrender any of its functions, least of all on the ground of its own incapacity to discharge them.

Should congress then of itself lay a revision of the articles of confederation before the states for their acceptance? Here

* Grayson to Madison, 22 March 1786. † Thomas Rodney's Journal.

Grayson, surveying his colleagues with a discerning eye, at once convinced himself that congress could never agree on amendments, even among themselves.* For himself, he held it essential that the general government should have power to regulate commerce; to prohibit the states from issuing paper money; to prohibit the slave-trade; to fix the site of the government in the centre of the union, that is to say, near Georgetown; and to change the method of voting by states to a vote according to population. Of effecting these reforms he had no hope. He was sure if the question of commerce should be settled, Massachusetts would be satisfied and refuse to go further. "Pinckney, the champion of powers over commerce," he said, "will be astounded when he meets with a proposition to prevent the states from importing any more of the seed of Cain." New York and Pennsylvania would feel themselves aggrieved if, by a national compact, the sessions of congress should always be held in the centre of the empire. Neither Maryland, nor Rhode Island, nor New Jersey, would like to surrender its equal vote for one proportioned to its real importance in the Union. Grayson, therefore, did not "think it would be for the advantage of the union that the convention at Annapolis should produce anything decisive," since it was restricted in its scope to commerce, and the question which he proposed to Madison was: "The state of Virginia having gone thus far, had she not better go further and propose to the other states to augment the powers of the delegates so as to comprehend all the grievances of the union?" †

But Pinckney of South Carolina was not daunted. Failing to secure the vote of congress for a general convention, he next obtained the appointment of a grand committee "to report such amendments to the confederation as it may be necessary to recommend to the several states for the purpose of obtaining from them such powers as will render the federal government adequate to the ends for which it was instituted." Congress, in a committee of the whole, devoted seven days of July and six of August to the solution of the great question, and before the end of August the report, which was made by a sub-committee consisting of Pinckney, Dane, and Johnson,

* Grayson to Madison, 28 May 1786. † Ibid.

and accepted by a grand committee, received its final amended form.*

To the original thirteen articles of confederation seven new ones were added.

The United States were to regulate foreign and domestic trade and collect duties on imports, but without violating the constitutions of the states. The revenue collected was to be paid to the state in which it should accrue.

Congress, on making requisitions on the states, was to fix "the proper periods when the states shall pass legislative acts giving full and complete effect to the same." In case of neglect, the state was to be charged at the rate of ten per cent per annum on its quota in money, and twelve per cent on the ascertained average expenses on its quota of land forces.

If a state should, for ten months, neglect to pass laws in compliance with the requisition, and if a majority of the states should have passed such laws, then, but not till then, the revenue required by congress was to be apportioned on towns or counties and collected by the collectors of the last state tax. Should they refuse to act, congress might appoint others with similar rights and powers, and with full power and authority to enforce the collections. Should a state, or citizens without the disapproval of the state, offer opposition, the conduct of the state was to be considered " as an open violation of the federal compact."

Interest was to be allowed on advances by states and charged on arrears.

A new system of revenue could be established by eleven states out of the thirteen; and so in proportion as the number of states might increase.

The United States were to have the sole and exclusive power to define and punish treason against them, misprision of treason, piracy or felonies on the high seas, and to institute, by appointments from the different parts of the union, a federal court of seven judges, of whom four would constitute a quorum, to hear appeals from the state courts on matters con-

* From reports of the committee. These amended resolutions may well be taken as representing the intentions of Charles Pinckney at that time. A copy of them, very greatly abridged, is preserved in the French archives.

cerning treaties with foreign powers, or the law of nations, or commerce, or the federal revenues, or important questions wherein the United States should be a party.

To enforce the attendance of members of congress, a state might punish its faulty delegate by a disqualification to hold office under the United States or any state.

These resolutions, though most earnestly discussed in congress, were left to repose among its countless reports. They did not offer one effective remedy for existing evils; they never could win a majority in congress; no one fancied that they could obtain the unanimous assent of the states; and, could they have gained it, the articles of confederation would have remained as feeble as before. Still less was it possible for congress to raise an annual revenue. The country was in arrears for the interest on its funded debt, and in the last two years had received not more than half a million dollars in specie from all the states—a sum not sufficient for the annual ordinary charges of the federal government. Pennsylvania had complied with the late requisitions almost with exactitude; Maryland and Virginia had furnished liberal supplies; New York exerted herself, and successfully, by the aid of her custom-house; but Massachusetts and all the other New England states were in arrears, and the three southernmost states had paid little money since the conclusion of the late war. Congress confessed that it could not raise a revenue unless measures were adopted for funding the foreign and domestic debts, and they went back to the system framed by Madison in April 1783; but the success of that measure depended on a unanimous grant of new power to the general government. All the states except New York had assented to the principle of deriving a federal revenue from imports, though the assenting acts of a majority of them still required modifications. Congress saw fit to assume that nothing remained but to obtain the consent of that one state.

In March a meeting of inhabitants of the city of New York unanimously petitioned the legislature to consent to the system which alone could give energy to the union or prosperity to commerce. On the other hand, it was contended that the confederation and the constitution of each state are the foundations which neither congress nor the legislatures of the states can alter, and on which it is the duty of both to build; that the surrender to congress of an independent authority to levy duties would be the surrender of an authority that inheres necessarily in the respective legislatures of each state; that deviation from the fundamental principles of the American constitutions would be ruinous, first, to the liberty of the states, and then to their existence; that congress, already holding in one hand the sword, would hold in the other the purse, and concentrate in itself the sovereignty of the thirteen states; that it is the division of the great republic into different republics of a middling size and confederated laws which save it from despotism.*

The legislature of New York conformed to these opinions, and, while on the fourth of May it imposed the duty of five per cent, it reserved to itself the revenue with the sole right of its collection. Nor was it long before Pennsylvania, which held a large part of the public debt, suspended its adhesion to the revenue plan of congress unless it should include supplementary funds. In August, King and Monroe were dispatched by congress to confer with its legislature. It is on record that the speech of King was adapted to insure applause even from an Attic audience;† but the subject was referred to the next assembly.

Congress joined battle more earnestly with New York. They recommended the executive to convene its legislature immediately for the purpose of granting the impost. The governor made reply: "I have not power to convene the legislature except on extraordinary occasions, and, as the present business has repeatedly been laid before them, and has so recently received their determination, it cannot come within that description." Congress repeated its demand, and it only served to call from Clinton a firm renewal of his refusal. The strife had degenerated into an altercation which only established before the country that congress, though it would not call a convention and could not of itself frame fit amendments to the confederation, had not power to raise an annual

* Report of the Austrian agent, Bertholff, 1 April 1786. MS.
† Henry Hill to Washington, 1 October 1786.

revenue for the wants of the government at home, or to rescue the honor of the nation from default in payments of interest on moneys borrowed to secure their independence.

The need of reform extended equally to the relation of the republic to foreign powers. Congress had no other means of fulfilling its treaty obligations than through the good-will and concurrence of every one of the states; though in theory the articles of confederation presented the United States to all other states as one nation.

The difficulty which caused these perpetual failures was inherent and incurable. Congress undertook to enact requisitions, and then direct the legislatures of thirteen independent states to pass laws to give them effect, itself remaining helpless till they should do so. A deliberative body ordering another independent deliberative body what laws to make is an anomaly; and, in the case of congress, the hopelessness of harmony was heightened by the immense extent of the United States, by the differences of time when the legislatures of the several states convened, and by a conflict of the interests, passions, hesitancies, and wills of thirteen legislatures, independent of each other and uncontrolled by a common head. No ray of hope remained but from the convention which Virginia had invited to assemble on the first Monday in September at Annapolis.

## CHAPTER VIII.

**VIRGINIA INVITES DEPUTIES OF THE SEVERAL LEGISLATURES OF THE STATES TO MEET IN CONVENTION.**

### SEPTEMBER 1786 TO MAY 1787.

CONGRESS having confessedly failed to find ways and means for carrying on the government, the convention which had been called to Annapolis became the ground of hope for the nation. The house of delegates of Maryland promptly accepted the invitation of Virginia, but the senate, in its zeal to strengthen the appeal which congress was then addressing to the states for a revenue, refused its concurrence. Neither Connecticut, nor South Carolina, nor Georgia sent delegates to the meeting. In Massachusetts two sets of nominees, among whom appears the name of George Cabot, declined the service; the third were, like the Rhode Island delegates, arrested on the way by tidings that the convention was over.

Every one of the commissioners chosen for New York, among whom were Egbert Benson and Hamilton, was engrossed by pressing duties. Egbert Benson, the guiding statesman in the Hartford convention of 1780, was engaged as attorney-general in the courts at Albany. With Schloss Hobart, the upright judge, he agreed that the present opportunity for obtaining a revision of the system of general government ought not to be neglected. He therefore consigned his public business to a friend, reported the conversation with Schloss Hobart to Hamilton in New York, and repaired with him to Annapolis. There, on the eleventh of September, they found Madison with the commissioners of Virginia aiming at a plenipotentiary general convention, and commissioners from New

Jersey instructed by their legislature to be content with nothing less than a new federal government. No state north of New York was represented, and no one south of Delaware save Virginia. It was a meeting of central states. One thought animated the assembly. Dickinson, a principal author of the articles of confederation, was unanimously elected chairman; and, with the same unanimity, a committee was raised to prepare a report. Hamilton, though not of the committee, made a draft; this the convention employed two days in considering and amending, when the resulting form was unanimously adopted. In clear and passionless language they expressed their conviction that it would advance the interests of the union if the states which they represented would agree, and use their endeavors to procure the concurrence of the other states to agree, "to meet at Philadelphia on the second Monday of the next May to consider the situation of the United States, and devise such further provisions as should appear necessary to render the constitution of the federal government adequate to the exigencies of the union; and to report to congress such an act as, when agreed to by them and confirmed by the legislatures of every state, would effectually provide for the same." * The proposition was explicit; the place for meeting wisely chosen; and the time within which congress and the thirteen states must decide and the convention meet for its work was limited to less than eight months.

In a few days the report, signed by the venerated name of Dickinson, was received by congress; but the delegation from Massachusetts, led by King, prevented the recommendation of the measure which the deputations at Annapolis had asked for.† The governor of New York was of opinion that the confederation as it stood was equal to the purposes of the union, or, with little alteration, could be made so; and that the commissioners from New York should have confined themselves to the purposes of their errand. ‡

On the tenth of October Rufus King appeared before the house of representatives of Massachusetts, and, in the presence of an audience which crowded the galleries, insisted that the

* Elliot, i., 117–120.    † Carrington to Madison, 18 December 1786.
‡ Hamilton, vi., 605.

confederation was the act of the people; that no part could be altered but on the initiation of congress and the confirmation of all the several legislatures; if the work should be done by a convention, no legislature could have a right to confirm it; congress, and congress only, was the proper body to propose alterations. In these views he was, a few days later, supported by Nathan Dane. The house of representatives, conforming to this advice, refused to adopt the suggestions that came from Annapolis; and there was not to be another session before the time proposed for the general convention at Philadelphia.*

From this state of despair the country was lifted by Madison and Virginia. The recommendation of a plenipotentiary convention was well received by the assembly of Virginia. The utter failure of congress alike in administration and in reform, the rapid advances of the confederation toward ruin, at length proselyted the most obstinate adversaries to a political renovation. On the motion of Madison, the assembly, showing the revolution of sentiment which the experience of one year had effected, gave its unanimous sanction to the recommendation from Annapolis.† We come now upon the week glorious for Virginia beyond any event in its annals, or in the history of any former republic. Madison had been calm and prudent and indefatigable, always acting with moderation, and always persistent of purpose. The hour was come for frank and bold words, and decisive action. Madison, giving effect to his own long-cherished wishes and the still earlier wishes of Washington, addressing as it were the whole country and marshalling all the states, recorded the motives to the action of his own commonwealth in these words:

"The commissioners who assembled at Annapolis, on the fourteenth day of September last, for the purpose of devising and reporting the means of enabling congress to provide effectually for the commercial interests of the United States, have represented the necessity of extending the revision of the federal system to all its defects, and have recommended that deputies for that purpose be appointed by the several legislatures, to meet in convention in the city of Philadelphia on the

* Carrington to Madison, 18 December 1786. † Madison, i., 259.

second day of May next—a provision preferable to a discussion of the subject in congress, where it might be too much interrupted by ordinary business, and where it would, besides, be deprived of the counsels of individuals who are restrained from a seat in that assembly. The general assembly of this commonwealth, taking into view the situation of the confederacy, as well as reflecting on the alarming representations made from time to time by the United States in congress, particularly in their act of the fifteenth day of February last, can no longer doubt that the crisis is arrived at which the people of America are to decide the solemn question whether they will, by wise and magnanimous efforts, reap the fruits of independence and of union, or whether, by giving way to unmanly jealousies and prejudices, or to partial and transitory interests, they will renounce the blessings prepared for them by the revolution. The same noble and extended policy, and the same fraternal and affectionate sentiments which originally determined the citizens of this commonwealth to unite with their brethren of the other states in establishing a federal government, cannot but be felt with equal force now as motives to lay aside every inferior consideration, and to concur in such further concessions and provisions as may be necessary to secure the objects for which that government was instituted, and render the United States as happy in peace as they have been glorious in war."

Such is the preamble adopted without a dissenting voice by the general assembly of the commonwealth of Virginia, as they acceded to the proposal from Annapolis with this one variation, that the new federal constitution, after it should be agreed to by congress, was to be established, not by the legislatures of the states, but by the states themselves, thus opening the way for special conventions of the several states.

In selecting her own delegates, Virginia placed Washington at their head, surrounded by Madison, Randolph, and Mason. Randolph, the newly elected governor of the state, adopting words of Washington, sent the act of his state to congress, and to the executive of each one of the states in the union, asking their concurrence.

Hardly had the tardy post of that day brought the gladdening news to New Jersey, when that state, first of the twelve, on the twenty-third of November, took its place at the side of Virginia. Pennsylvania did not let the year go by without joining them. North Carolina acceded in January 1787, and Delaware in the following February.

The solemn words of Virginia, the example of the three central states, the inspiring influence of Hamilton, the return to congress of Madison who was preparing himself for the convention and professed great expectations of good effects from the measure, caused the scales to fall from the eyes of King. The year was but six weeks old when he wrote to Gerry, who had thus far been his ally: "Although my sentiments are the same as to the legality of the measure, I think we ought not to oppose, but to coincide with this project. Events are hurrying us to a crisis. Prudent and sagacious men should be ready to seize the most favorable circumstances to establish a more perfect and vigorous government."*

A grand committee of the seventh congress reported in February, by a bare majority of one, that, "entirely coinciding with the proceedings of the commissioners, they did strongly recommend to the different legislatures to send forward delegates to the proposed convention at Philadelphia;" but they never ventured to ask for a vote upon their report. Meantime, the legislature of New York, in an instruction to their delegates in congress, taking no notice of the meeting at Annapolis, recommended a general convention to be initiated by congress itself. The proposition, as brought forward by the New York delegates, named no place or time for the convention, and knew nothing of any acts which had not proceeded from congress. It failed by a large majority. King of Massachusetts, seizing the opportunity to reconcile his present coalition with Madison and Hamilton with his old opinion that congress alone could initiate a reform of the constitution, substituted a motion which carefully ignored the act of the meeting at Annapolis, and recommended a convention as an original measure of congress, but identical in time and place with the appointment of the Annapolis commissioners. This motion, which was so framed as not to invalidate elections already made, was accepted without

* Austin's Gerry, ii., 3, 4, 7, and 8.

opposition.* In this way the self-love of congress was appeased, and its authority arrayed in favor of a general convention.

All parties in the legislature of New York then took up the subject of representation in the convention. Yates, in the senate, proposed that "the new provisions in the articles of confederation should not be repugnant to or inconsistent with the constitution of the state." The motion was rejected by the casting vote of the president. The house would have appointed five delegates to the convention, but the inflexible senate limited the number to three, and named Yates, Lansing, and Hamilton, who were elected in both branches without opposition.

In 1786, the sufferings of the debtors in Massachusetts, especially in its central and western counties, embittered by the devices of attorneys to increase their own emoluments, and aggrieved by the barbarous laws of that day which doomed the debtor, however innocent, to imprisonment at the caprice of his creditor, had driven them to interrupt the courts in Worcester. In the three western counties measures were taken to close the courts; and once, for a moment, the national armory at Springfield was menaced. The movement assumed the aspect of an insurrection, almost of a rebellion, which received support even from husbandmen otherwise firm supporters of the law. The measures of Bowdoin, in which he was throughout supported by Samuel Adams, were marked by decision, celerity, and lenity. The real cause of the distress was, in part, the failure of the state of Massachusetts itself to meet its obligations; and, still more, the bankruptcy of the general government, which owed large sums of money to inhabitants of almost every town for service in achieving the independence of their country. Wherever the insurgents gathered in numbers, Bowdoin sent a larger force than they could muster. In this way he gave authority to every branch of the government and peace to every town. He maintained the majesty of the law by opening the courts for the conviction of the worst offenders; but, interposing with his prerogative of mercy, he did not suffer the life of any one of them to be taken. For the restoration of the public and private finances, he called together the legislature of the commonwealth, which applauded his conduct, and

---

* Journals, iv., 723, 724. Gilpin, 587, 588, 619, 620. Elliot, v., 96, 106.

fulfilled the long desire of his heart. On the twenty-second of February 1787, six days in advance of New York, and as yet in ignorance of what had been done in congress, they acceded to the invitation from Annapolis. Before its delegates were chosen, the recommendation of a convention by that body was known; and Bowdoin, in their commissions, wisely made use of the words of congress.

The two southern states chose their delegates to the convention in April. Connecticut waited for its day of election in May. Then Elizur Goodrich, the preacher of the election sermon, proved from one of the prophets of Israel the duty of strengthening the national union and restoring the national honor, or they would be obliged themselves to repeat the lamentation that " from the daughter of Zion all her beauty was departed." " Gentlemen," he broke out to those to whom he was preaching, " Heaven unite the wisdom and patriotism of America in the proposed convention of the states in some equal system of federal subordination and sovereignty of the states." On the twelfth, Samuel Huntington, the governor, addressing the legislature, recommended a superintending power that should secure peace and justice between the states, and between all the states and foreign nations. " I am," he said, " an advocate for an efficient general government, and for a revenue adequate to its nature and its exigencies. Should the imposts be carried to excess, it will promote the growth of manufacture among yourselves of the articles affected by them, and proportionally increase our wealth and independence. Manufactures more than any other employment will increase our numbers, in which consists the strength and glory of a people." * The assembly then chose to the convention three men who were all closely united, and so able that scarce any delegation stood before them.

Maryland, rent by a faction eager for the issue of paper money, did not elect delegates till near the end of May. New Hampshire, from the poverty of her treasury, delayed its choice till June. Rhode Island alone, under the sway of a perverse party spirit which was fast ebbing, refused to be represented in the convention.

* Carey's Museum, ii., 396.

The people of the United States watched the result of the convention with trembling hope. "Shall we have a king?" asked Jay, and himself answered: "Not, in my opinion, while other expedients remain untried." * It was foreseen that a failure would be followed by the establishment of three separate confederacies.† The ministry of England harbored the thought of a constitutional monarchy, with a son of George III. as king; and they were not without alarm lest gratitude to France should place on an American throne a prince of the house of Bourbon. ‡

The task of preparing the outlines of a constitution as the basis for the deliberations of the convention was undertaken by Madison. His experience and his studies fitted him for the office. He had been a member of the convention which formed the first constitution for Virginia; of its first legislature as a state; of its executive council when Patrick Henry and Jefferson were governors; for three years a delegate in congress; then a member of the Virginia legislature; a commissioner at Annapolis; and, so soon as the rule of rotation permitted, once more a member of congress. From the declaration of independence he had devoted himself to the study of republican and of federal government. On the failure at Annapolis, Jefferson cheered him on to a broader reformation: to make the states one nation as to foreign concerns, and keep them distinct in domestic ones; to organize "the federal head into legislative, executive, and judiciary;" to control the interference of states in general affairs by an appeal to a federal court. With Edmund Randolph, Madison insisted that from him, as governor of Virginia, the convention would expect some leading proposition, and dwelt on the necessity of his bending his thoughts seriously to the great work of preparation; but Randolph declined, pleading his want of the necessary leisure. Madison proceeded without dismay. He held as a fixed principle that the new system should be ratified by the people of the several states, so that it might be clearly paramount to their individual legislative authority. He would make no material sacrifices to local or transient prejudices. To

---

* Sparks, ix., 511.

† Madison, i., 280.   ‡ Temple, infra; Adams, viii., 420.

him the independence of each separate state was utterly irreconcilable with the idea of an aggregate sovereignty, while a consolidation of the states into one simple republic was neither expedient nor attainable.* In the endeavor to reconcile the due supremacy of the nation with the preservation of the local authorities in their subordinate usefulness, he did not escape mistakes; but he saw clearly that a widely extended territory was the true domain for a republic, and in advance of the federal convention he sketched for his own use † and that of his friends, ‡ and ultimately of the convention, a thoroughly comprehensive constitutional government for the union.

Washington at Mount Vernon was equally studious. He made himself familiar with the reasonings of Montesquieu; and he obtained the opinions, not of Madison only, but of Knox and of Jay. From their letters and his own experience he drew three separate outlines of a new constitution, differing in manifold ways, and yet each of the three designed to restore and consolidate the union.#

* Madison, i., 287.   † Notes on the confederacy, Madison, i., 320–328.
‡ Madison to Jefferson, 19 March 1787, Madison, i., 284; to Randolph, Gilpin, 631; Elliot, 107; to Washington, Sparks, ix., 516.
# North American Review, xxv., 263.

# THE
# FORMATION OF THE CONSTITUTION
### OF THE
# UNITED STATES OF AMERICA.

*IN FIVE BOOKS.*

## BOOK THIRD.
### THE FEDERAL CONVENTION.
### MAY–SEPTEMBER 1787.

# CHAPTER I.

### THE CONSTITUTION IN OUTLINE.

### 14 MAY TO 13 JUNE 1787.

Do nations float darkling down the stream of the ages without hope or consolation, swaying with every wind and ignorant whither they are drifting? or, is there a superior power of intelligence and love, which is moved by justice and shapes their course?

From the ocean to the American outposts nearest the Mississippi, one desire prevailed for a closer connection, one belief that the only opportunity for its creation was come. Men who, from their greater attachment to the states, feared its hazards, neither coveted nor accepted an election to the convention, and in uneasy watchfulness awaited the course of events. Willie Jones of North Carolina, declining to serve, was replaced by Hugh Williamson, who had voted with Jefferson for excluding slavery from the territories. Patrick Henry, Thomas Nelson, and Richard Henry Lee refusing to be delegates, Edmund Randolph, then governor of Virginia and himself a delegate to the convention, named to one vacancy James McClurg, a professor in the college of William and Mary whom Madison had urged upon congress for the office of secretary of foreign affairs. No state except New York sent a delegation insensible to the necessity of a vigorous union. Discordant passions were repressed by the solemnity of the moment; and, as the statesmen who were to create a new constitution, veterans in the war and in the halls of legislation, journeyed for the most part on horseback to their place of meeting, the high-wrought hopes of the nation went along with them. Nor did they deserve the interest of the people of the United States alone; they felt the ennobling love for their fellow-men, and knew themselves to be forerunners of reform for the civilized world.

George Washington was met at Chester by public honors. From the Schuylkill the city light horse escorted him into Philadelphia, the bells chiming all the while. His first act was to wait upon Franklin, the president of Pennsylvania.

On the fourteenth of May, at the hour appointed for opening the federal convention, Virginia and Pennsylvania, the only states which were sufficiently represented, repaired to the state-house, and, with others as they gathered in, continued to do so, adjourning from day to day. Of deputies, the credentials of Connecticut and Maryland required but one to represent the state; of New York, South Carolina, and Georgia, two; of Massachusetts, New Jersey, Delaware, Virginia, and North Carolina, three; of Pennsylvania, four. The delay was turned to the best account by James Madison of Virginia. From the completion of the Virginia delegation by the arrival of George Mason, who came with unselfish zeal to do his part in fulfilling "the expectations and hopes of all the union," they not only attended the general session, but "conferred together by themselves two or three hours every day in order to form a proper correspondence of sentiments." * As their state had initiated the convention, they held it their duty at its opening to propose a finished plan for consideration.

The choice lay between an amended confederacy and "the new constitution" † for which Washington four years before had pleaded with the people of every state. "My wish is," so he had written to Madison, "that the convention may adopt no temporizing expedients, but probe the defects of the constitution to the bottom and provide a radical cure, whether agreed to or not. A conduct of this kind will stamp wisdom and dignity on their proceedings, and hold up a light which sooner or later will have its influence." ‡

We know from Randolph himself that before departing for the convention he was disposed to do no more than amend

---

* George Mason to his son, Philadelphia, 20 May 1787.
† Washington to Lafayette, 5 April 1783. Sparks, viii., 412.
‡ Sparks, ix., 250, 31 March 1787.

the confederation; and his decision was likely to have great weight in the councils of his own commonwealth. When his royalist father, attorney-general of Virginia, took refuge with the English, the son cleaved to his native land. At his own request and the solicitation of Richard Henry Lee, Washington received him as an aid during the siege of Boston. In 1776 he took a part in the convention for forming the constitution of Virginia; and the convention rewarded his patriotism by electing him at twenty-three years of age attorney-general of Virginia in the place of his father. In 1779 he preceded Madison by a year as a delegate to congress. In the effort for the reform of the confederation, he, with Ellsworth of Connecticut and Varnum of Rhode Island for his associates, was the chairman of the committee appointed to report on the defects of the confederacy and the new powers necessary for its efficiency. In 1786 he was elected governor of Virginia; and now in his thirty-fourth year he was sent to the convention, bringing with him a reputation for ability equal to his high position, and in the race for public honors taking the lead of James Monroe. But with all his merit there was a strain of weakness in his character, so that he was like a soft metal which needs to be held in place by coils of a harder grain than its own. That support he found in Madison, who had urged him to act a foremost part in the convention, and had laid before him the principles on which the new government should be organized; and in Washington, who was unceasing in his monitions and encouragement. Randolph, on his arrival in Philadelphia, at once yielded to their influence, and with them became persuaded that the confederacy was destitute of every energy which a constitution of the United States ought to possess.*

The result was harmony among the Virginia delegates. A plan for a national government, which imbodied the thoughts of Madison, altered and amended by their joint consultations, was agreed to by them all. To Randolph, as the official representative of the state, was unanimously assigned the office of bringing forward the outline which was to be known as the plan of Virginia. This forethought provided in

* Randolph to Speaker, 10 October 1787.

season a chart for the voyage, so that the ship, skilfully ballasted and trimmed from the beginning, could be steered through perilous channels to the wished-for haven.

A government founded directly on the people seemed to justify and require a distribution of suffrage in the national legislature according to some equitable ratio. Gouverneur Morris and other members from Pennsylvania in conversation urged the large states to unite from the first in refusing to the smaller states in the federal convention the equal vote which they enjoyed in the congress of the confederacy; but the Virginians, while as the largest state in extent and in numbers they claimed a proportioned legislative suffrage as an essential right which must be asserted and allowed, stifled the project, being of the opinion that the small states would be more willing to renounce this unequal privilege in return for an efficient government, than to disarm themselves before the battle without an equivalent.*

On the seventeenth, South Carolina appeared on the floor; on the eighteenth, New York; on the twenty first, Delaware; on the twenty-second, North Carolina. Of the delegates, some were for half-way measures from fear of displeasing the people; others were anxious and doubting. Just before there were enough to form a quorum, Washington, standing self-collected in the midst of them, his countenance more than usually solemn, his eye seeming to look into futurity, said: "It is too probable that no plan we propose will be adopted. Perhaps another dreadful conflict is to be sustained. If, to please the people, we offer what we ourselves disapprove, how can we afterward defend our work? Let us raise a standard to which the wise and the honest can repair; the event is in the hand of God." †

On the twenty-fifth, New Jersey, completing the seven states needed to form a house, was represented by William Churchill Houston, who had been detained by illness, and was too weak to remain long. There were from the South four states, from the North, three; from the South, nineteen members, from

---

\* Madison Papers, edited by Gilpin, 726. Stereotyped reprint of Elliot, 125.

† Oration by Gouverneur Morris upon the death of Washington, 31 December 1799, pp. 20, 21. Morris was, in May 1787, present in Philadelphia, and relates what he witnessed.

the North, ten. At the desire of Benjamin Franklin of Pennsylvania, Washington was unanimously elected president of the convention. During the organization it was noticed that the delegates from Delaware were prohibited from changing the article in the confederation establishing the equality of votes among the states.*

On the twenty-eighth, the representation was increased to nine states by the arrival of Massachusetts and Maryland. A letter was read from men of Providence, Rhode Island, among them John Brown, Jabez Bowen, Welcome Arnold, and William Barton, explaining why their state would send no delegates to the convention, and hopefully pledging their best exertions to effect the ratification of its proceedings.† The letter was forwarded and supported by Varnum, a member from Rhode Island in congress.

The delegates from Maryland, chosen at a time when the best men of the state were absorbed in a domestic struggle against new issues of paper money, and its senate by its stubborn resistance was estranged from the house, did not adequately represent its public spirit; yet the majority of them to the last promoted the national union. Of the fifty-five in the convention, nine were graduates of Princeton, four of Yale, three of Harvard, two of Columbia, one of Pennsylvania; five, six, or seven had been connected with William and Mary's; Scotland sent one of her sons, a jurist, who had been taught at three of her universities, and Glasgow had assisted to train another; one had been a student in Christ Church, Oxford, and he and three others had been students of law in the Temple. To many in the assembly the work of the great French magistrate on the "Spirit of Laws," of which Washington with his own hand had copied an abstract by Madison, was the favorite manual; some of them had made an analysis of all federal governments in ancient and modern times, and a few were well versed in the best English, Swiss, and Dutch writers on government. They had immediately before them the example of Great Britain; and they had a still better school of political wisdom in the republican constitutions of their several

* Gilpin, 723; Elliot, 124.
† Gilpin, 727; Elliot, 125, and Appendix No. 1.

states, which many of them had assisted to frame. Altogether they formed "the goodliest fellowship of" lawgivers "whereof this world holds record." In their standing rules they unanimously forbade any registry to be made of the votes of individuals, so that they might, without reproach or observation, mutually receive and impart instruction; and they sat with closed doors, lest the publication of their debates should rouse the country to obstinate conflicts before they themselves should have reached their conclusions.

On the twenty-ninth, Edmund Randolph, the governor of Virginia, opened the business of the convention in this wise: "To prevent the fulfilment of the prophecies of the downfall of the United States, it is our duty to inquire into the defects of the confederation and the requisite properties of the government now to be framed; the danger of the situation and its remedy.

"The confederation was made in the infancy of the science of constitutions, when the inefficiency of requisitions was unknown; when no commercial discord had arisen among states; when no rebellion like that in Massachusetts had broken out; when foreign debts were not urgent; when the havoc of paper money had not been foreseen; when treaties had not been violated; and when nothing better could have been conceded by states jealous of their sovereignty. But it offered no security against foreign invasion, for congress could neither prevent nor conduct a war, nor punish infractions of treaties or of the law of nations, nor control particular states from provoking war. The federal government has no constitutional power to check a quarrel between separate states; nor to suppress a rebellion in any one of them; nor to establish a productive impost; nor to counteract the commercial regulations of other nations; nor to defend itself against encroachments of the states. From the manner in which it has been ratified in many of the states, it cannot be claimed to be paramount to the state constitutions; so that there is a prospect of anarchy from the inherent laxity of the government. As the remedy, the government to be established must have for its basis the republican principle."

He then proposed fifteen resolutions, which he explained one by one.

"The articles of confederation ought to be so corrected and enlarged as to accomplish the objects proposed by their institution; namely, 'common defence, security of liberty, and general welfare.'

"The rights of suffrage in the national legislature ought to be proportioned to the quotas of contribution, or to the number of free inhabitants.

"The national legislature ought to consist of two branches, of which the members of the first or democratic house ought to be elected by the people of the several states; of the second, by those of the first, out of persons nominated by the individual legislatures.

"The national legislature, of which each branch ought to possess the right of originating acts, ought to enjoy the legislative rights vested in congress by the confederation, and moreover to legislate in all cases to which the separate states are incompetent, or in which the harmony of the United States might be interrupted by the exercise of individual legislation; to negative all laws passed by the several states contravening the articles of union; and to call forth the force of the union against any member of the union failing to fulfil its duty under the articles thereof.

"A national executive, chosen by the national legislature and ineligible a second time, ought to enjoy the executive rights vested in congress by the confederation, and a general authority to execute the national laws.

"The executive and a convenient number of the national judiciary ought to compose a council of revision, with authority to examine every act of the national legislature before it shall operate.

"A national judiciary ought to be established; to consist of supreme and inferior tribunals; to be chosen by the national legislature; to hold their offices during good behavior, with jurisdiction to hear and determine all piracies and felonies on the high seas; captures from an enemy; cases in which foreigners and citizens, a citizen of one state and a citizen of another state, may be interested; cases which respect the collection of the national revenue; impeachments of national officers; and questions which may involve the national peace and harmony.

"Provision ought to be made for the admission of states lawfully arising within the limits of the United States.

"A republican government and the territory of each state ought to be guaranteed by the United States to each state.

"Provision ought to be made for the completion of all the engagements of congress, and for its continuance until after the articles of union shall have been adopted.

"Provision ought to be made for the amendment of the articles of union; to which the assent of the national legislature ought not to be required.

"The legislative, executive, and judiciary powers, within the several states, ought to be bound by oath to support the articles of union.

"The amendments which shall be offered to the confederation by the convention ought, after the approbation of congress, to be submitted to assemblies of representatives, recommended by the several legislatures to be expressly chosen by the people to consider and decide thereon."

Randolph concluded with an exhortation to the convention not to suffer the present opportunity of establishing general harmony, happiness, and liberty in the United States to pass away unimproved.*

The new articles of union would form a representative republic. The nobleness of the Virginia delegation appeared in the offer of an option to found representation on "free inhabitants" alone. The proposed government would be truly national. Not the executive, not the judges, not one officer employed by the national government, not members of the first branch of the legislature, would owe their election to the states; even in the choice of the second branch of the national legislature, the states were only to nominate candidates.

It is worthy of note that, as Randolph declared the proportioned rule of suffrage to be "the basis upon which the larger states could assent to any reform," saying, "We ought to be one nation," William Paterson of New Jersey made note that "sovereignty is an integral thing," meaning that in the new union the states must be equal unless they all were to be merged into one.† The house referred the propositions of

* Gilpin, 731–735; Elliot, 126–128.    † Paterson MSS.

Virginia to a committee of the whole on the state of the union.*
Charles Pinckney of South Carolina, a young man of twenty-nine, then presented a plan for a constitution, "grounded on the same principles † as the resolutions" of Virginia. It received the same reference, but no part of it was used, and no copy of it has been preserved.

On the morning of the thirtieth, Nathaniel Gorham of Massachusetts having been elected chairman of the committee of the whole, Randolph offered a resolution, ‡ which Gouverneur Morris had formulated, "that a national government ought to be established, consisting of a supreme legislative, executive, and judiciary." The force of the word "supreme" was explained to be, that, should the powers to be granted to the new government clash with the powers of the states, the states were to yield.#

Pierce Butler of South Carolina advanced the business of the day by saying in the spirit of Montesquieu: "Heretofore I have opposed the grant of new powers to congress because they would all be vested in one body; the distribution of the powers among different bodies will induce me to go great lengths in its support." ‖

"In all communities," said Gouverneur Morris, "there must be one supreme power and one only. A confederacy is a mere compact, resting on the good faith of the parties; a national, supreme government must have a complete and compulsive operation." Mason argued "very cogently": "In the nature of things punishment cannot be executed on the states collectively; therefore such a government is necessary as can operate directly on individuals." △

Roger Sherman, who arrived that morning and enabled Connecticut to vote, was not yet ready to do more than vest in the general government a power to raise its own revenue; ◊ and against the negative of his state alone, New York being divided, the motion was carried by Massachusetts, Pennsylvania, Virginia, and the two Carolinas, on this day aided by Delaware.

---

\* Gilpin, 735; Elliot, 128.  † Yates in Elliot, i., 391.
‡ Gilpin, 747; Elliot, 132.  # Yates in Elliot, i., 392.
‖ Gilpin, 747, 748; Elliot, 133.
△ Gilpin, 748; Elliot, 133.  ◊ Gilpin, 748; Elliot, 133.

Alexander Hamilton of New York next moved that "the rights of suffrage in the national legislature ought to be proportioned to the number of free inhabitants;" and Richard Dobbs Spaight of North Carolina seconded him. But, to escape irritating debates, the resolution was postponed, and Madison, supported by Gouverneur Morris, moved, in more general terms, "that the equality of suffrage established by the articles of confederation ought not to prevail in the national legislature; and that an equitable ratio of representation ought to be substituted." *

Faithful to his instructions, George Read of Delaware asked that the consideration of the clause might be postponed; as on any change of the rule of suffrage it might become the duty of the deputies from his state to withdraw from the convention. "Equality of suffrage," said Madison, "may be reasonable in a federal union of sovereign states; it can find no place in a national government." But, from the spirit of conciliation, the request for delay was granted.†

The next day Georgia gained the right to vote by the arrival of William Pierce, a Virginian by birth, in the war an aid to Greene, and now a member of congress. The Virginia resolve, that the national legislature should be composed of two branches, passed without debate, and, but for Pennsylvania, unanimously; Hamilton and Robert Yates of New York voting together." ‡ Three weeks later, Pennsylvania, which had hesitated only out of forbearance toward its own constitution, gave in its adhesion. The decision, which was in harmony with the undisputed and unchanging conviction of the whole people of the United States, was adopted, partly to check haste in legislation by reciprocal watchfulness, and partly to prevent the fatal conflict which might one day take place between a single legislative body and a single executive.

On the method of electing the two branches, the upholders of the sovereignty of each state contended that the national government ought to seek its agents through the governments of the respective states; others preferred that the members of the first branch should be chosen directly by the people.

* Gilpin, 750, 751; Elliot, 134.
† Gilpin, 751, 752; Elliot, 134, 135.  ‡ Gilpin, 753; Elliot, 135.

"The people," said Sherman, "should have as little to do as may be about the government; they want information and are constantly liable to be misled; the election ought to be by the state legislatures." "The people do not want virtue; but they are the dupes of pretended patriots," added Elbridge Gerry of Massachusetts. To this arraignment of the people by men of New England, Mason of Virginia replied: "The larger branch is to be the grand depository of the democratic principle of the government. We ought to attend to the rights of every class of the people. I have often wondered at the indifference of the superior classes of society to this dictate of humanity and policy." "Without the confidence of the people," said James Wilson of Pennsylvania, "no government, least of all a republican government, can long subsist; nor ought the weight of the state legislatures to be increased by making them the electors of the national legislature." Madison, though for the senate, the executive, and the judiciary he approved of refining popular appointments by successive "filtrations," held the popular election of one branch of the national legislature indispensable to every plan of free government. This opinion prevailed.*

It was agreed, unanimously and without debate, that the national legislature should possess the legislative powers of the confederacy; but, to the extension of them to all cases to which the state legislatures were individually incompetent, Charles Pinckney, John Rutledge, and Butler, all the three of South Carolina, objected that the vagueness of the language might imperil the powers of the states. But Randolph disclaimed the intention of giving indefinite powers to the national legislature, and declared himself unalterably opposed to such an inroad on the state jurisdictions. Madison was strongly biased in favor of enumerating and defining the powers to be granted, although he could not suppress doubts of its practicability. "But," said he, "a form of government that will provide for the liberty and happiness of the community being the end of our deliberations, all the necessary means for attaining it must, however reluctantly, be submitted to." † The clause was

* Gilpin, 753, 754, 755, 756; Elliot, 135, 136, 137.
† Gilpin, 760; Elliot, 139.

adopted by nine states, including New York and New Jersey. Oliver Ellsworth of Connecticut, voting against Sherman, divided that state.

The clauses in the Virginia plan, giving to the national legislature the powers necessary to preserve harmony among the states, to negative all state laws contravening, in the opinion of the national legislature, the articles of union, or, as Benjamin Franklin of Pennsylvania added, "contravening treaties subsisting under the authority of the union," were agreed to without debate or dissent.

Madison struggled to confer on the national legislature the right to negative at its discretion any state law whatever, being of the opinion that a negative of which the rightfulness was unquestioned would strip a local law of every pretence to the character of legality, and thus suppress resistance at its inception. On another day, explaining his motives, he said: " A negative on state laws is the mildest expedient that can be devised for enforcing a national decree. Should no such precaution be engrafted, the only remedy would be coercion. The negative would render the use of force unnecessary. In a word, this prerogative of the general government is the great pervading principle that must control the centrifugal tendency of the states, which, without it, will continually fly out of their proper orbits, and destroy the order and harmony of the political system." * But the convention refused to adopt his counsel.

Lastly: the Virginia plan authorized the exertion of the force of the whole against a delinquent state. Madison, accepting the argument of Mason, expressed a doubt of the practicability, the justice, and the equity of applying force to a collective people. "To use force against a state," he said, "is more like a declaration of war than an infliction of punishment, and would be considered by the party attacked a dissolution of all previous contracts. I therefore hope that a national system, with full power to deal directly with individuals, will be framed, and the resource be thus rendered unnecessary." The clause was postponed.†

In this wise and in one day the powers of the legislature

* June 8, Gilpin, 822, 823; Elliot, 171.　　† Gilpin, 761; Elliot, 140.

which was to be the centre of the government were introduced, and, except the last, were with common consent established in their outlines. On points essential to union, Yates and Hamilton, New Jersey and Pennsylvania voted together. On the first day of June the convention took into consideration the national executive. The same spirit of conciliation prevailed, but with a chaos of ideas and a shyness in the members to declare their minds.

Should the national executive be one or many?—a question which, from a difference among themselves, the plan of the Virginia delegates had left undecided. Should it be chosen directly by the people? or by electors? or by the state legislatures? or by the executives of the states? or by one branch of the national legislature? or by both branches? And, if by both, by joint or concurrent ballot? or by lot? How long should be its term of service? And how far should its re-eligibility be limited? Should it have the sole power of peace and war? Should it have an absolute or a qualified veto on acts of legislation, or none at all? Should its powers be exercised with or without a council? Should it be liable to removal by the legislatures of the states, or by the national legislature? or by the joint action of both? or by impeachment alone?

Here the convention marched and countermarched for want of guides. Progress began to be made on the ascertainment that the members inclined to withhold from the executive the power over war and peace. This being understood, Wilson and Charles Pinckney proposed that the national executive should consist of a single person. A long silence prevailed, broken at last by the chairman asking if he should put the question. Franklin entreated the members first to deliver their sentiments on a point of so great importance. Rutledge joined in the request, and for himself supported Pinckney and Wilson.* On the other hand, Sherman, controlled by the precedents of the confederacy which appointed and displaced executive officers just as it seemed to them fit, replied: "The legislature are the best judges of the business to be done by the executive, and should be at liberty from time to time to appoint one or more, as experience may dictate." †

* Gilpin, 762; Elliot, 140.      † Gilpin, 763; Elliot, 140.
VOL. VI.—16

"I do not mean to throw censure on that excellent fabric, the British government," said Randolph; "if we were in a situation to copy it, I do not know that I should be opposed to it. But the fixed genius of the people of America requires a different form of government. The requisites for the executive department—vigor, dispatch, and responsibility—can be found in three men as well as in one. Unity in the executive is the fœtus of monarchy." * " Unity in the executive," retorted Wilson, "will rather be the best safeguard against tyranny. From the extent of this country, nothing but a great confederated republic will do for it." To calm the excitement, Madison led the convention, before choosing between unity or plurality in the executive, to fix the extent of its authority; and the convention agreed to clothe it "with power to carry into effect the national laws and to appoint to offices in cases not otherwise provided for." †

On the mode of appointing the executive, Wilson said: "Chimerical as it may appear in theory, I am for an election by the people. Experience in New York and Massachusetts shows that an election of the first magistrate by the people at large is both a convenient and a successful mode. The objects of choice in such cases must be persons whose merits have general notoriety." "I," replied Sherman, "am for its appointment by the national legislature, and for making it absolutely dependent on that body whose will it is to execute. An independence of the executive on the supreme legislature is the very essence of tyranny." Sherman and Wilson were for a period of office of three years and " against the doctrine of rotation, as throwing out of office the men best qualified to execute its duties." Mason asked for seven years at least, but without re-eligibility. " What," inquired Gunning Bedford of Delaware, " will be the situation of the country should the first magistrate elected for seven years be discovered immediately on trial to be incompetent?" He argued for a triennial election, with an ineligibility after three successive elections. The convention, by a vote of five and a half states against four and a half, decided for the period of seven years; ‡ and by at least

---

\* Gilpin, 763, 764; Elliot, 141.  † Gilpin, 765; Elliot, 141.
‡ Gilpin, 767; Elliot, 143.

seven states against Connecticut, that the executive should not be twice eligible.*

How to choose the executive remained the perplexing problem. Wilson, borrowing an idea from the constitution of Maryland, proposed that electors chosen in districts of the several states should meet and elect the executive by ballot, but not from their own body.† He deprecated the intervention of the states in its choice. ‡ Mason favored the idea of choosing the executive by the people ; Rutledge, by the national senate.# Gerry set in a clear light that the election by the national legislature would keep up a constant intrigue between that legislature and the candidates ; nevertheless, Wilson's motion was at that time supported only by Pennsylvania and Maryland ; and from sheer uncertainty what else to do, the convention left the choice of the executive to the national legislature. ‖

For relief from a bad selection of the executive, John Dickinson of Delaware, who did not like the plan of impeaching the great officers of state, proposed a removal on the request of a majority of the legislatures of the individual states.^ Sherman would give that power to the national legislature. "The making the executive the mere creature of the legislature," replied Mason, "is a violation of the fundamental principle of good government." ◊

"The occasion is so important," said Dickinson, "that no man ought to be silent or reserved. A limited monarchy is one of the best governments in the world. Equal blessings have never yet been derived from any of the republican forms. But, though a form the most perfect perhaps in itself be unattainable, we must not despair. Of remedies for the diseases of republics which have flourished for a moment only and then vanished forever, one is the double branch of the legislature, the other the accidental lucky division of this country into distinct states, which some seem desirous to abolish altogether. This division ought to be maintained, and considerable powers to be left with the states. This is the ground of my consola-

---

\* Gilpin, 779 ; Elliot, 149.     ‖ Gilpin, 770 ; Elliot, 144.
† Gilpin, 768 ; Elliot, 143.     ^ Gilpin, 776 ; Elliot, 147.
‡ Gilpin, 767 ; Elliot, 143.     ◊ Gilpin, 776 ; Elliot, 147.
# Gilpin, 768 ; Elliot, 143.

tion for the future fate of my country. In case of a consolidation of the states into one great republic, we may read its fate in the history of smaller ones. The point of representation in the national legislature of states of different sizes must end in mutual concession. I hope that each state will retain an equal voice, at least in one branch of the national legislature." *

The motion of Dickinson was sustained only by Delaware; and the executive was made removable on "impeachment and conviction of malpractice or neglect of duty." † But the advice on the distribution of suffrage in the national legislature sank deep into the minds of his hearers.

Randolph pleaded anew for an executive body of three members, one from each of the three geographical divisions of the country. "That would lead to a constant struggle for local advantages," replied Butler, who had travelled in Holland; and from his own observation he sketched the distraction of the Low Countries from a plurality of military heads. ‡ "Executive questions," said Wilson on the fourth, "have many sides; and of three members no two might agree.# All the thirteen states place a single magistrate at the head. Unity in the executive will favor the tranquillity not less than the vigor of the government." ‖ Assenting to unity in the executive, Sherman thought a council necessary to make that unity acceptable to the people. "A council," replied Wilson, "oftener covers malpractices than prevents them." The proposal for a single executive was sustained by seven states against New York, Delaware, and Maryland. In the Virginia delegation there would have been a tie but for Washington.△ The decision was reached after mature deliberation, and was accepted as final.

Wilson and Hamilton desired to trust the executive with an absolute negative on acts of legislation; but this was opposed, though from widely differing motives, by Gerry, Franklin, Sherman, Madison, Butler, Bedford, and Mason,◊ and was unanimously negatived.

\* Gilpin, 778; Elliot, 148.
† Gilpin, 779; Elliot, 149.
‡ Gilpin, 780; Elliot, 149.
# Gilpin, 782; Elliot, 150.
‖ Gilpin, 781; Elliot, 150.
△ Gilpin, 782, 783; Elliot, 151.
◊ Gilpin, 784–787; Elliot, 151–154.

When Wilson urged upon the convention the Virginia plan of vesting a limited veto on legislation in a council of revision composed of the executive and a convenient number of the judiciary, Gerry called to mind that judges had in some states, and with general approbation, set aside laws as being against the constitution; but that from the nature of their office they were unfit to be consulted on the policy of public measures; and, after the example of his own state, he proposed rather to confide the veto power to the executive alone, subject to be overruled by two thirds of each branch. "Judges," said Rufus King of Massachusetts, "should expound the law as it may come before them, free from the bias of having participated in its formation." * Gerry's motion was carried by eight states against Connecticut and Maryland.†

In a convention composed chiefly of lawyers, the organization of the judiciary engaged eager attention; at the close of a long sitting, the Virginia resolution, that a national judiciary be established, passed without debate and unanimously, with a further clause that the national judiciary should consist of one supreme tribunal and of one or more inferior tribunals. ‡

A night's reflection developed a jealousy of transferring business from the courts of the states to the courts of the union; and on the fifth Rutledge and Sherman insisted that state tribunals ought, in all cases, to decide in the first instance, yet without impairing the right of appeal. Madison replied: #
"Unless inferior tribunals are dispersed throughout the republic, in many cases with final jurisdiction, appeals will be most oppressively multiplied. A government without a proper executive and judiciary will be the mere trunk of a body, without arms or legs to act or move." The motion to dispense with the inferior national tribunals prevailed; but Dickinson, Wilson, and Madison, marking the distinction between establishing them and giving a discretion to establish them, obtained a great majority for empowering the national legislature to provide for their institution. ‖ On the thirteenth it was unanimously

* Gilpin, 783; Elliot, 151. † Gilpin, 790, 791; Elliot, 155.
‡ Gilpin, 791; Elliot, 155; and Elliot, i., 160.
# Gilpin, 798, 799; Elliot, 159.
‖ Gilpin, 800; Elliot, 160. Compare Elliot, i., 163, 397.

agreed "that the power of the national judiciary should extend to all cases of national revenue, impeachment of national officers, and questions which involve the national peace or harmony." *

The Virginia plan intrusted the appointment of the judges to the legislature; Wilson proposed to transfer it to the executive; Madison to the senate; and on the thirteenth the last mode was accepted without dissent.† All agreed that their tenure of office should be good behavior, and that their compensation should be safe from diminution during the period of their service.

On the sixth of June, Charles Pinckney, supported by Rutledge, made once more a most earnest effort in favor of electing the first branch of the legislature by the legislatures of the states, and not by the people. "Vigorous authority," insisted Wilson, "should flow immediately from the legitimate source of all authority, the people. Representation ought to be the exact transcript of the whole society; it is made necessary only because it is impossible for the people to act collectively." "If it is in view," said Sherman, "to abolish the state governments, the elections ought to be by the people. If they are to be continued, the elections to the national government should be made by them. I am for giving the general government power to legislate and execute within a defined province. The objects of the union are few: defence against foreign danger, internal disputes, and a resort to force; treaties with foreign nations; the regulation of foreign commerce and drawing revenue from it. These, and perhaps a few lesser objects, alone rendered a confederation of the states necessary. All other matters, civil and criminal, will be much better in the hands of the states." ‡

"Under the existing confederacy," said Mason, "congress represent the states, and not the people of the states; their acts operate on the states, not on individuals. In the new plan of government the people will be represented; they ought, therefore, to choose the representatives.# Improper elections in many cases are inseparable from republican governments.

---

* Gilpin, 855; Elliot, 188; Yates in Elliot, i., 409.
† Gilpin, 792, 793, 855; Elliot, 155, 156, 188.
‡ Gilpin, 801, 802, 803; Elliot, 160, 161.    # Gilpin, 803; Elliot, 161.

But compare these with the advantage of this form, in favor of the rights of the people, in favor of human nature!"

Approving the objects of union which Sherman had enumerated, "I combine with them," said Madison, "the necessity of providing more effectually for the security of private rights and the steady dispensation of justice." * And he explained at great length that the safety of a republic requires for its jurisdiction a large extent of territory, with interests so many and so various that the majority could never unite in the pursuit of any one of them. "It is incumbent on us," he said, "to try this remedy, and to frame a republican system on such a scale and in such a form as will control all the evils which have been experienced." †

"It is essential," said Dickinson, "that one branch of the legislature should be drawn immediately from the people; and it is expedient that the other should be chosen by the legislatures of the states. This combination of the state governments with the national government is as politic as it is unavoidable."

Pierce spoke for an election of the first branch by the people, of the second by the states; so that the citizens of the states will be represented both individually and collectively. ‡

When on the twenty-first the same question was revived in the convention, Charles Cotesworth Pinckney of South Carolina, seconded by Luther Martin of Maryland, adopting a milder form, proposed "that the first branch, instead of being elected by the people, should be elected in such manner as the legislature of each state should direct." #

"It is essential to the democratic rights of the community," said Hamilton, enouncing a principle which he upheld with unswerving consistency, "that the first branch be directly elected by the people." "The democratic principle," Mason repeated, "must actuate one part of the government. It is the only security for the rights of the people." "An election by the legislature," pleaded Rutledge, "would be a more refining process." "The election of the first branch by the people," said Wilson, "is not the corner-stone only, but the foundation

---

\* Gilpin, 804; Elliot, 162.    ‡ Gilpin, 807; Elliot, 163.
† Gilpin, 806; Elliot, 163.    # Gilpin, 925; Elliot, 223.

of the fabric." * South Carolina, finding herself feebly supported, gave up the struggle.

On the seventh of June, Dickinson moved that the members of the second branch, or, as it is now called, the senate, ought to be chosen by the individual legislatures.† The motion, without waiving the claim to perfect equality, clearly implied that each state should elect at least one senator. " If each of the small states should be allowed one senator," said Cotesworth Pinckney, " there will be eighty at least." " I have no objection to eighty or twice eighty of them," rejoined Dickinson. " The legislature of a numerous people ought to be a numerous body. I wish the senate to bear as strong a likeness as possible to the British house of lords, and to consist of men distinguished for their rank in life and their weight of property. Such characters are more likely to be selected by the state legislatures than in any other mode." " To depart from the proportional representation in the senate," said Madison, " is inadmissible, being evidently unjust. The use of the senate is to consist in its proceeding with more coolness, system, and wisdom than the popular branch. Enlarge their number, and you communicate to them the vices which they are meant to correct. Their weight will be in an inverse ratio to their numbers." Dickinson replied : " The preservation of the states in a certain degree of agency is indispensable. The proposed national system is like the solar system, in which the states are the planets, and they ought to be left to move more freely in their proper orbits." ‡

" The states," answered Wilson, " are in no danger of being devoured by the national government ; I wish to keep them from devouring the national government. Their existence is made essential by the great extent of our country. I am for an election of the second branch by the people in large districts, subdividing the districts only for the accommodation of voters." Gerry and Sherman declared themselves in favor of electing the senate by the individual legislatures. From Charles Pinckney came a proposal to divide the states periodically into three

---

\* Gilpin, 926, 927 ; Elliot, 223, 224. Yates in Elliot, i., 432, 433.
† Gilpin, 812 ; Elliot, 166.
‡ Gilpin, 813, 814, 815 ; Elliot, 166, 167.

classes according to their comparative importance; the first class to have three members, the second two, and the third one member each; but it received no attention. Mason closed the debate: "The state legislatures ought to have some means of defending themselves against encroachments of the national government. And what better means can we provide than to make them a constituent part of the national establishment? No doubt there is danger on both sides; but we have only seen the evils arising on the side of the state governments. Those on the other side remain to be displayed; for congress had not power to carry their acts into execution, as the national government will now have." The vote was then taken, and the choice of the second branch or senate was with one consent intrusted to the individual legislatures. In this way the states as states made their lodgment in the new constitution.*

The equality of the small states was next imperilled. On the ninth, David Brearley, the chief justice of New Jersey, vehemently protested against any change of the equal suffrage of the states. To the remark of Randolph, that the states ought to be one nation, Paterson replied: "The idea of a national government as contradistinguished from a federal one never entered into the mind of any of the states. If the states are as states still to continue in union, they must be considered as equals. Thirteen sovereign and independent states can never constitute one nation, and at the same time be states. If we are to be formed into a nation, the states as states must be abolished, and the whole must be thrown into hotchpot, and when an equal division is made there may be fairly an equality of representation. New Jersey will never confederate on the plan before the committee. I would rather submit to a despot than to such a fate. I will not only oppose the plan here, but on my return home will do everything in my power to defeat it there." †

When, on the eleventh, the committee of the whole was about to take the question, Franklin, ever the peace-maker, reproved the want of coolness and temper in the late debates.

---

* Gilpin, 817, 818, 821; Elliot, 168, 169, 170; and i., 165, 399.

† Paterson MSS. Gilpin, 831, 832; and compare 870, 902, 903; Elliot, 176, 177, 194, 211.

"We are sent here," he said, "to consult, not to contend with each other;" and, though he mingled crude proposals with wholesome precepts, he saw the danger of the pass into which they were entering. There were six states, two northern and four southern, demanding a representation in some degree proportioned to numbers—Massachusetts, Pennsylvania, Virginia, and the two Carolinas with Georgia, whose delegates, as they contemplated her vast and most fertile territory, indulged in glowing visions of her swift advances. There were two northern with one southern state for an equal representation of states—New York, New Jersey, and Delaware. Connecticut stood between the two. It was carried by the six national states and Connecticut against the three confederating states, Maryland being divided, that in the first branch, or house of representatives, of the national legislature, the suffrage ought to be according to some equitable ratio. In April 1783, congress had apportioned the supplies of the states for the common treasury to the whole number of their free inhabitants and three fifths of other persons; in this precedent the equitable ratio for representation in the popular branch was found.*

Connecticut then took the lead; and Sherman, acting upon a principle which he had avowed more than ten years before, moved that each state should have one vote in the second branch, or senate. "Everything," he said, "depends on this; the smaller states will never agree to the plan on any other principle than an equality of suffrage in this branch." Ellsworth shored up his colleague; but they rallied only five states against the six which had demanded a proportioned representation.

Finally Wilson and Hamilton proposed for the second branch the same rule of suffrage as for the first; and this, too, was carried by the phalanx of the same six states against the remaining five. So the settlement offered by Wilson, Hamilton, Madison, Rutledge, and others, to the small states, and adopted in the committee of the whole, was: The appointment of the senators among the states according to representative population, except that each state should have at least one.

* Gilpin, 843; Elliot, 181.

The convention speeded through the remainder of the Virginia plan. A guarantee to each state of its territory was declined. A republican constitution, the only one suited to the genius of the United States, to the principles on which they had conducted their war for independence, to their assumption before the world of the responsibility of demonstrating man's capacity for self-government, was guaranteed to each one of the United States.

The requirement of an oath from the highest state officers to support the articles of union was opposed by Sherman [*] as an intrusion into the state jurisdictions, and supported by Randolph as a necessary precaution. "An oath of fidelity to the states from national officers might as well be required," said Gerry. Martin observed: "If the new oath should conflict with that already taken by state officers, it would be improper; if coincident, it would be superfluous." [†] The clause was retained by the vote of the six national states. By the same vote the new system was referred for consideration and decision to assemblies chosen expressly for the purpose by the people of the several states. The articles of union were thereafter open to "amendment whensoever it should seem necessary."

Sherman and Ellsworth, speaking on the twelfth, wished the members of the popular branch to be chosen annually. "The people of New England," said Gerry, "will never give up annual elections." [‡] "We ought," replied Madison, "to consider what is right and necessary in itself for the attainment of a proper government;" and his proposal of a term of three years was adopted for the time; though, to humor the eastern states, it was afterward changed to two. The ineligibility of members of congress to national offices was limited to one year after their retirement; but, on the motion of Charles Pinckney, the restriction on their re-election was removed, and the power of recalling them, which was plainly inconsistent with their choice by the people, was taken away.[#]

The qualification of age was at a later day fixed at twenty-five years for the branch elected by the people. For senators

---

[*] Gilpin, 845; Elliot, 182.
[†] Gilpin, 845; Elliot, 183.
[‡] Gilpin, 847; Elliot, 184.
[#] Gilpin, 851; Elliot, 185.

the qualification of age was at that time fixed at thirty. Pierce would have limited their term of service to three years; Sherman to not more than five; but a great majority held seven years by no means too long.

The resolutions of the committee departed from the original plan of Virginia but rarely, and, for the most part, for the better. Thus amended, it formed a complete outline of a federal republic. The mighty work was finished in thirteen sessions, with little opposition except from the small states, and from them chiefly because they insisted on equality of suffrage in at least one branch of the legislature.

## CHAPTER II.

### NEW JERSEY CLAIMS AN EQUAL REPRESENTATION OF THE STATES.

### THE FIFTEENTH TO THE NINETEENTH OF JUNE 1787.

THE plan of Virginia divested the smaller states of the equality of suffrage, which they had enjoyed from the inception of the union. "See the consequence of pushing things too far," said Dickinson to Madison; the smaller states, though some of their members, like himself and the delegates from Connecticut, wished for a good national government with two branches of the legislature, were compelled, in self-defence, to fall back upon the articles of confederation.*

The project which in importance stands next to that of Virginia is the series of propositions of Connecticut. It consisted of nine sections, and in the sessions of the convention received the support of every one of the Connecticut delegation, particularly of Sherman and Ellsworth. It was framed while they were still contriving amendments of the articles of the confederation.† It gave to the legislature of the United

---

* Gilpin, 863, note; Elliot, 191.

† Therefore, certainly, before 19 June, and probably soon after the arrival of Sherman in Philadelphia. The Connecticut members were not chosen till Saturday, the twelfth of May. Ellsworth took his seat the twenty-eighth of May, Sherman the thirtieth, and Johnson the second of June. For the plan, see the Life of Roger Sherman by Jeremiah Evarts, in Biography of the Signers, Ed. of 1828, pp. 42–44. It may be that Sherman drew the paper; but one of the articles corresponds with the sixth recommendation of a committee on which Ellsworth served with Randolph in 1781; and is very similar to a proposition made in 1786 by a sub-committee of which Johnson was a member; and another, the sixth, does no more than adopt the report of a committee of which Ellsworth was a member with Hamilton and Madison in 1783. It is hard to say whether Sherman or Ells-

States the power over commerce with foreign nations and between the states in the union, with a revenue from customs and the post-office. The United States were to make laws in all cases which concerned their common interests; but not to interfere with the governments of the states in matters wherein the general welfare of the United States is not affected. The laws of the United States relating to their common interests were to be enforced by the judiciary and executive officers of the respective states. The United States were to institute ne supreme tribunal and other necessary tribunals, and to ascertain their respective powers and jurisdiction. The individual states were forbidden to emit bills of credit for a currency, or to make laws for the payment or discharge of debts or contracts in any manner differing from the agreement of the parties, whereby foreigners and the citizens of other states might be affected. The common treasury was to be supplied by the several states in proportion to the whole number of white and other free citizens and inhabitants and three fifths of all other persons, except Indians not paying taxes, in each state. Should any state neglect to furnish its quota of supplies, the United States might levy and collect the same on the inhabitants of such state. The United States might call forth aid from the people to assist the civil officers in the execution of their laws. The trial for a criminal offence must be by jury, and must take place within the state in which the offence shall have been committed.

The task of leading resistance to the large states fell to New Jersey. Paterson, one of its foremost statesmen, of Scotch-Irish descent, brought from Ireland in infancy, a graduate of Princeton, desired a thoroughly good general government. Cheerful in disposition, playful in manner, and of an even temper, he was undisturbed by resentments, and knew how to bring back his friends from a disappointment to a good humor with themselves and with the world.* In his present under-

---

worth was the greatest hater of paper money. Compare Gilpin, 1345, 1442; Elliot, 435, 485. For proof of their unity of action, compare their joint letter from New London, 26 September 1787, to Governor Huntington of Connecticut, in Elliot, i., 491.

* Dayton to Paterson, 1 February 1801. MS.

taking he was obliged to call around him a group of states agreeing in almost nothing. New York, his strongest ally, acted only from faction. New Jersey itself needed protection for its commerce against New York. Luther Martin could bring the support of Maryland only in the absence of a majority of his colleagues. The people of Connecticut * saw the need of a vigorous general government, with a legislature in two branches.

The plan of New Jersey, which Paterson presented on the fifteenth, was a revision of the articles of confederation. It preserved a congress of states in a single body; granted to the United States a revenue from duties, stamps, and the post-office, but nothing more except by requisitions; established a plural executive to be elected and to be removable by congress; and conferred on state courts original though not final jurisdiction over infractions of United States laws.†

"The New Jersey system," said John Lansing ‡ of New York, on the sixteenth, "is federal; the Virginia system, national. In the first, the powers flow from the state governments; in the second, they derive authority from the people of the states, and must ultimately annihilate the state governments. We are invested only with power to alter and amend defective parts of the present confederation." #

Now the powers granted by Virginia extended to "all further provisions necessary to render the federal constitution adequate to the exigencies of the Union." "Fully adequate," were the still more energetic words of Pennsylvania. New Jersey did not so much as name the articles of confederation; while Connecticut limited the discussions of its delegates only by "the general principles of republican government." ‖

The states, Lansing further insisted, would not ratify a

---

* Gilpin, 862, 863, Elliot, 191, note, wrongly classes New York and Connecticut together. In conduct and intention the delegates of Connecticut were very unlike Yates and Lansing.

† Paterson MSS.; Elliot, i., 175–177; Gilpin, 863–867; Elliot, 191–193.

‡ Yates in Elliot, i., 411; compared with Gilpin, 867; Elliot, 193; **Paterson MSS.**

# Gilpin, 867; Elliot, 193; Yates in Elliot, i., 411.

‖ Journals of Congress, iv. Appendix.

novel scheme, while they would readily approve an augmentation of the familiar authority of congress.*

Paterson next spoke with the skill of a veteran advocate, setting forth, "not his own opinions," as he frankly and repeatedly avowed,† but "the views of those who sent him."

"The system of government for the union which I have proposed accords with our own powers and with the sentiments of the people. ‡ If the subsisting confederation is so radically defective as not to admit of amendment, let us report its insufficiency and wait for enlarged powers. If no confederation at present exists, all the states stand on the footing of equal sovereignty; and all must concur before any one can be bound.# If a federal compact exists, an equal sovereignty is its basis; and the dissent of one state renders every proposed amendment null. The confederation is in the nature of a compact; and can any state, unless by the consent of the whole, either in politics or law, withdraw its powers? The larger states contribute most, but they have more to protect; a rich state and a poor state are in the same relation as a rich individual and a poor one: the liberty of the latter must be preserved. Two branches are not necessary in the supreme council of the states; the representatives from the several states are checks upon each other. Give congress the same powers that are intended for the two branches, and I apprehend they will act with more energy and wisdom than the latter. Congress is the sun of our political system." ‖

Wilson refuted Paterson by contrasting the two plans.△ "The congress of the confederacy," he continued, "is a single legislature. Theory and practice both proclaim that in a single house there is danger of a legislative despotism." ◊ Cotesworth Pinckney added: "The whole case comes to this: give New Jersey an equal vote, and she will dismiss her scruples and concur in the national system." ‡

* Gilpin, 868, 869; Elliot, 194.
† Paterson MSS. The informants of England name Governor Livingston as author of the system. ‡ Gilpin, 869; Elliot, 194; Yates in Elliot, i., 412.
# Gilpin, 869; Elliot, 194. ‖ Paterson MSS.
△ Gilpin, 871; Elliot, 195; Elliot, i., 414; Paterson MSS.
◊ Gilpin, 874; Elliot, 196.
‡ Gilpin, 875; Yates in Elliot, i., 415; Elliot, 197; Paterson MSS.

## CHAPTER II.

### NEW JERSEY CLAIMS AN EQUAL REPRESENTATION OF THE STATES.

### THE FIFTEENTH TO THE NINETEENTH OF JUNE 1787.

THE plan of Virginia divested the smaller states of the equality of suffrage, which they had enjoyed from the inception of the union. "See the consequence of pushing things too far," said Dickinson to Madison; the smaller states, though some of their members, like himself and the delegates from Connecticut, wished for a good national government with two branches of the legislature, were compelled, in self-defence, to fall back upon the articles of confederation.*

The project which in importance stands next to that of Virginia is the series of propositions of Connecticut. It consisted of nine sections, and in the sessions of the convention received the support of every one of the Connecticut delegation, particularly of Sherman and Ellsworth. It was framed while they were still contriving amendments of the articles of the confederation.† It gave to the legislature of the United

---

\* Gilpin, 863, note; Elliot, 191.

† Therefore, certainly, before 19 June, and probably soon after the arrival of Sherman in Philadelphia. The Connecticut members were not chosen till Saturday, the twelfth of May. Ellsworth took his seat the twenty-eighth of May, Sherman the thirtieth, and Johnson the second of June. For the plan, see the Life of Roger Sherman by Jeremiah Evarts, in Biography of the Signers, Ed. of 1828, pp. 42–44. It may be that Sherman drew the paper; but one of the articles corresponds with the sixth recommendation of a committee on which Ellsworth served with Randolph in 1781; and is very similar to a proposition made in 1786 by a sub-committee of which Johnson was a member; and another, the sixth, does no more than adopt the report of a committee of which Ellsworth was a member with Hamilton and Madison in 1783. It is hard to say whether Sherman or Ells-

States the power over commerce with foreign nations and between the states in the union, with a revenue from customs and the post-office. The United States were to make laws in all cases which concerned their common interests; but not to interfere with the governments of the states in matters wherein the general welfare of the United States is not affected. The laws of the United States relating to their common interests were to be enforced by the judiciary and executive officers of the respective states. The United States were to institute ne supreme tribunal and other necessary tribunals, and to ascertain their respective powers and jurisdiction. The individual states were forbidden to emit bills of credit for a currency, or to make laws for the payment or discharge of debts or contracts in any manner differing from the agreement of the parties, whereby foreigners and the citizens of other states might be affected. The common treasury was to be supplied by the several states in proportion to the whole number of white and other free citizens and inhabitants and three fifths of all other persons, except Indians not paying taxes, in each state. Should any state neglect to furnish its quota of supplies, the United States might levy and collect the same on the inhabitants of such state. The United States might call forth aid from the people to assist the civil officers in the execution of their laws. The trial for a criminal offence must be by jury, and must take place within the state in which the offence shall have been committed.

The task of leading resistance to the large states fell to New Jersey. Paterson, one of its foremost statesmen, of Scotch-Irish descent, brought from Ireland in infancy, a graduate of Princeton, desired a thoroughly good general government. Cheerful in disposition, playful in manner, and of an even temper, he was undisturbed by resentments, and knew how to bring back his friends from a disappointment to a good humor with themselves and with the world.* In his present under-

worth was the greatest hater of paper money. Compare Gilpin, 1345, 1442; Elliot, 435, 485. For proof of their unity of action, compare their joint letter from New London, 26 September 1787, to Governor Huntington of Connecticut, in Elliot, i., 491.

* Dayton to Paterson, 1 February 1801. MS.

"When the salvation of the republic is at stake," said Randolph, "it would be treason to our trust not to propose what we find necessary.* The insufficiency of the federal plan has been fully displayed by trial. The end of a general government can be attained only by coercion, or by real legislation. Coercion is impracticable, expensive, and cruel, and trains up instruments for the service of ambition. We must resort to a national legislation over individuals. To vest such power in the congress of the confederation would be blending the legislative with the executive. Elected by the legislatures who retain even a power of recall, they are a mere diplomatic body, with no will of their own, and always obsequious to the states who are ever encroaching on the authority of the United States.† A national government, properly constituted, will alone answer the purpose; and this is the only moment when it can be established." ‡

On the morning of the eighteenth, Dickinson, to conciliate the conflicting parties, induced the convention to proceed through a revision of the articles of the confederation to a government of the United States, adequate to the exigencies, preservation, and prosperity of the union.#

Hamilton could no longer remain silent. Embarrassed by the complete antagonism of both his colleagues, he yet insisted that even the New York delegates need not doubt the ample extent of their powers, and under them the right to the free exercise of their judgment. The convention could only propose and recommend; to ratify or reject remained "in the states." ‖

Feeling that another ineffectual effort "would beget despair," he spoke for "a solid plan without regard to temporary opinions." "Our choice," he said, "is to engraft powers on the present confederation, or to form a new government with complete sovereignty." △ He set forth the vital defects of the confederacy, and that it could not be amended except by investing it with most important powers. To do so would estab-

---

* Gilpin, 876; Elliot, 197; Paterson MSS.　† Gilpin, 876, 877; Elliot, 198.
‡ Yates in Elliot, i., 417; Gilpin, 877-879; Elliot, 198; Paterson MSS.
# Gilpin, 878; Elliot, 198.　　　‖ Yates in Elliot, i., 418.
△ Hamilton's Works, ii., 410.
　VOL. VI.—17

lish a general government in one hand without checks; a sovereignty of the worst kind, the sovereignty of a single body. This is a conclusive objection to the Jersey plan.*

"I have great doubts," he continued, "whether a national government on the Virginia plan can be effectual.† Gentlemen say we need to be rescued from the democracy. But what are the means proposed? A democratic assembly is to be checked by a democratic senate, and both these by a democratic chief magistrate. ‡ The Virginia plan is but pork still with a little change of the sauce.# It will prove inefficient, because the means will not be equal to the object. ‖

"The general government must not only have a strong soul, but strong organs by which that soul is to operate.△ I despair that a republican form of government can remove the difficulties; I would hold it, however, unwise to change it. ◊ The best form of government, not attainable by us, but the model to which we should approach as near as possible, ⟡ is the British constitution, ⟢ praised by Necker as 'the only government which unites public strength with individual security.' ⟣ Its house of lords is a most noble institution. It forms a permanent barrier against every pernicious innovation, whether attempted on the part of the crown or of the commons.**

"It seems to be admitted that no good executive can be established upon republican principles.†† The English model is the only good one. The British executive is placed above temptation, and can have no interest distinct from the public welfare. ‡‡ The inference from these observations is, that, to obtain stability and permanency, we ought to go to the full length that republican principles will admit.## And the government will be republican so long as all officers are appointed by

---

\* Hamilton's Works, ii., 412; Yates in Elliot, i., 420, 421.
† Yates in Elliot, i., 417.  ‡ Hamilton, ii., 415.
# Yates in Elliot, i., 423; Gilpin, 893, note; Elliot, 205.
‖ Hamilton, ii., 415.  △ Hamilton, ii., 413.
◊ Yates in Elliot, i., 421.  ⟢ Hamilton, ii., 413.
⟡ Yates in Elliot, i., 421; Hamilton, ii., 413.  ⟣ Gilpin, 886; Elliot, 202
** Gilpin, 886, 887; Elliot, 203.  †† Gilpin, 887; Elliot, 203.
‡‡ Yates in Elliot, i., 422.
## Gilpin, 888; Elliot, 203; Yates in Elliot, i., 422.

the people, or by a process of election originating with the people."

Hamilton then read and commented on his sketch of a constitution for the United States. It planted no one branch of the general government on the states; but, by methods even more national than that of the Virginia plan, derived them all from the people.

The assembly, which was to be the corner-stone of the edifice, was to consist of persons elected directly by the people for three years. It was to be checked by a senate elected by electors chosen by the people,* and holding office during good behavior. The supreme executive, whose term of office was to be good behavior, was to be elected by electors, chosen by electors, chosen by the people.† "It may be said," these were his words, "this constitutes an elective monarchy; but by making the executive subject to impeachment the term monarchy can not apply." ‡ The courts of the United States were so instituted as to place the general government above the state governments in all matters of general concern.# To prevent the states from passing laws contrary to the constitution or laws of the United States, the executive of each state was to be appointed by the general government with a negative on all state legislation.

Hamilton spoke, not to refer a proposition to the committee, but only to present his own ideas, and to indicate the amendments which he might offer to the Virginia plan. He saw evils operating in the states which must soon cure the people of their fondness for democracies, and unshackle them from their prejudices; so that they would be ready to go as far at least as he had suggested. ‖ But for the moment he held it the duty of the convention to balance inconveniences and dangers, and choose that which seemed to have the fewest objections.△

Hamilton "was praised by everybody, but supported by none." ◊ It was not the good words for the monarchy of

---

\* I think Hamilton meant the choice of electors to be made by the landholders; see his fuller plan, written out by himself and given to Madison near the close of the convention. The senate of New York was so chosen.
  † Elliot, i., 179.     ‡ Yates in Elliot, i., 422.     # Ibid., 423.
  ‖ Gilpin, 890; Elliot, 204.     △ Hamilton, ii., 415.     ◊ Yates in Elliot, i., 431.

Great Britain that enstranged his hearers. Hamilton did not go far beyond the language of Randolph,* or Dickinson,† or Gerry, ‡ or Charles Pinckney.# The attachment to monarchy in the United States had not been consumed by volcanic fire; it had disappeared because there was nothing left in them to keep it alive. The nation imperceptibly and without bitterness outgrew its old habits of thought. Gratitude for the revolution of 1688 still threw a halo round the house of lords. But Hamilton, finding a home in the United States only after his mind was near maturity, did not cherish toward the states the feeling of those who were born and bred on the soil, and had received into their affections the thought and experience of the preceding generation. His speech called forth from many sides the liveliest defence of the rights of the states.

On the nineteenth the convention in committee rejected the milder motion of Dickinson; and, after an exhaustive analysis by Madison ‖ of the defects in the New Jersey plan, they reported the amended plan of Virginia by the vote of the six national states, aided by the vote of Connecticut.▲

* Gilpin, 763; Elliot, 141.
† Gilpin, 778; Elliot, 148.
‡ Yates in Elliot, i., 408.
# Gilpin, 947; Elliot, 234.
‖ Gilpin, 893; Elliot, 206.
▲ Gilpin, 904; Elliot, 212; Yates in Elliot, i., 425.

## CHAPTER III.

### THE CONNECTICUT COMPROMISE.

### FROM 19 JUNE TO 2 JULY 1787.

The convention, which had shown itself so resolute for consolidating the union, next bethought itself of home rule. In reply to what had fallen from Hamilton, Wilson said, on the nineteenth of June: "I am for a national government, but not one that will swallow up the state governments; these are absolutely necessary for purposes which the national government cannot reach."

"I did not intend yesterday," exclaimed Hamilton, "a total extinguishment of state governments; but that a national government must have indefinite sovereignty; for if it were limited at all, the rivalship of the states would gradually subvert it.* The states must retain subordinate jurisdictions." † "If the states," said King, "retain some portion of their sovereignty, they have certainly divested themselves of essential portions of it. If, in some respects, they form a confederacy, in others they form a nation."

Martin held that the separation from Great Britain placed the thirteen states in a state of nature toward each other. ‡ This Wilson denied, saying: "In the declaration of independence the united colonies were declared to be free and independent states, independent, not individually, but unitedly." #

Connecticut, which was in all sincerity partly federal and partly national, was now compelled to take the lead. As a

---

\* Gilpin, 904; Elliot, 212.
† Yates in Elliot, i., 426.
‡ Gilpin, 906, 907; Elliot, 213.
# Gilpin, 907; Elliot, 213.

state she was the most homogeneous and the most fixed in the character of her consociate churches and her complete system of home government. Her delegation to the convention was thrice remarkable: they had precedence in age; in experience, from 1776 to 1786 on committees to frame or amend a constitution for the country; and in illustrating the force of religion in human life.

Roger Sherman was a unique man. No one in the convention had had so large experience in legislating for the United States. Next to Franklin the oldest man in the convention, like Franklin he had had no education but in the common school of his birthplace hard by Boston; and as the one learned the trade of a tallow-chandler, so the other had been apprenticed to a shoemaker.

Left at nineteen an orphan on the father's side, he ministered to his mother during her long life; and having suffered from the want of a liberal education, he provided it for his younger brothers. Resolved to conquer poverty, at the age of two-and-twenty he wrapped himself in his own manliness, and, bearing with him the tools of his trade, he migrated on foot to New Milford, in Connecticut, where he gained a living by his craft or by traffic, until in December 1754, after careful study, he was admitted to the bar.

There was in him kind-heartedness and industry, penetration and close reasoning, an unclouded intellect, superiority to passion, intrepid patriotism, solid judgment, and a directness which went straight to its end; so that the country people among whom he lived, first at New Milford and then at New Haven, gave him every possible sign of their confidence. The church made him its deacon; Yale college its treasurer; New Haven its representative, and, when it became a city, its first mayor, re-electing him as long as he lived. For nineteen years he was annually chosen one of the fourteen assistants, or upper house of the legislature; and for twenty-three years a judge of the court of common pleas, or of the superior court.

A plurality of offices being then allowed, Sherman was sent to the first congress in 1774, and to every other congress to the last hour of his life, except when excluded by the fundamental law of rotation. In congress he served on most of the important committees, the board of war, the board of the marine, the board of finance. He signed the declaration of 1774, which some writers regard as the date of our nationality; was of the committee to write, and was a signer of the declaration of independence; was of the committee to frame the articles of the confederation, and a signer of that instrument. No one is known to have complained of his filling too many offices, or to have found fault with the manner in which he filled them. In the convention he never made long speeches, but would intuitively seize on the turning-point of a question, and present it in terse language which showed his own opinion and the strength on which it rested.

By the side of Sherman stood William Samuel Johnson, then sixty years of age. He took his first degree at Yale, his second, after a few months' further study, at Harvard; became a representative in the Connecticut assembly; was a delegate to the stamp-act congress of 1765, and assisted in writing its address to the king. He became the able and faithful agent of his state in England, where Oxford made him a doctor of civil law. After his return in 1771, he was chosen one of the fourteen assistants, and one of the judges of the superior court. He was sent by Connecticut on a peace mission to Gage at Boston; but from the war for independence he kept aloof. His state, nevertheless, appointed him its leading counsel in its territorial disputes with Pennsylvania. A delegate to the fifth congress and the sixth, he acted in 1786 on a grand committee and its sub-committee for reforming the federal government. He had just been unanimously chosen president of Columbia college. His calm and conservative character made him tardy in coming up to a new position, so that he had even opposed the call of the federal convention.* He was of good-humor, composedness, and candor, and he knew how to conciliate and to convince.

The third member of the Connecticut delegation was Oliver Ellsworth, whom we have seen on the committee of 1781 for amending the constitution, and on the committee of 1783 for addressing the states in behalf of further reforms. A native of Connecticut, he was at Yale for two years, and in

---

* Gale to Johnson, 19 April 1787; Gilpin, 589; Elliot, 96.

1766, after two years more of study, graduated in the college of New Jersey, where Luther Martin was his classmate. Of a robust habit of mind, he was full of energy and by nature hopeful; devoid of sentimentality and safe against the seductions of feeling or the delusions of imagination, he was always self-possessed. Free from rancor and superior to flattery, he could neither be intimidated nor cajoled. His mind advanced cautiously, but with great moving force. Knowing what he needed, he could not be turned from its pursuit; obtaining it, he never wrangled for more. He had been the attorney of his own state, a member of its assembly, one of its delegates in congress, a colleague of Sherman in its superior court; and now, at the age of two-and-forty, rich in experience, he becomes one of the chief workmen in framing the federal constitution.

By Paterson, in his notes for a New Jersey plan, the proposed new government was named "the federal government of the United States;" by Dickinson, in his resolution, "the government of the United States." In the Virginia plan it was described as "national" nineteen times, and in the report from the convention in committee of the whole to the house, twenty-six times. Ellsworth, who then and ever after did not scruple to use the word "national," moved to substitute in the amended Virginia plan the phrase of Dickinson as the proper title.* To avoid alarm, the friends to the national plan unhesitatingly accepted the colorless change.† Lansing then moved "that the powers of legislation ought to be vested in the United States in congress." He dwelt again on the want of power in the convention, the probable disapprobation of their constituents, the consequent dissolution of the union, the inability of a general government to pervade the whole continent, the danger of complicating the British model of government with state governments on principles which would gradually destroy the one or the other.

Mason protested against a renewed agitation of the question between the two plans, and against the objection of a want of ample powers in the convention; with impassioned wisdom, he continued:

"On two points the American mind is well settled: an at

---

* Gilpin, 908, 909; Elliot, 214. † Martin in Elliot, i., 362.

tachment to republican government, and an attachment to more than one branch in the legislature. The general accord of their constitutions in both these circumstances must either have been a miracle, or must have resulted from the genius of the people. Congress is the only single legislature not chosen by the people themselves, and in consequence they have been constantly averse to giving it further powers. They never will, they never can, intrust their dearest rights and liberties to one body of men not chosen by them, and yet invested with the sword and the purse; a conclave, transacting their business in secret and guided in many of their acts by factions and party spirit. It is acknowledged by the author of the New Jersey plan that it cannot be enforced without military coercion. The most jarring elements of nature, fire and water, are not more incompatible than such a mixture of civil liberty and military execution.

"Notwithstanding my solicitude to establish a national government, I never will agree to abolish the state governments, or render them absolutely insignificant. They are as necessary as the general government, and I shall be equally careful to preserve them. I am aware of the difficulty of drawing the line between the two, but hope it is not insurmountable. That the one government will be productive of disputes and jealousies against the other, I believe; but it will produce mutual safety. The convention cannot make a faultless government; but I will trust posterity to mend its defects." *

The day ended in a definitive refusal to take up the proposition of Lansing; the six national states standing together against the three federal ones and Connecticut, Maryland being divided. The four southernmost states aimed at no selfish advantages, when in this hour of extreme danger they came to the rescue of the union. Moreover, the people of Maryland were by a large majority on the side of the national states, and the votes of Connecticut and Delaware were given only to pave the way to an equal vote in the senate.

Weary of supporting the New Jersey plan, Sherman † pleaded for two houses of the national legislature and an equal

* Gilpin, 912–915; Elliot, 216, 217; Yates in Elliot, i., 428, 429.
† Gilpin, 918; Elliot, 219.

vote of the states in one of them. On the next morning Johnson* took up the theme. Avoiding every appearance of dictation, he invited the convention to harmonize the individuality of the states as proposed by New Jersey with the general sovereignty and jurisdiction of the Virginia plan. He wished it to be well considered, whether the portion of sovereignty which was to remain with the states could be preserved without allowing them in the second branch of the national legislature a distinct and equal vote.

The six national states, re-enforced by Connecticut, then resolved † that the general legislature should consist of two branches. Upon this decision, which was carried by more than two states to one, the New Jersey plan fell hopelessly to the ground.

It was on the twenty-fifth, in the course of these debates, that Wilson said: "When I consider the amazing extent of country, the immense population which is to fill it, the influence which the government we are to form will have, not only on the present generation of our people and their multiplied posterity, but on the whole globe, I am lost in the magnitude of the object. ‡ We are laying the foundation of a building in which millions are interested, and which is to last for ages.# In laying one stone amiss we may injure the superstructure; and what will be the consequence if the corner-stone should be loosely placed? A citizen of America is a citizen of the general government, and is a citizen of the particular state in which he may reside.‖ The general government is meant for them in the first capacity; the state governments in the second. Both governments are derived from the people, both meant for the people; both, therefore, ought to be regulated on the same principles.△ In forming the general government we must forget our local habits and attachments, lay aside our state connections, and act for the general good of the whole. ◊ The general government is not an assemblage of states, but of

---

\* Gilpin, 920; Elliot, 220; Yates in Elliot, i., 431.
† Gilpin, 925; Elliot, 223; i., 184; Yates in Elliot, i., 432.
‡ Gilpin, 956; Elliot, 239.   # Yates in Elliot, i., 446.
‖ Yates in Elliot, i., 445, 446.   △ Gilpin, 956; Elliot, 239.
◊ Yates in Elliot, i., 446.

individuals, for certain political purposes; it is not meant for the states, but for the individuals composing them; the individuals, therefore, not the states, ought to be represented in it." * He persisted to the last in demanding that the senate should be elected by electors chosen by the people.

Ellsworth replied: "Whether the member of the senate be appointed by the people or by the legislature, he will be a citizen of the state he is to represent. Every state has its particular views and prejudices, which will find their way into the general council, through whatever channel they may flow. † The state legislatures are more competent to make a judicious choice than the people at large. Without the existence and co-operation of the states, a republican government cannot be supported over so great an extent of country. We know that the people of the states are strongly attached to their own constitutions. If you hold up a system of general government, destructive of their constitutional rights, they will oppose it. The only chance we have to support a general government is to graft it on the state governments." ‡

That the members of the second branch should be chosen by the individual legislatures, which in the committee had been unanimously accepted, was then affirmed in convention by all the states except Pennsylvania and Virginia, which looked upon this mode of choice as the stepping-stone to an equal representation.#

For the term of office of the senators, who, as all agreed, were to go out in classes, Randolph proposed seven years; Cotesworth Pinckney, four; Gorham and Wilson, six with biennial rotation. Read desired the tenure of good behavior, but, hardly finding a second, ‖ moved for a term of nine years as the longest which had a chance for support.

Madison came to his aid. "The second branch, as a limited number of citizens, respectable for wisdom and virtue, will be watched by and will keep watch over the representatives of the people; it will seasonably interpose between impetuous counsels; and will guard the minority who are placed

* Gilpin, 957; Elliot, 239. † Ibid. ‡ Yates in Elliot, i., 446, 447.
# Gilpin, 959; Elliot, 240; Yates in Elliot, i., 447.
‖ Compare Gilpin, 960, or Elliot, 241, with Yates in Elliot, i., 448.

above indigence against the agrarian attempts of the ever-increasing class who labor under all the hardships of life, and secretly sigh for a more equal distribution of its blessings. The longer the members of the senate continue in office, the better will these objects be answered. The term of nine years can threaten no real danger." *

Sherman replied : " The more permanency a government has, the worse, if it be a bad one. I shall be content with six years for the senate ; but four will be quite sufficient." †

" We are now to decide the fate of republican government," said Hamilton ; " if we do not give to that form due stability, it will be disgraced and lost among ourselves, disgraced and lost to mankind forever. ‡ I acknowledge I do not think favorably of republican government; but I address my remarks to those who do, in order to prevail on them to tone their government as high as possible. I profess myself as zealous an advocate for liberty as any man whatever; and trust I shall be as willing a martyr to it, though I differ as to the form in which it is most eligible. Real liberty is neither found in despotism nor in the extremes of democracy, but in moderate governments. # Those who mean to form a solid republic ought to proceed to the confines of another government. If we incline too much to democracy, we shall soon shoot into a monarchy." The term of nine years received only the votes of Pennsylvania, Delaware, and Virginia; and that for six years, with the biennial renewal of one third of its members, was carried by the voice of seven states against four. ‖

On the twenty-seventh, Rutledge brought the convention to consider the rule of suffrage in the two branches of the national legislature. For the rest of the day, and part of the next, Martin vehemently denounced any general government that could reach individuals, and intimated plainly that Clinton of New York would surely prevent its adoption in that state. Lansing renewed the proposal to vote by states in the first branch of the legislature. Madison summed up a most

---

\* Gilpin, 964 ; Elliot, 242, 243 ; Yates in Elliot, i., 450.
† Gilpin, 965; Elliot, 243 ; Yates in Elliot, i., 450.
‡ Gilpin, 965, 966 ; Elliot, 244.    # Yates in Elliot, i., 450.
‖ Gilpin, 969 ; Elliot, 245 ; i., 451.

elaborate statement by saying: "The two extremes before us are, a perfect separation, and a perfect incorporation of the thirteen states. In the first case, they will be independent nations, subject only to the law of nations; in the last, they will be mere counties of one entire republic, subject to one common law. In the first, the smaller states will have everything to fear from the larger; in the last, nothing. Their true policy, therefore, lies in promoting that form of government which will most approximate the states to the condition of counties." * Johnson and Sherman and Ellsworth, Paterson and Dickinson, even at the risk of union, opposed King, the most eloquent orator, Wilson, the most learned civilian, and Madison, the most careful statesman, of the convention. It was in vain for the smaller states to say they intended no injustice, and equally in vain for Madison to plead that the large states, from differing customs, religion, and interests, could never unite in perilous combinations. In the great diversity of sentiment, Johnson could not foresee the result of their deliberations; † and at a later day Martin reported that the convention was "on the verge of dissolution, scarce held together by the strength of a hair." ‡

To restore calm, Franklin, just as the house was about to adjourn, proposed that the convention should be opened every morning by prayer. Having present in his mind his own marvellous career from the mocking skepticism of his boyhood, he said: "The longer I live, the more convincing proofs I see that God governs in the affairs of men. I firmly believe that 'except the Lord build the house, they labor in vain that build it.' Without his concurring aid, we shall be divided by our little local interests, succeed no better than the builders of Babel, and become a reproach and by-word to future ages. What is worse, mankind may hereafter, from this unfortunate instance, despair of establishing government by human wisdom, and leave it to chance and war." # The motion was avoided by adjournment.

The concurring aid which Franklin invoked implied a

---

* Gilpin, 982; Elliot, 252.
† William Samuel Johnson to his son, Philadelphia, 27 June 1787.
‡ Elliot, i., 358.   # Gilpin, 985; Elliot, 253, 254.

purification from the dominion of selfish interests. In the next meeting the members were less absorbed by inferior motives.* The debate was opened by Johnson. "A state," he said, "exists as a political society, and it exists as a district of individual citizens. The aristocratic and other interests, and the interests of the states, must be armed with some power of self-defence. In one branch of the general government the people ought to be represented; in the other, the states." † Gorham brought together arguments for union alike from the point of view of small and of large states; and his last word was: "A union of the states is necessary to their happiness, and a firm general government is necessary to their union. I will stay here as long as any state will remain, in order to agree on some plan that can be recommended to the people." ‡

"I do not despair," said Ellsworth; "I still trust that some good plan of government will be devised and adopted."

"If this point of representation is once well fixed," said Madison, "we shall come nearer to one another in sentiment.# The necessity will then be discovered of circumscribing more effectually the state governments, and enlarging the bounds of the general government. There is a gradation from the smallest corporation with the most limited powers to the largest empire with the most perfect sovereignty. ‖ The states never possessed the essential rights of sovereignty; these were always vested in congress. Voting as states in congress is no evidence of sovereignty. The state of Maryland voted by counties. Did this make the counties sovereign? The states, at present, are only great corporations, having the power of making by-laws not contradictory to the general confederation.△ The proposed government will have powers far beyond those exercised by the British parliament when the states were part of the British empire.

"The mixed nature of the government ought to be kept in view; but the exercise of an equal voice by unequal portions of the people is confessedly unjust, and would infuse

---

\* Compare Walter Scott in The Heart of Midlothian, vol. i., chap. xiv.
† Gilpin, 987; Elliot, 255.     ‡ Gilpin, 989; Elliot, 255.
# Elliot, i., 461.   ‖ Gilpin, 990; Elliot, 256.   △ Yates in Elliot, i., 461.

mortality into the constitution which we wish to last forever. A total separation of the states from each other or partial confederacies would alike be truly deplorable; and those who may be accessory to either can never be forgiven by their country, nor by themselves." *

"In all the states," said Hamilton, "the rights of individuals with regard to suffrage are modified by qualifications of property. In like manner states may modify their right of suffrage, the larger exercising a larger, the smaller a smaller share of it. Will the people of Delaware be less free if each citizen has an equal vote with each citizen of Pennsylvania? The contest is for power, not for liberty.

"No government can give us happiness at home which has not the strength to make us respectable abroad. This is the critical moment for forming such a government. As yet we retain the habits of union. We are weak, and sensible of our weakness. Our people are disposed to have a good government; † but henceforward the motives will become feebler and the difficulties greater. It is a miracle that we are now here, exercising free deliberation; it would be madness to trust to future miracles. ‡ We must therefore improve the opportunity, and render the present system as perfect as possible. The good sense of the people, and, above all, the necessity of their affairs, will induce them to adopt it." #

It was then decided, by the six national states to four, Maryland being divided, that the rule of suffrage in the first branch ought to bear proportion to the population of the several states. A reversal of this decision was never attempted.

Ellsworth now put forth all his strength as he moved that in the second branch the vote should be taken by states: ‖ "I confess that the effect of this motion is to make the general government partly federal and partly national. I am not sorry that the vote just passed has determined against this rule in the first branch; I hope it will become a ground of compromise with regard to the second. On this middle ground,

* Gilpin, 990, 992; Elliot, 256, 257; Yates in Elliot, i., 462.
† Yates in Elliot, i., 463.   ‡ Gilpin, 995; Elliot, 259.
# Yates in Elliot, i., 464.   ‖ Yates in Elliot, i., 464.

and on no other, can a compromise take place.* If the great states refuse this plan, we shall be forever separated.

"In the hour of common danger we united as equals; is it just to depart from this principle now, when the danger is over?† The existing confederation is founded on the equality of the states in the article of suffrage, ‡ and is declared to be perpetual.# Is it meant to pay no regard to this plighted faith?∥ We then associated as free and independent states. To perpetuate that independence, I wish to establish a national legislature, executive, and judiciary; for under these we shall preserve peace and harmony." ᐃ

Abraham Baldwin, a native of Connecticut, a graduate of Yale college, for four years one of its tutors, a recent emigrant to Georgia, from which state he was now a deputy, stepped forth to the relief of Ellsworth, saying: "The second branch ought to be the representation of property,◊ and ought not to be elected as the first." ‡

"If a minority will have their own will, or separate the union," said Wilson, on the thirtieth, "let it be done. I cannot consent that one fourth shall control the power of three fourths. The Connecticut proposal removes only a part of the objection. We all aim at giving the general government more energy. The state governments are necessary and valuable. No liberty can be obtained without them. On this question of the manner of taking the vote in the second branch depend the essential rights of the general government and of the people." ⫷

Ellsworth replied: "No salutary measure has been lost for want of a majority of the states to favor it. ⫸ If the larger states seek security, they have it fully in the first branch of the general government. But are the lesser states equally secure? We are razing the foundation of the building, when we need only repair the roof.** And let it be remembered that these remarks are not the result of partial or local

* Gilpin, 996, 997; Elliot, 260.
† Elliot, i., 464, 465.
‡ Gilpin, 998; Elliot, 260.
# Yates in Elliot, i., 465.
∥ Gilpin, 998; Elliot, 260.
ᐃ Yates in Elliot, i., 465.
◊ Gilpin, 998; Elliot, 260.
‡ Yates in Elliot, i., 465.
⫷ Yates in Elliot, i., 466, 467.
⫸ Gilpin, 1003; Elliot, 263.
** Gilpin, 1003; Elliot, 263; Yates in Elliot, i., 468.

views. In importance, the state I represent holds a middle rank." *

"If there was real danger to the smaller states," said Madison, "I would give them defensive weapons. But there is none. The great danger to our general government is, that the southern and northern interests of the continent are opposed to each other, † not from their difference of size, but from climate, and principally from the effects of their having or not having slaves. ‡ Look to the votes in congress; most of them stand divided by the geography of the country, not by the size of the states.# Defensive power ought to be given, not between the large and small states, but between the northern and southern. Casting about in my mind for some expedient that will answer this purpose, it has occurred that the states should be represented in one branch according to the number of free inhabitants only; and in the other according to the whole number, counting the slaves as free. The southern scale would have the advantage in one house, and the northern in another." ‖ By this willingness to recede from the strict claim to representation in proportion to population for the sake of protecting slavery, Madison stepped from firm ground. The argument of Ellsworth drawn from the faith plighted to the smaller states in the existing federal compact, he answered only by taunts: "The party claiming from others an adherence to a common engagement ought at least to be itself guiltless of its violation. Of all the states, Connecticut is perhaps least able to urge this plea." △

Fixing his eyes on Washington, Ellsworth rejoined: "To you I can with confidence appeal for the great exertions of my state during the war in supplying both men and money. ◊ The muster rolls will show that she had more troops in the field than even the state of Virginia. ‡ We strained every nerve to raise them; and we spared neither money nor exertions to complete our quotas. This extraordinary exertion ha-

---

\* Gilpin, 1004; Elliot, 264.
† Yates in Elliot, i., 465, 466.   ‡ Gilpin, 1006; Elliot, 264.
# Yates in Elliot, i., 466.   The date in Madison is 30 June.
‖ Gilpin, 1006; Elliot, 264, 265.   △ Gilpin, 1005; Elliot, 264.
◊ Gilpin, 1007; Elliot, 265.   ‡ Yates in Elliot, i., 469.

VOL. VI.—18

greatly impoverished us, and has accumulated our state debts; but we defy any gentleman to show that we ever refused a federal requisition. If she has proved delinquent through inability only, it is not more than others have been without the same excuse. It is the ardent wish of the state to strengthen the federal government." *

Davie of North Carolina, breaking the phalanx of national states, preferred the proposition of Ellsworth to the proportional representation, which would in time make the senate a multitudinous body.† Connecticut had won the day.

Startled by the appearance of defeat, Wilson hastily offered to the smallest states one senator, to the others one for every hundred thousand souls. This expedient Franklin brushed aside, saying: "On a proportional representation the small states contend that their liberties will be in danger; with an equality of votes, the large states say their money will be in danger. A joiner, when he wants to fit two boards, takes a little from both." ‡ And he suggested for the several states a like number of delegates to the senate, with proportionate votes on financial subjects, equal votes on questions affecting the rights of the states.

King inveighed against the "phantom of state sovereignty:" "If the adherence to an equality of votes is unalterable, we are cut asunder already. My mind is prepared for every event, rather than to sit down under a government which must be as short-lived as it would be unjust." #

Dayton replied: "Assertion for proof and terror for argument, however eloquently spoken, will have no effect. It should have been shown that the evils we have experienced proceeded from the equality of representation."

"The plan in its present shape," said Madison, "makes the senate absolutely dependent on the states; it is, therefore, only another edition of the old confederation, and can never answer. Still I would preserve the state rights as carefully as the trial by jury." ‖

* Yates in Elliot, i., 469, 470.
† Gilpin, 1007; Elliot 265, 266; Yates in Elliot, i., 470; Paterson MS.
‡ Gilpin, 1009; Elliot, 266; Yates in Elliot, i., 471.
# Gilpin, 1010, 1011; Elliot, 266, 267.
‖ Gilpin, 1012; Elliot, 267; Yates in Elliot, i., 471.

Bedford scoffed at Georgia, proud of her future greatness; at South Carolina, puffed up with wealth and negroes; at the great states, ambitious, dictatorial, and unworthy of trust; and defied them to dissolve the confederation, for ruin would then stare them in the face.*

To a question from King, whether by entering into a national government he would not equally participate in national security, Ellsworth answered: "I confess I should; but a general government cannot know my wants, nor relieve my distress. I depend for domestic happiness as much on my state government as a new-born infant depends upon its mother for nourishment. If this is not an answer, I have no other to give." †

On the second of July five states voted with Ellsworth for equal suffrage in the senate; five of the six national states answered, No. All interest then centred upon Georgia, the sixth national state and the last to vote. Baldwin, fearing a disruption of the convention, and convinced of the hopelessness of assembling another under better auspices, dissented from his colleague, and divided the vote of his state. So the motion was lost by a tie; ‡ but as all believed that New Hampshire and Rhode Island, had they been present, would have voted with Connecticut, the convention moved rapidly toward its inevitable decision.

For a moment Charles Pinckney made delay by calling up his scheme for dividing the United States into northern, middle, and southern groups, and apportioning the senators between the three; # a measure which, with modifications, he repeatedly brought forward.

Cotesworth Pinckney liked better the motion of Franklin, and proposed that a committee of one from each state, taking into consideration both branches of the legislature, should devise and report a compromise. ‖ "Such a committee," said Sherman, "is necessary to set us right." △

Gouverneur Morris, who, after a month's absence, had just returned, spoke abruptly for a senate for life to be appointed

---

\* Gilpin, 1012–1014; Elliot, 268.
† Yates in Elliot, i., 473, 474.
‡ Gilpin, 1016; Elliot, 269, 270.
\# Gilpin, 1017; Elliot, 270.
‖ Ibid.
△ Yates in Elliot, i., 475.

by the executive;* but the committee was ordered by a great majority; and the house showed its own inclination by selecting Franklin, Gerry, Ellsworth, Yates, Paterson, even Bedford and Martin, Mason, Davie, Rutledge, and Baldwin. To give them time for their task, and to all the opportunity of celebrating the anniversary of independence, the convention adjourned for three days. †

* Gilpin, 1019, 1020; Elliot, 271, 272. † Gilpin, 1023, 1024; Elliot, 273.

## CHAPTER IV.

### THE ADJUSTMENT OF REPRESENTATION.

FROM THE THIRD TO THE TWENTY-THIRD OF JULY 1787.

On the morning of the third of July the grand committee accepted as a basis for a compromise* the proposal of Franklin,† that in the first branch of the first congress there should be one member for every forty thousand inhabitants, counting all the free and three fifths of the rest; that in the second branch each state should have an equal vote; and that, in return for this concession to the small states, the first branch should be invested with the sole power of originating taxes and appropriations. The settlement of the rule of representation for new states was considered, but was left to the convention.

"The committee have exceeded their powers," ‡ cried Wilson, when Gerry, on the fifth, delivered the report to the convention. Madison encouraged the large states to oppose it steadfastly. Butler denounced the plan as unjust.# Gouverneur Morris, delighting to startle by his cynicism, condemned alike its form and substance,‖ adding: "State attachments and state importance have been the bane of the country. We cannot annihilate the serpents, but we may perhaps take out their teeth.△ Suppose the larger states agree, the smaller states must come in. Jersey would follow the opinions of New York and Pennsylvania. If persuasion does not unite the small states with the others, the sword will. The strongest party

---

\* Yates in Elliot, i., 478.  
† Martin in Elliot, i., 358.  
‡ Gilpin, 1025; Elliot, 274.  
\# Gilpin, 1028; Elliot, 275.  
‖ Gilpin, 1028; Elliot, 276.  
△ Gilpin, 1030; Elliot, 277.

will make the weaker traitors, and hang them. The larger states are the most powerful; they must decide." * Ellsworth enforced the necessity of compromise, and saw none more convenient or reasonable than that proposed by the committee. †

"We are neither the same nation, nor different nations," said Gerry; "we therefore ought not to pursue the one or the other of these ideas too closely. Without a compromise a secession will take place, and the result no man can foresee." "There must be some accommodation on this point," said Mason, "or we shall make little further progress in the work. It cannot be more inconvenient to any gentleman to remain absent from his private affairs than it is for me; but I will bury my bones in this city rather than expose my country to the consequences of a dissolution of the convention without anything being done." ‡

A throng of questions on representation thrust themselves into the foreground. Gouverneur Morris objected to the rule of numbers alone in the distribution of representatives. "Not liberty," said he; "property is the main object of society. The savage state is more favorable to liberty than the civilized, and was only renounced for the sake of property. A range of new states will soon be formed in the West. The rule of representation ought to be so fixed as to secure to the Atlantic states a prevalence in the national councils." Rutledge repeated: "Property is certainly the principal object of society. If numbers should be the rule of representation, the Atlantic states will soon be subjected to the western." "If new states," said Mason and Randolph, "make a part of the union, they ought to be subject to no unfavorable discriminations." #

On the morning of the sixth, Gouverneur Morris moved to refer the ratio of representation in the popular branch to a committee of five. ‖ Wilson, who still strove to defeat the compromise between the federal and the national states, seconded the motion. In the distribution of representatives, Gorham thought the number of inhabitants the true guide. "Property," said King, "is the primary object of society, and,

---

\* Paterson MSS.  # Gilpin, 1034, 1035; Elliot, 278, 279.
† Gilpin, 1032; Elliot, 278.  ‖ Gilpin, 1036, 1039; Elliot, 280, 281.
‡ Gilpin, 1032, 1033; Elliot, 278.

in fixing a ratio, ought not to be excluded from the estimate." *
" Property," said Butler, "is the only just measure of representation."† To Charles Pinckney the number of inhabitants appeared the true and only practicable rule,‡ and he acquiesced in counting but three fifths of the slaves. The motion of Morris was carried by New England, Pennsylvania, and the four southernmost slaveholding states. Gouverneur Morris, Gorham, Randolph, Rutledge, and King, were chosen the committee.

On the seventh the clause allowing each state an equal vote in the senate was retained as part of the report by six states against three, New York being present and voting with the majority, Massachusetts and Georgia being divided.

The number and distribution of the members of the first branch of the legislature in the first congress, the rule for every future congress, the balance of legislative power between the South and the North; between the carrying states which asked for a retaliatory navigation act and the planting states which desired free freight and free trade; between the original states and new ones; the apportionment of representation according to numbers or wealth, or a combination of the two; the counting of all, or three fifths, or none, of the slaves; the equal suffrage in the senate—became the subjects of motions and counter-motions, postponements and recalls. To unravel the tangled skein it is necessary to trace each subject for itself to its preliminary settlement.

On the ninth Gouverneur Morris presented the report of the committee of five. It changed the distribution of representation in the first congress to the advantage of the South; for the future, no one opposing except Randolph, it authorized, but purposely refrained from enjoining, the legislature, from time to time, to regulate the number of representatives of each state by its wealth and the number of its inhabitants. #

"The report," said Sherman, "corresponds neither with any rule of numbers, nor any requisition by congress;" ‖ and on his motion its first paragraph was referred to a committee of one member from each state.△ Gouverneur Morris sec-

\* Gilpin, 1037; Elliot, 280.
† Gilpin, 1038; Elliot, 281.
‡ Gilpin, 1039; Elliot, 281.
\# Gilpin, 1051, 1052; Elliot, 287, 288.
‖ Gilpin, 1052; Elliot, 288.
△ Elliot, i., 197.

onded and Randolph approved the motion.* Paterson could regard negro slaves in no light but as property; to grant their masters an increase of representation for them he condemned as an indirect encouragement of the slave-trade.† Madison revived his suggestion of a representation of free inhabitants in the popular branch; of the whole number, including slaves, in the senate; which, as the special guardian of property, would rightly be the protector of property in slaves. ‡ "The southern states are the richest," said King, who yet should have known that they were not so, or perhaps was thinking only of the exports of the country; "they will not league themselves with the northern unless some respect is paid to their superior wealth. The North must not expect to receive from the connection preferential distinctions in commerce without allowing some advantage in return." #

The committee of one from each state on the very next morning, the tenth of July, produced their well-considered report. The committee of five had fixed the number of representatives at fifty-six; or thirty from the North, twenty-six from the South; and Maryland and Virginia had each given up one member to South Carolina, raising her number to five.‖

In the confederacy each state might send to congress as many as seven delegates, so that the whole number in congress might be ninety-one. This number was adopted for the new constitution: as there were to be two branches of the legislature, two members for each state were assigned to the branch representing the states, the remaining sixty-five were assigned to the popular branch. Thirty-five were parcelled out to the North, to the South thirty. Of the new members for the South, two were allotted to Maryland, one to Virginia, and one to Georgia. In this way Connecticut, North Carolina, and South Carolina, having each five votes in the popular branch, retained in the house exactly one thirteenth of all the votes in that body, and so would hold in each branch exactly the same relative power as in the confederacy. The first census established the justice of this relative distribution between

---

\* Gilpin, 1054; Elliot, 288, 289.     ‡ Gilpin, 1055; Elliot, 289, 290.
† Gilpin, 1055; Elliot, 289.     # Gilpin, 1056; Elliot, 290.
‖ Gilpin, 1062, 1063; Elliot, 293; Elliot, i., 197, 198.

the North and the South; though, within the South, Georgia and South Carolina had each at least one more than its share.

The final division was approved by all except South Carolina and Georgia; and these two favored states now opened a resolute but not stormy debate to gain still more legislative strength. To this end Rutledge moved to reduce the absent state of New Hampshire from three to two members, pleading its deficiency in population and its poverty.*

King, after demonstrating the rights of New Hampshire, proceeded: " The difference of interests lies not between the great and small states, but between the southern and eastern. For this reason I have been ready to yield something in the proportion of representatives for the security of the southern. I am not averse to yielding more, but do not see how it can be done. They are brought as near an equality as is possible; no principle will justify giving them a majority." † Cotesworth Pinckney replied: " If the southern states are to be in such a minority, and the regulation of trade is to be given to the general government, they will be nothing more than overseers for the northern states. I do not expect the southern states to be raised to a majority of the representatives; but I wish them to have something like an equality." Randolph, speaking the opinions of Richard Henry Lee and of Mason as well as his own, announced that he had it in contemplation to require more than a bare majority of votes for laws regulating trade.

For reducing New Hampshire none voted but South Carolina and Georgia. ‡ There followed successive motions to give one additional vote to each of the three southernmost states. They were all lost; Georgia alone obtaining the voice of Virginia.

On that day Robert Yates and John Lansing of New York were on the floor for the last time. The governor of their state had unreservedly declared that no good was to be expected from the deliberations at Philadelphia; that the confederation on more full experiment might be found to answer all the purposes of the union.# The state which had borne itself with unselfish magnanimity through the war of the revo-

* Gilpin, 1057; Elliot, 290.   ‡ Gilpin, 1059; Elliot, 291; Elliot, i., 198.
† Gilpin, 1057, 1058; Elliot, 290, 291.   # Penn. Packet, 26 July 1787.

lution had fallen under the sway of factious selfishness. Yielding to this influence, Yates and Lansing, renouncing the path to glory and the voice of duty, deserted their post, leaving to the South the power to mould the commercial policy of the union at its will. Hamilton, being left alone, had no vote, and from this day to the end was absent more than half the time, taking very little part in the formation of the constitution.

In the convention, from its organization to its dissolution, there was always a majority of at least one on the side of the southern states. After the defection of New York the proportion remained six to four till New Hampshire arrived.

Slavery in the United States was a transient form, not an original element of their colonization, nor its necessary outgrowth. In the division between northern and southern states the criterion was, whether a state retained the power and the will by its own inward energy to extricate itself from slavery. Seven had abolished, or were preparing to abolish it. Madison[*] and others counted the southern states as no more than five; but Delaware, like all south of it, gave signs of being not equal to the high endeavor of setting all its bondmen free; and its votes in the convention prove that it was rightly classed by Dayton[†] with the South. The boundary between the two sections was Mason and Dixon's line. Pennsylvania, purely popular, without family aristocracies or the ascendency of any one form of religion, first in agriculture and commerce, and not surpassed in ship-building, stood midway between six northern states and six southern ones, the stronghold of an undivided, inseparable federal republic.

The abolition of slavery in the North, which was aided by the long British occupation of Boston, Rhode Island, and New York, had not been accomplished without a quickening of conscience on the wrongfulness of hereditary bondage and its inconsistency with the first principles of American polity. By the act of Pennsylvania of 1780 for the gradual abolition of slavery, persons merely sojourning in the state were permitted to retain their slaves for a term of six months; delegates in congress from other states, foreign ministers and consuls, as long as they continued in their public characters. The right of

---

[*] Gilpin, 1104; Elliot, 315.　　　　　[†] Gilpin, 1058; Elliot, 291.

the masters of absconding slaves to take them away remained as before. But the recovery of a slave through the interposition of the courts was resisted with zeal by self-appointed agents; * and the southern master sometimes had no relief but to seize the runaway and bring him back to bondage by force.

Abolition and manumission societies were formed in various parts of the North. Of one of these Hamilton was the secretary, with Jay, Duane, and Robert R. Livingston for associates. Just at this time Franklin was elected president of the society in Pennsylvania. The newspapers of all parties at the North teemed with essays against slavery. The opposition to it prevailed in nearly all religious and political sects, but flamed the brightest among those of extreme democratic tendencies.

In 1783 deputies from the yearly meeting of the Quakers were admitted to the floor † of congress, and delivered their address, entreating that body to use its influence for the general abolition of the slave-trade, and in several later years the meeting renewed the petition. ‡ The Presbyterian synod which met at Philadelphia in the same week as the federal convention resolved " to procure eventually the final abolition of slavery in America." # The Pennsylvania Abolition Society adopted a memorial to the convention to suppress the slave-trade, ‖ though, from motives of prudence, it was not presented.

This conspicuous action at the North on the slave-trade and slavery might have baffled every hope of a consolidated union but for the wide distinction between those states that were least remote from the West Indies and those that lay nearer the North; between the states which planted indigo and rice and those which cultivated by slave labor maize and wheat and tobacco; between Georgia and South Carolina which had ever been well affected to the slave-trade, and the great slave-hold-

---

\* Dallas, i., 179, 180; ii., 224.     † Journals of Congress, iv., 289.

‡ Address presented 8 October 1783, MS., at State Dept., Vol. of Remonstrances and Addresses, 339; Letter to R. H. Lee, President, 21 January 1785; Ibid., 347. See the MS. Records of the Friends, 20 October 1786, and October 1789.

\# Acts and Proceedings of the Synod of New York and Philadelphia, A. D. 1787.

‖ Penn. Packet of 14 February 1788; Independent Gazetteer of 7 March 1788.

ing state to the north of them which had wrestled with England for its abolition.

In the three northernmost of the southern states slavery maintained itself, not as an element of prosperity, but as a baleful inheritance. The best of the statesmen of Virginia, without regard to other questions which divided them, desired its abolition—alike Washington, Richard Henry Lee, Jefferson, Randolph, Madison, and Grayson. George Mason had written to the legislature of Virginia against it with the most terrible invectives and gloomiest forebodings.

This comparative serenity of judgment in Virginia was shared, though not completely, by North Carolina, of whose population three parts out of four were free, and whose upland country attracted emigrants by its fertility, salubrity, and beauty.

The difference between the two classes of slave states was understood by themselves, and was a guarantee that questions on slavery would neither inflame nor unite them. Virginia and North Carolina held the balance of power, and knew how to steer clear of a fatal collison.

The preliminary distribution of representatives having been agreed upon, Gouverneur Morris on the ninth desired to leave the control of future changes to the national legislature.* Perceiving peril in confiding so vast a discretion to those who might be tempted to keep to themselves an undue share of legislative power, Randolph, following the precedent of 1781, on the tenth insisted on an absolute constitutional requirement of a census of population and an estimate of wealth, to be taken within one year after the first meeting of the legislature, and ever thereafter periodically; and that the representation should be arranged accordingly.†

Gouverneur Morris, supported by King and others, resisted this "fettering of the legislature," by which a preponderance might be thrown into the western scale. In various debates it was urged by Morris and King and others that the western people would in time outnumber those of the Atlantic states, while they would be less wealthy, less cultivated, less favorable to foreign commerce, and less willing to bide the right moment for acquiring the free navigation of the lower Mississippi;

* Gilpin, 1052; Elliot, 288.   † Gilpin, 1063; Elliot, 293.

that the busy haunts of men are the proper school for statesmen; that the members from the back country are always most averse to the best measures; that, if the western people should get the power into their hands, they would ruin the Atlantic interests; and therefore that, in every future legislature, the original states should keep the majority in their own hands.*

To this Mason replied: " A revision from time to time, according to some permanent and precise standard, is essential to fair representation. According to the present population of America, the northern part of it has a right to preponderate; and I cannot deny it. But, unless there shall be inserted in the constitution some principle which will do justice to the southern states hereafter, when they shall have three fourths of the people of America within their limits, I can neither vote for the system here nor support it in my state. The western states as they arise must be treated as equals, or they will speedily revolt. The number of inhabitants is a sufficiently precise standard of wealth." †

"Congress," said Randolph, "have pledged the public faith to the new states that they shall be admitted on equal terms. They never will, they never ought to accede on any other." ‡ Madison demonstrated that no distinctions unfavorable to the western states were admissible, either in point of justice or policy.#

By a vote of seven to three the first legislature under the new constitution was required to provide for a census; ‖ a periodical census ever after was then accepted without a division. Its period, first fixed at fifteen years, after repeated debates, was reduced to ten.△

Yet an ineradicable dread of the coming power of the South-west lurked in New England, especially in Massachusetts. On the fourteenth, only three days after the subject appeared to have been definitively disposed of, Gerry and King moved that the representatives of new states should never col-

---

\* Gilpin, 1063, 1064, 1072; Elliot, 294, 298.
† Gilpin, 1065, 1066; Elliot, 294, 295.
‡ Gilpin, 1067; Elliot, 295.
\# Gilpin, 1073; Elliot, 299.
‖ Gilpin, 1078; Elliot, 301.
△ Gilpin, 1086; Elliot, 305.

lectively exceed in number the representatives from such of the old thirteen states as should accede to the new confederation.* The motion came from New England; and from New England came the reply. "We are providing for our posterity," said Sherman, who had taken the principal part in securing to Connecticut a magnificent reserve of lands in northern Ohio. "Our children and our grandchildren will be as likely to be citizens of new western states as of the old states." † His words were lost upon his own colleagues. The motion was defeated by the narrowest majority, Massachusetts being sustained by Connecticut, Delaware, and Maryland, against New Jersey and the four southernmost states, Pennsylvania being divided. ‡ The vote of Maryland and Delaware was but the dying expression of old regrets about the proprietaryship of western lands, from which they had been excluded; that of Massachusetts sprung from a jealousy which grew stronger with the ever-increasing political power of the South-west. But in spite of renewed murmurs the decision was never reversed.

The final concession on the representation for slaves proceeded from North Carolina. On the eleventh of July, Williamson accepted for the permanent basis the free inhabitants and three fifths of all others.# Randolph agreed to the amendment. On the instant Butler and Cotesworth Pinckney demanded that the blacks should be counted equally with the whites. ‖

New York, New Hampshire, and Rhode Island not being on the floor, the southern states were left with ample power to settle the question as they pleased. "The motion," said Mason, " is favorable to Virginia, but I think it unjust. As slaves are useful to the community at large, they ought not to be excluded from the estimate for representation; I cannot, however, vote for them as equals to freemen." △ On the question, Delaware alone joined South Carolina and Georgia.

Rutledge next insisted on proportioning representation periodically according to wealth as well as population. This was

---

\* Gilpin, 1095; Elliot, 310.  
† Ibid.  
‡ Ibid.  
\# Gilpin, 1066; Elliot, 295.  
‖ Gilpin, 1067; Elliot, 296.  
△ Gilpin, 1068; Elliot, 296.

condemned by Mason as indefinite and impracticable, leaving to the legislature a pretext for doing nothing.* Madison saw no substantial objection to fixing numbers for the perpetual standard of representation.† In like manner Sherman, Johnson, Wilson, and Gorham looked upon population as the best measure of wealth; and accepted the propriety of establishing numbers as the rule.

King refused to be reconciled to any concession of representation for slaves. ‡ Gouverneur Morris, always a hater of slavery, closed the debate by saying : " I am reduced to the dilemma of doing injustice to the southern states, or to human nature, and I must do it to the former; I can never agree to give such encouragement to the slave-trade as would be given by allowing them a representation for their negroes." #

On the division, those who insisted on enumerating all the slaves and those who refused to enumerate any of them, as elements of representation, partially coalesced; and Connecticut, Virginia, and North Carolina, though aided by Georgia, were outvoted by Massachusetts, New Jersey, Pennsylvania, Delaware, Maryland, and South Carolina. ‖

The aspect of affairs at the adjournment was not so dangerous as it seemed. Virginia with a united delegation had her hand on the helm, while North Carolina kept watch at her side.

But Gouverneur Morris brooded over the deep gulf by which the convention seemed to him rent in twain; and rashly undertook to build a bridge over the chasm. To that end he proposed the next morning that taxation should be in proportion to representation.△ His motion was general, extending to every branch of revenue.

The convention was taken by surprise. South Carolina scorned to be driven from her object by the menace of increased contributions to the general treasury; and again demanded a full representation for all blacks. ◊ Mason pointed out that the proposal of Gouverneur Morris would so embarrass the legis-

* Gilpin, 1071; Elliot, 297.  # Gilpin, 1078; Elliot, 301.
† Gilpin, 1074; Elliot, 299.  ‖ Ibid.
‡ Gilpin, 1076; Elliot, 300.  △ Gilpin, 1079; Elliot, 302.
◊ Gilpin, 1079, 1080; Elliot, 302.

lature in raising a revenue that they would be driven back to requisitions on the states. Appalled at discovering that his motion was a death-blow to the new constitution, Morris limited it to direct taxation, saying: "It would be inapplicable to indirect taxes on exports and imports and consumption." * Cotesworth Pinckney took fire at the idea of taxing exports. Wilson came to the partial rescue of Morris; and the convention, without a dissentient, agreed that "direct taxation ought to be in proportion to representation." † In this short interlude, by the temerity of one man, the United States were precluded from deriving an equitable revenue from real property. Morris soon saw what evil he had wrought, but he vainly strove to retrieve it.

The moderating states of the South grew restless. "North Carolina," said Davie, "will never confederate on terms that do not rate their blacks at least as three fifths." ‡ Johnson, holding the negro slave to be a man, and nothing less than a man, could not forego the conclusion "that blacks equally with the whites ought to fall within the computation," and his votes conformed to his scruples. Contrary to the wishes of Gouverneur Morris and King, Randolph insisted that the representation allowed for slaves should be imbodied in the constitution, saying: "I lament that such a species of property exists; but, as it does exist, the holders of it will require this security." # Ellsworth seconded Randolph, whose motion was tempered in its form by Wilson, so as to avoid the direct mention of slavery or slave. "The southern states," said King, "threaten to separate now in case injury shall be done them. There will be no point of time at which they will not be able to say, 'Do us justice or we will separate.'" The final motion to make blacks equal with whites in fixing the ratio of representation received no support but from South Carolina and Georgia; ‖ and the compromise, proportioning representation to direct taxation, and both to the number of the free and three fifths of others, was established by the southern states, even Georgia approving, and South Carolina relenting so far as to divide its vote.^

---

\* Gilpin, 1080; Elliot, 302.
† Gilpin, 1081; Elliot, 302.
‡ Gilpin, 1081; Elliot, 302, 303.
\# Gilpin, 1083; Elliot, 304.
‖ Gilpin, 1084–1087; Elliot, 304–306.
^ Gilpin, 1086, 1087; Elliot, 306.

Randolph, on the thirteenth, seized the opportunity to propose numbers as the sole rule of representation. Gouverneur Morris " stated the result of his deep meditation " : " The southern gentlemen will not be satisfied unless they see the way open to their gaining a majority in the public councils. The consequence of such a transfer of power from the maritime to the interior and landed interest will, I foresee, be an oppression to commerce. In this struggle between the two ends of the union, the middle states ought to join their eastern brethren. If the southern states get the power into their hands and be joined as they will be with the interior country, everything is to be apprehended."

By the interior, Morris had specially in his mind the rising states of Kentucky and Tennessee. Butler replied: " The southern states want security that their negroes may not be taken from them, which some gentlemen within or without doors have a very good mind to do. North Carolina, South Carolina, and Georgia will have relatively many more people than they now have. The people and strength of America are evidently bearing to the South and South-west." *

"The majority," said Wilson, "wherever found, ought to govern. The interior country, should it acquire this majority, will avail itself of its right whether we will or no. If numbers be not a proper rule, why is not some better rule pointed out? Congress have never been able to discover a better. No state has suggested any other. Property is not the sole nor the primary end of government and society; the improvement of the human mind is the most noble object. With respect to this and other personal rights, numbers are surely the natural and precise measure of representation, and could not vary much from the precise measure of property." †

The apportionment of representation according to numbers was adopted without a negative, Delaware alone being divided.‡ The American declaration of independence proclaimed all men free and equal; the federal convention founded representation on numbers alone.

The equality of votes of the states in the senate being re-

---

\* Gilpin, 1091–1093 ; Elliot, 308, 309.

† Gilpin, 1093, 1094 ; Elliot, 309.      ‡ Gilpin, 1094 ; Elliot, 309.

ported to the convention on the fourteenth, was resisted by Wilson, King, and Madison to the last as contrary to justice. On the other hand, Sherman held that the state governments could not be preserved unless they should have a negative in the general government.

Caleb Strong, a statesman of consummate prudence, from the valley of the Connecticut, a graduate of Harvard, and a fit representative of the country people of Massachusetts, lucidly reviewed the case, and, from the desire to prevent the dissolution of the union, found himself compelled to vote for the compromise. Madison replied in an elaborate speech, which closed with these words: "The perpetuity which an equality of votes in the second branch will give to the preponderance of the northern against the southern scale is a serious consideration. It seems now well understood that the real difference of interests lies, not between the large and small, but between the northern and southern states. The institution of slavery and its consequences form the line of discrimination. Should a proportional representation take place, the northern will still outnumber the other; but every day will tend toward an equilibrium." *

The great poet of the Hellenic race relates how the most famed of its warriors was lured by one of the heavenly powers from the battle-field to chase a phantom. Had the South joined with the smaller states to establish the suffrage by states in both branches of the general legislature, it would, in less than ten years,† have arrived at an equality, alike in the house and in the senate. But it believed that swarms of emigrants were about to throng every path to the South-west, bearing with them affluence and power. It did not yet know the dynamic energy of freedom in producing wealth, and attracting and employing and retaining population. The equality of the vote in the senate, which Virginia and South Carolina vehemently resisted, was to gain and preserve for the slave-holding states a balance in one branch of the legislature; in the other, where representation was apportioned to population, the superiority of the free commonwealths would increase from decade to decade till slavery in the United States should be no

* Gilpin, 1104; Elliot, 315. † In 1796, on the admission of Tennessee.

more. Shrinking from the final vote on the question, the house adjourned.

On Monday, the sixteenth, as soon as the convention assembled, the question was taken on the amended report which included an equality of votes in the senate.* The six southern states were present, and only four of the northern. Four of the six states which demanded a proportioned representation stubbornly refused to yield. It was of decisive influence on the history of the country that Strong and Gerry, balancing the inflexible King and Gorham, pledged Massachusetts at least to neutrality. On the other side, Connecticut, New Jersey, Delaware, and Maryland spurned the thought of surrender. The decision was given by North Carolina, which broke from her great associates and gave a majority of one to the smaller states. More than ten years before, Jefferson had most earnestly proposed this compromise, seeking to proselyte John Adams, to whom he wrote: "The good whigs will so far cede their opinions for the sake of union." † He heard with great joy that his prophecy had come to pass. ‡

The large states accepted the decision as final. When, on the seventeenth, Gouverneur Morris proposed a reconsideration of the resolution of the former day, no one would second his motion.

On the twenty-third the number of senators for each state was fixed at two, and each of these, as had been proposed by Gerry and supported by Sherman, was personally to have one vote.#

From the day when every doubt of the right of the smaller states to an equal vote in the senate was quieted, they—so I received it from the lips of Madison, and so it appears from the records—exceeded all others in zeal for granting powers to the general government. Ellsworth became one of its strongest pillars. Paterson of New Jersey was for the rest of his life a federalist of federalists.

\* Gilpin, 1107–1109 ; Elliot, 316, 317.
† Works of John Adams, ix., 465–467.   ‡ Jefferson, ii., 329.
\# Gilpin, 1098, 1185, 1186 ; Elliot, 311, 312, 356, 357.

## CHAPTER V.

**THE OUTLINE OF THE CONSTITUTION COMPLETED AND REFERRED.**

### FROM THE 17TH TO THE 27TH OF JULY 1787.

THE distribution of powers between the general government and the states was the most delicate and most difficult task before the convention. Startled by the vagueness of language in the Virginia resolve, Sherman on the seventeenth of July proposed the grant of powers "to make laws in all cases which may concern the common interests of the union, but not to interfere with the government of the individual states in any matters of internal police which respect the government of such states only, and wherein the general welfare of the United States is not concerned." * Wilson seconded the amendment, as better expressing the general principle. But, on scanning its probable interpretation by the separate states, the objection prevailed that it would be construed to withhold from the general government the authority to levy direct taxes and the authority to suppress the paper money of the states.

Bedford moved to empower the national legislature "to legislate for the general interests of the union, for cases to which the states are severally incompetent, or in which the harmony of the United States might be interrupted by the exercise of individual legislation." † This Gouverneur Morris gladly seconded; and, though Randolph resisted, the current ran with such increasing vehemence for union that the amendment was adopted at first by six states, and then by every state but South Carolina and Georgia.

As to giving power to the national legislature "to negative

\* Gilpin, 1115; Elliot, 319, 320. † Gilpin, 1116; Elliot, 320.

laws passed by the several states," Gouverneur Morris, opposing it as terrible to the states,* looked where Jefferson invited Madison to look—to the judiciary department to set aside a law that ought to be negatived.† Sherman insisted that state laws, contravening the authority of the union, ‡ were invalid and inoperative from the beginning. Madison put forth all his strength to show that a power of negativing the improper laws of the states is the most mild and certain means of preserving the harmony of the system. He was supported by Massachusetts, Virginia, and North Carolina.#

From the New Jersey plan it was taken, without one dissentient, that the laws and treaties of the United States should be the supreme law of the states, and bind their judiciaries, anything in their laws to the contrary notwithstanding. ‖ That all power not granted to the general government remained with the states was the opinion of every member of the convention; but they held it a work of supererogation to place in the constitution an express recognition of the reservation. Thus in one half of a morning the convention began and ended its distribution of power between the states and the union. The further development of the central government brought to it a wider scope of action and new ascendency over the states.

The construction of the executive department was fraught with bewildering difficulties, of which a new set rose up as fast as the old ones were overcome. The convention, though it devoted many days in July to the subject, did but acquiesce for the moment in the Virginia resolve, with which its deliberations had yet made it thoroughly discontented.

Mason and the Pinckneys would have required a qualification of landed property for the executive, judiciary, and members of the national legislature.△ Gerry approved securing property by property provisions. "If qualifications are proper," said Gouverneur Morris, "I should prefer them in the electors rather than the elected;" ◊ and Madison agreed

---

\* Gilpin, 1117; Elliot, 321.     ‖ Gilpin, 1119; Elliot, 322.
† Gilpin, 1118; Elliot, 321.     △ Gilpin, 1211, 1213; Elliot, 370, 371.
‡ Gilpin, 1117, 1118; Elliot, 321, 322.    ◊ Gilpin, 1211; Elliot, 370.
# Gilpin, 1118, 1119; Elliot, 322.

with him. "I," said Dickinson, "doubt the policy of interweaving into a republican constitution a veneration for wealth. A veneration for poverty and virtue is the object of republican encouragement. No man of merit should be subjected to disabilities in a republic where merit is understood to form the great title to public trust, honors, and rewards." * The subject came repeatedly before the convention; but it never consented to require a property qualification for any office in the general government. In this way no obstruction to universal suffrage was allowed to conquer a foothold in the constitution, but its builders left the enlargement of suffrage to time and future lawgivers. They disturbed no more than was needed for the success of their work. They were not restless in zeal for one abstract rule of theoretical equality to be introduced instantly and everywhere. They were like the mariner in mid-ocean, on the rolling and tossing deck of a ship, who learns how to keep his true course by watching the horizon as well as the sun. In leading a people across the river that divided their old condition from the new, the makers of the new form of government anchored the supporting boats of their bridge up stream. The qualifications of the electors it left to be decided by the states, each for itself.

All agreed "that a supreme tribunal should be established," † and that the national legislature should be empowered to create inferior tribunals. ‡ By the report of the committee, on the eighteenth, the judges were to be appointed by the senate. Gorham, supported by Gouverneur Morris, proposed their appointment "by the executive with the consent of the second branch"; a mode, he said, which had been ratified by the experience of a hundred and forty years in Massachusetts.# The proposal was gradually gaining favor; but for the moment failed by an equal division.

The trial of impeachments of national officers was taken from the supreme court; and then, in the words of Madison, its jurisdiction was unanimously made to "extend to all cases arising under the national laws, or involving the national peace

---

\* Gilpin, 1213–1215; Elliot, 371, 372.     ‡ Gilpin, 1137; Elliot, 331.
† Gilpin, 1130; Elliot, 328.     # Gilpin, 1134; Elliot, 330.

and harmony."* Controversies which began and ended in the several states were not to be removed from the courts of the states.

The convention had still to decide how the new constitution should be ratified. "By the legislatures of the states," proposed Ellsworth, on the twenty-third, and he was seconded by Paterson. "The legislatures of the states have no power to ratify it," said Mason. "And, if they had, it would be wrong to refer the plan to them, because succeeding legislatures, having equal authority, could undo the acts of their predecessors, and the national government would stand in each state on the tottering foundation of an act of assembly. Whither, then, must we resort? To the people, with whom all power remains that has not been given up in the constitutions derived from them."

"One idea," said Randolph, "has pervaded all our proceedings, that opposition, as well from the states as from individuals, will be made to the system to be proposed. Will it not, then, be highly imprudent to furnish any unnecessary pretext by the mode of ratifying it? The consideration of this subject should be transferred from the legislatures, where local demagogues have their full influence, to a field in which their efforts can be less mischievous. Moreover, some of the states are averse to any change in their constitution, and will not take the requisite steps unless expressly called upon to refer the question to the people." †

"The confederation," said Gerry, "is paramount to the state constitutions; and its last article authorizes alterations only by the unanimous concurrence of the states." "Are all the states," replied his colleague Gorham, "to suffer themselves to be ruined, if Rhode Island, if New York, should persist in opposition to general measures? Provision ought to be made for giving effect to the system, without waiting for the unanimous concurrence of the states." ‡

"A new set of ideas," said Ellsworth, "seems to have crept in since the articles of confederation were established. Conventions of the people, with power derived expressly from

---
\* Gilpin, 1138; Elliot, 332, and i., 210.   ‡ Gilpin, 1180; Elliot, 354.
† Gilpin, 1177–1179; Elliot, 352, 353.

the people, were not then thought of." \* "A reference to the authority of the people expressly delegated to conventions," insisted King, "is most likely to draw forth the best men in the states to decide on the new constitution, and to obviate disputes and doubts concerning its legitimacy." †

Madison spoke with intense earnestness. "The difference between a system founded on the legislatures only and one founded on the people is the difference between a treaty and a constitution. A law violating a treaty ratified by a preexisting law might be respected by the judges; a law violating a constitution established by the people themselves would be considered by the judges as null and void. A breach of any one article of a treaty by any one of the parties frees the other parties from their engagements; a union of the people, under one constitution, by its nature excludes such an interpretation." ‡

After a full debate, the convention, by nine states against Delaware, referred the ratification of the new constitution to an assembly in each state to be chosen specially for that purpose by the people.#

In the following three days the resolutions of the federal convention for the establishment of a national government, consisting of twenty-three in number, were finished and referred to a committee of detail, five in number, who were ordered to prepare and report them in the form of a constitution. With them were referred the propositions of Charles Pinckney and the plan of New Jersey.

The federal convention selected for its committee of detail three members from the North and two from the South—Gorham, Ellsworth, Wilson, Randolph, and John Rutledge, of whom the last was the chairman. By ancestry Scotch-Irish, in early youth carefully but privately educated, afterward a student of law in the Temple at London, Rutledge became the foremost statesman of his time south of Virginia. At the age of twenty-six he began his national career in the stamp-act congress of 1765, and from that time was employed by his state wherever the aspect of affairs was the gravest. Patrick Henry

---

\* Gilpin, 1181; Elliot, 354.  ‡ Gilpin, 1183, 1184; Elliot, 355, 356.
† Gilpin, 1183; Elliot, 355.  # Gilpin, 1185; Elliot, 356.

pronounced him the most eloquent man in the congress of 1774; his sincerity gave force to his words. In the darkest hours he was intrepid, hopeful, inventive of resources, and resolute, so that timidity and wavering disappeared before him. To the day when disease impaired his powers he was, in war and in peace, the pride of South Carolina. That state could not have selected an abler representative of its policy on the payment of the members of the national legislature from the treasuries of the states, on the slave-trade, the taxation of exports, and the requisition of more than a bare majority of the legislature to counteract European restrictions on navigation.

Of his associates, Gorham was a merchant of Boston, who from his own experience understood the commercial relations of his country, and knew where the restrictive laws of England, of France, and of Spain injured American trade and shipping. Ellsworth, who had just established harmony between the small and the larger states by a wise and happy compromise, now found himself the umpire between the extreme South and the North.

Cotesworth Pinckney called to mind that if the committee should fail to insert some security to the southern states against an emancipation of slaves, and against taxes on exports, he should be bound by duty to his state to vote against their report.* After this the convention, on the twenty-sixth of July, unanimously adjourned till Monday, the sixth of August, that the committee of detail might have time to prepare and report the constitution.†

The committee in joint consultation gave their unremitting attention to every question that came before them. ‡ Their best guides were the constitutions of the several states, which furnished most striking expressions, and regulations approved by long experience. There is neither record nor personal narrative of their proceedings, though they were invested with the largest constructive powers; but the conduct of its several members may be determined by light reflected from their own words and actions before and after. Meanwhile the interest and

---

\* Gilpin, 1187; Elliot, 357. † Gilpin, 1220; Elliot, 374, 375.
‡ Wilson in Gilpin, 1249; Elliot, 385, and Rutledge in Gilpin, 1284; Elliot, 403.

anxiety of the country were on the increase. In May Grayson had written to Monroe: "The weight of General Washington is very great in America, but I hardly think it is sufficient to induce the people to pay money or part with power." * "If what the convention recommend should be rejected," so wrote Monroe to Jefferson the day after the adjournment, "they will complete our ruin. But I trust that the presence of General Washington will overawe and keep under the demon of party, and that the signature of his name to the result of their deliberations will secure its passage through the union."

* Grayson to Monroe, 29 May 1787.

## CHAPTER VI.

### THE COLONIAL SYSTEM OF THE UNITED STATES.

### From January 1786 to July 1787.

Before the federal convention had referred its resolutions to a committee of detail, an interlude in congress was shaping the character and destiny of the United States of America. Sublime and humane and eventful in the history of mankind as was the result, it will take not many words to tell how it was brought about. For a time wisdom and peace and justice dwelt among men, and the great ordinance, which could alone give continuance to the union, came in serenity and stillness. Every man that had a share in it seemed to be led by an invisible hand to do just what was wanted of him; all that was wrongfully undertaken fell to the ground to wither by the wayside; whatever was needed for the happy completion of the mighty work arrived opportunely, and just at the right moment moved into its place.

By the order of congress a treaty was to be held, in January 1786, with the Shawnees, at the mouth of the Great Miami. Monroe, who had been present as a spectator at the meeting of the United States commissioners with the representatives of the Six Nations at Fort Stanwix, in 1784, desired to attend this meeting with a remoter tribe. He reached Fort Pitt, and with some of the American party began the descent of the Ohio; but, from the low state of the water, he abandoned the expedition at Limestone, and made his way to Richmond through Kentucky and the wilderness. As the result of his inquiries on the journey, he took with him to congress the opinion that a great part of the western territory, especially that near Lakes Michigan and Erie, was miserably poor; that the land on the Mississippi and the Illinois consisted of extensive plains which had not a single bush on them, and would not have for ages; that the western settlers, in many of the most important objects of a federal government, would be either opposed to the interests of the old states or but little connected with them. He would form the territory into no more than five states; but he adhered to the principle of Jefferson, that they ought as soon as possible to take part in governing themselves, and at an early day share "the sovereignty, freedom, and independence" of the other states.

In the course of the winter the subject of the division of the western territory into states was, on the motion of Monroe, referred to a grand committee. Its report, which was presented on the twenty-fourth of March, traced the division of the territory into ten states to the resolution of congress of September 1780, by which no one was to contain less territory than one hundred nor more than one hundred and fifty miles square. This resolution had controlled the ordinance of April 1784; and, as the first step toward a reform, every part of that ordinance which conflicted with the power of congress to divide the territory into states according to its own discretion was to be repealed.*

Virginia had imbodied the resolve of congress of September 1780 in its cession of its claims to the land north-west of the Ohio. A further report proposed that Virginia should be asked to revise its act of cession.†

At this stage of the proceedings Dane made a successful motion to raise a committee for considering and reporting the form of a temporary government for the western states. ‡ Its chairman was Monroe, with Johnson and King of New Eng-

---

* This first report of the grand committee is found in Reports of Committees, Papers of Old Congress, xxx., 75, in the State Department, and is indorsed as having been "read 24th of March 1780, to be considered Thursday, March 30th."

† This second report of the grand committee is found likewise in vol. xxx., 79, and following, of Papers of Old Congress; but it has no indorsement as to the time when it was entered, read, or considered.

‡ The day on which this motion was made is not given, nor is the motion entered in the Journal. It was probably in April. We get the fact from page 85 of vol. xxx. of the Papers of the Old Congress.

land, John Kean and Charles Pinckney of South Carolina, as his associates. On the tenth of May this committee read their report. It asked the consent of Virginia to a division of the territory into not less than two nor more than five states; presented a plan for their temporary colonial government; and promised them admission into the confederacy on the principle of the ordinance of Jefferson. Not one word was said of a restriction on slavery. No man liked better than Monroe to lean for support on the minds and thoughts of others. He loved to spread his sails to a favoring breeze, but in threatening weather preferred quiet under the shelter of his friends. When Jefferson, in 1784, moved a restriction on slavery in the western country from Florida to the Lake of the Woods, Monroe was ill enough to be out of the way at the division. When King in the following year revived the question, he was again absent at the vote; now, when the same subject challenged his attention, he was silent.

At first Monroe flattered himself that his report was generally approved;* but no step was taken toward its adoption. All that was done lastingly for the West by this congress was the fruit of independent movements. On the twelfth of May, at the motion of Grayson seconded by King, the navigable waters leading into the Mississippi and the St. Lawrence, and the carrying places between them, were declared to be common highways, forever free to all citizens of the United States, without any tax, impost, or duty.

The assembly of Connecticut, which in the same month held a session, was resolved on opening a land office for the sale of six millions of acres west of the Pennsylvania line which their state had reserved in its cession of all further claims by charter to western lands. The reservation was not excessive in extent; the right of Connecticut under its charter had been taken away by an act of the British parliament of which America had always denied the validity. The federal constitution had provided no mode of settling a strife between a state and the United States; a war would cost more than the land was worth.† Grayson ceased his opposition; and on the

* Monroe to Jefferson, New York, 11 May 1786.
† Grayson to Madison, 28 May 1786.

fourteenth of the following September congress accepted the deed of cession by which Connecticut was confirmed in the possession of what was called her "western reserve." The compact establishment of the culture of New England in that district had the most beneficent effect on the character of Ohio and the development of the union.

For diminishing the number of the states to be formed out of the western territory, Monroe might hope for a favorable hearing. At his instance the subject was referred to a grand committee, which on the seventh of July reported in favor of obtaining the assent of Virginia to the division of the territory north-west of the Ohio into not less than two nor more than five states.

With singular liberality Grayson proposed to divide the country at once into not less than five states. He would run a line east and west so as to touch the most southern part of Lake Michigan, and from that line draw one meridian line to the western side of the mouth of the Wabash, and another to the western side of the mouth of the Great Miami, making three states between the Mississippi and the western lines of Virginia and Pennsylvania. The peninsula of Michigan was to form a fourth state; the fifth would absorb the country between Lake Michigan, Lake Superior, and the line of water to the northern boundary in the Lake of the Woods on the one side and the Mississippi on the other. This division, so unfavorable to southern influence, was voted for by Maryland, Virginia, North Carolina, and Georgia, South Carolina being divided; the North did not give one state in its favor; and the motion was lost. It was then agreed that the district should ultimately be divided at least into three states, the states and individuals being unanimous, except that Grayson adhered to his preference of five.*

The cause which arrested the progress of the ordinance of Monroe was a jealousy of the political power of the western states, and a prevailing desire to impede their admission into the union. To Jefferson he explained with accurate foresight the policy toward which congress was drifting.

When the inhabitants of the Kaskaskias presented a peti-

* Journals of Congress, iv., 662, 663.

tion for the organization of a government over their district, Monroe took part in the answer, that congress had under consideration the plan of a temporary government for their district in which it would manifest a due regard to their interest.* This is the last act of congress relating to the West in which Monroe participated. With the first Monday of the coming November the rule of rotation would exclude him from congress.

During the summer Kean was absent from congress, and his place on the committee was taken by Melancthon Smith † of New York. In September, Monroe and King went on a mission from Congress to the legislature of Pennsylvania, and their places were filled by Henry of Maryland and Dane. The committee with its new members represented the ruling sentiment of the house; and its report, which was made on the nineteenth of September, required of a western state before its admission into the union a population equal to one thirteenth part of the citizens of the thirteen original states according to the last preceding enumeration. Had this report been adopted, and had the decennial census of the population of territories and states alone furnished the rule, Ohio must have waited twenty years longer for admission into the union; Indiana would have been received only after 1850; Illinois only after 1860; Michigan could not have asked admittance till after the census of 1880; and after that census Wisconsin must still have remained a colonial dependency.

The last day of September 1786 was given to the consideration of the report; but before anything was decided the seventh congress expired.

The new congress, to which Madison and Richard Henry Lee, as well as Grayson and Edward Carrington, were sent by Virginia, had no quorum till February 1787, and then was occupied with preparations for the federal convention and with the late insurrection in Massachusetts. But the necessity of providing for a territorial government was urgent; and near the end of April the committee of the late congress revived

---

* Journals of Congress, iv., 688, 689.

† The name of Smith as one of the committee occurs in August 1786. Journals of Congress, iv., 688.

its project of the preceding September. On the ninth of May it was read a second time; the clause which would have indefinitely delayed the admission of a western state was cancelled;* a new draft of the bill as amended was directed to be transcribed, and its third reading was made the order of the next day,† when of a sudden the further progress of the ordinance was arrested.

Rufus Putnam, of Worcester county, Massachusetts, who had drawn to himself the friendly esteem of the commander-in-chief, and before the breaking up of the army received the commission of brigadier-general, was foremost in promoting a petition to congress of officers and soldiers of the revolution for leave to plant a colony of the veterans of the army between Lake Erie and the Ohio, in townships of six miles square, with large reservations "for the ministry and schools." For himself and his associates he entreated Washington to represent to congress the strength of the grounds on which their petition rested. ‡ Their unpaid services in the war had saved the independence and the unity of the land; their settlement would protect the frontiers of the old states against alarms of the savages; their power would give safety along the boundary line on the north; under their shelter the endless procession of emigrants would take up its march to fill the country from Lake Erie to the Ohio.

With congress while it was at Princeton, and again after its adjournment to Annapolis, Washington exerted every power of which he was master to bring about a speedy decision. The members with whom he conversed acquiesced in the reasonableness of the petition and approved its policy, but they excused their inertness by the want of a cession of the north-western lands.

When, in March 1784, the lands were ceded by Virginia, Rufus Putnam again appeals to Washington: "You are sensible of the necessity as well as the possibility of both officers and soldiers fixing themselves in business somewhere as soon as

---

* This appears from the erasures on the printed bill, which is still preserved.
† Journals of Congress, iv., 747.
‡ S. P. Hildreth, Pioneer Settlers of Ohio, 88. Walker, 29. Letter of Rufus Putnam, 16 June 1783.

possible; many of them are unable to lie long on their oars;" but congress did not mind the spur. In the next year, under the land ordinance of Grayson, Rufus Putnam was elected a surveyor of land in the western territory for Massachusetts; and as he could not at once enter on the service, another brigadier-general, Benjamin Tupper of Chesterfield, in the same state, was appointed for the time in his stead.* Tupper repaired to the West to superintend the work confided to him; but disorderly Indians prevented the survey; without having advanced farther west than Pittsburgh, he returned home; and, like almost every one who caught glimpses of the West, he returned with a mind filled with the brightness of its promise.

Toward the end of 1785, Samuel Holden Parsons, the son of a clergyman in Lyme, Connecticut, a graduate of Harvard, an early and a wise and resolute patriot, in the war a brigadier-general of the regular army, travelled to the West on public business, descended the Ohio as far as its falls, and, full of the idea of a settlement in that western country, wrote, before the year went out, that on his way he had seen no place which pleased him so much for a settlement as the country on the Muskingum.†

In the treaty at Fort Stanwix, in 1784, the Six Nations renounced to the United States all claims to the country west of the Ohio. A treaty of January 1785, with the Wyandotte, Delaware, Chippewa, and Ottawa nations, released the country east of the Cuyahoga, and all the lands on the Ohio, south of the line of portages from that river to the Great Miami and the Maumee. On the last day of January 1786, George Rogers Clark, the conqueror of the North-west, Richard Butler, late a colonel in the army, and Samuel Holden Parsons, acting under commissions from the United States, met the Shawnees at the mouth of the Great Miami, and concluded with them a treaty by which they acknowledged the sovereignty of the United States over all their territory as described in the treaty of peace with Great Britain, and for themselves renounced all claim to property in any land east of the main branch of

* Journals of Congress, iv., 520, 527, 547.
† William Frederick Poole in N. A. Review, liii., 331.

the Great Miami.* In this way the Indian title to southern Ohio, and all Ohio to the east of the Cuyahoga, was quieted.

Six days before the signature of the treaty with the Shawnees, Rufus Putnam and Benjamin Tupper, after a careful consultation at the house of Putnam, in Rutland, published in the newspapers of Massachusetts an invitation to form "the Ohio Company" for purchasing and colonizing a large tract of land between the Ohio and Lake Erie. The men chiefly engaged in this enterprise were husbandmen of New England, nurtured in its schools and churches, laborious and methodical, patriots who had been further trained in a seven years' war for freedom. Have these men the creative power to plant a commonwealth? And is a republic the government under which political organization for great ends is the most easy and the most perfect?

To bring the Ohio company into formal existence, all persons in Massachusetts who wished to promote the scheme were invited to meet in their respective counties on Wednesday, the fifteenth day of the next February, and choose delegates to meet in Boston on Wednesday, the first day of March 1786, at ten of the clock, then and there to consider and determine on a general plan of association for the company. On the appointed day and hour, representatives of eight counties of Massachusetts came together; among others, from Worcester county, Rufus Putnam; from Suffolk, Winthrop Sargent; from Essex, Manasseh Cutler, lately a chaplain in the army, then minister at Ipswich; from Middlesex, John Brooks; from Hampshire, Benjamin Tupper. Rufus Putnam was chosen chairman of the meeting, Winthrop Sargent its secretary. On the third of March, Putnam, Cutler, Brooks, Sargent, and Cushing, its regularly appointed committee, reported an association of a thousand shares, each of one thousand dollars in continental certificates, which were then the equivalent of one hundred and twenty-five dollars in gold, with a further liability to pay ten dollars in specie to meet the expenses of the agencies. Men might join together and subscribe for one share.

A year was allowed for subscription. At its end, on the eighth of March 1787, a meeting of the subscribers was held at Boston, and Samuel Holden Parsons, Rufus Putnam, and

* U. S. Statutes at Large, vii., 15, 16–18, 26.

Manasseh Cutler were chosen directors to make application to congress for a purchase of lands adequate to the purposes of the company.

The basis for the acquisition of a vast domain was settled by the directors, and Parsons repaired to New York to bring the subject before congress. On the ninth of May 1787, the same day on which the act for the government of the North-west was ordered to a third reading on the morrow, the memorial of Samuel Holden Parsons, agent of the associators of the Ohio company, bearing date only of the preceding day, was presented.* It interested every one. For vague hopes of colonization, here stood a body of hardy pioneers; ready to lead the way to the rapid absorption of the domestic debt of the United States; selected from the choicest regiments of the army; capable of self-defence; the protectors of all who should follow them; men skilled in the labors of the field and of artisans; enterprising and laborious; trained in the severe morality and strict orthodoxy of the New England villages of that day. All was changed. There was the same difference as between sending out recruiting officers and giving marching orders to a regular corps present with music and arms and banners. On the instant the memorial was referred to a committee consisting of Edward Carrington, Rufus King, Nathan Dane, Madison, and Egbert Benson—a great committee: its older members of congress having worthy associates in Carrington and Benson, of whom nothing was spoken but in praise of their faultless integrity and rightness of intention.

On the fourth day of July 1787, for the first time since the eleventh of May, congress had a quorum. There were present from the North, Massachusetts, New York, and New Jersey; from the South, Virginia, the two Carolinas, and Georgia, soon to be joined by Delaware. The South had all in its own way. The president of congress being absent, William Grayson of Virginia was elected the temporary president.

* The memorial of Parsons is in his own handwriting. It is contained in vol. xli. of Papers of the Old Congress, vol. viii., 226, of the Memorials. It is indorsed in the handwriting of Roger Alden, "Memorial of Samuel H. Parsons, agent of the associators for the purchase of lands on the Ohio. Read May ninth 1787. Referred to Mr. Carrington, Mr. King, Mr. Dane, Mr. Madison, Mr. Benson. Acted on July 23, 1787. See committee book."

On Friday, the fifth, there was no quorum. In the evening arrived Manasseh Cutler, one of the three agents of the Ohio company, sent to complete the negotiations for western lands. On his way to New York, Cutler had visited Parsons, his fellow-director, and now acted in full concert with him. Carrington gave the new envoy a cordial welcome, introduced him to members on the floor of congress, devoted immediate attention to his proposals, and already, on the tenth of July, his report granting to the Ohio company all that they desired was read in congress.*

This report, which is entirely in the handwriting of Edward Carrington, assigns as gifts a lot for the maintenance of public schools in every township; another lot for the purpose of religion; and four complete townships, " which shall be good land, and near the centre," for the purpose of a university. The land, apart from the gifts, might be paid for in loan-office certificates reduced to specie value or certificates of liquidated debts of the United States. For bad land, expenses of surveying, and incidental circumstances, the whole allowance was not to exceed one third of a dollar an acre. The price, therefore, was about sixty-six cents and two thirds for every acre, in United States certificates of debt. But as these were then worth only twelve cents on the dollar, the price of land in specie was between eight and nine cents an acre.

On the ninth of July, Richard Henry Lee took his seat in congress. His presence formed an era. On that same day the report for framing a western government, which was to have had its third reading on the tenth of May, was referred to a new committee † of seven, composed of Edward Carrington

---

* The business of congress was done with closed doors and with rigid secrecy. Hence some slight misconceptions in the journal of Cutler. N. A. Review, liii., 334, etc. He says that on July sixth a committee was appointed to consider his proposal. The committee was appointed not on July sixth, but on the ninth of May, and was not changed. Its report is to be found in vol. v. of the Reports of Committees, and in Old Papers of Congress, xix., 27. The report is in the handwriting of Edward Carrington, and by his own hand is indorsed: "Report of Committee on Memorial of S. H. Parsons." Mr. Thomson's hand indorses further: "Report of Mr. Carrington, Mr. King, Mr. Dane, Mr. Madison, Mr. Benson. Read July 10th, 1787. Order of the day for the eleventh." On what day it was presented is not recorded.

† In the Journals of Congress, iv., 751, for the 11th of July, mention is made

and Dane, Richard Henry Lee, Kean of South Carolina, and Melancthon Smith of New York. There were then in congress five southern states to three of the North; on the committee two northern men to three from the South, of whom the two ablest were Virginians.

The committee, animated by the presence of Lee, went to its work in good earnest. Dane, who had been actively employed on the colonial government for more than a year, and for about ten months had served on the committee which had the subject in charge, acted the part of scribe. Like Smith and Lee, he had opposed a federal convention for the reform of the constitution. The three agreed very well together, though Dane secretly harbored the wish of finding in the West an ally for "eastern politics." They were pressed for time, and found it necessary finally to adopt the best system they could get. At first they took up the plan reported by Monroe; but new ideas were started; and they worked with so much industry that on the eleventh of July their report of an ordinance for the government of the territory of the United States north-west of the river Ohio was read for its first time in congress.

The ordinance imbodied the best parts of the work of their predecessors. For the beginning they made the whole north-western territory one district, of which all the officers appointed by congress were to take an oath of fidelity as well as of office. Jefferson, in his ordinance for the sale of lands, had taken care for the equal descent of real estate, as well as other property, to children of both sexes. This was adopted and expressed in the forms of the laws of Massachusetts. The rule of Jefferson was followed in requiring no property qualification for an elector; but was not extended, as Jefferson had done, to the officers to be elected.

The committee then proceeded to establish articles of compact, not to be repealed except by the consent of the original states and the people and states in the territory. Among these,

that the report of a committee touching the temporary government for the western territory had been referred to the committee. I find an indorsement in the State Department on one of the papers that the day on which that reference was made was July ninth.

as in Massachusetts and Virginia, were freedom of religious worship and of religious thought; and various articles from the usual bills of rights of the states.

The next clause bears in every word the impress of the mind of Richard Henry Lee. "No law ought ever to be made in said territory that shall in any manner whatever interfere with or conflict with private contracts or engagements, *bona fide* and without fraud previously formed." This regulation related particularly to the abuse of paper money.*

The third article recognised, like the constitution of Massachusetts, and like the letter of Rufus Putnam of 1783,† that religion, morality, and knowledge are necessary to good government and the happiness of mankind, and declared that schools and the means of education shall forever be encouraged.

The utmost good faith was enjoined toward the Indians; their lands and property, their rights and liberty, were ordered to be protected by laws founded in justice and humanity; so that peace and friendship with them might ever be preserved.

The new states, by compact which neither party alone could change, became, and were forever to remain, a part of the United States of America. The waters leading into the Mississippi and St. Lawrence, and the carrying places between them, according to the successful motion of Grayson and King, were made common highways and forever free. The whole territory was divided into three states only, the population required for the admission of any one of them to the union was fixed at sixty thousand; but both these clauses were subject to the future judgment of congress. The prayer of the Ohio

* "Cette disposition porte particulièrement sur l'abus du papier monnaie." Otto to Montmorin, successor of Vergennes at Versailles, 20 July 1787. R. H. Lee to George Mason, Chantilly, 15 May 1787. Life of Richard Henry Lee, ii., 71–73. Lee hated paper money, and therefore had entreated his friends in the convention at Philadelphia to take from the states the right of issuing it. Moreover, he piqued himself upon the originality of his suggestion: "a proposition that I have not heard mentioned." Compare Lee to Washington, in Sparks's Letters to Washington, iv., 174. More than forty-two years later Dane claimed for himself "originality" in regard to the clause against impairing contracts [Massachusetts Historical Society Proceedings, 1867 to 1869, p. 479], but contemporary evidence points to R. H. Lee as one with whom he must at least divide the honor.

† The proposals presented by Cutler are in the handwriting of Parsons.

company had been but this: "The settlers shall be under the immediate government of congress in such mode and for such time as congress shall judge proper;" the ordinance contained no allusion to slavery; and in that form it received its first reading and was ordered to be printed.

Grayson, then the presiding officer of congress, had always opposed slavery. Two years before he had wished success to the attempt of King for its restriction; and everything points to him * as the immediate cause of the tranquil spirit of disinterested statesmanship which took possession of every southern man in the assembly. Of the members of Virginia, Richard Henry Lee had stood against Jefferson on this very question; but now he acted with Grayson, and from the states of which no man had yielded before, every one chose the part which was to bring on their memory the benedictions of all coming ages. Obeying an intimation from the South, Nathan Dane copied from Jefferson the prohibition of involuntary servitude in the territory, and quieted alarm by adding from the report of King a clause for the delivering up of the fugitive slave. This at the second reading of the ordinance he moved as a sixth article of compact, and, on the thirteenth day of July 1787, the great statute forbidding slavery to cross the river Ohio was passed by the vote of Georgia, South Carolina, North Carolina, Virginia, Delaware, New Jersey, New York, and Massachusetts, all the states that were then present in congress. Pennsylvania and three states of New England were absent;

* William Grayson voted for King's motion of reference, by which the prohibition of slavery was to be immediate; he expressed the hope that congress would be liberal enough to adopt King's motion; he gave, more than any other man in congress, efficient attention to the territorial questions; in 1785 he framed and carried through congress an ordinance for the sale of western lands; his influence as president of congress was great; his record as against slavery is clearer than that of any other southern man who was present in 1787. The assent of Virginia being requisite to the validity of the ordinance, he entreated Monroe to obtain that consent. The consent was not obtained. Though in shattered health, he then became a member of the next Virginia legislature, and was conspicuous in obtaining the assent of Virginia. Add to this in the debate on excluding slavery from the territory of Arkansas, Hugh Nelson of Virginia was quoted as having ascribed the measure to Grayson. Austin Scott fell upon, and was so good as to point out to me, this passage in Annals of Congress for February 1819, column 1225. Thus far no direct report of Nelson's speech has been found.

Maryland only of the South. Of the eighteen members of congress who answered to their names, every one said "aye" excepting Abraham Yates the younger of New York, who insisted on leaving to all future ages a record of his want of good judgment, right feeling, and common sense.

Thomas Jefferson first summoned congress to prohibit slavery in all the territory of the United States; Rufus King lifted up the measure when it lay almost lifeless on the ground, and suggested the immediate instead of the prospective prohibition; a congress composed of five southern states to one from New England, and two from the middle states, headed by William Grayson, supported by Richard Henry Lee, and using Nathan Dane as scribe, carried the measure to the goal in the amended form in which King had caused it to be referred to a committee; and, as Jefferson had proposed, placed it under the sanction of an irrevocable compact.*

The ordinance being passed, the terms of a sale between the United States and Manasseh Cutler and Winthrop Sargent, as agents of the Ohio company, were rapidly brought to a close, substantially on the basis of the report of Carrington.†

The occupation of the purchased lands began immediately, and proceeded with the order, courage, and regularity of men accustomed to the discipline of soldiers. "No colony in America," said Washington in his joy, "was ever settled under such favorable auspices as that which has just commenced at the Muskingum. Information, property, and strength will be its characteristics. I know many of the settlers personally, and there never were men better calculated to promote the welfare of such a community." ‡ Before a year had passed by, free labor kept its sleepless watch on the Ohio.

But this was not enough. Virginia had retained the right to a very large tract north-west of the Ohio; and should she consent that her own sons should be forbidden to cross the river with their slaves to her own lands?

It was necessary for her to give her consent before the ordinance could be secure; and Grayson earnestly entreated

---

* Nathan Dane to Rufus King, 16 July 1787.

† Compare Carrington's report with its amended form in Journals of Congress, iv., Appendix 17.   ‡ Sparks, ix., 385.

Monroe to gain that consent before the year should go out. But Monroe was not equal to the task, and nothing was accomplished.

At the next election of the assembly of Virginia, Grayson, who was not a candidate in the preceding or the following year, was chosen a delegate; and then a powerful committee, on which were Carrington, Monroe, Edmund Randolph, and Grayson, successfully brought forward the bill by which Virginia confirmed the ordinance for the colonization of all the territory then in the possession of the United States by freemen alone.

The white men of that day everywhere held themselves bound to respect and protect the black men in their liberty and property. The suffrage was not as yet regarded as a right incident to manhood, and could be extended only according to the judgment of those who were found in possession of it. When in 1785 an act providing for the gradual abolition of slavery within the state of New York, while it placed the children born of slaves in the rank of citizens, deprived them of the privileges of electors, the council of revision, Clinton and Sloss Hobart being present, and adopting the report of Chancellor Livingston, negatived the act, because, "in violation of the rules of justice and against the letter and spirit of the constitution," it disfranchised the black, mulatto, and mustee citizens who had heretofore been entitled to a vote. The veto prevailed;[*] and in the state of New York the colored man retained his impartial right of suffrage till the constitution of 1821. Virginia, which continued to recognise free negroes as citizens, in the session in which it sanctioned the north-western ordinance, enacted that any person who should be convicted of stealing or selling any free person for a slave shall suffer death without benefit of clergy.[†] This was the protection which Virginia, when the constitution was forming, extended to the black man.

[*] Street's New York Council of Revision, 268, 269.    [†] Hening, xii., 531.

## CHAPTER VII.

### THE CONSTITUTION IN DETAIL. THE POWERS OF CONGRESS.

### 6 AUGUST TO 10 SEPTEMBER 1787.

THE twenty-three resolutions of the convention were distributed by the committee of detail into as many articles, which included new subjects of the gravest moment. On the sixth of August 1787 every member of the convention received a copy of this draft of a constitution, printed on broadsides in large type, with wide spaces and margin for minutes of amendments.* The experience of more than two months had inspired its members with the courage and the disposition to make still bolder grants of power to the union.

The instrument † opens with the sublime words: "We, the people of the states," enumerating New Hampshire and every other of the thirteen, "do ordain, declare, and establish the following constitution for the government of ourselves and our posterity." ‡

When in 1776 "the good people" of thirteen colonies, each having an organized separate home government, and each hitherto forming an integral part of one common empire, jointly prepared to declare themselves free and independent states, it was their first care to ascertain of whom they were composed. The question they agreed to investigate and decide

---

\* Of these copies six have been examined, including that of the president of the convention, and, as is believed, that of its secretary.

† Gilpin, 1226; Elliot, 376.

‡ "We the people of Massachusetts—do—ordain and establish the following —constitution of civil government for ourselves and posterity." Preamble to the first constitution of Massachusetts.

by a joint act of them all. For this end congress selected from its numbers five of its ablest jurists and most trusted statesmen: John Adams of Massachusetts, Thomas Jefferson of Virginia, Edward Rutledge of South Carolina, James Wilson of Pennsylvania, and Robert R. Livingston of New York; the fairest representation that could have been made of New England, of the South, and of the central states. The committee thought not of embarrassing themselves with the introduction of any new theory of citizenship; they looked solely for existing facts. They found colonies with well-known territorial boundaries; and inhabitants of the territory of each colony; and their unanimous report, unanimously accepted by congress, was: "All persons abiding within any of the United Colonies, and deriving protection from the laws of the same, owe allegiance to the said laws, and are members of such colony." *
From "persons making a visitation or temporary stay," only a secondary allegiance was held to be due.

When the articles of confederation were framed with the grand principle of intercitizenship, which gave to the American confederation a superiority over every one that preceded it, the same definition of membership of the community was repeated, except that intercitizenship was not extended to the pauper, or the vagabond, or the fugitive from justice, or the slave. And now these free inhabitants of every one of the United States, this collective people, proclaim their common intention, by their own innate life, to institute a general government.

For the name of the government they chose "The United States of America"; words which expressed unity in plurality and being endeared by usage were preferred to any new description.

That there might be no room to question where paramount allegiance would be due, the second article declared: "The government shall consist of supreme legislative, executive, and judicial powers." †

To maintain that supremacy, the legislature of the United States was itself authorized to carry into execution all powers vested by this new constitution in the government of the Unit-

* Journals of Congress for 5, 17, and 24 June 1776.   † Gilpin, 1226; Elliot, 377.

ed States, or in any of its departments or offices.* The name congress was adopted to mark the two branches of the legislature, which were now named the house of representatives and the senate; the house still taking precedence as the first branch. The executive was henceforward known as "the President."

The scheme of erecting a general government on the authority of the state legislatures was discarded; and the states were enjoined to prescribe for the election of the members of each branch regulations subject to be altered by the legislature of the United States; but the convention itself, in its last days, unanimously reserved to the states alone the right to establish the places for choosing senators.†

To ensure the continuous succession of the government, the legislature was ordered to meet on the first Monday in December in every year, ‡ "unless," added the convention, "congress should by law appoint a different day."

To complete the independence of congress, provision needed to be made for the support of its members. The committee of detail left them to be paid for their services by their respective states; but this mode would impair the self-sustaining character of the government. Ellsworth, avowing a change of opinion, moved that they should be paid out of the Treasury of the United States.# "If the general legislature," said Dickinson, "should be left dependent on the state legislatures, it would be happy for us if we had never met in this room." The motion of Ellsworth was carried by nine states against Massachusetts and South Carolina. ‖ The compensation which he and Sherman would have fixed at five dollars a day, and the same for every thirty miles of travel, was left "to be ascertained by law." △

In the distribution of representatives among the states no change was made; but to the rule of one member of the house for every forty thousand inhabitants Madison objected that in the coming increase of population it would render the number excessive. "The government," replied Gorham, "will not

* Gilpin, 1233; Elliot, 379.
† Gilpin, 1229, 1279, 1281, 1282, 1546, 1608; Elliot, 377, 401, 402, 559.
‡ Gilpin, 1227; Elliot, 377.   # Gilpin, 931, 1326; Elliot, 226, 425.
‖ Gilpin, 1329; Elliot, 427.   △ Gilpin, 1330; Elliot, 427.

last so long as to produce this effect. Can it be supposed that this vast country, including the western territory, will one hundred and fifty years hence remain one nation?"* The clause was for the time unanimously made to read: "not exceeding one for every forty thousand."

As the first qualification for membership of the legislature, it was agreed, and it so remains, that the candidate at the time of his election should be an inhabitant of the state in which he should be chosen. It is not required that a representative should reside in the district which he may be elected to represent.

Citizenship was indispensable; and, before a comer from a foreign country could be elected to the house, he must, according to the report, have been a citizen of the United States for at least three years; before eligibility to the senate, for at least four. "I do not choose," said Mason, "to let foreigners and adventurers make laws for us and govern us without that local knowledge which ought to be possessed by the representative." And he moved for seven years instead of three.† To this all the states agreed except Connecticut.

From respect to Wilson, who was born and educated in Scotland, the subject was taken up once more. Gerry, on the thirteenth, wished none to be elected but men born in the land. Williamson preferred a residence of nine years to seven. ‡ Hamilton proposed to require only citizenship and inhabitancy,# and Madison seconded him. In proof of the advantage of encouraging emigration, Wilson cited Pennsylvania, the youngest settlement on the Atlantic except Georgia, yet among the foremost in population and prosperity; almost all the general officers of her line in the late army and three of her deputies to the convention—Robert Morris, Fitzsimons, and himself—were not natives. ‖ But Connecticut, Pennsylvania, Maryland, and Virginia, which voted with Hamilton and Madison, were overpowered by the seven other states, of which, on this question, New Hampshire, South Carolina, and Georgia were the most stubborn.△

* Gilpin, 1263; Elliot, 392.
† Gilpin, 1256, 1257; Elliot, 389.
‡ Gilpin, 1299; Elliot, 411.
# Gilpin, 1299, 1300; Elliot, 411.
‖ Gilpin, 1300, 1301; Elliot, 412.
△ Gilpin, 1301; Elliot, 412.

Gouverneur Morris desired that the proviso of seven years should not affect any person then a citizen. On this candid motion New Jersey joined the four more liberal states; but Rutledge, Charles Pinckney, Mason, and Baldwin spoke with inveterate tenacity for the disfranchisement against Gorham, Madison, Morris, and Wilson; and the motion was lost by five states to six.*

For a senator, citizenship for nine years was required; Connecticut, Pennsylvania, and Maryland alone finding the number of years excessive.† Three days later, power was vested in the legislature of the United States to establish a uniform rule of naturalization throughout the United States. ‡

The committee of detail had evaded the question of a property qualification for the members of the federal legislature and other branches of the government by referring it to legislative discretion. Charles Pinckney, who wished to require for the president a fortune of not less than a hundred thousand dollars, for a judge half as much, and a like proportion for the members of the national legislature, ventured no more than to move generally that a property qualification should be required of them all.# Franklin made answer: "I dislike everything that tends to debase the spirit of the common people. If honesty is often the companion of wealth, and if poverty is exposed to peculiar temptation, the possession of property increases the desire for more. Some of the greatest rogues I was ever acquainted with were the richest rogues. Remember, the scripture requires in rulers that they should be men hating covetousness. If this constitution should betray a great partiality to the rich, it will not only hurt us in the esteem of the most liberal and enlightened men in Europe, but discourage the common people from removing to this country." ‖ The motion was rejected by a general "no." The question was for a while left open, but the constitution finally escaped without imposing a property qualification on any person in the public employ.

Various efforts were made by Gorham, Mercer, King, and

* Gilpin, 1301–1305; Elliot, 412–414.
† Gilpin, 1305; Elliot, 414.
‡ Elliot, i., 245.
# Gilpin, 1283, 1284; Elliot, 402, 403.
‖ Gilpin, 1284, 1285; Elliot, 403.

Gouverneur Morris to follow the precedent of the British parliament, and constitute a less number than a majority in each house sufficient for a quorum, lest the secession of a few members should fatally interrupt the course of public business. But, by the exertions of Wilson and Ellsworth, Randolph and Madison, power was all but unanimously given to each branch to compel the attendance of absent members, in such manner and under such penalties as each house might provide. Moreover, each house received the power, unknown to the confederacy, to expel a member with the concurrence of two thirds of those voting.*

What should distinguish the "electors" of the United States from their citizens? the constituency of the house of representatives of the United States from the people? The report of the committee ran thus: "The qualifications of the electors shall be the same, from time to time, as those of the electors in the several states of the most numerous branch of their own legislatures." † Gouverneur Morris desired to restrain the right of suffrage to freeholders; and he thought it not proper that the qualifications of the national legislature should depend on the will of the states. "The states," said Ellsworth, "are the best judges of the circumstances and temper of their own people." ‡ "Eight or nine states," remarked Mason, "have extended the right of suffrage beyond the freeholders. What will the people there say if any should be disfranchised?" # "Abridgments of the right of suffrage," declared Butler, "tend to revolution." "The freeholders of the country," replied Dickinson, "are the best guardians of liberty; and the restriction of the right to them is a necessary defence against the dangerous influence of those multitudes without property and without principle, with which our country, like all others, will in time abound. As to the unpopularity of the innovation, it is chimerical. The great mass of our citizens is composed at this time of freeholders, and will be pleased with it." "Ought not every man who pays a tax," asked Ellsworth, "to vote for the representative who is to levy and dispose of his money?" ‖ "The time," said Gouverneur

* Gilpin, 1291; Elliot, 407.  † Gilpin, 1227; Elliot, 377.
‡ Gilpin, 1250; Elliot, 386.  # Ibid.  ‖ Gilpin, 1251; Elliot, 386.

Morris, "is not distant when this country will abound with mechanics and manufacturers, who will receive their bread from their employers. Will such men be the secure and faithful guardians of liberty—the impregnable barrier against aristocracy? The ignorant and the dependent can be as little trusted with the public interest as children. Nine tenths of the people are at present freeholders, and these will certainly be pleased with the restriction." * "The true idea," said Mason, "is that every man having evidence of attachment to the society, and permanent common interest with it, ought to share in all its rights and privileges." "In several of the states," said Madison, "a freehold is now the qualification. Viewing the subject in its merits alone, the freeholders of the country would be the safest depositories of republican liberty. In future times, a great majority of the people will not only be without property in land, but property of any sort. These will either combine under the influence of their common situation, in which case the rights of property and the public liberty will not be secure in their hands, or, what is more probable, they will become the tools of opulence and ambition; in which case there will be equal danger on another side." † Franklin reasoned against the restriction from the nobleness of character that the possession of the electoral franchise inspires. ‡ "The idea of restraining the right of suffrage to the freeholders," said Rutledge, "would create division among the people, and make enemies of all those who should be excluded." # The movement of Morris toward a freehold qualification gained no vote but that of Delaware; and the section as reported was unanimously approved.

Each state was therefore left to fix for itself within its own limits its conditions of suffrage; but where, as in New York and Maryland, a discrimination was made in different elections, the convention applied the most liberal rule adopted in the state to the elections of members of congress, accepting in advance any extensions of the suffrage that in any of the states might grow out of the development of republican institutions. Had the convention established a freehold or other

* Gilpin, 1252; Elliot, 386, 387.     ‡ Gilpin, 1254; Elliot, 388.
† Gilpin, 1253; Elliot, 387.     # Gilpin, 1255; Elliot, 388.

qualification of its own, it must have taken upon itself the introduction of this restriction into every one of the states of the union.

On the question of representation the only embarrassment that remained grew out of that part of the report of the committee of detail which sanctioned the perpetual continuance of the slave-trade. Everywhere, always, by everybody, in statutes alike of Virginia and South Carolina, in speeches, in letters, slavery in those days was spoken of as an evil. Everywhere in the land, the free negro always, the slave from the instant of his emancipation, belonged to the class of citizens, though in Virginia, South Carolina and Georgia, and in Delaware, for all except those who before 1787 had already acquired the elective franchise,* color barred the way to the ballot-box. The convention did nothing to diminish the rights of black men; and, to the incapacities under which they labored in any of the states, it was careful to add no new one. Madison, in the following February, recommending the constitution for ratification, writes: "It is admitted that, if the laws were to restore the rights which have been taken away, the negroes could no longer be refused an equal share of representation with the other inhabitants." † The convention had agreed to the enumeration of two fifths of the slaves in the representative population; but a new complication was introduced by the sanction which the committee of detail had lent to the perpetuity of the slave-trade.

"I never can agree," said King, in the debate of the eighth, "to let slaves be imported without limitation of time, and be represented in the national legislature." ‡

Gouverneur Morris then moved that there should be no representation but of "free inhabitants." "I never will concur in upholding domestic slavery. It is a nefarious institution. It is the curse of heaven on the states where it prevails. Compare the free regions of the middle states, where a rich and noble cultivation marks the prosperity and happiness of

---

\* I so interpret the Delaware statute of 1787.
† Federalist, No. liv.
‡ Gilpin, 1262; Elliot, 392.

the people, with the misery and poverty which overspread the barren wastes of Virginia, Maryland, and the other states having slaves. Travel through the whole continent, and you behold the prospect continually varying with the appearance and disappearance of slavery. The moment you leave the eastern states and enter New York, the effects of the institution become visible. Passing through the Jerseys and entering Pennsylvania, every criterion of superior improvement witnesses the change; proceed southwardly, and every step you take through the great regions of slaves presents a desert increasing with the increasing proportion of these wretched beings. Upon what principle shall slaves be computed in the representation? Are they men? Then make them citizens, and let them vote. Are they property? Why, then, is no other property included? The houses in this city are worth more than all the wretched slaves who cover the rice-swamps of South Carolina. The admission of slaves into the representation, when fairly explained, comes to this: that the inhabitant of Georgia and South Carolina who goes to the coast of Africa, and in defiance of the most sacred laws of humanity tears away his fellow-creatures from their dearest connections and damns them to the most cruel bondage, shall have more votes in a government instituted for protection of the rights of mankind than the citizen of Pennsylvania or New Jersey, who views with a laudable horror so nefarious a practice. I will add, that domestic slavery is the most prominent feature in the aristocratic countenance of the proposed constitution. The vassalage of the poor has ever been the favorite offspring of aristocracy. And what is the proposed compensation to the northern states for a sacrifice of every principle of right, of every impulse of humanity? They are to bind themselves to march their militia for the defence of the southern states against those very slaves of whom they complain. They must supply vessels and seamen, in case of foreign attack. The legislature will have indefinite power to tax them by excises and duties on imports, both of which will fall heavier on them than on the southern inhabitants. On the other side, the southern states are not to be restrained from importing fresh supplies of wretched Africans, at once to increase the danger of attack and the difficulty of defence; nay, they are to be encouraged to it by an assurance of having their votes in the national government increased in proportion; and are, at the same time, to have their exports and their slaves exempt from all contributions for the public service. I will sooner submit myself to a tax for paying for all the negroes in the United States than saddle posterity with such a constitution." * Dayton seconded the motion, that his sentiments on the subject might appear, whatever might be the fate of the amendment.† Charles Pinckney "considered the fisheries and the western frontier as more burdensome to the United States than the slaves." ‡ Wilson thought an agreement to the clause would be no bar to the object of the motion, which itself was premature. New Jersey voted aye, ten states in the negative. So ended the skirmish preliminary to the struggle on the continuance of the slave-trade.

Great as was the advance from the articles of the confederacy, the new grants, not less than the old ones, of power to the legislature of the United States to lay taxes, duties, imposts, and excises, and collect them; to regulate foreign and domestic commerce; alone to coin money and regulate the value of foreign coin; to fix the standard of weights and measures; and establish post-offices, were accepted on the sixteenth, with little difference of opinion.#

No one disputed the necessity of clothing the United States with power " to borrow money." The committee of detail added a continuance of the permission "to emit bills on the credit of the United States." ‖ Four years before, Hamilton, in his careful enumeration of the defects in the confederation, pronounced that this authority " to emit an unfunded paper as the sign of value ought not to continue a formal part of the constitution, nor ever, hereafter, to be employed; being, in its nature, pregnant with abuses, and liable to be made the engine of imposition and fraud; holding out temptations equally pernicious to the integrity of government and to the morals of the people." △

\* Gilpin, 1263–1265; Elliot, 392, 393.　# Gilpin, 1343; Elliot, 434.
† Gilpin, 1265; Elliot, 393.　‖ Gilpin, 1232; Elliot, 378.
‡ Gilpin, 1265, 1266; Elliot, 393–397.　△ Hamilton's Works, ii., 271.

Gouverneur Morris on the fifteenth recited the history of paper emissions and the perseverance of the legislative assemblies in repeating them, though well aware of all their distressing effects, and drew the inference that, were the national legislature formed and a war to break out, this ruinous expedient, if not guarded against, would be again resorted to.* On the sixteenth he moved to strike out the power to emit bills on the credit of the United States. "If the United States," said he, "have credit, such bills will be unnecessary; if they have not, they will be unjust and useless." † Butler was urgent for disarming the government of such a power, and seconded the motion. ‡ It obtained the acquiescence of Madison.

Mason of Virginia "had a mortal hatred to paper money, yet, as he could not foresee all emergencies, he was unwilling to tie the hands of the legislature. The late war could not have been carried on had such a prohibition existed." # "The power," said Gorham, "as far as it will be necessary or safe, is involved in that of borrowing money." ‖ Mercer of Maryland was unwilling to deny to the government a discretion on this point; besides, he held it impolitic to excite the opposition to the constitution of all those who, like himself, were friends to paper money.△ "This," said Ellsworth, "is a favorable moment to shut and bar the door against paper money, which can in no case be necessary. The power may do harm, never good. Give the government credit, and other resources will offer." ◊ Randolph, notwithstanding his antipathy to paper money, could not foresee all the occasions that might arise. ‡ "Paper money," said Wilson, "can never succeed while its mischiefs are remembered; and, as long as it can be resorted to, it will be a bar to other resources." ‡ "Rather than give the power," said John Langdon of New Hampshire, "I would reject the whole plan." ‡

With the full recollection of the need, or seeming need, of paper money in the revolution, with the menace of danger in

---

\* Gilpin, 1334; Elliot, 429.    △ Gilpin, 1344, 1345; Elliot, 435.
† Gilpin, 1343; Elliot, 434.    ◊ Gilpin, 1345; Elliot, 435.
‡ Gilpin, 1344; Elliot, 434.    ‡ Ibid.
\# Ibid.    ‡ Ibid.
‖ Gilpin, 1344; Elliot, 435.    ‡ Gilpin, 1346; Elliot, 435.

future time of war from its prohibition, authority to issue bills of credit that should be legal-tender was refused to the general government by the vote of nine states against New Jersey and Maryland. It was Madison who decided the vote of Virginia; and he has left his testimony that "the pretext for a paper currency, and particularly for making the bills a tender, either for public or private debts, was cut off." This is the interpretation of the clause, made at the time of its adoption alike by its authors and by its opponents,* accepted by all the statesmen of that age, not open to dispute because too clear for argument, and never disputed so long as any one man who took part in framing the constitution remained alive.

History can not name a man who has gained enduring honor by causing the issue of paper money. Wherever such

* For Madison's narrative and opinion, see Gilpin, 1344–1346, and note on 1346; Elliot, 434, 435. The accuracy of the historical sketch of Luther Martin, officially addressed, 27 January 1788, to the speaker of the house of delegates of Maryland, has in ninety-six years never been questioned. It may be found in Elliot, i., 369, 370, and is as follows:

"By our original Articles of Confederation, the congress have power to borrow money and emit bills of credit on the credit of the United States; agreeable to which was the report on this system as made by the committee of detail. When we came to this part of the report, a motion was made to strike out the words 'to emit bills of credit.' Against the motion we urged that it would be improper to deprive the congress of that power; that it would be a novelty unprecedented to establish a government which should not have such authority; that it was impossible to look forward into futurity so far as to decide that events might not happen that should render the exercise of such a power absolutely necessary; and that we doubted whether, if a war should take place, it would be possible for this country to defend itself without having recourse to paper credit, in which case there would be a necessity of becoming a prey to our enemies or violating the constitution of our government; and that, considering the administration of the government would be principally in the hands of the wealthy, there could be little reason to fear an abuse of the power by an unnecessary or injurious exercise of it. But, sir, a majority of the convention, being wise beyond every event, and being willing to risk any political evil rather than admit the idea of a paper emission in any possible case, refused to trust this authority to a government to which they were lavishing the most unlimited powers of taxation, and to the mercy of which they were willing blindly to trust the liberty and property of the citizens of every state in the union; and they erased that clause from the system."

With regard to the paper money issued during the late civil war, congress healed the difficulty by obtaining, in the fourteenth amendment, from the whole country what may be regarded as an act of indemnity; and, while the country made itself responsible for the debt which was contracted, the amendment preserved the original clause of the constitution in its full integrity and vigor.

er has been employed, it has in every case thrown upon its authors the burden of exculpation under the plea of pressing necessity.

Paper money has no hold, and from its very nature can acquire no hold, on the conscience or affections of the people. It impairs all certainty of possession, and taxes none so heavily as the class who earn their scant possession by daily labor. It injures the husbandman by a twofold diminution of the exchangeable value of his harvest. It is the favorite of those who seek gain without willingness to toil; it is the deadly foe of industry. No powerful political party ever permanently rested for support on the theory that it is wise and right. No statesman has been thought well of by his kind in a succeeding generation for having been its promoter.*

In the plan of government, concerted between the members from Connecticut, especially Sherman and Ellsworth, there was this further article: "That the legislatures of the individual states ought not to possess a right to emit bills of credit for a currency, or to make any tender laws for the payment or discharge of debts or contracts in any manner different from the agreement of the parties, or in any manner to obstruct or impede the recovery of debts, whereby the interests of foreigners or the citizens of any other state may be affected."†

The committee of detail had reported: "No state, without the consent of the legislature of the United States, shall emit bills of credit." With a nobler and safer trust in the power of truth and right over opinion, Sherman on the twenty-eighth, scorning compromise, cried out: "This is the favorable crisis for crushing paper money," and, joining Wilson, they two proposed to make the prohibition absolute. Gorham feared that

---

\* This paragraph is a very feeble abstract of the avowed convictions of the great statesmen and jurists who made the constitution. Their words are homely and direct condemnation; and they come not from one party. Richard Henry Lee is as strong in his denunciation as Washington, Sherman, or Robert R. Livingston. William Paterson of New Jersey wrote in 1786 as follows: "An increase of paper money, especially if it be a tender, will destroy what little credit is left; will bewilder conscience in the mazes of dishonest speculations; will allure some and constrain others into the perpetration of knavish tricks; will turn vice into a legal virtue; and sanctify iniquity by law," etc.—From the holograph of William Paterson.

† Sherman's Life, in Biography of the Signers, ii., 43.

the absolute prohibition would rouse the most desperate opposition; but four northern states and four southern states, Maryland being divided, New Jersey absent, and Virginia alone in the negative, placed in the constitution these unequivocal words: "No state shall emit bills of credit." The second part of the clause, "No state shall make anything but gold and silver coin a tender in payment of debts," was accepted without a dissentient state. So the adoption of the constitution is to be the end forever of paper money, whether issued by the several states or by the United states, if the constitution shall be rightly interpreted and honestly obeyed.

It was ever the wish of Sherman and Ellsworth to prohibit "the discharge of debts or contracts in any manner different from the agreement of the parties." Among the aggressions made by the states on the rights of other states, Madison, in his enumeration,* names the enforced payment of debts in paper money, the enforced discharge of debts by the conveyance of land or other property, the instalment of debts, and the "occlusion" of courts. For the two last of these wrongs no remedy was as yet provided.

King moved to add, as in the ordinance of congress for the establishment of new states, "a prohibition on the states to interfere in private contracts." † "This would be going too far," interposed Gouverneur Morris. "There are a thousand laws relating to bringing actions, limitations of actions, and the like, which affect contracts. The judicial power of the United States will be a protection in cases within their jurisdiction; within the state itself a majority must rule, whatever may be the mischief done among themselves." ‡ "Why, then, prohibit bills of credit?" inquired Sherman. Wilson was in favor of King's motion. Madison admitted that inconveniences might arise from such a prohibition, but thought on the whole its utility would overbalance them. He conceived, however, that a negative on the state laws could alone secure the end. Evasions might and would be devised by the ingenuity of legislatures.# His colleague Mason replied: "The motion" of King "is carrying the restraint too far. Cases will

* Madison, i., 321.  
† Gilpin, 1443; Elliot, 485.  
‡ Ibid.  
# Ibid.

happen that cannot be foreseen, where some kind of interference will be proper and essential." He mentioned the case of limiting the period for bringing actions on open account, that of bonds after a lapse of time, asking whether it was proper to tie the hands of the states from making provision in such cases.*

"The answer to these objections is," Wilson explained, " that retrospective interferences only are to be prohibited." " Is not that already done," asked Madison, " by the prohibition of *ex post facto* laws, which will oblige the judges to declare such interferences null and void?" † But the prohibition which, on the motion of Gerry and McHenry, had been adopted six days before, was a limitation on the powers of congress. Instead of King's motion, Rutledge advised to extend that limitation to the individual states; ‡ and accordingly they, too, were now forbidden to pass bills of attainder or *ex post facto* laws by the vote of seven states against Connecticut, Maryland, and Virginia, Massachusetts being absent. So the motion of King, which had received hearty support only from Wilson, was set aside by a very great majority.

The next morning " Dickinson mentioned to the house that, on examining Blackstone's Commentaries, he found that the term *ex post facto* related to criminal cases only; that the words would consequently not restrain the states from retrospective laws in civil cases; and that some further provision for this purpose would be requisite." # Of this remark the convention at the moment took no note; and the clause of Rutledge was left in the draft then making of the constitution, as the provision against the "stay laws and occlusion of courts" so much warned against by Madison, "the payment or discharge of debts or contracts in any manner different from the agreement of the parties," as demanded by Sherman and Ellsworth. ‖

* Gilpin, 1443; Elliot, 485.      † Gilpin, 1399, 1444; Elliot, 462, 485.

‡ *Ex post facto*, not retrospective, was the form used by Rutledge. Correct Gilpin, 1444, by the Journal of the Convention, in Elliot, i., 271, and compare Elliot, i., 257.      # Gilpin, 1450; Elliot, 488.

‖ That no other motion in form or substance was adopted by the convention till after the draft went into the hands of the committee of style and revision, appears from a most careful comparison of the printed journal of the convention, of

Among the prohibitions on the states which the committee of detail reported on the twenty-eighth, was that of laying duties on imports. "Particular states," observed Mason, "may wish to encourage by impost duties certain manufactures for which they enjoy natural advantages, as Virginia the manufacture of hemp, etc." * Madison replied: "The encouragement of manufactures in that mode requires duties, not only on imports directly from foreign countries, but from the other states in the union, which would revive all the mischiefs experienced from the want of a general government over commerce." † King proposed to extend the prohibition not to imports only, but also to exports, so as to prohibit the states from taxing either. Sherman added, that, even with the consent of the United States, the several states should not levy taxes on importations except for the use of the United States. This movement Gouverneur Morris supported as a regulation necessary to prevent the Atlantic states from endeavoring to tax the western states and promote their separate interest by opposing the navigation of the Mississippi, which would drive the western people into the arms of Great Britain. George Clymer of Pennsylvania "thought the encouragement of the western country was suicide on the part of the old states. If the states have such different interests that they cannot be left to regulate their own manufactures, without encountering the interests of other states, it is a proof that they are not fit to compose one nation." ‡ King did not wish to "interfere too much with the policy of states respecting their manufactures," holding that such a policy of protection in a separate state might be necessary. "Revenue," he reminded the house, "was the object of the general legislature." # By a large majority the prohibition on the several states of taxing imports was made dependent on the consent of the legislature of the United States;

---

its journal as preserved in manuscript, of every scrap of paper containing any motion or sketch of a motion preserved among the records of the convention in the state department, of the debates of the convention as reported by Madison, and of the several copies of the broadside which were used for the entry of amendments by Washington, by Madison, by Brearley, by Gilman, by Johnson, and another, which seems to be that of the secretary, Jackson.

* Gilpin, 1445; Elliot, 486.  ‡ Gilpin, 1446, 1447; Elliot, 487.
† Ibid.  # Gilpin, 1447; Elliot, 478.

and with this limitation it was carried without a dissentient vote. The extending of the prohibition to exports obtained a majority of but one. That taxes on imports or exports by the states, even with the consent of the United States, should be exclusively for the use of the United States, gained every state but Massachusetts and Maryland. The power to protect domestic manufactures by imposts was taken away from the states, and, so far as it is incident to the raising of revenue, was confined to the United States.

The country had been filled with schemes for a division of the thirteen states into two or more separate groups; the convention, following its committee of detail, would suffer no state to enter into any confederation, or even into a treaty or alliance with any confederation. The restriction was absolute. To make it still more clear and peremptory, it was repeated and enlarged in another article, which declared not only that "no state shall enter into any agreement or compact with any foreign power," but that "no state shall enter into any agreement or compact with any other state." * Each state was confined in its government strictly to its own duties within itself.

As to slavery, it was by a unanimous consent treated as a sectional interest; freedom existed in all the states; slavery was a relation established within a state by its own law. Under the sovereignty of the king of Great Britain the laws of a colony did not on British soil prevail over the imperial law. In like manner in America, a slave in one American colony, finding himself on the soil of another, was subject only to the laws of the colony in which he might be found. It remained so on the declaration of independence; not as an innovation, but as the continuance of an established fact. The articles of confederation took no note of slavery, except by withholding the privileges of intercitizenship from the slave. The enumeration of slaves was in the distribution of political power a matter of indifference so long as congress voted by states and proportioned its requisitions of revenue to wealth alone.

In framing a constitution in which representation in one branch of the legislature was made to depend on population, it became the political interest of the states in which slaves

* Article xiii. Gilpin, 1239, 1447; Elliot, 381, 487.

abounded to have them included in the enumeration of the population equally with the free negroes and the whites. They so far succeeded that the slave inhabitants were held to be a part of the grand aggregate of the people of the United States, and as such were entitled to bring a proportional increase of representation to the state in which they abode. For this purpose of representation the slaves were by a compromise allowed to be counted, but only as three out of five; should the master see fit to liberate the slave, he became at once a free inhabitant and a citizen with the right of intercitizenship, and of being counted equally in the representative population.

Intercitizenship was the life-blood of the union. The report of the committee of detail, changing only the words " free inhabitants" for "citizens," followed the articles of confederation in declaring that " the citizens of each state shall be entitled to all privileges and immunities of citizens in the several states." * The slave remained a slave, but only in states whose local laws permitted it.

After three weeks' reflection, Cotesworth Pinckney, on the twenty-eighth of August, avowed himself not satisfied with the article; he wished that "some provision should be included in favor of property in slaves." The article was nevertheless adopted, but not unanimously; South Carolina voted against it, and Georgia was divided, showing that discontent with the want of the protection to slavery was seated in their breasts, even so far as to impugn the great principle which was a necessary condition of union.†

The convention proceeded with its work, and proposed that any person who should flee from justice should be delivered up on the demand of the executive of the state from which he fled. Butler and Charles Pinckney moved, as an amendment, to require fugitive slaves to be delivered up like criminals. " This," answered Wilson, " would oblige the executive of the state to do it at the public expense." "The public," said Sherman, "can with no more propriety seize and surrender a slave or servant than a horse." Butler withdrew his motion and the article as proposed was unanimously adopted. ‡

---

\* Gilpin, 1240; Elliot, 381. † Gilpin, 1447; Elliot, 487.
‡ Gilpin, 1447, 1448; Elliot, 487.

The convention was not unprepared to adopt a fugitive slave law, for such a clause formed a part of the ordinance of 1787, adopted in the preceding July for the government of the north-western territory. On the twenty-ninth, Butler, after the opportunity of reflection and consultation, offered a proposal: "That the fugitive slaves escaping into another state shall be delivered up to the person justly claiming their service or labor." This for the moment was agreed to without dissent.[*] The trouble and expense of making the claim fell on the slave-holder; the language of the article did not clearly point out by whom the runaway slave was to be delivered up.

[*] Gilpin, 1456; Elliot, 492. Compare Gilpin, 1558; Elliot, 564.

## CHAPTER VIII.

**THE CONSTITUTION IN DETAIL. THE POWERS OF CONGRESS, CONTINUED.**

From the Middle to the End of August 1787.

On the eighteenth of August, Rutledge insisted that it was necessary and expedient for the United States to assume "all the state debts." A committee of eleven, to whom the subject was referred, on the twenty-first reported a grant of power to the United States to assume "the debts of the several states incurred during the late war for the common defence and general welfare." But the states which had done the most toward discharging their obligations were unwilling to share equally the burdens of those which had done the least; and the convention, adopting on the twenty-fifth the language of Randolph, affirmed no more than that the engagements of the confederation should be equally valid against the United States under this constitution.*

The convention, on the seventeenth, agreed with its committee in giving jurisdiction to the United States over the crime of counterfeiting their coins and over crimes committed on the high seas, or against the law of nations.†

The report of the committee of detail gave power to congress "to subdue a rebellion in any state on the application of its legislature." Martin, on the seventeenth, approved the limitation to which Charles Pinckney, Gouverneur Morris, and Langdon objected. Ellsworth moved to dispense with the application of the legislature of the rebellious state when that body could not meet. "Gerry was against letting loose the

---

* Gilpin, 1426; Elliot, 476. † Gilpin, 1349; Elliot, 437.

myrmidons of the United States on a state without its own consent. The states will be the best judges in such cases. More blood would have been spilt in Massachusetts in the late insurrection if the general authority had intermeddled." The motion of Ellsworth was adopted; but it weighed down the measure itself, which obtained only four votes against four.*

We come to a regulation where the spirit of republicanism exercised its humanest influence. The world had been retarded in civilization, impoverished and laid waste by wars of the personal ambition of its kings. The committee of detail and the convention, in the interest of peace, intrusted the power to declare war, not to the executive, but to the deliberate decision of the two branches of the legislature,† each of them having a negative on the other; and the executive retaining his negative on them both.

On the eighteenth Madison offered a series of propositions, granting powers to dispose of the lands of the United States; to institute temporary governments for new states; to regulate affairs with the Indians; to exercise exclusively legislative authority at the seat of general government; to grant charters of incorporation where the public good might require them and the authority of a single state might be incompetent; to secure to authors their copyrights for a limited time; to establish a university; to encourage discoveries and the advancement of useful knowledge. ‡ In that and the next sitting Charles Pinckney proposed, among other cessions, to grant immunities for the promotion of agriculture, commerce, trades, and manufactures. They were all unanimously referred to the committee of detail.

Gerry would have an army of two or three thousand # at the most; a number in proportion to population greater than the present army of the United States. The power to raise and support armies was, however, accepted unanimously, with no "fetter on" it, except the suggestion then made by Mason and soon formally adopted, that "no appropriation for that use should be for a longer term than two years."

* Gilpin, 1350, 1351; Elliot, 437, 438.　　# Gilpin, 1360; Elliot, 443.
† Gilpin, 1351; Elliot, 438.　Elliot, i., 247.
‡ Gilpin, 1353, 1354, 1355; Elliot, 439, 440.

The idea of a navy was welcome to the country. Jefferson thought a small one a necessity.* The convention accepted unanimously the clause giving power "to build and equip fleets;" or, as the power was more fitly defined, "to provide and maintain a navy." †

The report gave to the general government only power to call forth the aid of the militia. ‡ Mason moved to grant the further power of its regulation and discipline, for "thirteen states would never concur in any one system"; # but he reserved "to the states the appointment of the officers." In the opinion of Ellsworth, the motion went too far. "The militia should be under rules established by the general government when in actual service of the United States. The whole authority over it ought by no means to be taken from the states. Their consequence would pine away to nothing after such a sacrifice of power. The general authority could not sufficiently pervade the union for the purpose, nor accommodate itself to the local genius of the people." Sherman supported him. "My opinion is," said Dickinson, "that the states never ought to give up all authority over the militia, and never will." ‖

Swayed by Dickinson, Mason modified his original motion, which Cotesworth Pinckney instantly renewed. A grand committee of eleven, to which this among other subjects was referred, on the twenty-first reported △ that the legislature should have power "to make laws for organizing, arming, and disciplining the militia, and for governing such part of them as may be employed in the service of the United States." Ellsworth and Sherman, on the twenty-third, accepted the latter part of the clause, but resisted the former. "The discipline of the militia," answered Madison, "is evidently a national concern, and ought to be provided for in the national constitution." And the clause was adopted by nine states against Connecticut and Maryland. ◊

---

\* Notes on Virginia, end of the answer to query 22; Jefferson, i., 592, 606; ii., 211, 218; Madison, i., 196.     # Gilpin, 1355; Elliot, 440.
† Gilpin, 1360; Elliot, 443.     ‖ Gilpin, 1361, 1362; Elliot, 443, 444.
‡ Gilpin, 1233; Elliot, 379.     △ Gilpin, 1378; Elliot, 451.
◊ Gilpin, 1406, 1407; Elliot, 466.

Madison always wished to reserve to the United States the appointment of general officers in the militia. This Sherman pronounced absolutely inadmissible. "As the states are not to be abolished," said Gerry, "I wonder at the attempts to give powers inconsistent with their existence. A civil war may be produced by the conflict between people who will support a plan of vigorous government at every risk and others of a more democratic cast." "The greatest danger," said Madison, "is disunion of the states; it is necessary to guard against it by sufficient powers to the common government; the greatest danger to liberty is from large standing armies; it is best to prevent them by an effectual provision for a good militia." Madison gained for his motion only New Hampshire, South Carolina, and Georgia. The appointment of officers by the states was then agreed to; and the states were to train the militia, but according to the discipline prescribed by the United States.*

The power "to make all laws necessary and proper for carrying into execution the powers vested by this constitution in the government of the United States, or in any department or office thereof," was so clearly necessary that, without cavil or remark, it was unanimously agreed to.†

The definition of treason against the United States, though made in language like that of the English law, took notice of the federal character of the American government by defining it as levying war against the United States or any one of them; thus reserving to the United States the power to punish treason, whether by war against the United States or by war against a state. Johnson was of opinion that there could be no treason against a particular state even under the confederation, much less under the proposed system. Mason answered: "The United States will have a qualified sovereignty only; the individual states will retain a part of the sovereignty." "A rebellion in a state," said Johnson, "would amount to treason against the supreme sovereign, the United States." "Treason against a state," said King, "must be treason against the United States." Sherman differed from him, saying: "Resistance against the laws of the United States is distin-

* Gilpin, 1407, 1408; Elliot, 466, 467.  † Gilpin, 1370; Elliot, 447.

guished from resistance against the laws of a particular state." Ellsworth added: "The United States are sovereign on one side of the line dividing the jurisdictions, the states on the other. Each ought to have power to defend their respective sovereignties." * "War or insurrection against a member of the union," said Dickinson, "must be so against the whole body." The clause as amended, evading the question, spoke only of treason by levying war against the United States or adhering to their enemies, giving them aid or comfort. No note was taken of the falsification of election returns, or the dangers peculiar to elective governments. Martin relates that he wished an amendment excepting citizens of any state from the penalty of treason, when they acted expressly in obedience to the authority of their own state; but seeing that a motion to that effect would meet with no favor, he at the time shut up the thought within his own breast.†

The members of the convention long held in "recollection the pain and difficulty which the subject of slavery caused in that body," and which "had well-nigh led southern states to break it up without coming to any determination." ‡ The members from South Carolina and Georgia were moved by the extreme desire of preserving the union and obtaining an efficient government; but as their constituents could not be reconciled to the immediate prohibition of the slave-trade by the act of the United States, they demanded that their states should retain on that subject the liberty of choice which all then possessed under the confederation. Unwilling to break the union into fragments, the committee of detail proposed limitations of the power of congress to regulate commerce. No tax might be laid on exports, nor on the importation of slaves. As to the slave-trade, each state was to remain, as under the articles of confederation, free to import such persons as it "should think proper to admit." The states might, one by

---

* Gilpin, 1375; Elliot, 450.

† Elliot, i., 382, 383. I think Martin did not make the motion, as it is found neither in the journal nor in Madison. His narrative is, perhaps, equivocal. His words are: "I wished to have obtained"; and again: "But this provision was not adopted." Here is no assertion that he made the motion.

‡ Baldwin's Speech in the House, 12 February 1790.

VOL. VI.—22

one, each for itself, prohibit the slave-trade; not the United States by a general law. This decision was coupled with no demand of privileges for the shipping interest. Ellsworth, in the committee, had consented, unconditionally, that no navigation act should be passed without the assent of two thirds of the members present in each house.

On the twenty-first the prohibition to tax exports was carried by Massachusetts and Connecticut with the five most southern states. Thus absolute free trade as to exports became a part of the fundamental law of the United States. The vote of Virginia was due to Mason, Randolph, and Blair; Washington and Madison were always unwilling to seem to favor a local interest, especially a southern one, and were ready to trust the subject to the general government.*

From Maryland came a voice against the slave-trade. For three reasons Martin proposed to prohibit or to tax the importation of slaves: "The importation of slaves affects the apportionment of representation, weakens one part of the union which the other parts are bound to protect, and dishonors the principles of the revolution and the American character."

Rutledge answered: "Religion and humanity have nothing to do with this question; interest alone is the governing principle with nations. The true question at present is, whether the southern states shall or shall not be parties to the union? If the northern states consult their interest they will not oppose the increase of slaves, which will increase the commodities of which they will become the carriers." Ellsworth, speaking consistently with the respect which he had always shown for the rights of the states, answered: "I am for leaving the clause as it stands. Let every state import what it pleases. The morality or wisdom of slavery are considerations belonging to the states themselves. The old confederation did not meddle with this point; and I do not see any greater necessity for bringing it within the policy of the new one." "South Carolina," said Charles Pinckney, "can never receive the plan if it prohibits the slave-trade."

The debate was continued through the next day. Sherman was perplexed between his belief in the inherent right of man

* Gilpin, 1388; Elliot, 456.

to freedom and the tenet of the right of each state to settle for itself its internal affairs, and said: "I disapprove of the slave-trade; yet, as the states are now possessed of the right to import slaves, and as it is expedient to have as few objections as possible to the proposed scheme of government, I think it best to leave the matter as we find it."

Mason, compressing the observation of a long life into a few burning words, replied: "This infernal traffic originated in the avarice of British merchants; the British government constantly checked the attempts of Virginia to put a stop to it. The present question concerns not the importing states alone, but the whole union. Maryland and Virginia have already prohibited the importation of slaves expressly; North Carolina has done the same in substance. All this would be in vain if South Carolina and Georgia be at liberty to import them. The western people are already calling out for slaves for their new lands, and will fill that country with slaves if they can be got through South Carolina and Georgia. Slavery discourages arts and manufactures. The poor despise labor when performed by slaves. They prevent the emigration of whites, who really enrich and strengthen a country. They produce the most pernicious effect on manners. Every master of slaves is born a petty tyrant. They bring the judgment of heaven on a country. As nations cannot be rewarded or punished in the next world, they must be in this. By an inevitable chain of causes and effects, Providence punishes national sins by national calamities. I lament that some of our eastern brethren have, from a lust of gain, embarked in this nefarious traffic. As to the states being in possession of the right to import, this is the case with many other rights, now to be properly given up. I hold it essential in every point of view, that the general government should have power to prevent the increase of slavery." Mason spoke from his inmost soul, anxious for freedom and right, for the happiness of his country and the welfare of mankind.

To words of such intense sincerity Ellsworth answered with almost mocking irony: "As I have never owned a slave I cannot judge of the effects of slavery on character. If, however, it is to be considered in a moral light, we ought to go further and free the slaves already in the country. Besides, slaves multiply so fast in Virginia and Maryland that it is cheaper to raise than import them, whilst in the sickly rice-swamps foreign supplies are necessary; if we go no further than is urged, we shall be unjust toward South Carolina and Georgia. Let us not intermeddle. As population increases, poor laborers will be so plenty as to render slaves useless. Slavery, in time, will not be a speck in our country. Provision is made in Connecticut for abolishing it; and the abolition has already taken place in Massachusetts."

"If the southern states are let alone," said Charles Pinckney, "they will probably of themselves stop importations. I would myself, as a citizen of South Carolina, vote for it."

In the same vein Cotesworth Pinckney remarked: "If I and all my colleagues were to sign the constitution and use our personal influence, it would be of no avail toward obtaining the assent of our constituents. South Carolina and Georgia cannot do without slaves. Virginia will gain by stopping the importations. Her slaves will rise in value, and she has more than she wants. It would be unequal to require South Carolina and Georgia to confederate on such terms. Slaves should be dutied like other imports; but a rejection of the clause is the exclusion of South Carolina from the union." Baldwin, with opinions on the rights of the states like those of Ellsworth and Sherman, continued: "The object before the convention is not national, but local. Georgia cannot purchase the advantage of a general government by yielding the abridgment of one of her favorite prerogatives. If left to herself, she may probably put a stop to the evil."

"If South Carolina and Georgia," observed Wilson, "are themselves disposed to get rid of the importation of slaves in a short time, they will never refuse to unite because the importation might be prohibited." To this Cotesworth Pinckney made answer: "I think myself bound to declare candidly that I do not believe South Carolina will stop her importations of slaves in any short time, except occasionally as she now does."

"On every principle of honor and safety," said Dickinson, "it is inadmissible that the importation of slaves should be authorized to the states by the constitution. The true question is whether the national happiness will be promoted or impeded by the importation; and this question ought to be left to the national government, not to the states particularly interested. I cannot believe that the southern states will refuse to confederate on that account, as the power is not likely to be immediately exercised by the general government." Here was the opening to a grant of the power, coupled with a prospect of delay in using it.

Williamson, himself no friend of slavery, distinctly intimated that North Carolina would go with her two neighbors on the south. Cotesworth Pinckney now moved to commit the clause, that slaves might be made liable to an equal tax with other imports. "If the convention," said Rutledge, "thinks that North Carolina, South Carolina, and Georgia will ever agree to the plan, unless their right to import slaves be untouched, the expectation is vain;" and he seconded the motion for a commitment. Gouverneur Morris wished the whole subject to be committed, including the clauses relating to taxes on exports and to a navigation act. These things might form a bargain among the northern and southern states. "Rather than to part with the southern states," said Sherman, " it is better to let them import slaves. But a tax on slaves imported makes the matter worse, because it implies they are property."

"Two states," said Randolph, "may be lost to the union; let us, then, try the chance of a commitment." The motion for commitment was adopted by the votes of Connecticut, New Jersey, and the five southernmost states, against New Hampshire, Pennsylvania, and Delaware; Massachusetts was absent.

Charles Pinckney and Langdon then moved to commit the section relating to a navigation act. "I desire it to be remembered," said Gorham, remotely hinting at possible secession, "the eastern states have no motive to union but a commercial one." Ellsworth, maintaining the position which he had deliberately chosen, answered: "I am for taking the plan as it is. If we do not agree on this middle and moderate ground, I am afraid we shall lose two states with others that may stand aloof;

and fly, most probably, into several confederations, not without bloodshed." *

Had the convention listened to no compromise on the slave-trade, Georgia and South Carolina would not have accepted the new constitution; North Carolina would have clung to them, from its internal condition; Virginia, however earnest might have been the protest against it by Madison and Washington, must have acted with North Carolina, and, as a consequence, there would from the beginning have been a federation of slave-holding states. The committee to which the whole subject of restriction on the power over commerce was referred consisted of Langdon, King, Johnson, the aged William Livingston of New Jersey, Clymer, Dickinson, Martin, Madison, Williamson, Cotesworth Pinckney, and Baldwin,† a large majority of them venerable for uprightness and ability. Their report, made on the twenty-fourth, denied to the United States the power to prohibit the slave-trade prior to the year 1800, but granted the power to impose a tax or duty on such migration or importation at a rate not exceeding the average of the duties laid on imports. ‡

On the twenty-fifth, when the report of the committee of eleven was taken up, Cotesworth Pinckney immediately moved to extend the time allowed for the importation of slaves till the year 1808. Gorham was his second. Madison spoke earnestly against the prolongation; # but, without further debate, the motion prevailed by the votes of the three New England states, Maryland, and the three southernmost states, against New Jersey, Pennsylvania, Delaware, and Virginia. ‖

Sherman once more resisted the duty "as acknowledging men to be property" by taxing them as such under the character of slaves; and Madison supported him, saying: "I think it wrong to admit in the constitution the idea that there can be property in men." ᐃ But, as the impost which had been proposed on all imported articles was of five per cent and the slave was deemed to have an average value of two hundred dollars, the rate was fixed definitively at ten dollars on every

---

\* Gilpin, 1388–1396; Elliot, 456–461.    # Gilpin, 1427; Elliot, 477.
† Gilpin, 1397; Elliot, 461.    ‖ Gilpin, 1429; Elliot, 478.
‡ Gilpin, 1415; Elliot, 471.    ᐃ Gilpin, 1429, 1430; Elliot, 478.

imported slave, and the clause thus amended was unanimously held fast as a discouragement of the traffic.

"It ought to be considered," wrote Madison near the time, "as a great point gained in favor of humanity, that a period of twenty years may terminate forever within these states a traffic which has so long and so loudly upbraided the barbarism of modern policy. Happy would it be for the unfortunate Africans if an equal prospect lay before them of being redeemed from the oppressions of their European brethren!" *

The confederation granted no power to interfere with the slave-trade. The new constitution gave power to prohibit it in new states immediately on their admission, in existing states at the end of the year 1807. Louisiana, by annexation to the union, lost the license to receive slaves from abroad. On the second day of December 1806, Thomas Jefferson, president of the United States of America, addressed this message to congress: † "I congratulate you, fellow-citizens, on the approach of the period at which you may interpose your authority constitutionally to withdraw the citizens of the United States from all further participation in those violations of human rights which have been so long continued on the unoffending inhabitants of Africa, and which the morality, the reputation, and the best interests of our country have long been eager to proscribe."

Unanimous legislation followed the words from the president, and, as the year 1808 broke upon the United States, the importation of slaves had ceased. And did slavery have as peaceful an end? Philanthropy, like genius and like science, must bide its time. Man cannot hurry the supreme power, to which years are as days.

Two members of the convention, with the sincere integrity which clears the eye for prophetic vision, read the doom of slave-holding. Mason, fourteen years before, in a paper prepared for the legislature of Virginia, had given his opinion that as the natural remedy for political injustice the constitution should by degrees work itself clear by its own innate strength, the virtue and resolution of the community; and added: "The laws of impartial Providence may avenge upon

* The Federalist, No. xlii.      † Journals of Congress, v., 468.

our posterity the injury done to a set of wretches whom our injustice hath debased almost to a level with the brute creation. These remarks were extorted by a kind of irresistible, perhaps an enthusiastic, impulse; and the author of them, conscious of his own good intentions, cares not whom they please or offend." \*

During a previous debate on the value of slaves, Mason had observed of them that they might in cases of emergency themselves become soldiers.† On the twenty-second of August ‡ he called to mind that Cromwell, when he sent commissioners to Virginia to take possession of the country, gave them power to arm servants and slaves. He further pointed out that the British might have prevailed in the South in the war of the revolution had they known how to make use of the slaves; that in Virginia the royal governor invited them to rise at a time when he was not in possession of the country, and, as the slaves were incapable of self-organization and direction, his experiments by proclamation, addressed to them in regions not within his sway, totally failed; but that in South Carolina, where the British were in the full possession of the country, they might have enfranchised the slaves and enrolled them for the consolidation and establishment of the royal authority. But the civil and military officers in those days of abject corruption chose rather to enrich themselves by shipping the slaves to the markets of the West Indies. Five months later Madison, in a paper addressed to the country, remarked: "An unhappy species of population abounds in some of the states who, during the calm of the regular government, are sunk below the level of men; but who, in the tempestuous scenes of civil violence, may emerge into the human character, and give a superiority of strength to any party with which they may associate themselves." # Slave-holding was to be borne down on the field of battle.

The dignity and interests of the United States alike de-

---

\* George Mason's extracts from the Virginia charters, with some remarks on them, made in the year 1773. MS. The paper, though communicated to the legislature of Virginia, has not been found in its archives. My copy, which is, perhaps, the only one now in existence, I owe to the late James M. Mason.

† Gilpin, 1068; Elliot, 296.          ‡ Gilpin, 1390; Elliot, 458.

# Madison in the Federalist, No. xliii., published 25 January 1788.

manded a grant of power to the general government for the regulation of foreign as well as domestic trade. Without it the navigation of the country would have been at the mercy of foreign restrictions. For this regulation the new constitution required, as in all other acts of legislation, no more than a majority of the two houses of congress. A strong opposition started up in the South under the lead of Charles Pinckney and Martin, inflamed by Mason and by Randolph; but it was in vain. On the twenty-ninth, Madison, Spaight, and Rutledge defended the report of the eleven like statesmen, free from local influences or prejudice. It was clearly stated that the ships of nations in treaty with the United States would share in their carrying trade; that a rise in freight could be but temporary, because it would be attended by an increase of southern as well as of northern shipping; that the West India trade was a great object to be obtained only through the pressure of a navigation act. Cotesworth Pinckney owned that he had been prejudiced against the eastern states, but had found their delegates as liberal and as candid as any men whatever. On the question, Delaware and South Carolina joined the united North against Maryland, Virginia, North Carolina, and Georgia. After this vote the convention accepted unanimously the proposition to grant to the majority in the two branches of congress full power to make laws regulating commerce and navigation. Randolph was so much dissatisfied that he expressed a "doubt whether he should be able to agree to the constitution." Mason, more deeply in earnest, as yet held his emotions in check.

Of new states, the Virginia plan knew those only "lawfully arising within the limits of the United States," and for their admission vaguely required less than a unanimous vote; the committee of detail demanded the consent of two thirds of each house of congress, as well as the concurrence of the states within whose "limits" the new states should arise.

At this stage Gouverneur Morris enlarged the scope and simplified the language of the article. The confederation had opened the door to Canada at its own choice alone, and to any other territory that could obtain the consent of two thirds of congress. It was no longer decent to hold out to Canada an invitation to annex itself to the union; but the American mind, in the strength of independence, foresaw its expansion. The rising states beyond the mountains were clamorous for the unobstructed navigation of the Mississippi, which might lead to the acquisition by treaty of all the land east of that river; and the boundary on the south, as well of Georgia as of Florida, had never been adjusted with Spain. Gouverneur Morris had at an early day desired to restrict the limits of the United States; he now gave his ancient fears to the winds, and, acceding in advance to the largest eventual annexations, he proposed these few and simple words: "New States may be admitted by the legislature into the union," with the full understanding and intention that an ordinary act of legislation should be sufficient by a bare majority to introduce foreign territory as a state into the union.* This clause the convention accepted without a debate, and without a division.

On the thirtieth, Maryland, impelled by a desire to guard the right of the United States to the back lands, and to be the champion of Kentucky, of Maine, of Vermont, and of the settlements on the Tennessee river and its branches, would have granted to the legislature of the United States unlimited power to dismember old states, but was supported only by Delaware and New Jersey. Vermont might once have been included within "the limits" of New York, but certainly remained no longer within its jurisdiction. By changing the word "limits" to "jurisdiction," the convention, still following Gouverneur Morris, provided for its future admission to the union without the consent of New York. In regard to the south-western settlements, the preliminary consent of the states of which they then formed a part was not dispensed with. In like manner no state could be formed by the junction of two or more states or parts thereof without the concurrence of such states. The country north-west of the Ohio having already been provided for, the rule for the admission of new states was thus completed for every part of the territory of the states or of the United States. The convention, still using the language of Gouverneur Morris, and no one but Maryland dissenting, assigned to the legislature the power to dispose of and make

* Gilpin, 1458; Elliot, 493. Life and Writings of Gouverneur Morris by Sparks, iii., 183, 185, 290. Cooley's Story, 1282, etc.

all needful rules and regulations respecting the territory or other property belonging to the United States.

Every word in the constitution bearing on the subject of slavery was chosen with the greatest caution; every agreement was jealously guarded. After the section relating to the slave-trade, the committee of detail inserted: "No capitation tax shall be laid unless in proportion to the census hereinbefore directed to be taken." * This was intended to prevent congress from enforcing a general emancipation by the special taxation of slaves.†

* Gilpin, 1234, 1415; Elliot, 379, 471.
† Speech of Baldwin in the house of representatives, 12 February 1790.

## CHAPTER IX.

### THE PRESIDENT.

### July, August, and September 1787.

How to call forth one of the people to be their executive chief for a limited period of years, and how to clothe him with just sufficient powers, long baffled the convention. Federal governments, in Greece, in Switzerland, and in Holland, like the confederation of the United States, had been without a separate executive branch; and the elective monarchies of Poland, of the Papal states, and of Germany, offered no available precedents. The report of the committee of detail of the sixth of August introduced no improvement in the manner of selecting a president; and it transferred to the senate the power to make treaties and to appoint ambassadors and judges of the supreme court.* Questions relating to the duties of the president long remained in doubt; the mode of his election was reached only just before the close of the convention.

The Virginia plan confided the choice of the executive to the national legislature. "An election by the national legislature," objected Gouverneur Morris, on the seventeenth of July, "will be the work of intrigue, of cabal, of corruption, and of faction; it will be like the election of a pope by a conclave of cardinals; of a king by the diet of Poland; real merit will rarely be the title to the appointment." He moved for an election by the " citizens of the United States." † Sherman preferred a choice by the national legislature. Wilson insisted on an election by the people; should no one have a majority, then, and then only, the legislature might decide between the

* Gilpin, 1234; Elliot, 379. † Gilpin, 1120; Elliot, 322.

candidates.* Charles Pinckney opposed the election by the people, because it would surrender the choice to a combination of the populous states led by a few designing men.† "To refer the choice of a proper character for a chief magistrate to the people," protested Mason, " would be as unnatural as to refer a trial of colors to a blind man." ‡ " An election by the people," observed Williamson, " is an appointment by lot." On the first vote Pennsylvania stood alone against nine states. Martin proposed to intrust the appointment to the legislatures of the states; and was supported only by Delaware and Maryland.

On the mode of choosing the president, the length of his period of office and his re-eligibility would be made to depend. The convention, in committee, had fixed that period at seven years with a prohibition of re-election. On the motion of William Houston of Georgia, supported by Sherman and Gouverneur Morris, this compulsory rotation was struck out by six states, against Delaware, Virginia, and the two Carolinas. The executive becoming re-eligible, Jacob Broom of Delaware revived the idea of a shorter period of service. McClurg held that the independence of the executive was no less essential than the independence of the judiciary; that a president, elected for a small number of years by the national legislature, and looking to that body for re-election, would be its dependent. To escape from corrupt cabals and yet preserve a good officer in place, he moved that the tenure of office should be good behavior. Gouverneur Morris beamed with joy. Broom found all his difficulties obviated. "Such a tenure," interposed Sherman, "is neither safe nor admissible; re-election will depend on good behavior." #

Madison, who to the last refused with unabated vigor to intrust the choice of the national executive to the national legislature, and at heart would not have been greatly disinclined to the longest period of service for the executive if " an easy and effectual removal by impeachment could have been settled," ‖ argued from the necessity of keeping the executive, legislative, and judiciary powers independent of each other,

---

\* Gilpin, 1121; Elliot, 323.   ‡ Gilpin, 1123; Elliot, 324.
† Gilpin, 1121; Elliot, 323.   # Gilpin, 1125, 1126; Elliot, 325.
   ‖ Madison's Writings, i, 345; Gilpin, 1127; Elliot, 326.

that the tenure of good behavior for the executive was a less evil than its dependence on the national legislature for re-election.

Mason replied: "An executive during good behavior is only a softer name for an executive for life; the next easy step will be to hereditary monarchy. Should the motion succeed, I may myself live to see such a revolution." "To prevent the introduction of monarchy," rejoined Madison, "is, with me, the real object. Experience proves a tendency in our governments to throw all power into the legislative vortex. The executives of the states are in general little more than ciphers; the legislatures omnipotent. If no effectual check be devised on the encroachments of the latter, a revolution will be inevitable." After explanations by McClurg, four states—New Jersey, Pennsylvania, Delaware, and Virginia, Madison voting with McClurg—expressed their preference for the tenure of good behavior to the tenure of seven years with a perpetual re-eligibility by the national legislature.* Massachusetts was among the six states in the negative, though to King, who "relied on the vigor of the executive as a great security for the public liberties," the tenure of good behavior would have been most agreeable, "provided an independent and effectual forum could be devised for the trial of the executive on an impeachment." †

This discussion brought the convention unanimously ‡ to the opinion that if the executive was to be chosen by the national legislature, he ought not to be re-eligible. Those, therefore, who agreed with Sherman, that the statesman who had proved himself most fit for an office ought not to be excluded by the constitution from holding it, were bound to devise some other acceptable mode of election.

The first thought was an immediate choice by the people. But here Madison pointed out that "the right of suffrage was much more diffusive in the northern states than in the southern; and that the latter would have no influence in the election on the score of the negroes." # To meet this difficulty, King revived Wilson's proposition for the appointment of the ex-

* Gilpin, 1127, 1128, 1129; Elliot, 326, 327.     ‡ Gilpin, 1147; Elliot, 337.
† Gilpin, 1157; Elliot, 342.     # Gilpin, 1148; Elliot, 337.

ecutive by electors chosen by the people expressly for the purpose; * and Madison promptly accepted it as, " on the whole, liable to fewest objections." † So, too, in part, thought the convention, which, on the motion of Ellsworth, decided, by six states to three, that the national executive should be appointed by electors; and, by eight states to two, that the electors should be chosen by the state legislatures. ‡ From confidence in the purity of the electoral body thus established, the re-eligibility of the executive was again affirmed by a vote of eight states against the two Carolinas; # and, in consequence of the re-eligibility, the term of office was, at Ellsworth's motion, reduced by the vote of all the states but Delaware from seven years to six. ‖ So the convention hoped to escape from the danger of a corrupt traffic between the national legislature and candidates for the executive by assembling in one place one grand electoral college, chosen by the legislatures of the several states for the sole purpose of electing that officer.

To this system Caleb Strong of Massachusetts started this grave objection: "A new set of men, like the electors, will make the government too complex; nor will the first characters in the state feel sufficient motives to undertake the office." ᐃ On the previous day Houston of Georgia had directed the thoughts of the convention "to the expense and extreme inconvenience of drawing together men from all the states for the single purpose of electing the chief magistrate." ◊ To him, likewise, it now seemed improbable that capable men would undertake the service. He was afraid to trust to it. Moved by these considerations, but still retaining its conviction of the greater purity of an electoral college, the convention, by seven votes against four, in the weariness of vacillation, returned to the plan of electing the national executive by the national legislature. ‡ But the vote was sure to reopen the question of his re-eligibility.

The convention was now like a pack of hounds in full chase, suddenly losing the trail. It fell into an anarchy of opinion,

---

\* Gilpin, 1147; Elliot, 336.
† Gilpin, 1148; Elliot, 337.
‡ Gilpin, 1150; Elliot, 338.
\# Gilpin, 1150, 1151; Elliot, 338.
‖ Gilpin, 1151, 1152; Elliot, 339.
ᐃ Gilpin, 1189; Elliot, 358.
◊ Gilpin, 1186; Elliot, 357.
‡ Gilpin, 1190; Elliot, 359.

and one crude scheme trod on the heels of another. Williamson, pleading the essential difference of interests between the northern and southern states, particularly relating to the carrying trade, "wished the executive power to be lodged in three men, taken from three districts, into which the states should be divided." * "At some time or other," said he, "we shall have a king; to postpone the event as long as possible, I would render the executive ineligible." †

In the event of the ineligibility of the executive, Martin, forgetting the state of anarchy and faction that would attend a long period of service by an incompetent or unworthy incumbent, proposed that the term of executive service should be eleven years. ‡ "From ten to twelve," said Williamson.# "Fifteen," said Gerry; and King mocked them all by proposing "twenty years, the medium life of princes." ‖ Wilson, seeing no way of introducing a direct election by the people, made the motion △ that the executive should be chosen by electors to be taken from the national legislature by lot.

Ellsworth, on the twenty-fifth, pointed out that to secure a candidate for re-election against an improper dependence on the legislature, the choice should be made by electors.◊ Madison liked best an election of the executive by the qualified part of the people at large. "Local considerations," he said, "must give way to the general interest. As an individual from the southern states, I am willing to make the sacrifice." ⁀

And now came into consideration an element which exercised a constant bias on the discussion to the last. Ellsworth complained that the executive would invariably be taken from one of the larger states. "To cure the disadvantage under which an election by the people would place the smaller states," Williamson proposed that each man should vote for three candidates. ‡ Gouverneur Morris accepted the principle, but desired to limit the choice of the voters to two, of whom at least

---

\* Gilpin, 1189; Elliot, 358.   ‖ Gilpin, 1191; Elliot, 360.
† Gilpin, 1189, 1190; Elliot, 359.   △ Gilpin, 1196; Elliot, 362.
‡ Gilpin, 1191; Elliot, 360.   ◊ Gilpin, 1198; Elliot, 363.
# Gilpin, 1190; Elliot, 359.   ⁀ Gilpin, 1201; Elliot, 365.
⁀ Gilpin, 1204; Elliot, 366.

one should not be of his own state. This Madison approved, believing that the citizens would give their second vote with sincerity to the next object of their choice.* We shall meet the proposition again.

Lastly, Dickinson said: "Insuperable objections lie against an election of the executive by the national legislature, or by the legislatures or executives of the states. I have long leaned toward an election by the people, which I regard as the best and the purest source. Let the people of each state choose its best citizen, and out of the thirteen names thus selected an executive magistrate may be chosen, either by the national legislature or by electors appointed by it." †

From hopelessness of an agreement, Gerry and Butler were willing to refer the resolution relating to the executive to a committee, but Wilson insisted that a general principle must first be fixed by a vote of the house. ‡

On the morning of the next day # Mason recapitulated all the seven different ways that had been proposed of electing the chief magistrate: by the people at large; by the legislatures of the states; by the executives of the states; by electors chosen by the people; by electors chosen by lot; by the legislature on the nomination of three or two candidates by each several state; by the legislature on the nomination of one candidate from each state. After reviewing them all, he concluded that an election by the national legislature, as originally proposed, was the best. At the same time he held it to be the very palladium of civil liberty, that the great officers of state, and particularly the executive, should at fixed periods return to that mass from which they were taken. Led for the moment by this train of thought, the convention by six states, against Pennsylvania, Delaware, and Maryland, with Virginia equally divided, resolved that a national executive be instituted; to consist of a single person; who should be chosen by the national legislature; for the term of seven years; and be ineligible a second time. ‖

Foremost in undiminished disapproval of the choice of the executive by the legislature were Washington, Madison, Wil-

* Gilpin, 1205; Elliot, 367.  ‡ Gilpin, 1207; Elliot, 368.
† Gilpin, 1206; Elliot, 367.  # Ibid.   ‖ Gilpin, 1211; Elliot, 370.
VOL. VI.—23

son, Gouverneur Morris, and Gerry; foremost for the election by that body were Rutledge, Mason, and, in a moderate degree, Strong. During the debate Gouverneur Morris had declared: "Of all possible modes of appointing the executive, an election by the people is the best; an election by the legislature is the worst.* I prefer a short period and re-eligibility, but a different mode of election." † In this he spoke the mind of Pennsylvania; and he refused to accept the decision of that day as final.

On the twenty-fourth of August the report of the committee of detail relating to the executive came before the convention. All agreed that the executive power should be vested in a single person, to be styled: the President of the United States of America; and none questioned that his title might be: His Excellency. ‡ According to the report, he was to be elected by ballot by the legislature for a term of seven years, but might not be elected a second time.#

The strife on the manner of his election revived. Daniel Carroll of Maryland, seconded by Wilson, renewed the motion, that he should be elected by the people; but the house was weary or unprepared to reopen the subject, and at the moment the motion received only the votes of Pennsylvania and Delaware. ‖ Rutledge then moved that the election of the president be made by the legislature in "joint ballot."

The conducting of business, especially of elections, by the two branches of the legislature in joint session was from early days familiar to the states, and was at that time established in every one of them which had prepared a constitution of its own with two branches of the legislature, so that the regulations for that mode of choice were perfectly well understood. New Hampshire had had the experience of both methods; many of its officers were chosen annually by joint ballot, while its representatives to congress were appointed by the concurrent vote of the two houses. Unhappily, throughout this part of the work, the equal vote of the smaller states with the larger

* Gilpin, 1193, 1204; Elliot, 361, 366.
† Gilpin, 1195; Elliot, 362.
‡ Gilpin, 1417; Elliot, 472.
# Gilpin, 1236; Elliot, 380.
‖ Gilpin, 1418; Elliot, 472.

ones in the senate persistently biased the movements of the convention.

In the special interest of the smaller states Sherman objected to a vote of the two houses in joint ballot, because it would deprive the senate of a negative on the more numerous branch. "It is wrong," said Gorham, "to be considering at every turn whom the senate will represent; the public good is the object to be kept in view; delay and confusion will ensue if the two houses vote separately, each having a negative on the choice of the other." Dayton and Brearley, following in the wake of Sherman, opposed a joint ballot, as impairing the power of the smaller states;* but Langdon of New Hampshire, enlightened by experience at home, dwelt on the great difficulties of which the mode of separate votes by the two houses was productive; and, like a good patriot as he was, he approved the joint ballot, "though unfavorable to New Hampshire as a small state." Wilson remarked "that the senate might have an interest in throwing dilatory obstacles in the way, if its separate concurrence should be required." On the same side spoke Madison; and the motion of Rutledge prevailed by seven states, against Connecticut, New Jersey, Maryland, and Georgia.†

These four states, joined by Delaware, then demanded that, on the joint ballot, the vote should be taken by states; the decision turned on New Hampshire; and following the patriotic opinion of Langdon, it joined the five larger states and negatived the proposal. For an election of president, a majority of the votes of the members present was required, New Jersey alone dissenting. ‡ "In case the votes of the two highest should be equal," Read of Delaware, taking a clause from the constitution of his own state, moved that the president of the senate should have an additional vote; but it was disagreed to by a general negative.

At this moment Gouverneur Morris interposed with decisive effect. He set forth the danger of legislative tyranny that would follow from leaving the executive dependent on the legislature for his election; he dwelt once more on the

* Gilpin, 1418; Elliot, 472.     † Gilpin, 1419; Elliot, 473.
‡ Gilpin, 1420; Elliot, 473.

"cabal and corruption " * which would attach to that method of choice. The plan of choosing the president by electors, which he now revived, had made such progress that five states voted with him, among them Pennsylvania and Virginia. A reference of the subject to a committee was lost for the moment by a tie vote, Connecticut being divided.† But opinion ripened so fast that, on the thirty-first of August, the mode of choosing the president, his powers, and the question of his reeligibility, was with other unfinished business referred to a grand committee of one from each state. The Eleven, appointed by ballot, were Gilman, King, Sherman, Brearley, Gouverneur Morris, Dickinson, Carroll, Madison, Williamson, Butler, and Baldwin. ‡

Gouverneur Morris had loudly put forward his wish to make of the senate a thoroughly aristocratic body, and of the president a tenant for life. It agreed with this view to repose the eventual election of the president in the senate. The electoral colleges, in the want of all means of rapid intercommunication, would have rarely cast a majority for one man; and the requisition on the electors to vote each for two men increased the chances that there would be no election, and that one of the candidates at least would be a citizen of a smaller state. He was aware that the outgoing president would be apt to be a candidate for re-election; and desired nothing better than such a junction between the president and senate as would secure a re-election during life.

Sherman hated aristocracy; but he was specially watchful of the equal power of the smaller states, and saw that, on the first ballot of the election, the large states, having many votes, would always bring forward their candidates with superior strength. To gain a chance for electing a president from the small states, they insisted that, in case there should be no election by the colleges, not less than five names should be reported as candidates for the eventual election, and among five names there was a great probability that there would be one from the smaller states. They therefore insisted that the eventual election should be made by the senate; and this was carried by a

* Gilpin, 1420; Elliot, 473. † Gilpin, 1421; Elliot, 474.
‡ Gilpin, 1478; Elliot, 503.

coalition of aristocratic tendencies in Gouverneur Morris and others from the large states with the passion of the small states for disproportionate chances for power.

The committee, having considered the subject in all its bearings, made their report on the fourth day of September.* The term of the presidency was limited to four years; and the election was confided to electors to be appointed in each state as its legislature might direct; and to be equal to the whole number of its senators and representatives in congress; so that the electoral colleges collectively were to be the exact counterpart of the joint convention of the legislature.

The electors of each state were to meet † in their respective states and vote by ballot for two persons, of whom one, at least, should not be an inhabitant of the same state with themselves. A certified list of these votes, under the seal of the electoral college, was to be transmitted to the president of the senate. ‡

" The president of the senate," discharging a purely ministerial office, " shall in that house open all the certificates, and the votes shall be then and there counted. The person having the greatest number of votes shall be the president, if such number be a majority of that of the electors; and if there be more than one who has such a majority and an equal number of votes—a case that would most rarely, perhaps never, occur—then the senate shall # choose by ballot one of them for president; but if no person has a majority, then, from the five highest on the list, 'the senate,'" in which body the smallest state had an equal vote with the largest, "shall choose by ballot the president." " After the choice of the president, the person having the greatest number of votes," whether a majority of them or not, " shall be vice-president "—an officer now for the first time introduced; "but if there should remain two or more who have equal votes, then the senate shall choose from them the vice-president." ‖

Mason, who thought the insulated electoral colleges would hardly ever unite their votes on one man, spoke earnestly:

* Gilpin, 1485–1488; Elliot, 506, 507.   † Gilpin, 1486; Elliot, 507.
‡ Ibid.
# " Immediately," not in original report. It was inserted 6 September. Gilpin, 1509; Elliot, 518, and i., 283, 289.   ‖ Gilpin, 1486, 1487; Elliot, 507.

"The plan is liable to this strong objection, that nineteen times in twenty the president will be chosen by the senate, an improper body for the purpose." To the objection of Charles Pinckney, that electors would be strangers to the several candidates, and unable to decide on their comparative merits, Baldwin answered: "The increasing intercourse among the people of the states will render important characters less and less unknown." * "This subject," said Wilson, "has greatly divided the house, and will divide the people. It is, in truth, the most difficult of all on which we have had to decide. I have never made up an opinion on it entirely to my own satisfaction." The choice by electors "is, on the whole, a valuable improvement on the former plan. It gets rid of cabal and corruption; and continental characters will multiply as we more and more coalesce, so as to enable the electors in every part of the union to know and judge of them. It clears the way for a discussion of the question of the re-eligibility of the president on its own merits, which the former mode of election seemed to forbid. It may, however, be better to refer the eventual appointment to the legislature than to the senate, and to confine it to a smaller number than five of the candidates." †

"I wish to know," asked Randolph, chiming in with Wilson, "why the eventual election is referred to the senate, and not to the legislature? I see no necessity for this, and many objections to it." ‡

On the fifth, Mason, supported by Gerry, attempted to reduce the number of candidates to be voted for from five to three; # but the small states, who saw their best chance of furnishing a president in the larger number, were humored by the convention, and to the last the number of five was not changed.

One great objection of Mason would be removed by depriving the senate of the eventual election. ‖ Wilson proposed the capital amendment, to transfer the eventual election from the senate to the "legislature." ᐃ This change Dickinson approved. But the convention was not yet ripe for the motion,

* Gilpin, 1491; Elliot, 509.
† Gilpin, 1491, 1492; Elliot, 509.
‡ Gilpin, 1492; Elliot, 510.
# Gilpin, 1502; Elliot, 514.
‖ Gilpin, 1498, 1499; Elliot, 513.
ᐃ Gilpin, 1500; Elliot, 513.

all the smaller states voting against it, except New Hampshire, which was divided.

"The mode of appointment as now regulated," said Mason at the close of the day, "is utterly inadmissible. I should prefer the government of Prussia to one which will put all power into the hands of seven or eight men"—a majority of a quorum of the senate—"and fix an aristocracy worse than absolute monarchy." *

On the sixth, Gerry, supported by King and Williamson, proposed that the eventual election should be made by the legislature. Sherman, sedulously supporting the chances of the small states, remarked, that if the legislature, instead of the senate, were to have the eventual appointment of the president, it ought to vote by states.†

Wilson himself, on the same morning, spoke with singular energy, disapproving alike the eventual choice of the president by the equal vote of the states and the tendency to clothe the senate with special powers: "I have weighed carefully the report of the committee for remodelling the constitution of the executive; and, on combining it with other parts of the plan, I am obliged to consider the whole as having a tendency to aristocracy, as throwing a dangerous power into the hands of the senate. They will have, in fact, the appointment of the president, and, through his dependence on them, the virtual appointment to offices—among others, the officers of the judiciary department; they are to make treaties; and they are to try all impeachments. The legislative, executive, and judiciary powers are all blended in one branch of the government. The power of making treaties involves the case of subsidies; and here, as an additional evil, foreign influence is to be dreaded. According to the plan as it now stands, the president will not be the man of the people, as he ought to be, but the minion of the senate. He cannot even appoint a tide-waiter without it. I have always thought the senate too numerous a body for making appointments to office. With all their powers, and the president in their interest, they will depress the other branch of the legislature, and aggrandize themselves in proportion. The new mode of appointing the

* Gilpin, 1503; Elliot, 515.   † Gilpin, 1504; Elliot, 516.

president by electors is a valuable improvement; but I can never agree to purchase it at the price of the ensuing parts of the report." *

" The mutual connection of the president and senate," said Hamilton, " will perpetuate the one and aggrandize both. I see no better remedy than to let the highest number of ballots, whether a majority or not, appoint the president." † The same motion had the day before been offered by Mason, ‡ but the convention, especially the smaller states, inflexibly required a majority.

Williamson, to avoid favoring aristocracy in the senate, and yet to secure the assent of the small states, wished to transfer the eventual choice to the legislature, voting by states. To the legislature Sherman preferred the house of representatives, the members from each state having one vote; # and the convention so decided by ten states out of eleven.

Nor would the convention intrust the counting of the votes to the senate alone. By amendments adopted on the sixth,‖ it was thus finally established: "The president of the senate shall, in the presence of the senate and house of representatives, open all the certificates, and the votes shall then be counted." In every stage of the proceeding the convention suffered no chance for the failure of an election, and had specially guarded against the failure of an election by the negative of one house upon the other, leaving the rules for the conduct of the electoral colleges, or of the two houses when in presence of each other, to be supplied by the familiar experience of the states. On one point, and on one point only, the several states of that day differed in their manner of counting votes. In Virginia the ballot of the two houses was taken in each house respectively, and the boxes examined jointly by a committee of each house. In Massachusetts the whole work was done by the senators and representatives assembled in one room. On this point, therefore, and on this point only, there was need of a special regulation; and, accordingly, the constitution enjoined the counting of the votes in the presence of

\* Gilpin, 1504, 1505; Elliot, 516.  # Gilpin, 1510; Elliot, 519.
† Gilpin, 1507; Elliot, 517.   ‖ Gilpin, 1509, 1513; Elliot, 518, 520.
‡ Gilpin, 1498, 1499; Elliot, 513.

the senate and house of representatives after the manner of Massachusetts.*

The language of this clause of the constitution is a concise, clear, and imperative command: "The votes shall then be counted." The convention is left with no one but itself to interpret its duties and prescribe its rules of action. No power whatever over the counting of the votes is devolved on the house of representatives or on the senate; whatever is granted is granted to the two houses "in the presence of" each other; representing the states and the people according to the compromise adopted for the electoral colleges.

And now the whole line of march to the mode of the election of the president can be surveyed. The convention at first reluctantly conferred that office on the national legislature; and to prevent the possibility of failure by a negative of one house on the other, to the legislature voting in joint ballot. To escape from danger of cabal and corruption, it next transferred full and final power of choice to an electoral college

---

* Constitution of VIRGINIA, of 1776. B. P. Poore's edition, 1910, 1911. A governor, or chief magistrate, shall be chosen annually by joint ballot of both houses (to be taken in each house respectively) deposited in the conference room; the boxes examined jointly by a committee of each house, and the numbers severally reported to them that the appointments may be entered (which shall be the mode of taking the joint ballot of both houses, in all cases). . . .

A privy council, or council of state, consisting of eight members, shall be chosen by joint ballot of both houses of assembly.

The delegates for Virginia to the continental congress shall be chosen annually, or superseded in the mean time, by joint ballot of both houses of assembly.

The two houses of assembly shall, by joint ballot, appoint judges of the supreme court of appeals, and general court, judges in chancery, judges of admiralty, secretary, and the attorney-general, to be commissioned by the governor, and continue in office during good behavior.

Constitution of MASSACHUSETTS, of 1780. B. P. Poore's edition, 967, 969. Ch. II., Art. II. Nine councillors shall be annually chosen from among the persons returned for councillors and senators, on the last Wednesday in May, by the joint ballot of the senators and representatives assembled in one room.

Ch. II., Art. I. The secretary, treasurer, and receiver-general, and the commissary-general, notaries public, and naval officers, shall be chosen annually, by joint ballot of the senators and representatives, in one room.

Ch. IV. The delegates of this commonwealth to the congress of the United States shall, some time in the month of June, annually, be elected by the joint ballot of the senate and house of representatives assembled together in one room.

that should be the exact counterpart of the joint convention of the two houses in the representation of the states as units, as well as the population of the states, and should meet at the seat of government. Then, fearing that so large a number of men would not travel to the seat of government for that single purpose, or might be hindered on the way, they most reluctantly went back to the choice of the president by the two houses in joint convention. At this moment the thought arose that the electors might cast their votes in their own several states, and transmit the certificates of their ballots to the seat of government. Accordingly, the work of electing a president was divided; the convention removed the act of voting from the joint session of the two houses to electoral colleges in the several states, the act of voting to be followed by the transmission of authenticated certificates of the votes to a branch of the general legislature at the seat of government; and then it restored to the two houses in presence of each other the same office of counting the collected certificates which they would have performed had the choice remained with the two houses of the legislature. Should no one have a majority, the eventual election of the president, to satisfy the rising jealousy of the prerogatives of the senate, was assigned to the house of representatives, and, to please the small states, to the representatives voting by states. And the house of representatives was in the clearest language ordered "immediately" to choose by ballot one of two, when their vote was equal, one of five where no person had a majority. In this way a collision between the two houses, by a negative vote of one on the other, was completely guarded against in every stage of the procedure.*

\* When, thirteen years later, this clause came up for consideration, Madison and Baldwin, two surviving members of the grand committee to whom the federal convention had referred everything relating to the choice of the president, left on record their interpretation of the clause. For the opinion of Madison, see Madison to Jefferson, 4 April 1800, in writings of Madison, ii., 158, where the name "Nicholson's" is erroneously printed for "Nicholas's," as appears from a comparison which has been made of the printed letter with the original. The opinion of Baldwin is found in "Counting Electoral Votes," page 19. Baldwin gives his vote with Langdon and Pinckney, both of whom had been members of the federal convention, for the right of the joint convention to count the votes. By the kindness of Miss Sarah Nicholas Randolph, granddaughter of Governor Wilson Cary Nicholas of Virginia, and great-granddaughter of Thomas Jefferson, I have been al-

The almost certain election of the vice-president was secured by declaring the candidate having the most votes to be duly elected. In the extremely improbable case, that two persons should lead all the candidates with an exactly equal number of votes, the election was to devolve on the senate.

"Such an officer as vice-president," said Williamson on the seventh, "is not wanted." * To make an excuse for his existence, the convention decreed that he should be president of the senate. "That," said Mason, "is an encroachment on the senate's rights; and, moreover, it mixes too much the legislative and the executive." It was seen that the vice-president brings to the chair of the senate the dignity of one of the two highest officers in the land chosen by the whole country; and yet that he can have no real influence in a body upon which he is imposed by an extraneous vote.

That the vice-president should, in the event of a vacancy, act as president, prevents the need of a new election before the end of the regular term; but an immediate appeal to the people might give a later and truer expression of its wishes.

While the method to be adopted for the election of the president still engaged the untiring efforts of the convention, it proceeded in the ascertainment of his powers. His style was

lowed to take from the holograph of Jefferson a copy of his paper on this subject, written by him for the use of W. C. Nicholas when senator from Virginia in congress in 1800.

The question as voted upon in congress in 1800 was decided not by any bearing on the selection of Jefferson or Burr for the presidency, for the party opposed to Jefferson had a majority in each branch, but on the unwillingness of the senate to give to the house of representatives superior weight in the decision of elections. Jefferson, iv., 322. The vice-president was *never* charged with the power to count the votes. The person who counted the first votes for president and vice-president was no vice-president, but a senator elected by the senate as its presiding officer for that act under a special authority conferred by the constitution for that one occasion when the constitution was to be set in motion.

On any pretence of a right in the vice-president to count the votes, compare the words spoken in the senate by Senator Conkling, 23 and 24 January 1877, and Senator Edmunds, 20 November 1877. The laws of historical criticism require the historian to study the words of the state constitutions from which the article in the United States constitution is taken, and the practice of the state legislatures of that day under the original articles in the state constitutions; and these must decide on the right interpretation of the language employed in the constitution of the United States. * Gilpin, 1517; Elliot, 522.

declared to be " the President of the United States of America;" the clause that his title should be "His Excellency" was still suffered to linger in the draft. He was to be the minister to carry out the will of the legislature, and see that the laws are executed. It was made his duty to give information of the state of the union; and to recommend necessary and expedient measures. He could not prorogue the two branches of the legislature nor either of them; nor appeal to the people by dissolving them. They alone had the power to adjourn; but on extraordinary occasions to him belonged the prerogative to convene them, or to convene the senate alone.

Wilson was most apprehensive that the legislature, by swallowing up all the other powers, would lead to a dissolution of the government, no adequate self-defensive power having been granted either to the executive or judicial department.* To strengthen the president and raise a strong barrier against rash legislation, Gouverneur Morris would have granted the president a qualified veto on the repeal of a law, an absolute veto on every act of legislation.†

In June the convention had agreed that the veto of the president on an act of congress could be overruled by two thirds of each house; on the fifteenth of August, at the instance of Williamson, it was agreed that the veto of the president could be overruled only by three fourths of each branch of congress, and on the next day the same rule was applied to every order, resolution, or vote to which the concurrence of the two houses might be necessary, except it were a question of adjournment.‡

Sherman, on the twenty-fifth of August, had proposed that pardons should require the consent of the senate; but no state except his own was willing thus to restrict the clemency of the president.#

All agreed that he should be commander-in-chief of the army and the navy; but, on the twenty-seventh of August, at Sherman's instance, he was to command the militia only when it should be called into the actual service of the United States.‖

The men who made the constitution had taken to heart the

---

\* Gilpin, 1336, 1337; Elliot, 430.
† Gilpin, 1334; Elliot, 429.
‡ Gilpin, 1337, 1338; Elliot, 431.

\# Gilpin, 1433; Elliot, 480.
‖ Gilpin, 1434; Elliot, 480.

lesson that the three great powers—legislative, judicial, and executive—should be lodged in different hands. "Executing the laws and appointing officers not appertaining to and appointed by the legislature," Wilson had said, so early as the first of June, "are strictly executive powers." * Yet it seemed needful to keep watch over the president, and Gerry † and Sherman had favored the appointment of an executive council.‡ Charles Pinckney wished the president to consult the heads of the principal departments.# "A superfluous proposition," said Hamilton, "for the president will at any rate have that right." Mercer, on the fourteenth of August, suggested "a council composed of members of both houses of the legislature to stand between the aristocracy and the executive." ‖ But the thought did not take root.

The convention was anxious to reconcile a discreet watchfulness over the executive with his independence. In August Ellsworth had recommended a council to be composed of the president of the senate, the chief justice, and the ministers, or secretaries as Gouverneur Morris named them, of the foreign, the interior, war, treasury, and navy departments, " to advise, but not conclude the president." ᐃ Gerry pronounced the nomination of the chief justice particularly exceptionable. ◊ Dickinson urged that the great appointments of the heads of departments should be made by the legislature, in which case they might properly be consulted by the executive. The elaborate plan of a council of state which Gouverneur Morris proposed on the twentieth differed from that of Ellsworth mainly in its exclusion of the president of the senate.

The persistent convention next consulted its committee of detail, which on the twenty-second reported: that "the privy council of the president of the United States shall consist of the president of the senate, the speaker of the house of representatives, the chief justice of the supreme court, and the principal officer in each of five departments as they shall from time to time be established; their duty shall be to advise him in

* Gilpin, 763; Elliot, 141.
† Ibid.
‡ Gilpin, 782; Elliot, 150.
# Gilpin, 811; Elliot, 165.
‖ Gilpin, 1318; Elliot, 421.
ᐃ Gilpin, 1358, 1359; Elliot, 442.
◊ Gilpin, 1359; Elliot, 442.

matters which he shall lay before them; but their advice shall not conclude him, nor affect his responsibility." * The report did not satisfy the convention, which, still hopeful and persevering, referred the subject to the grand committee of the eleven states.

The report of the committee, made on the fourth of September, did no more than permit the executive to "require the opinion in writing of the principal officer in each of the executive departments, upon any subject relating to the duties of his office." † "In rejecting a council to the president," such were the final words of Mason, "we are about to try an experiment on which the most despotic government has never ventured; the Grand Seignior himself has his Divan;" and he proposed an executive council to be appointed by the legislature or by the senate, and to consist of two members from the eastern, two from the middle, and two from the southern states; with a rotation and duration of office similar to those of the senate. ‡ He was seconded by Franklin, who "thought a council would be a check on a bad president, a relief to a good one." # Wilson "approved of a council, in preference to making the senate a party to appointments." So did Dickinson and Madison; but the motion gained only three states; ‖ and then by a unanimous vote the president was authorized to take written opinions of the heads of departments,△ who thus became his constitutional advisers.

The failure to establish an efficient council led the convention most reluctantly to vest the senate with some control over acts of the executive. On the seventh it was agreed "that the president shall have the power to make treaties by and with the advice and consent of the senate." ◊ "And of the house of representatives," Wilson would have added; saying: "As treaties are to have the operation of laws, they ought to have the sanction of laws." But Sherman represented that the necessity of secrecy forbade a reference to both houses, and every state assented except Pennsylvania. ‡

\* Gilpin, 1398, 1399; Elliot, 462.
† Gilpin, 1488; Elliot, 507.
‡ Gilpin, 1523; Elliot, 525.
# Ibid.
‖ Gilpin, 1524; Elliot, 526.
△ Ibid.
◊ Gilpin, 1519, Elliot, 523.
‡ Gilpin, 1519; Elliot, 523.

It has already been related that to diminish the temptation to war, the power to declare it was confided to the legislature. In treaties of peace, Madison, fearing in a president a passion for continuing war, proposed to dispense with his concurrence. "The means of carrying on the war," said Gorham, "will not be in the hands of the president, but of the legislature." "No peace," insisted Gouverneur Morris, "ought to be made without the concurrence of the president, who is the general guardian of the nation." And Maryland, South Carolina, and Georgia alone voted for the amendment.*

On the seventh, the advice and consent of the senate was, by a unanimous vote, required for the appointment of ambassadors, other public ministers, consuls, and judges of the supreme court;† and for all other officers of the United States by nine states against Pennsylvania and South Carolina. ‡ But eight days later the legislature was authorized to vest the appointment of inferior officers in the president alone, in the courts of law, or in the heads of departments.#

All agreed in giving the president power to fill up, temporarily, vacancies that might happen during the recess of the senate. ‖

Had the consent of the senate been made necessary to displace as well as to appoint, the executive would have suffered degradation; and the relative importance of the house of representatives a grave diminution. To change the tenure of office from the good opinion of the president, who is the employer and needs efficient agents in executing the laws, to the favor of the senate, which has no executive powers, would create a new fealty alien to the duties of an officer of the United States.

"The three distinct powers, legislative, judicial, and executive," said Ellsworth, as senator, in 1789, explaining the constitution which he had done so much to frame, "should be placed in different hands. *He shall take care that the laws be faithfully executed*, are sweeping words. The officers should be attentive to the president, to whom the senate is not a coun-

---

* Gilpin, 1521, 1522; Elliot, 524, 525.    # Gilpin, 1588, 1589; Elliot, 550.
† Gilpin, 1520; Elliot, 523, 524.    ‖ Gilpin, 1520; Elliot, 524.
‡ Gilpin, 1520; Elliot, 524.

cil. To turn a man out of office is an exercise neither of legislative nor of judicial power. The advice of the senate does not make the appointment; the president appoints: there are certain restrictions in certain cases, but the restriction is as to the appointment and not as to the removal." *

One question on the qualifications of the president was among the last to be decided. On the twenty-second of August the committee of detail, fixing the requisite age of the president at thirty-five, on their own motion and for the first time required that the president should be a citizen of the United States, and should have been an inhabitant of them for twenty-one years.† The idea then arose that no number of years could properly prepare a foreigner for the office of president; but as men of other lands had spilled their blood in the cause of the United States, and had assisted at every stage of the formation of their institutions, the committee of states who were charged with all unfinished business proposed, on the fourth of September, that "no person except a natural-born citizen, or a citizen of the United States at the time of the adoption of this constitution, should be eligible to the office of president," and for the foreign-born proposed a reduction of the requisite years of residence to fourteen. On the seventh of September the modification, with the restriction as to the age of the president, was unanimously adopted.

No majorities of the legislature could force a president to retire before the end of his term; but he might be impeached by the house of representatives for treason, bribery, or other high crimes and misdemeanors. The tribunal for his arraignment was at first the supreme court of the United States; but they would be few in number; the president, after condemnation, might be further amenable to them; and besides, they would be of his appointment. Hamilton had suggested a forum composed of the chief justice of each state. ‡ Contrary to the opinion of Madison, the English precedent was followed, and the senate was made the court to try all officers liable to impeachment; and, on conviction by a two thirds vote, to remove them. As the vice-president, on the president's removal,

---
* MS. report of Ellsworth's speech by William Paterson.
† Gilpin, 1398; Elliot, 462.    ‡ Gilpin, 892, 1158; Elliot, 205, 342.

would succeed to his place, the chief justice was directed to preside on the trial of the president.

At so late a day as the fourteenth of September, Rutledge and Gouverneur Morris moved that persons impeached be suspended from their offices until they be tried and acquitted; but Madison defeated the proposition by pointing out that this intermediate suspension would put it in the power of one branch only to vote a temporary removal of the existing magistrate.*

Judgment in cases of impeachment could extend only to removal from office and disqualification; but the party remained liable to indictment, trial, and punishment, according to law. The trial of all crimes, except in cases of impeachment, could be only by jury.

* Gilpin, 1572; Elliot, 542.

## CHAPTER X.

### THE FEDERAL JUDICIARY.

### AUGUST AND SEPTEMBER 1787.

THE resolution on the federal judiciary which went from the convention to the committee of detail purposely described the extent of its jurisdiction in vague and general terms. The very able lawyers on that committee, Rutledge, Wilson, Randolph, and Ellsworth, proceeding with equal boldness and precision, shrinking from aggressions on the rights of the states and yet entertaining efficient and comprehensive designs, brought in a report, which caused little diversity of opinion, and was held to need no essential amendment. But on one point they kept silence. A deeply-seated dread of danger from hasty legislation pervaded the mind of the convention; and Mason, Madison, and others persistently desired to vest in the supreme court a revisionary power over the acts of congress, with an independent negative, or a negative in conjunction with the executive. Though the measure had been repeatedly brought forward and as often put aside, Madison, on the fifteenth of August, proposed once more that "Every bill which shall have passed the two houses shall, before it becomes a law, be severally presented to the president of the United States, and to the judges of the supreme court, for the revision of each;"* the veto of the judges not to be overthrown by less than two thirds, nor, if the president joined them, by less than three fourths of each house. He was seconded by Wilson.

Charles Pinckney opposed the interference of the judges in legislation, because it would involve them in the conflict of

* Gilpin, 1332; Elliot, 428.

parties and tinge their opinions before their action in court. "The judiciary," said John Francis Mercer of Maryland, "ought to be separate from the legislative and independent of it. I disapprove the doctrine that the judges should, as expositors of the constitution, have authority to declare a law void. Laws ought to be well and cautiously made, and then to be uncontrollable." * To the regret of Gouverneur Morris, the motion of Madison was supported only by Maryland, Delaware, and Virginia. Dickinson was strongly impressed with the objection to the power of the judges to set aside the law. He thought no such power ought to exist, but was at a loss for a substitute. "The justiciary of Aragon," he observed, "became by degrees the law-giver." †

On the morning of the twentieth Charles Pinckney submitted numerous propositions; among them was one that "Each branch of the legislature, as well as the supreme executive, shall have authority to require the opinions of the supreme judicial court upon important questions of law, and upon solemn occasions." ‡ This article, as well as the rest, was referred to the committee of detail, without debate or consideration by the house, and was never again heard of.

On the twenty-seventh the article on the judiciary reported by the committee of detail was taken up; and it was agreed that "the judicial power of the United States shall be vested in one supreme court, and such inferior courts as shall, when necessary, from time to time, be constituted by the legislature of the United States." # "The judges of the supreme court, and of the inferior courts, shall hold their offices during good behavior. They shall, at stated times, receive for their services a compensation which shall not be diminished during their continuance in office." ‖ Judges of inferior courts were clothed with the same independence of the two other branches of the government as the judges of the supreme court.

Dickinson thought that the tenure of office was made too absolute; and, following the example of Great Britain and Massachusetts, he desired that the judges should be removable

---

* Gilpin, 1333; Elliot, 429.  # Gilpin, 1435; Elliot, 481.
† Gilpin, 1334; Elliot, 429.  ‖ Gilpin, 1437; Elliot, 482.
‡ Gilpin, 1365; Elliot, 445; i., 249.

by the executive on application of the senate and the house of representatives.* "If the supreme court," said Rutledge, "is to judge between the United States and particular states, this alone is an insuperable objection to the motion." The clause gained no vote but that of Connecticut, Massachusetts being absent. In England the highest judicial officer is liable to change with every change of administration, and every one may be removed on the request of a majority in each house of parliament; every judge of the United States, from the highest to the lowest, is an officer for life, unless on impeachment he should be convicted by the vote of two thirds of the senate.

The judicial power was by a motion of Johnson extended to cases in law and equity. He further proposed to extend it "to all cases arising under the constitution;" and the motion was agreed to without dissent, because in the opinion of the convention the jurisdiction given was constructively limited to cases of a judiciary nature.†

In this way Madison's scheme of restraining unconstitutional legislation of the states by reserving to the legislature of the union a veto on every act of state legislation was finally abandoned; and the power of revising and reversing a clause of a state law that conflicted with the federal constitution was confided exclusively to the federal judiciary, but only when a case should be properly brought before the court. The decision of the court in all cases within its jurisdiction is final between the parties to a suit, and must be carried into effect by the proper officers; but, as an interpretation of the constitution, it does not bind the president or the legislature of the United States. Under the same qualification the constitution gives to the judges the power to compare any act of congress with the constitution. But the supreme bench can set aside in an act of congress or of a state only that which is at variance with the constitution; if it be merely one clause, or even but one word, they can overrule that word or that clause, and no more. The whole law can never be set aside unless every part of it is tainted with unconstitutionality. ‡

Rutledge next observed that the jurisdiction of the court

---

* Gilpin, 1436; Elliot, 481.   † Gilpin, 1438, 1439; Elliot, 483.
‡ Curtis in Howard, xix., 628.

should extend to treaties made, or to be made, under the authority of the United States; and this proposal was readily adopted.*

The proposition that the courts should conduct the trial of impeachments was put aside, and that duty was afterward assigned to the senate. Two clauses in the report of the committee of detail, which, after a precedent in the confederacy, confided to the senate the settlement of all controversies between two or more states respecting jurisdiction or territory, and all controversies concerning grants of the same lands by two or more states, were in the course of the discussion removed from the senate and made over to the federal courts.

In constructing the judiciary, extreme care was taken to keep out of the United States courts all questions which related to matters that began and ended within a separate commonwealth. This intention is stamped alike on the federal proposals of Virginia, of New Jersey, and of Connecticut; it was carefully respected in those clauses which limit the action of the individual states.

The original jurisdiction of the supreme court embraces only cases affecting ambassadors, other public ministers and consuls. Cases in which a state should be a party were added for the single purpose of authorizing a state as plaintiff to seek justice in a federal court; it was as little intended to permit individuals to bring a state there as defendant as to arraign an ambassador. The appellate power included cases of admiralty and maritime jurisdiction. In these three classes the jurisdiction of the court, original in two of them, appellate in the third, is in imperative language extended "to all cases." But as " to controversies to which the United States shall be a party; to controversies between two or more states; between a state and citizens of another state; between citizens of different states; between citizens of the same state claiming lands under grants of different states, and between a state or the citizens thereof and foreign states, citizens or subjects," the judicial power is limited. The section implies that only a part of the controversies in each of the enumerated classes may come under the jurisdiction of the federal courts; and it was left to

* Gilpin, 1439; Elliot, 483.

the federal legislature to make the discrimination which in its judgment public policy might dictate.* Here congress, and congress alone, selects the controversies to which the appellate judicial power may extend, and at its own judgment limits the right of appeal. The convention purposely made it the duty of congress to watch over the development of the system, and restrict accordingly the appellate jurisdiction. By reserving to the tribunals of the states jurisdiction over cases that may properly belong to them, it may rescue the federal court from the danger of losing its efficiency beneath larger masses of business than it can dispose of.

The method of choosing the federal judiciary was settled without strife. The motion for its appointment by the executive, with the advice and consent of the senate, when first proposed, gained an equal vote; and on the seventh of September was agreed to without a division.†

The supreme court was to be the "bulwark of a limited constitution against legislative encroachments." ‡ A bench of a few, selected with care by the president and senate from the nation, seemed a safer tribunal than a multitudinous assembly elected for a short period under the sway of passing currents of thought, or the intrepid fixedness of an uncompromising party. There always remains danger of erroneous judgments, arising from mistakes, imperfect investigation, the bias of previous connections, the seductions of ambition, or the instigations of surrounding opinions; and a court from which there is no appeal is apt to forget circumspection in its sense of security. The passage of a judge from the bar to the bench does not necessarily divest him of prejudices; nor chill his relations to the particular political party to which he may owe his advancement; nor blot out of his memory the great interests which he may have professionally piloted through doubtful straits; nor quiet the ambition which he is not required to renounce, even though his appointment is for life; nor cure predilections which sometimes have their seat in his own inmost nature.

But the constitution retains the means of protecting itself against the errors of partial or interested judgments. In the

---

\* Story in Curtis, iii., 569; Ellsworth in Curtis, i., 243.
† Gilpin, 1520; Elliot, 524. ‡ Federalist, lxxviii.

first place, the force of a judicial opinion of the supreme court, in so far as it is irreversible, reaches only the particular case in dispute; and to this society submits, in order to escape from anarchy in the daily routine of business. To the decision on an underlying question of constitutional law no such finality attaches. To endure, it must be right. If it is right, it will approve itself to the universal sense of the impartial. A judge who can justly lay claim to integrity will never lay claim to infallibility; but with indefatigable research will add, retract, and correct whenever more mature consideration shows the need of it.* The court is itself inferior and subordinate to the constitution; it has only a delegated authority, and every opinion contrary to the tenor of its commission is void, except as settling the case on trial. The prior act of the superior must be preferred to the subsequent act of an inferior; otherwise it might transform the limited into an unlimited constitution. When laws clash, the latest law is rightly held to express the corrected will of the legislature; but the constitution is the fundamental code, the law of laws; and where there is a conflict between the constitution and a decision of the court, the original permanent act of the superior outweighs the later act of the inferior, and retains its own supreme energy unaltered and unalterable except in the manner prescribed by the constitution itself. To say that a court, having discovered an error, should yet cling to it because it has once been delivered as its opinion, is to invest caprice with inviolability and make a wrong judgment of a servant outweigh the constitution to which he has sworn obedience. An act of the legislature at variance with the constitution is pronounced void; an opinion of the supreme court at variance with the constitution is equally so.

Next to the court itself, the men who framed the constitution relied upon the power and the readiness of congress to punish through impeachment the substitution of the personal will of the judge for the law.

A third influence may rise up "as the rightful interpreter of this great charter" of American rights and American power in "the good sense" † of the land, wiser than the judges alone,

---

* Wilson's Works, i., 29.   † Cooley's Constitutional Law, 224; Curtis, iv., 390.

because it includes within itself the wisdom of the judges themselves; and this may lead either to the better instruction of the court, or to an amendment of the constitution by the collective mind of the country.

The consolidation of the union was to be made visible to the nation and the world by the establishment of a seat of government for the United States under their exclusive jurisdiction; and like authority was to be exercised over all places purchased for forts, dock-yards, and other needful buildings.* It was not doubted that the government of the union should defend each state against foreign enemies and concurrently against domestic violence; and should guarantee to every one of the states the form of a republic.†

Sherman hesitated about granting power to establish uniform laws on the subject of bankruptcies, lest they might be made punishable even with death. "This," said Gouverneur Morris, "is an extensive and delicate subject. I see no danger of abuse of the power by the legislature of the United States." ‡ On the question the clause was agreed to, Connecticut alone being in the negative.

So soon as it was agreed that the states should have an equal representation in the senate, the small states ceased to be jealous of its influence on money bills; finally, on the eighth of September, it was settled that, while all bills for raising revenue should originate in the house of representatives, the senate might propose or concur with amendments as on other bills.#

On the same day, just before the adjournment, Williamson strove to increase the number of the first house of representatives; and was seconded by Madison. Hamilton spoke with earnestness and anxiety for the motion. "I am," said he, "a friend to a vigorous government; at the same time I hold it essential that the popular branch of the government should rest on a broad foundation. The house of representatives is on so narrow a scale as to warrant a jealousy in the people for their

* Gilpin, 740, 1218, 1295, 1612; Elliot, 130, 374, 409, 561.
† Gilpin, 734, 801, 1141, 1241,1621; Elliot, 128, 190, 333, 381, 564.
‡ Gilpin, 1481; Elliot, 504.
# Gilpin, 1494, 1530, 1531; Elliot, 510, 529; Elliot, i., 285, 294, **295.**

liberties. The connection between the president and the senate will tend to perpetuate him by corrupt influence; on this account a numerous representation in the other branch of the legislature should be established." The motion was lost by one majority; Pennsylvania and the four states nearest her on the south being outvoted by New Jersey and the New England states at one extreme, and South Carolina and Georgia at the other.*

It remained to mark out the way in which the new constitution should be ratified. The convention had shown a disinclination to ask for it the approbation of congress. Hamilton saw in the omission an indecorum, and made the rash motion that congress, if they should agree to the constitution, should transmit it for ratification to the legislatures of the several states. Gerry seconded him.† Wilson strongly disapproved "the suspending the plan of the convention on the approbation of congress." He declared it worse than folly to rely on the concurrence of the Rhode Island members of congress. Maryland had voted, on the floor of the convention, for requiring the unanimous assent of the thirteen states to the change in the federal system; for a long time New York had not been represented; deputies from other states had spoken against the plan. "Can it then be safe to make the assent of congress necessary? We are ourselves, at the close, throwing insuperable obstacles in the way of its success." ‡ Clymer thought the proposed mode would fetter and embarrass congress; and King and Rutledge concurring with him, Hamilton's motion was supported only by Connecticut.# It was then voted, in the words of the report of the committee of detail: "This constitution shall be laid before the United States in congress assembled; and it is the opinion of this convention that it should be afterward submitted to a convention chosen in each state, under the recommendation of its legislature, in order to receive the ratification of such convention." In substance this method was never changed; in form it was removed from the constitution and imbodied in a directory resolution. ‖

* Gilpin, 1533; Elliot, 530.     † Gilpin, 1539; Elliot, 533.
‡ Gilpin, 1540; Elliot, 534.     # Gilpin, 1541; Elliot, 534.
‖ Art. xxii. of draft of the constitution submitted to the committee of revision, September 10th. Gilpin, 1570; Elliot, 541.

Randolph now began to speak of the constitution as a plan which would end in tyranny; and proposed that the state conventions, on receiving it, should have power to adopt, reject, or amend it; after which another general convention should meet with full power to adopt or reject the proposed alterations, and to establish finally the government. Franklin seconded the motion.* Out of respect to its authors, the proposition was allowed to remain on the table; but by a unanimous vote it was ordered that the constitution should be established on its ratification by the conventions of nine states.† Finally, a committee of five was appointed to revise its style and the arrangement of its articles.

* Gilpin, 1542; Elliot, 535.     † Gilpin, 1571; Elliot, 541.

## CHAPTER XI.

#### THE LAST DAYS OF THE CONVENTION.

##### SEPTEMBER 12 TO SEPTEMBER 17, 1787.

THE committee to whom the constitution was referred for the arrangement of its articles and the revision of its style were Johnson, Hamilton, Gouverneur Morris, Madison, and King. The final draft of the instrument was written by Gouverneur Morris,* who knew how to reject redundant and equivocal expressions, and to use language with clearness and vigor; but the convention itself had given so minute, long-continued, and oft-renewed attention to every phrase in every section, that there scarcely remained room for improvement except in the distribution of its parts.

Its first words are: "We the people of the United States, in order to form a more perfect union, to establish justice, ensure domestic tranquillity, provide for the common defence, promote the general welfare, and secure the blessings of liberty to ourselves and our posterity, do ordain and establish this constitution for the United States of America." Here is no transient compact between parties: it is the institution of government by an act of the highest sovereignty; the decree of many who are yet one; their law of laws, inviolably supreme, and not to be changed except in the way which their forecast has provided.

The names of the thirteen states, so carefully enumerated in the declaration of independence and in the treaty of peace, were omitted, because the constitution was to go into effect on its acceptance by nine of them, and the states by which it would

* G. Morris to T. Pickering, 22 December 1814, in Life by Sparks, iii., 323.

be ratified could not be foreknown. The deputies in the convention, representing but eleven states, did not pretend to be "the people;" and could not institute a general government in its name. The instrument which they framed was like the report of a bill beginning with the words "it is enacted," though the binding enactment awaits the will of the legislature; or like a deed drawn up by an attorney for several parties, and awaiting its execution by the principals themselves. Only by its acceptance could the words "we the people of the United States" become words of truth and power.

The phrase "general welfare," * adopted from the articles of confederation, though seemingly vague, was employed in a rigidly restrictive sense to signify "the concerns of the union at large, not the particular policy of any state." † The word "national" was excluded from the constitution, because it might seem to present the idea of the union of the people without at the same time bringing into view that the one republic was formed out of many states. Toward foreign powers the country presented itself as one nation.

The arrangement of the articles and sections is faultless; the style of the whole is nearly so. The branches of the legislature are definitively named senate and house of representatives, the senate, at last, having precedence; the two together take the historic name of congress.

The veto of the president could still be overruled only by three fourths of each branch of congress; the majority of the convention, fearing lest so large a requisition would impose too great a difficulty in repealing bad laws, ‡ at this last moment substituted the vote of two thirds.

Williamson pointed out the necessity of providing for juries in civil cases. "It is not possible," said Gorham, "to discriminate equity cases from those in which juries would be proper; and the matter may safely be trusted to the representatives of the people." # Gerry urged the necessity of juries as a safeguard against corrupt judges. "A general principle laid down on this and some other points would be sufficient,"

---

* Gilpin, 1543; Elliot, 558.
† Washington to William Gordon, 8 July 1783.
‡ Gilpin, 1563; Elliot, 537.   # Gilpin, 1565; Elliot, 538.

said Mason, and he joined with Gerry in moving for a bill of rights.

The declaration of American independence, by the truths which it announced, called forth sympathy in all parts of the world. Could the constitution of the United States have been accompanied by a like solemn declaration of the principles on which it rested, the states would have been held together by the holiest and strongest bonds.* But the motion was lost by the unanimous vote of ten states, Massachusetts being absent, and Rhode Island and New York not represented.

The style of the executive, as silently carried forward from the committee of detail, was still "his Excellency;" this vanished in the committee of revision, so that he might be known only as the president of the United States.

Following a precedent of the first congress, Mason, on the thirteenth, seconded by Johnson, moved for a committee to report articles of association for encouraging economy, frugality, and American manufactures.† It was adopted without debate and without opposition. The proposal was referred to Mason, Franklin, Dickinson, Johnson, and William Livingston; but they made no report.

From the work of the committee of detail the word "servitude" survived as applied to the engagement to labor for a term of years; on the motion of Randolph the word "service"

---

* Here manuscripts and printed texts differ in an astonishing manner.
*Text of Madison in Elliot, i., 306.*
It was moved and seconded to appoint a committee to prepare a bill of rights; which passed UNANIMOUSLY in the negative.
*Manuscript of Madison.*
On the question for a committee to prepare a bill of rights—
N. H. no, Mas. abst., Ct. no, N. J. no, Pa. no, Del. no, Md. no, Va. no, N. C. no, S. C. no, Geo. no.
*Text of Madison in Gilpin,* 1566; *in Elliot,* 538.
On the question for a committee to prepare a bill of rights—
New Hampshire, Connecticut, New Jersey, Pennsylvania, Delaware, aye—5; Maryland, Virginia, North Carolina, South Carolina, Georgia, no—5; Massachusetts, absent.

The manuscript of Madison, which is plainly written, represents the motion as negatived unanimously; the printed edition, as lost by a purely geographical division. The change remains as yet a mystery.

† Gilpin, 1568; Elliot, 540.

was unanimously substituted for it, servitude being thought to express the condition of slaves, service an obligation of free persons.*

On the same day Johnson, from the committee on style, reported † resolutions for the ratification of the constitution through congress by conventions of the people of the several states; and then for the election of senators, representatives, and electors, and through them of president. Nothing was omitted to make it certain that at a fixed time and place the government under the constitution would start into being.

On the fourteenth it was confirmed without dissent that congress should have no right to change the places of the election of senators.

The appointment of the treasurer as the keeper of the purse had thus far been jealously reserved to the two houses of congress. ‡ It marks the confidence of the convention in its own work, that at this period the selection of that officer was confided to the president and senate.

On the same day Franklin, seconded by Wilson, moved to add, after the authority to establish post-offices and post-roads, a power " to provide for cutting canals." # " The expense," objected Sherman, " will fall on the United States, and the benefit accrue to the places where the canals are cut." " Canals," replied Wilson, " instead of being an expense to the United States, may be made a source of revenue." Madison, supported by Randolph, suggested an enlargement of the motion into a warrant to grant charters of incorporation which might exceed the legislative provisions of individual states, and yet be required by the interest of the United States; political obstacles to an easy communication between the states being removed, a removal of natural ones ought to follow. The necessity of the power was denied by King. " It is necessary," answered Wilson, " to prevent a state from obstructing the general welfare." " The states," rejoined King, " will be divided into parties to grant charters of incorporation, in Philadelphia and New York to a bank, in other places to mercantile

---

* Gilpin, 1233, 1544, 1569; Elliot, 379, 540, 559.
† Gilpin, 1570, 1571; Elliot, 541.
‡ Gilpin, 1574; Elliot, 542.     # Gilpin, 1576; Elliot, 543.

monopolies." Wilson mentioned the importance of facilitating by canals the communication with the western settlements. The motion, even when limited to the case of canals, gained no votes but those of Pennsylvania, Virginia, and Georgia.*

Madison and Charles Pinckney asked for congress permission to establish a university in which no preferences should be allowed on account of religion. "The exclusive power of congress at the seat of government will reach the object," said Gouverneur Morris. The motion was sustained only by Pennsylvania, Virginia, and North and South Carolina; in Connecticut, Johnson divided against Sherman.†

In framing the constitution, Madison kept in mind that the functions of the general government should extend to the prevention of "trespasses of the states on the rights of each other." ‡ "The rights of individuals," he said in the convention, "are infringed by many of the state laws, such as issuing paper money, and instituting a mode to discharge debts differing from the form of the contract." # It has already been told how the delegates from Connecticut had agreed among themselves, "that the legislatures of the individual states ought not to possess a right to make any laws for the discharge of contracts in any manner different from the agreement of the parties." ‖ Stringent clauses in the constitution already prohibited paper money. For the rest, King, as we have seen, proposed a clause forbidding the states to interfere in private contracts; but the motion had been condemned as reaching too far; and instead of it, at the instance of Rutledge, the convention denied to the states the power "to pass bills of attainder or *ex post facto* laws." ᐃ In this manner it was supposed that laws for closing the courts, or authorizing the debtor to pay his debts by more convenient instalments than he had covenanted for, were effectually prohibited. But Dickinson, as we have seen, after consulting Blackstone, mentioned to the house that the term *ex post facto* related to criminal

---

\* Gilpin, 1576, 1577; Elliot, 544. † Gilpin, 1577, 1578; Elliot, 544.
‡ Madison, i., 321.
# Yates's Minutes, Elliot, i., 424, 425. Compare Gilpin, 898; Elliot, 208.
‖ Sherman by J. Evarts in Biography of the Signers, ii., 43.
ᐃ Elliot, i., 271.

cases only; and that restraint of the states from retrospective law in civil cases would require some further provision.* Before an explanatory provision had been made, the section came into the hands of the committee on revision and style. That committee had no authority to bring forward any new proposition, but only to make corrections of style. Gouverneur Morris retained the clause forbidding *ex post facto* laws; and, resolute not "to countenance the issue of paper money and the consequent violation of contracts," † he of himself added the words: "No state shall pass laws altering or impairing the obligation of contracts." The convention reduced the explanatory words to the shorter form: "No state shall pass any law impairing the obligation of contracts." ‡ In this manner an end was designed to be made to barren land laws, laws for the instalment of debts, and laws closing the courts against suitors.

On the fifteenth, from fresh information, it appeared to Sherman that North Carolina was entitled to another representative; and Langdon moved to allow one more member to that state, and likewise one more to Rhode Island.# "If Rhode Island is to be allowed two members," said King, "I can never sign the constitution."

Charles Pinckney urged separately the just claim of North Carolina; on which Bedford put in a like claim for Rhode Island and for Delaware; and the original proposition was hopelessly defeated. ‖

Randolph and Madison disliked leaving the pardon for treason to the president alone; but the convention would not suffer the legislature or the senate to share that power.△

The committee of revision had described a fugitive slave as "a person legally held to service or labor in one state." The language seemed to imply that slavery was a "legal" condition; the last word of the convention relating to the subject defined the fugitive slave to be "a person held to service or labor in one state under the laws thereof," making it clear that, in the meaning of the constitution, slavery was local and not federal.◊

* Gilpin, 1450; Elliot, 488.    # Gilpin, 1583; Elliot, 547.
† G. Morris by Sparks, iii., 323.    ‖ Gilpin, 1583, 1584; Elliot, 547.
‡ Gilpin, 1552, 1581; Elliot, 546, 561.    △ Gilpin, 1587; Elliot, 549.
◊ Gilpin, 1558, 1589, 1620; Elliot, 550, 564.

The convention gave the last touches to the modes of amending the constitution. In August the committee of detail had reported that, "on the application of the legislatures of two thirds of the states in the union, the legislature of the United States shall call a convention for that purpose." * On the thirtieth day of August, Gouverneur Morris had suggested that congress "should be at liberty to call a convention whenever it pleased." † "An easier mode of introducing amendments," said Hamilton, reviving the question, "is desirable. The state legislatures will not apply for alterations but with a view to increase their own powers. The national legislature will be the first to perceive the necessity of amendments; and on the concurrence of each branch ought to be empowered to call a convention, reserving the final decision to the people." ‡ Madison supported Hamilton.

Here Sherman suggested an alternative: the legislature may propose amendments directly to the several states, not to be binding until consented to by them all.# "To be binding when consented to by two thirds of the several states," interposed Wilson. To facilitate amendments, the convention authorized two thirds of congress to introduce amendments to the constitution; but, to prevent hasty changes, required for their ratification the assent of three fourths of the legislatures or conventions of the states.

Madison, summing up the ideas that had found favor, moved that the legislature of the United States, upon a vote of two thirds of both houses, or upon the application of two thirds of the legislatures of the states, shall propose amendments to the constitution which shall be valid when they shall have been ratified by three fourths at least of the several states in their legislatures or conventions, as one or the other mode of ratification may be proposed by the legislature of the United States. ‖

This motion was accepted, but not till it had been agreed that the clauses in the constitution forming special covenants with the South on slavery should not be liable to change.

* Gilpin, 1241; Elliot, 381.
† Gilpin, 1468; Elliot, 498.
‡ Gilpin, 1534; Elliot, 531.
# Gilpin, 1535; Elliot, 531.
‖ Ibid.

Five days later the fears of the small states were quieted by a proviso that no state without its own consent should ever be deprived of its equality in the senate.*

Finally, on maturest reflection, the proposition of the committee of detail, obliging congress to call a convention on application of two thirds of the states, was restored. Amendments to the constitution might proceed from the people as represented in the legislatures of the states; or from the people as represented in congress; or from the people as present in a convention; in every case to be valid only with the assent of three fourths of the states.

Mason, in sullen discontent at the grant of power to a bare majority of congress to pass navigation acts, and dreading that "a few rich merchants in Philadelphia, New York, and Boston" might by that means monopolize the staples of the southern states and reduce their value perhaps fifty per cent, moved " that no law in the nature of a navigation act be passed before the year eighteen hundred and eight, without the consent of two thirds of each branch of the legislature;" but he was supported only by Maryland, Virginia, and Georgia.†

Next, Randolph, whose weight as governor of Virginia might turn the scale in that state, declared his intention to withhold his signature from the constitution that he might retain freedom as to his ultimate action; and, agreeing exactly with Richard Henry Lee, ‡ he moved " that state conventions might have the power to offer to the constitution which was to be laid before them as many amendments as they pleased; and that these amendments, together with the constitution, should be submitted to another general convention " # for a final decision. He was seconded by Mason, who said: "The government as established by the constitution will surely end either in monarchy or a tyrannical aristocracy. As it now stands, I can neither give it my support in Virginia, nor sign it here. With the expedient of another convention I could sign." ‖

" I, too," said Charles Pinckney, " object to the power of a majority of congress over commerce; but, apprehending the

---

* Gilpin, 1592; Elliot, 552. † Gilpin, 1593; Elliot, 552.
‡ Compare R. H. Lee to Chancellor Pendleton, 22 May 1788, in Life, ii., 93, 94.
# Gilpin, 1593; Elliot, 552. ‖ Gilpin, 1594; Elliot, 552, 553.

danger of a general confusion and an ultimate decision by the sword, I shall give the plan my support." Then Gerry counted up eight objections to the constitution, " all " of which he could yet get over, were it not that the legislature had general power to make " necessary and proper" laws, to raise "armies and money" without limit, and to establish "a star chamber as to civil cases;" and he, too, contended for a second general convention.

On the proposition for another convention all the states answered " No." Washington then put the question of agreeing to the constitution in its present form; and all the states present answered "Aye." The constitution was then ordered to be engrossed, and late on the evening of Saturday the house adjourned.*

One morning Washington, in a desultory conversation with members of the convention before the chair was taken, observed how unhappy it would be, should any of them oppose the system when they returned to their states.† On Monday, the seventeenth of September, Franklin made a last effort to win over the dissenting members. "Mr. President," said he, "several parts of this constitution I do not at present approve, but I am not sure I shall never approve them. It astonishes me to find this system approaching so near to perfection. I consent to this constitution because I expect no better, and because I am not sure that it is not the best. The opinions I have had of its errors I sacrifice to the public good.

"On the whole, sir, I cannot help expressing a wish that every member of the convention, who may still have objections to it, would with me on this occasion doubt a little of his own infallibility, and, to manifest our unanimity, put his name to this instrument." ‡ He then moved that the constitution be signed by the members; and he offered as the form of signature a simple testimony that the constitution had received "the unanimous consent of the states present." # But this ample concession induced neither Mason, nor Gerry, nor Randolph to relent.

* Gilpin, 1595; Elliot, 553.
† Luther Martin in Maryland Journal of 21 March 1788.
‡ Gilpin, 1597, 1598; Elliot, 554, 555.     # Gilpin, 1598; Elliot, 555.

Before the question was put, Gorham, obeying an intimation from Washington, proposed to render the house of representatives a more popular body by allowing one member for every thirty thousand inhabitants. He was warmly seconded by King and Carroll.*

Rising to put the question, the president, after an apology for offering his sentiments, said: "I would make objections to the plan as few as possible. The smallness of the number of representatives has been considered by many members as insufficient security for the rights and interests of the people; and to myself has always appeared exceptionable; late as is the moment, it will give me much satisfaction to see the amendment adopted." † And at his word it was adopted unanimously.

On the question to agree to the engrossed constitution, all the states answered "Aye." ‡

Randolph then apologized for refusing to sign the constitution, "notwithstanding the vast majority and the venerable names which gave sanction to its wisdom and its worth. I do not mean by this refusal," he continued, "to decide that I shall oppose the constitution without doors; I mean only to keep myself free to be governed by my duty, as it shall be prescribed by my future judgment." #

"I, too, had objections," said Gouverneur Morris; "but considering the present plan the best that can be attained, I shall take it with all its faults. The moment it goes forth, the great question will be: 'Shall there be a national government, or a general anarchy?'"

"I am anxious," said Hamilton, "that every member should sign. A few by refusing may do infinite mischief. No man's ideas are more remote from the plan than my own are known to be; but is it possible to deliberate between anarchy and convulsion on the one side, and the chance of good to be expected from the plan on the other?" ‖

"I," said Gerry, "fear a civil war. In Massachusetts there are two parties: one devoted to democracy, the worst, I think, of all political evils; the other as violent in the opposite ex-

---

* Gilpin, 1599; Elliot, 555.    † Gilpin, 1599, 1600; Elliot, 555, 556.
‡ Gilpin, 1600; Elliot, 556.    # Ibid.    ‖ Gilpin, 1601; Elliot, 556.

treme. From the collision of these, confusion is greatly to be feared."

"I shall sign the constitution with a view to support it with all my influence," said Cotesworth Pinckney, "and I wish to pledge myself accordingly." * Jared Ingersoll of Pennsylvania considered the signing as a recommendation of what, all things considered, was the most eligible.

The form proposed by Franklin was accepted with no dissent, except that South Carolina was impatient at its want of an affirmative expression of unhesitating approval. The journals and papers of the convention were confided to the care of the president, subject to the order of the new government when it should be formed.† Hamilton successively inscribed on the great sheet of parchment the name of each state as the delegations one after the other came forward in geographical order and signed the constitution. When it appeared that the unanimous consent of all the eleven states present in convention was recorded in its favor, Franklin, looking toward a sun which was blazoned on the president's chair, said of it to those near him: "In the vicissitudes of hope and fear I was not able to tell whether it was rising or setting; now I know that it is the rising sun." ‡

The members were awe-struck at the result of their councils; the constitution was a nobler work than any one of them had believed it possible to devise. They all on that day dined together, and took a cordial leave of each other. Washington at an early hour of the evening retired "to meditate on the momentous work which had been executed." #

* Gilpin, 1603, 1604; Elliot, 557, 558.   ‡ Gilpin, 1624; Elliot, 565.
† Gilpin, 1605; Elliot, 558.   # Diary of Washington for the day.

# THE
# FORMATION OF THE CONSTITUTION
### OF THE
# UNITED STATES OF AMERICA.

*IN FIVE BOOKS.*

## BOOK FOURTH.
### THE PEOPLE OF THE STATES IN JUDGMENT ON THE CONSTITUTION.

1787–1788.

# CHAPTER I.

### THE CONSTITUTION IN CONGRESS AND IN VIRGINIA.

### SEPTEMBER TO NOVEMBER 1787.

On the twentieth of September the letter of the president of the convention to the president of congress, the full text of the proposed constitution, and the order of the convention, were laid before congress, and on the next day appeared in the daily papers of New York.

The letter of Washington said: The powers necessary to be vested in "the general government of the union" are too extensive to be delegated to "one body of men." "It is impracticable, in the federal government of these states, to secure all rights of independent sovereignty to each, and yet provide for the interest and safety of all; it is difficult to draw with precision the line between those rights which must be surrendered and those which may be reserved; on the present occasion this difficulty was increased by a difference among the several states as to their situation, extent, habits, and particular interests. We kept steadily in view the consolidation of our union, in which is involved our prosperity, felicity, safety, perhaps our national existence. And thus the constitution which we now present is the result of that mutual deference and concession which the peculiarity of our political situation rendered indispensable."

The constitution instantly met with opposition from the indefatigable Richard Henry Lee,* supported by Nathan Dane † and all the delegates from New York, of whom Melancthon

---

\* Carrington to Madison, Sunday, 23 September 1787.
† Gilpin, 643, 650; Elliot, 566, 568.

Smith was the ablest. Till Madison returned, the delegates from Virginia were equally divided, Grayson opposing the government because it was too feeble, and Lee because it was too strong.* Already the New York faction was actively scattering the seeds of opposition, and Hamilton dauntlessly opposing them in the public papers by arguments for union.†

It was only out of the ashes of the confederation that the new constitution could spring into being; and the letter of the convention did indeed invite congress to light its own funeral pyre. On the twenty-sixth it was first contended that congress could not properly give any positive countenance to a measure subversive of the confederation to which they owed their existence. To this it was answered, that in February congress itself had recommended the convention as "the most probable means of establishing a firm national government," and that it was not now more restrained from acceding to the new plan than the convention from proposing it. If the plan was within the powers of the convention, it was within those of congress; if beyond those powers, the necessity which justified the one would justify the other; and the necessity existed if any faith was due to the representations of congress themselves, confirmed by twelve states in the union and by the general voice of the people.

Lee next attempted to amend the act of the convention before it should go forth from congress to the people. "Where," said he, "is the contract between the nation and the government? The constitution makes mention only of those who govern, and nowhere speaks of the rights of the people who are governed." ‡ He wished to qualify the immense power of the government by a bill of rights, which had always been regarded as the palladium of a free people. The bill of rights was to relate to the rights of conscience, the freedom of the press, the trial by jury in civil cases as well as criminal, the prohibition of standing armies, freedom of elections, the independence of the judges, security against excessive bails, fines, or punishments, against unreasonable searches or seizure of

---

\* Carrington to Jefferson, 23 October 1787.
† Carrington to Madison, 23 September 1787.
‡ Minister Otto to Count Montmorin, New York, 23 October 1787.

persons, houses, papers, or property; and the right of petition. He further proposed amendments to the constitution; a council of state or privy council, to be joined with the president in the appointment of all officers, so as to prevent the blending of legislative and executive powers; no vice-president; an increase of the number of the representatives; and the requisition of more than a majority to make commercial regulations.

The restraint on the power of regulating commerce and navigation would have been fatal to the wealth and prosperity of New York. Nevertheless, the propositions of Lee were supported by Melancthon Smith, who insisted that congress had the undoubted right and the duty to amend the plan of the federal constitution, in which the essential safeguards of liberty had been omitted. To this it was replied that congress had certainly a right of its own to propose amendments, but that these must be addressed to the legislatures of the states, and would require ratification by all the thirteen; but that the act of the federal convention was to be addressed to conventions of the several states, of which any nine might adopt it for themselves. So the first day's debate ended without admitting the proposed amendments to consideration.*

The next day Lee, seconded by Smith, offered a resolution that congress had no power whatever to assist † in creating a "new confederacy of nine" states; and therefore he would do no more than, as a mark of respect, forward the acts of the convention to the executives of every state to be laid before their respective legislatures. On the instant Abraham Clarke of New Jersey, seconded by Nathaniel Mitchell of Delaware, proposed to add: "In order to be by them submitted to conventions of delegates to be chosen agreeably to the said resolutions of the convention." On the question, Georgia and the two Carolinas voted unanimously against Lee; so did Delaware and the only member from Maryland, with Pennsylvania, New Jersey, Connecticut, Massachusetts, New Hampshire. Virginia, on the return of Madison, joined them by the inflexible majority of Madison, Carrington, and Henry Lee,

---

* Madison to Washington, New York, 30 September 1787; R. H. Lee to Samuel Adams, New York, 5 October 1787; Life of R. H. Lee, ii., 74, 76.

† Gilpin, 643; Elliot, 566.

against Grayson and Richard Henry Lee. All the states except New York were for the motion; and all except New York and Virginia were unanimously so. The majority in congress was impatient to express its approval of the acts of the convention in still stronger language; Carrington of Virginia, therefore, seconded by Bingham of Pennsylvania, proposed that it be recommended to the legislatures of the several states to cause conventions to be held as speedily as may be, to the end that the same may be adopted, ratified, and confirmed.*

In this stage of the business congress adjourned. The friends of the new constitution desired to send it to the states by the unanimous vote of congress. The members from New York would not consent to any language that implied approval. To win their vote the resolution of congress must be neutral. On the other hand, the idea of unanimity required the effacement of every motion adverse to the reference of the constitution. Accordingly, congress, when it next assembled, expunged from its journal the proposed amendments of Richard Henry Lee, and the vote of the preceding day; † and having obliterated every record of opposition, it resolved on the twenty-eighth unanimously, eleven states being present, Maryland having one delegate, Rhode Island alone being altogether unrepresented, that the said report, with the resolutions and letter accompanying the same, be transmitted to the several legislatures, in order to be submitted to a convention of delegates chosen in each state by the people thereof in conformity to the resolves of the convention. ‡

Baffled within the convention, Richard Henry Lee appealed to the world through the press in a series of "Letters from the Federal Farmer," of which thousands of copies were scattered through the central states. He acknowledged the necessity of reforming the government, but claimed to discern a strong tendency to aristocracy in every part of the proposed constitution, which he slighted as the work of visionary young men,# bent on changing the thirteen distinct independent republics under a federal head into one consolidated government.△ He way-

* MS. Journals of Congress in State Department.
† MS. Journals of Congress.      # Letters from the Federal Farmer, 8.
‡ Journals of Congress, iv., 782.    △ Letters from the Federal Farmer, 6.

laid Gerry when bound for home, and assisted him in preparing an official letter to explain his refusal to sign the constitution. He addressed himself to Samuel Adams, the "dear friend with whom he had long toiled in the vineyard of liberty," submitting to his wisdom and patriotism the objections to the new constitution which he had proposed in congress in the form of amendments, but disingenuously substituting other words for his remonstrance against vesting congress with power to regulate commerce. He extended his intrigues to Pennsylvania and Delaware, hoping to delay their decisions.

"I am waiting with anxiety for the echo from Virginia, but with very faint hopes of its corresponding with my wishes," wrote Madison from New York city to Washington.* The party in power in New York was passionately opposed to the constitution; but already day had begun to scatter the dusk of earliest morning.

In the first moment after his return to Mount Vernon, Washington sent a copy of the constitution to Patrick Henry,† to Harrison, and to Nelson, each of whom had been governor of Virginia. In a propitiatory letter he appealed to their experience of the difficulties which had ever arisen in attempts to reconcile the interests and local prejudices of the several states. "I wish," he continued, "the constitution which is offered had been more perfect; but it is the best that could be obtained at this time, and a door is opened for amendments hereafter. The political concerns of this country are suspended by a thread. The convention has been looked up to by the reflecting part of the community with a solicitude which is hardly to be conceived; and if nothing had been agreed on by that body, anarchy would soon have ensued, the seeds being deeply sown in every soil."

A visitor at Mount Vernon, just after this letter was sent out, writes of Washington: "He is in perfect health, and looks almost as well as he did twenty years ago. I never in my life saw him so keen for anything as he is for the adoption of the new form of government." ‡ Throughout the whole country he

---
\* Madison to Washington. Gilpin, 646; Elliot, 567.
† Washington to Henry, 24 September 1787. Sparks, ix., 265.
‡ A. Donald to Jefferson, 12 November 1787.

was the centre of interest; in Virginia of power. The leaders of opposition answered him frankly, but with expressions of deference and affection.

"The seeds of civil discord," replied Harrison, "are plentifully sown in very many of the powers given both to the president and congress. If the constitution is carried into effect, the states south of the Potomac will be little more than appendages to those to the northward of it. My objections chiefly lie against the unlimited powers of taxation, the regulation of trade, and the jurisdictions that are to be established in every state altogether independent of their laws. The sword and such powers will, nay, must, sooner or later establish a tyranny." *

Avowing very sincerely "the highest reverence" for Washington, Patrick Henry answered positively: "I cannot bring my mind to accord with the proposed constitution." †

George Mason, who had rendered the highest and wisest service in shaping the constitution, now from wounded pride resisted his inmost convictions, enumerating to his old friend his objections, of which the grant to congress of power to regulate commerce by a bare majority was the capital one. ‡

Next Richard Henry Lee, professing himself "compelled by irresistible conviction of mind to doubt about the new system for federal government," wrote: "It is, sir, in consequence of long reflection upon the nature of man and of government, that I am led to fear the danger that will ensue to civil liberty from the adoption of the new system in its present form." And, having at once fixed in his mind the plan on which resistance to its adoption should be conducted, he avowed his wish "that such amendments as would give security to the rights of human nature and the discordant interests of the different parts of this union might employ another convention." #

But the influence of Washington outweighed them all. He was embosomed in the affections and enshrined in the pride of the people of Virginia; and in all their waverings during

---

* Sparks, ix., 266, 267. Note. † Sparks, ix., 266. Note.
‡ George Mason to Washington, 7 October 1787. Sparks, ix., 267, 268. Note.
# R. H. Lee to Washington, New York, 11 October 1787. Letters to W., iv., 180, 181.

the nine months following the federal convention he was the anchor of the constitution. His neighbors of Alexandria to a man agreed with him; and Fairfax county unanimously instructed its representatives, of whom George Mason was one, "that the peace, security, and prosperity of Virginia and of the United States depended on the speedy adoption of the federal constitution." *

In the close division of parties in the state it was of vital importance to secure the influence of Edmund Randolph, its governor; and his old military chief in due time received from him an elaborate paper which he had prepared in the form of an address to the speaker of the house of delegates. In this letter, not yet pledging himself to the unconditional support of the constitution, he avowed that he prized the intimate and unshaken friendship of Washington and Madison as among the happiest of all his acquisitions; but added: "Dreadful as the total dissolution of the union is to my mind, I entertain no less horror at the thought of partial confederacies. The utmost limit of any partial confederacy which Virginia could expect to form would comprehend the three southern and her nearest northern neighbor. But they, like ourselves, are diminished in their real force by the mixture of an unhappy species of population." †

Monroe wrote to Madison that his "strong objections" to the constitution "were overbalanced by the arguments in its favor." ‡

The legislature of Virginia was to hold its regular meeting on the third Monday of October; this year there was a quorum on the first day of the session, which had not happened since the revolution.

On the nineteenth the vote of congress transmitting the constitution came before the house; Patrick Henry, refusing to make an issue where he would have met with defeat, declared that the constitution must go before a conven-

---

* Meeting of Fairfax county, Tuesday, 2 October 1787. Carey's Museum, ii., 392, 393.

† Edmund Randolph to the speaker of the house of delegates of Virginia, 10 October 1787. Elliot, i., 487.

‡ Monroe to Madison, 13 October 1787.

tion, as it transcended the power of the house to decide on it.*

But when, on the twenty-fifth, Francis Corbin proposed "a convention to be called according to the recommendation of congress," Henry objected that under that limitation its members "would have power to adopt or reject the new plan, but not to propose amendments" of its "errors and defects." His motion to give this power to the convention of the state was seconded by Mason, who added: "I declare that from the east of New Hampshire to the south of Georgia there is not a man more fully convinced of the necessity of establishing some general government than I am; that I regard our perfect union as the rock of our political salvation." †

After some debate, John Marshall of Richmond, conceding the point as to "leaving the door open for amendments," ‡ pleaded that the legislature should not seem to disapprove the new federal government, and, for the form of the resolution, proposed that "the new constitution should be laid before the convention for their free and ample discussion." # This form was silently accepted by Henry, while Mason declared "that the house had no right to suggest anything to a body paramount to itself." The vote was unanimous, the form of the resolution being that of Marshall, while in substance it yielded up all that Henry and Mason required. ‖ From "unfriendly intentions toward the constitution," ⌐ the choice of the convention was postponed till the court days in March, and its time of meeting to the first Monday in June. Should many of the states then be found against the constitution, Virginia could assume the office of mediator between contending parties, and dictate to all the rest of the union. ◊

* Bushrod Washington to G. W., 19 October 1787. Sparks, ix., 273.
† Report of Debate in Packet, 10 November 1787.
‡ Madison, i., 363, 364.
# Report of the Debate from Penn. Packet, 10 November 1787.
‖ Compare George Mason to G. W., 6 November 1787, in Letters to G. W., iv., 190. Report of Debates in Penn. Packet, 10 November 1787. Bushrod Washington in Sparks, ix., 287.
⌐ Edward Carrington to T. Jefferson, 10 November 1787. Bushrod Washington was inexperienced, and at first judged the disposition of the legislature too favorably; Carrington had keener-eyed correspondents.
◊ Monroe to Madison, 7 February 1788. Carrington to Madison, 18 January

Since amendments had been unanimously authorized, it seemed fair that any expense of an attempt to make them should be provided for with the other charges of the convention.* A letter from Richard Henry Lee, a representative from Virginia in congress, to the governor of the commonwealth, recommended, as a policy open to "no objection and promising great safety and much good," † that amendments adopted severally by the states should all be definitively referred to a second federal convention.

To carry out this policy, resolutions were on the last day of November introduced into the house, and supported by Henry and Mason, pledging the general assembly to defray the expense of a deputy or deputies which the convention of the commonwealth in the following June might think proper to send to confer with a convention of any one or more of the sister states, " as well as the allowance to be made to the deputies to a federal convention, in case such a convention should be judged necessary." The friends of the constitution, who now perceived the direction in which they were drifting, made a rally; but they were beaten by a majority of about fifteen. A bill pursuant to the resolutions, reported by a committee composed mainly of the most determined "malcontents," soon became a law. ‡ Friends of the constitution who had been jubilant at the first aspect of the legislature now doubted whether it any longer had a majority in its favor; its enemies claimed a decisive victory. Early in December, Monroe reported to Madison: "The cloud which hath hung over us for some time past is not likely soon to be dispelled." #

But on Washington's mind no cloud rested. On the last day of November he had replied to David Stuart of his own state: "I am sorry to find by your favor that the opposition gains strength. If there are characters who prefer disunion or separate confederacies to the general government which is offered to them, their opposition may, for aught I know, proceed from principle; but as nothing, according to my conception of the matter, is more to be deprecated than a disunion or

---

1788. Washington to Carter, 14 December 1787, in Penn. Packet of 11 January 1788.   * Sparks, ix., 287.   † Lee's Life, ii., 81; Elliot, i., 505.

‡ Hening, xii., 462.   # Monroe to Madison, 6 December. MS.

VOL. VI.—26

three distinct confederacies, as far as my voice can go it shall be offered in favor of the general government." *

Nor did he lose heart or trust; on the fourteenth of December, in a letter which soon reached the people of Virginia through the newspapers, he wrote to Charles Carter of Fredericksburg: "I am pleased that the proceedings of the convention have met your approbation. My decided opinion on the matter is, that there is no alternative between the adoption of it and anarchy. If one state, however important it may conceive itself to be," and here he meant Virginia, " or a minority of them," meaning the five southernmost states, "should suppose that they can dictate a constitution to the union, unless they have the power of applying the *ultima ratio* to good effect, they will find themselves deceived. All the opposition to it that I have yet seen is addressed more to the passions than to reason; and clear I am, if another federal convention is attempted, that the sentiments of the members will be more discordant or less accommodating than the last. In fine, they will agree upon no general plan. General government is now suspended by a thread; I might go further, and say it is really at an end; and what will be the consequence of a fruitless attempt to amend the one which is offered before it is tried, or of the delay of the attempt, does not in my judgment need the gift of prophecy to predict.

"I saw the imperfections of the constitution I aided in the birth of, before it was handed to the public; but I am fully persuaded it is the best that can be obtained at this time, that it is free from many of the imperfections with which it is charged, and that it or disunion is before us to choose from. If the first is our election, when the defects of it are experienced, a constitutional door is opened for amendments and may be adopted in a peaceable manner, without tumult or disorder." † But as Virginia has delayed her convention till June, our narrative must turn to the states which were the first to meet in convention.

* In Sparks, ix., 284, for "these distinct confederacies" read "*three* distinct confederacies."

† Washington to Charles Carter, 14 December 1787, in Penn. Packet of 11 January 1788. The original draft of the letter is preserved in the State Department.

## CHAPTER II.

### THE CONSTITUTION IN PENNSYLVANIA, DELAWARE, AND NEW JERSEY; AND IN GEORGIA.

### FROM 18 SEPTEMBER 1787 TO 2 JANUARY 1788.

OUR happy theme leads from one great act of universal interest to another. A new era in the life of the race begins: a people select their delegates to state conventions to pronounce their judgment on the creation of a federal republic.

One more great duty to his fellow-citizens and to mankind is to be fulfilled by Franklin; one more honor to be won by Philadelphia as the home of union; one new victory by Pennsylvania as the citadel of the love of the one indivisible country. That mighty border commonwealth, extending its line from Delaware bay to the Ohio, and holding convenient passes through the Alleghanies, would not abandon the South, nor the West, nor the North; she would not hear of triple confederacies nor of twin confederacies; but only of one government embracing all. Its people in their multifarious congruity had nothing adverse to union; the faithful of the proprietary party were zealous for a true general government; so too was every man in public life of the people called Quakers;* so was an overwhelming majority of the Germans;† so were the Baptists, as indeed their synod authoritatively avowed for every state. The perfect liberty of conscience prevented religious differences from interfering with zeal for a closer union.

In the first period of the confederacy the inhabitants of Philadelphia did not extend their plans for its reform beyond the increase of its powers, but, after the flight of congress

---
\* Independent Gazetteer, 15 January 1788.      † Independent Gazetteer.

from their city, they began to say to one another that "it would be more easy to build a new ship of state than to repair the old one;" that there was need of a new constitution with a legislature in two branches. Merchants, bankers, holders of the national debt, the army officers, found no party organized against this opinion; Dickinson was magnanimous enough to become dissatisfied with the confederation which he had chiefly assisted to frame; and he and Mifflin and McKean and George Clymer and Rush manifested no opposition to the policy of Wilson, Robert Morris, Gouverneur Morris, and Fitzsimons; although remoter counties, and especially the backwoodsmen on each side of the mountains, loved their wild personal liberty too dearly to welcome a new supreme control.

At eleven in the morning of the eighteenth, Benjamin Franklin, then president of Pennsylvania, more than fourscore years of age, fulfilling his last great public service, was ushered into the hall of the assembly, followed by his seven colleagues of the convention. After expressing in a short address their hope and belief that the measure recommended by that body would produce happy effects to the commonwealth of Pennsylvania as well as to every other of the United States, he presented the constitution and accompanying papers.

For the next ten days the house, not willing to forestall the action of congress, confined itself to its usual business; but as it had resolved to adjourn *sine die* on Saturday, the twenty-ninth, Clymer, on the morning of the last day but one of the session, proposed to refer the acts of the federal convention to a convention of the state. That there might be time for reflection, Robert Whitehill of Carlisle, on behalf of the minority, requested the postponement of the question at least until the afternoon. This was conceded; but in the afternoon the minority, nineteen in number, did not attend, and refused to obey the summons of the speaker delivered by the sergeant-at-arms, so that no quorum could be made. This factious secession so enraged the inhabitants that early the next morning a body of "respectable men" made a search for the delinquents; and finding two of them, just sufficient to form a house, dragged them into the assembly, where, in spite of their protests, they were compelled to stay. Meantime a fleet messenger, sent from New York by William Bingham, a delegate in congress from Pennsylvania, arrived with an authentic copy of a resolution of congress of the preceding day, unanimously recommending the reference of the constitution to conventions of the several states; and within twenty hours* from the adoption of the resolution, the Pennsylvania assembly called a convention of the state for the third Tuesday in November.† The vote was received by the spectators with three heartfelt cheers; the bells of the churches were rung; and signs of faith in the speedy return of prosperity were everywhere seen. But the minority, trained in resistance to influences which were thought to be aristocratic, refused to be reconciled, and became the seed of a permanent national party.

Richard Henry Lee had disseminated in Philadelphia the objections of himself and George Mason to the constitution; and seventeen of the seceding members imbodied them in an appeal to their constituents. ‡ But the cause of the inflammation in Pennsylvania was much more in their state factions than in the new federal system.#

The efforts of Richard Henry Lee were counteracted in Philadelphia by Wilson, whom Washington at the time called "as able, candid, and honest a member as was in the convention." On the sixth of October, at a great meeting in Philadelphia, he held up the constitution as the best which the world had as yet seen. To the objection derived from its want of a bill of rights, he explained that the government of the United States was a limited government, which had no powers except those which were specially granted to it. The speech was promptly reprinted in New York as a reply to the insinuations of Lee; and through the agency of Washington it was republished in Richmond. ‖ But the explanation of the want of a bill of rights satisfied not one state.

Great enthusiasm was awakened among the people of Penn-

* Carey's Museum, vol. ii., Chronicle, pp. 6, 7.
† Lloyd's Debates of Pennsylvania Legislature, p. 137.  P. Bond to Lord Carmarthen, Philadelphia, 29 September 1787.
‡ Washington to Madison, 10 October 1787, in Letter Book at State Department.
# Madison to Jefferson, 19 February 1788, in Madison, i., 377.
‖ Sparks, ix., 271.

sylvania in the progress of the election of their delegates; they rejoiced at the near consummation of their hopes. The convention was called to meet on Tuesday, the twentieth of November; a quorum appeared on the next day. Before the week was over the constitution on two successive days received its first and second reading. Its friends, who formed a very large and resolute majority, were intensely in earnest, and would not brook procrastination.

On Saturday, the twenty-fourth,* Thomas McKean of Philadelphia, seconded by John Allison of Franklin county, offered the resolution in favor of ratifying the constitution; and Wilson, as the only one present who had been a member of the federal convention, opened the debate:

"The United States exhibit to the world the first instance of a nation unattacked by external force, unconvulsed by domestic insurrections, assembling voluntarily, deliberating fully, and deciding calmly concerning that system of government under which they and their posterity should live. To form a good system of government for a single city or an inconsiderable state has been thought to require the strongest efforts of human genius; the views of the convention were expanded to a large portion of the globe.

" The difficulty of the business was equal to its magnitude. The United States contain already thirteen governments mutually independent; their soil, climates, productions, dimensions, and numbers are different; in many instances a difference and even an opposition subsists among their interests, and is imagined to subsist in many more. Mutual concessions and sacrifices, the consequences of mutual forbearance and conciliation, were indispensably necessary to the success of the great work.

" The United States may adopt any one of four different systems. They may become consolidated into one government in which the separate existence of the states shall be entirely absolved. They may reject any plan of union and act as unconnected states. They may form two or more confederacies.

* Correct the date in Elliot, ii., 417, by Independent Gazette of 29 November 1787. Especially, Centinel in the same, 4 December. Mr. W. [Wilson] in a speech on Saturday, 24 instant, Pa. Packet of 27 November.

They may unite in one federal republic. Neither of these systems found advocates in the late convention. The remaining system is a union in one confederate republic.*

"The expanding quality of a government by which several states agree to become an assemblage of societies that constitute a new society, capable of increasing by means of further association, is peculiarly fitted for the United States. But this form of government left us almost without precedent or guide. Ancient history discloses, and barely discloses, to our view some confederate republics. The Swiss cantons are connected only by alliances; the United Netherlands constitute no new society; from the Germanic body little useful knowledge can be drawn.

"Since states as well as citizens are represented in the constitution before us, and form the objects on which that constitution is proposed to operate, it is necessary to mention a kind of liberty which has not yet received a name. I shall distinguish it by the appellation of federal liberty. The states should resign to the national government that part, and that part only, of their political liberty which, placed in that government, will produce more good to the whole than if it had remained in the several states. While they resign this part of their political liberty, they retain the free and generous exercise of all their other faculties, so far as it is compatible with the welfare of the general and superintending confederacy.

"The powers of the federal government and those of the state governments are drawn from sources equally pure. The principle of representation, unknown to the ancients, is confined to a narrow corner of the British constitution. For the American states were reserved the glory and happiness of diffusing this vital principle throughout the constituent parts of government.

"The convention found themselves embarrassed with another difficulty of peculiar delicacy and importance; I mean that of drawing a proper line between the national government and the governments of the several states. Whatever object of government is confined in its operation and effects within the bounds of a particular state should be considered as belong-

* Elliot, ii., 427, 428.

ing to the government of that state; whatever object of government extends in its operation or effects beyond the bounds of a particular state should be considered as belonging to the government of the United States. To remove discretionary construction, the enumeration of particular instances in which the application of the principle ought to take place will be found to be safe, unexceptionable, and accurate.

"To control the power and conduct of the legislature by an overruling constitution limiting and superintending the operations of legislative authority was an improvement in the science and practice of government reserved to the American states. Oft have I marked with silent pleasure and admiration the force and prevalence through the United States of the principle that the supreme power resides in the people, and that they never part with it. There can be no disorder in the community but may here receive a radical cure. Error in the legislature may be corrected by the constitution; error in the constitution, by the people. The streams of power run in different directions, but they all originally flow from one abundant fountain. In this constitution all authority is derived from the people."

Already much had been gained for the friends of the constitution. "I am sensible," said John Smilie of Fayette county, "of the expediency of giving additional strength and energy to the federal head." The question became on the one side the adoption of the constitution as sent forth by the convention; on the other, with amendments. Smilie spoke against a system of precipitancy which would preclude deliberation on questions of the highest consequence to the happiness of a great portion of the globe. "Is the object," he asked, "to bring on a hasty and total adoption of the constitution? The most common business of a legislative body is submitted to repeated discussion upon different days." Robert Whitehill of Carlisle, in Cumberland county, fearing a conveyance to the federal government of rights and liberties which the people ought never to surrender, asked a reference to a committee of the whole. He was defeated on the twenty-sixth, by a vote of forty-three to twenty-four; but each member obtained leave to speak in the house as often as he pleased. When it was observed that the federal convention had exceeded the powers given to them by their respective legislatures, Wilson answered: "The federal convention did not proceed at all upon the powers given to them by the states, but upon original principles; and having framed a constitution which they thought would promote the happiness of their country, they have submitted it to their consideration, who may either adopt or reject it as they please." *

On the twenty-seventh, Whitehill, acting in concert with the Virginia opposition and preparing the way for entering on the journals a final protest against the proceedings of the majority, proposed that upon all questions where the yeas and nays were called any member might insert the reason of his vote upon the journal of the convention. This was argued all the day long, and leave was refused by a very large majority.†

The fiercest day's debate, and the only one where the decision of the country was finally in favor of the minority, took place on the twenty-eighth of November. There was a rising discontent at the omission of a declaration of rights. To prove that there was no need of a bill of rights, Wilson said: "The boasted Magna Charta of England derives the liberties of the inhabitants of that kingdom from the gift and grant of the king, and no wonder the people were anxious to obtain bills of rights; but here the fee simple remains in the people; and by this constitution they do not part with it. The preamble to the proposed constitution, 'We the people of the United States do establish,' contains the essence of all the bills of rights that have been or can be devised." ‡ The defence was imperfect both in sentiment and in public law. To the sentiment, Smilie answered: "The words in the preamble of the proposed system, however superior they may be to the terms of the great charter of England, must yield to the expressions in the Pennsylvania bill of rights and the memorable declaration of the fourth of July 1776." As a question of public law, the answer of Smilie was equally conclusive: "It is not enough to

---

\* Independent Gazetteer, 29 November 1787.
† Independent Gazetteer for 3 December; and especially for 7 December 1787.
‡ Elliot's Debates, ii., 434–439.

reserve to the people a right to alter and abolish government, but some criterion should be established by which it can easily and constitutionally ascertain how far the government may proceed and when it transgresses its jurisdiction." "A bill of rights," interposed McKean, "though it can do no harm, is an unnecessary instrument. The constitutions of but five out of the thirteen United States have bills of rights." The speaker was ill informed. South Carolina and Georgia had alone declined the opportunity of establishing a bill of rights; every state to the north of them had one except Rhode Island and Connecticut, which as yet adhered to their original charters, and New Jersey, which still adhered to its government as established just before the declaration of independence. New York had incorporated into its constitution the whole of that declaration.

Wilson asserted that in the late convention the desire of "a bill of rights had never assumed the shape of a motion." Here his memory was at fault; but no one present could correct him. "In civil governments," he proceeded, "bills of rights are useless, nor can I conceive whence the contrary notion has arisen. Virginia has no bill of rights." Smilie interrupted him to cite the assurance of George Mason himself that Virginia had a bill of rights; and he repeated the remark that Mason* had made in the convention: "The laws of the general government are paramount to the laws and constitutions of the several states; and as there is no declaration of rights in the new constitution, the declarations of rights in the constitutions of the several states are no security. Every stipulation for the most sacred and invaluable privileges of man is left at the mercy of government." †

On Saturday, the first of December, William Findley, the third leading member of the opposition, in a long and elaborate argument endeavored to prove that the proposed plan of government was not a confederation of states, but a consolidation of government. He insisted that the constitution formed a contract between individuals entering into society, not a

---

\* Gilpin, 1566; Elliot, 538.

† Independent Gazetteer, December 10, 13, 18, 20, 24, 27. Review of the Constitutions by De La Croix, English translation, ii., 386, note.

union of independent states; that in the legislature it established the vote by individuals, not by states; that between two parties in the same community, each claiming independent sovereignty, it granted an unlimited right of internal taxation to the federal body, whose stronger will would thus be able to annihilate the power of its weaker rival; that it conceded a right to regulate and judge of elections; that it extended the judicial power as widely as the legislative; that it raised the members of congress above their states, for they were paid not by the states as subordinate delegates, but by the general government; and finally, that it required an oath of allegiance to the federal government, and thus made the allegiance to a separate sovereign state an absurdity.*

Meantime the zeal of the majority was quickened by news from "the Delaware state," whose people were for the most part of the same stock as the settlers of Pennsylvania, and had grown up under the same proprietary. On the proposal for the federal convention at Philadelphia, its general assembly declared that "they had long been fully convinced of the necessity of revising the federal constitution," "being willing and desirous of co-operating with the commonwealth of Virginia and the other states in the confederation." † Now that an equality of vote in the senate had been conceded, the one single element of opposition disappeared. The legislature of Delaware met on the twenty-fourth of October, and following "the sense and desire of great numbers of the people of the state, signified in petitions to their general assembly," "adopted speedy measures to call together a convention." ‡

The constituent body, which met at Dover in the first week of December, encountered no difficulty but how to find language strong enough to express their joy in what had been done. On the sixth "the deputies of the people of the Delaware state fully, freely, and entirely approved of, assented to, ratified, and confirmed the federal constitution," to which they all on the next day subscribed their names.#

* Independent Gazetteer, 6 December, 1787.
† Laws of Delaware, page 892, in edition of 1797.
‡ Packet, 17 November 1787.
# Journals of Congress, iv. Appendix, 46.

When it became known that Delaware was leading the way at the head of the grand procession of the thirteen states, McKean, on Monday, the tenth of December, announced to the Pennsylvania convention that he should on the twelfth press the vote for ratification.

On the next day Wilson summed up his defence of the constitution, and repeated: "This system is not a compact; I cannot discern the least trace of a compact; the introduction to the work is not an unmeaning flourish; the system itself tells you what it is, an ordinance, an establishment of the people." * The opposition followed the line of conduct marked out by the opposition in Virginia. On the twelfth, before the question for ratification was taken, Whitehill presented petitions from seven hundred and fifty inhabitants of Cumberland county against adopting the constitution without amendments, and particularly without a bill of rights to secure liberty in matters of religion, trial by jury, the freedom of the press, the sole power in the individual states to organize the militia; the repeal of the executive power of the senate, and consequent appointment of a constitutional council; a prohibition of repealing or modifying laws of the United States by treaties; restrictions on the federal judiciary power; a confirmation to the several states of their sovereignty, with every power, jurisdiction, and right not expressly delegated to the United States in congress assembled. In laboring for this end, he showed a concert with the measure which Mason and Randolph had proposed in the federal convention and Richard Henry Lee in congress, and which led the Virginia legislature on that very day to pass the act for communicating with sister states.†

The amendments which Whitehill proposed were not suffered to be entered in the journal. His motion was rejected by forty-six to twenty-three; and then the new constitution was ratified by the same majority.

On Thursday the convention marched in a procession to the court-house, where it proclaimed the ratification. Returning to the place of meeting, the forty-six subscribed their names to their act. The opposition were invited to add their names as a fair and honorable acquiescence in the principle that the

* Elliot, ii., 497, 499. † Hening, xii., 463.

majority should govern. John Harris refused, yet held himself bound by the decision of the majority. Smilie answered: "My hand shall never give the lie to my heart and tongue." Twenty-one of the minority signed an exceedingly long address to their constituents, complaining that the extent of the country did not admit of the proposed form of government without danger to liberty; and that the powers vested in congress would lead to an iron-handed despotism, with unlimited control of the purse and the sword.

The ratification gave unbounded satisfaction to all Pennsylvania east of the Susquehanna; beyond that river loud murmurs were mingled with threats of resistance in arms. On the fifteenth the convention dissolved itself, after offering a permanent and a temporary seat of government to the United States.

The population of New Jersey at that time was almost exclusively rural; in the west chiefly the descendants of Quakers, in the east of Dutch and Scottish Calvinists. This industrious, frugal, and pious people, little agitated by political disputes, received the federal constitution with joy, and the consciousness that its own sons had contributed essentially to its formation.*

On the twenty-sixth of October its legislature called a state convention by a unanimous vote. On the eleventh of December the convention of New Jersey, composed of accomplished civilians, able judges, experienced generals, and fair-minded, intelligent husbandmen, assembled in Trenton. The next day was spent in organizing the house, all the elected members being present save one. John Stevens was chosen president by ballot; Samuel Whitham Stockton, secretary. The morning began with prayer. Then with open doors the convention proceeded to read the federal constitution by sections, giving opportunity for debates and for votes if called for; and, after a week's deliberation, on Tuesday, the eighteenth, determined unanimously to ratify and confirm the federal constitution. A committee, on which appear the names of Brearley, a member of the federal convention, Witherspoon, Neilson, Beatty, former members of congress, was appointed to draw up the

* Penn. Journal, 7 November 1787.

form of the ratification; and the people of the state of New Jersey, " by the unanimous consent of the members present, agreed to, ratified, and confirmed the proposed constitution and every part thereof." *

On the next day, the resolve for ratification having been engrossed in duplicate on parchment, one copy for the congress of the United States and one for the archives of the state, every member of the convention present subscribed his name.

In the shortest possible time, Delaware, Pennsylvania, and New Jersey, the three central states, one by a majority of two thirds, the others unanimously, accepted the constitution.

The union of the central states was of the best omen. Before knowing their decision, Georgia at the extreme south had independently taken its part; its legislature chanced to be in session when the message from congress arrived. All its relations to the United States were favorable; it was in possession of a territory abounding in resources and large enough to constitute an empire; its people felt the need of protection against Spain, which ruled along their southern frontier from the Mississippi to the Atlantic, and against the savages who dwelt in their forests and hung on the borders of their settlements. A convention which was promptly called met on Christmas-day, with power to adopt or reject any part or the whole of the proposed constitution. Assembled at Augusta, its members, finding themselves all of one mind, on the second day of the new year, unanimously, for themselves and for the people of Georgia, fully and entirely assented to, ratified, and adopted the proposed constitution. They hoped that their ready compliance would " tend to consolidate the union " and " promote the happiness of the common country." The completing of the ratification by the signing of the last name was announced by a salute of thirteen guns in token of faith that every state would accede to the new bonds of union.†

* Penn. Journal and Penn. Packet, 22 and 29 December.
† Stevens, History of Georgia, ii., 387.

## CHAPTER III.

### THE CONSTITUTION IN CONNECTICUT AND MASSACHUSETTS.

### FROM 26 SEPTEMBER 1787 TO 6 FEBRUARY 1788.

ON the twenty-sixth of September Roger Sherman and Oliver Ellsworth, two of the delegates from Connecticut to the federal convention, transmitted to Samuel Huntington, then governor of the state, a printed copy of the constitution to be laid before the legislature. In an accompanying official letter they observed that the proportion of suffrage accorded to the state remained the same as before; and they gave the assurance that the " additional powers vested in congress extended only to matters respecting the common interests of the union, and were specially defined; so that the particular states retained their sovereignty in all other matters." [*] The restraint on the legislatures of the several states respecting emitting bills of credit, making anything but money a tender in payment of debts, or impairing the obligation of contracts by *ex post facto* laws, was thought necessary as a security to commerce, in which the interest of foreigners as well as of the citizens of different states may be affected.[†]

The governor was a zealous friend of the new constitution. The legislature, on the sixteenth of October, unanimously [‡] called a convention of the state. To this were chosen the retired and the present highest officers of its government; the judges of its courts; "ministers of the Gospel;" and nearly sixty who had fought for independence. Connecticut had a special interest in ratifying the constitution; the compromise

---

[*] Compare the remark of Wilson, *supra*, 385, 386.
[†] Elliot, i., 491, 492.      [‡] Madison, i., 359.

requiring for acts of legislation a majority of the states and a majority of the representatives of the people had prevailed through its own delegates.

In January 1788, the convention, having been organized in the state-house in Hartford, moved immediately to the North Meeting House, where, in the presence of a multitude, the constitution was read and debated section by section, under an agreement that no vote should be taken till the whole of it should have been considered.*

On the fourth, Oliver Ellsworth explained the necessity of a federal government for the national defence, for the management of foreign relations, for preserving peace between the states, for giving energy to the public administration. He pointed out that a state like Connecticut was specially benefited by the restraint on separate states from collecting duties on foreign importations made through their more convenient harbors.

Johnson added: While under the confederation states in their political capacity could be coerced by nothing but a military force; the constitution introduces the mild and equal energy of magistrates for the execution of the laws. "By a signal intervention of divine providence, a convention from states differing in circumstances, interests, and manners, have harmoniously adopted one grand system; if we reject it, our national existence must come to an end." †

The grave and weighty men who listened to him approved his words; but when the paragraph which gave to the general government the largest powers of taxation was debated, James Wadsworth, who had served as a general officer in the war, objected to duties on imports as partial to the southern states. "Connecticut," answered Ellsworth, "is a manufacturing state; it already manufactures its implements of husbandry and half its clothes." Wadsworth further objected, that authority which unites the power of the sword to that of the purse is despotic. Ellsworth replied: "The general legislature ought to have a revenue; and it ought to have power to defend the state against foreign enemies; there can be no government without the power of the purse and the sword." "So well guarded is this constitution," observed Oliver Wolcott, then lieutenant-gov-

* Penn. Packet for 18 January 1788. † Penn. Packet, 24 January 1788.

ernor, "it seems impossible that the rights either of the states or of the people should be destroyed." When on the ninth the vote was taken, one hundred and twenty-eight appeared for the constitution; forty only against it.*

The people received with delight the announcement of this great majority of more than three to one; at the next election the "wrong-headed" James Wadsworth was left out of the government; and opposition grew more and more faint till it wholly died away.

The country from the St. Croix to the St. Mary's now fixed its attention on Massachusetts, whose adverse decision would inevitably involve the defeat of the constitution. The representatives of that great state, who came together on the seventeenth of October, had been chosen under the influence of the recent insurrection; and the constitution, had it been submitted to their judgment, would have been rejected.† In communicating it to the general court, the governor most wisely avoided provoking a discussion on its merits, and simply recommended its reference to a convention from regard to the worth of its authors and their unanimity on questions affecting the prosperity of the nation and the complicated rights of each separate state. ‡

Following his recommendation with exactness, the senate, of which Samuel Adams was president, promptly adopted a resolve to refer the new constitution to a convention of the commonwealth. On motion of Theophilus Parsons, of Newburyport, a lawyer destined to attain in his state the highest professional honors, the resolve of the senate was opened in the house. Spectators crowded the galleries and the floor.

* Penn. Packet, 24 January 1788.
† B. Lincoln to Washington, Boston, 19 March 1788.
‡ The conduct of Hancock in support of the constitution was from beginning to end consistent; and so wise that the afterthought of the most skilful caviller can not point out where it could be improved. Nathaniel Gorham, who had known Hancock long and well, in a letter to Madison of 27 January 1788, the darkest hour, places Hancock and Bowdoin foremost in the list of the managers of the cause of the constitution, naming them with equal confidence. Hancock, who was not wanting in sagacity, may have seen, and others may have let him know that they too saw, how much the support of the constitution would strengthen his position in public life; but at that time he had nothing to fear from the rivalry of Bowdoin, who had definitively retired.

VOL. VI.—27

Signs of a warm opposition appeared; the right to supersede the old confederation was denied alike to the convention and to the people; the adoption of a new constitution by but nine of the thirteen states would be the breach of a still valid compact. An inalienable power, it was said in reply, resides in the people to amend their form of government. An array of parties was avoided; and with little opposition a convention was ordered.

The choice took place at a moment when the country people of Massachusetts were bowed down by cumulative debts, and quivering in the agonies of a suppressed insurrection; the late disturbers of the peace were scarcely certain of amnesty; and they knew that the general government, if established, must array itself against violence. The election resulted in the choice of at least eighteen of the late insurgents. The rural population were disinclined to a change. The people in the district of Maine, which in territory far exceeded Massachusetts, had never willingly accepted annexation; the desire for a government of their own outweighed their willingness to enter into the union as a member of Massachusetts; and one half of their delegates were ready to oppose the constitution. On the other hand, the commercial towns of Maine, all manufacturers, men of wealth, the lawyers, including the judges of all the courts, and nearly all the officers of the late army, were in favor of the new form of general government. The voters of Cambridge rejected Elbridge Gerry in favor of Francis Dana; in Beverly, Nathan Dane was put aside[*] for George Cabot; the members from Maine were exactly balanced; but of those from Massachusetts proper a majority of perhaps ten or twelve was opposed to the ratification of the constitution. Among the elected were King, Gorham, and Strong, who had been of the federal convention; the late and present governors, Bowdoin and Hancock; Heath and Lincoln of the army; of rising statesmen, John Brooks and Christopher Gore; Theophilus Parsons, Theodore Sedgwick, John Davis, and Fisher Ames; and about twenty ministers of various religious denominations. So able a body had never met in Massachusetts. Full of faith that the adoption of the constitution was the

[*] Ind. Gazetteer, 8, 9 January 1788.

greatest question of the age, the federalists were all thoroughly in earnest, and influenced by no inferior motives; so that there could be among them neither cabals in council nor uncertainty in action. They obeyed an immovable determination to overcome the seemingly adverse majority. As a consequence, they had discipline and concerted action.

It was consistent with the whole public life of Samuel Adams, the helmsman of the revolution at its origin, the truest representative of the home rule of Massachusetts in its town-meetings and general court, that he was startled when, on entering the new "building, he met with a national government instead of a federal union of sovereign states;" but, in direct antagonism to George Mason and Richard Henry Lee, he had always approved granting to the general government the power of regulating commerce.* Before he had declared his intentions, perhaps before they had fully ripened, his constituents of the industrial classes of Boston, which had ever been his main support, came together, and from a crowded hall a cry went forth that on the rejection of the constitution "navigation" would languish and "skilful mechanics be compelled to emigrate," so that "any vote of a delegate from Boston against adopting it would be contrary to the interests, feelings, and wishes of the tradesmen of the town."

The morning betokened foul weather, but the heavy clouds would not join together. The enterprising and prosperous men of Maine, though they desired separation from Massachusetts, had no sympathy with the late insurrection; and the country people, though they could only by slow degrees accustom their minds to untried restraints on their rustic liberty, never wavered in their attachment to the union. The convention was organized with the governor of the commonwealth as its president.† The federalists of Philadelphia had handled their opponents roughly; the federalists of Massachusetts re-

---

* The activity and wise and efficient support of the constitution by Samuel Adams I received from my friend John Davis, who was a member of the convention, and who was singularly skilful in weighing evidence. The account which he gave me is thoroughly supported by the official record.

† Debates and Proceedings in the Convention, etc., published by the legislature of Massachusetts, edited by B. K. Peirce and C. Hale. The best collection on the subject.

solved never in debate to fail in gentleness and courtesy. A motion to request Elbridge Gerry to take a seat in the convention, that he might answer questions of fact, met no objection; and he was left to grow sick of sitting in a house to which he had failed of an election, and in whose debates he could not join. On motion of Caleb Strong, no vote was to be taken till the debate, which assumed the form of a free conversation, should have gone over the several paragraphs of the constitution.*

Massachusetts had instructed its delegates in the federal convention to insist on the annual election of representatives; Samuel Adams asked why they were to be chosen for two years. Strong explained that it was a necessary compromise among so many states; and Adams answered: "I am satisfied." † This remark the federal leaders entreated him to repeat; all the house gave attention as he did so, and the objection was definitively put to rest.

Referring to the power of congress to take part in regulating the elections of senators and representatives, Phineas Bishop of Rehoboth proclaimed "the liberties of the yeomanry at an end." It is but "a guarantee of free elections," said Cabot. "And a security of the rights of the people," added Theophilus Parsons. "Our rulers," observed Widgery of Maine, "ought to have no power which they can abuse." ‡ "All the godly men we read of," added Abraham White of Bristol, "have failed; I would not trust a flock, though every one of them should be a Moses."

On the seventeenth an official letter from Connecticut announced the very great majority by which it had adopted the constitution; but its enemies in Massachusetts were unmoved. Samuel Thompson of Maine condemned it for not requiring of a representative some property qualification, saying: "Men who have nothing to lose have nothing to fear." "Do you wish to exclude from the federal government a good man because he is not rich?" asked Theodore Sedgwick. "The men who have most injured the country," said King, "have commonly been rich men."

On the eighteenth the compromise respecting the taxation

---

* Elliot, ii., 3.      † From John Davis.      ‡ Elliot, ii., 28.

and representation of slaves was cried against. Thomas Dawes of Boston answered: "Congress in the year 1808 may wholly prohibit the importation of them, leaving every particular state in the mean time its own option totally to prohibit their introduction into its own territories. Slavery could not be abolished by an act of congress in a moment; but it has received a mortal wound." *

On the nineteenth a farmer of Worcester county complained: "There is no provision that men in power should have any religion; a Papist or an infidel is as eligible as Christians." John Brooks and Parsons spoke on the other side; and Daniel Shute, the minister of Hingham, said: "No conceivable advantage to the whole will result from a test." William Jones of Maine rejoined: "It would be happy for the United States if our public men were to be of those who have a good standing in the church." Philip Payson, the minister of Chelsea, retorted: "Human tribunals for the consciences of men are impious encroachments upon the prerogatives of God. A religious test, as a qualification for office, would have been a great blemish."

William Jones of Maine objected to the long period of office for the senators. "One third of the senators," observed Fisher Ames, "are to be introduced every second year; the constitution, in practice as in theory, will be that of a federal republic." "We cannot," continued Jones, "recall the senators." "Their duration," answered King, "is not too long for a right discharge of their duty."

On the twenty-first, King explained the nature of the transition † from a league of states with only authority to make requisitions on each state, to a republic instituted by the people with the right to apply laws directly to the individual members of the states. He showed that without the power over the purse and the sword no government can give security to the people; analyzed and defended the grant of revenue alike from indirect and direct taxes, and insisted that the proposed constitution is the only efficient federal government that can be substituted for the old confederation.

Thomas Dawes of Boston defended the power of laying

* Elliot, ii., 41. † Elliot, ii., 54–57.

imposts and excises in this wise: "For want of general laws of prohibition through the union, our coasting trade, our whole commerce, is going to ruin. A vessel from Halifax with its fish and whalebone finds as hearty a welcome at the southern ports as though built and navigated and freighted from Salem or Boston. South of Delaware three fourths of the exports and three fourths of the returns are made in British bottoms. Of timber, one half of the value—of other produce shipped for London from a southern state, three tenths—go to the British carrier in the names of freight and charges. This is money which belongs to the New England states, because we can furnish the ships much better than the British. Our sister states are willing that these benefits should be secured to us by national laws; but we are slaves to Europe. We have no uniformity in duties, imposts, excises, or prohibitions. Congress has no authority to withhold advantages from foreigners in order to obtain reciprocal advantages from them. Our manufacturers have received no encouragement by national duties on foreign manufactures, and they never can by any authority in the confederation. The very face of our country, our numerous falls of water and places for mills, lead to manufactures: have they been encouraged? Has congress been able by national laws to prevent the importation of such foreign commodities as are made from such raw materials as we ourselves raise? The citizens of the United States within the last three years have contracted debts with the subjects of Great Britain to the amount of near six millions of dollars. If we wish to encourage our own manufactures, to preserve our own commerce, to raise the value of our own lands, we must give congress the powers in question." *

Every day that passed showed the doubtfulness of the convention. "The decision of Massachusetts either way," wrote Madison from congress, "will involve the result in New York," and a negative would rouse the minority in Pennsylvania to a stubborn resistance. Langdon of New Hampshire, and men from Newport and Providence who came to watch the course of the debates, reported that New Hampshire and Rhode Island would accept the constitution should it be adopted by

* Elliot, ii., 57-60.

Massachusetts. Gerry, under the influence of Richard Henry Lee, had written a letter to the two houses of Massachusetts, insinuating that the constitution needed amendments, and should not be adopted till they were made. These same suggestions had been circulated throughout Virginia, where, as has already been related,* Washington threw himself into the discussion and advised, as the only true policy, to accept the constitution and amend it by the methods which the constitution itself had established. The letter in which he had given this advice reached Boston in season to be published in the Boston "Centinel" of the twenty-third of January. In the convention the majority still seemed adverse to the constitution. To win votes from the ranks of its foes, its friends, following the counsels of Washington, resolved to combine with its ratification a recommendation of amendments. For this end Bowdoin and Hancock, Theophilus Parsons and Gorham, Samuel Adams, Heath, and a very few other resolute and trusty men, matured in secret council a plan of action.†

Meantime Samuel Thompson could see no safety but in a bill of rights. Bowdoin spoke at large for the new government with its ability to pay the public debts and to regulate commerce. "Power inadequate to its object is worse than none; checks are provided to prevent abuse. The whole constitution is a declaration of rights. It will complete the temple of American liberty, and consecrate it to justice. May this convention erect Massachusetts as one of its pillars on the foundation of perfect union, never to be dissolved but by the dissolution of nature." ‡

Parsons recapitulated and answered the objections brought against the constitution, and closed his remarks by saying: "An increase of the powers of the federal constitution by usurpation will be upon thirteen completely organized legislatures having means as well as inclination to oppose it successfully. The people themselves have power to resist it without an appeal to arms. An act of usurpation is not law, and therefore is not obligatory; and any man may be justified in his resistance. Let him be considered as a criminal by the general

---

* See page 380 of this volume.
† King to Madison, quoted in Madison's Writings, i., 373.   ‡ Elliot, ii., 80–88.

government; his own fellow-citizens are his jury; and if they pronounce him innocent, not all the powers of congress can hurt him." *

On the morning of the twenty-fourth, Nason of Maine, an implacable enemy of the constitution, proposed to cease its discussion by paragraphs so as to open the whole question. This attempt "to hurry the matter" was resisted by Samuel Adams in a speech so effective that the motion was negatived without a division.

On the next day Amos Singletary of Sutton, a husbandman venerable from age and from patriotic service from the very beginning of the troubles with England, resisted the constitution as an attempt to tax and bind the people in all cases whatsoever.

Jonathan Smith of Lanesborough, speaking to men who like himself followed the plough for their livelihood, began a reply by arguments drawn from the late insurrection, when he was called to order. Samuel Adams instantly said with authority: "The gentleman is in order; let him go on in his own way." The "plain man" then proceeded in homely words to show that farmers in the western counties, in their great distress during the insurrection, would have been glad to snatch at anything like a government for protection. "This constitution," he said, "is just such a cure for these disorders as we wanted. Anarchy leads to tyranny."

Attention was arrested by the clause on the slave-trade. "My profession," said James Neal of Maine, "obliges me to bear witness against anything that favors making merchandise of the bodies of men, and unless this objection is removed I cannot put my hand to the constitution." "Shall it be said," cried Samuel Thompson, "that after we have established our own independence and freedom we make slaves of others? How has Washington immortalized himself! but he holds those in slavery who have as good a right to be free as he has." Dana and Samuel Adams rejoiced that a door was to be opened for the total annihilation of the slave-trade after twenty years; but hatred of slavery influenced the final vote.†

On the morning of the thirty-first of January, Hancock,

\* Elliot, ii., 94. † Elliot, ii., 107, 120.

who till then had been kept from his place by painful illness, took the chair, and the concerted movement began. Conversation came to an end; and Parsons proposed "that the convention do assent to and ratify the constitution." * Heath suggested that in ratifying it they should instruct their members of congress to endeavor to provide proper checks and guards in some of its paragraphs, and that the convention should correspond with their sister states, to request their concurrence." †

Hancock then spoke earnestly for the necessity of adopting the proposed form of government; and brought forward nine general amendments. Taken from the letters of Richard Henry Lee, the remonstrance of the minority in Pennsylvania, and the objections made in the Massachusetts debates, "they were the production of the federalists after mature deliberation," and were clad in terse and fittest words, which revealed the workmanship of Parsons. "All powers not expressly delegated to congress," so ran the most important of them, " are reserved to the several states."

"I feel myself happy," thus Samuel Adams addressed the chair, "in contemplating the idea that many benefits will result from your Excellency's conciliatory proposition to this commonwealth and to the whole United States. The objections made to this constitution as far as Virginia are similar. I have had my doubts; other gentlemen have had theirs; the proposition submitted will tend to remove such doubts, and conciliate the minds of the convention and of the people out-of-doors. The measure of Massachusetts will from her importance have the most salutary effect in other states where conventions have not yet met, and throughout the union. The people should be united in a federal government to withstand the common enemy and to preserve their rights and liberties; I should fear the consequences of large minorities in the several states.

"The article which empowers congress to regulate commerce and to form treaties I esteem particularly valuable. For want of this power in our national head our friends are grieved; our enemies insult us; our minister at the court of

* Elliot, ii., 120.        † Elliot, ii., 122.

London is a cipher. A power to remedy this evil should be given to congress, and applied as soon as possible. I move that the paper read by your Excellency be now taken into consideration." *

Samuel Adams, on the first day of February, invited members to propose still further amendments; but Nason of Maine, the foremost in opposition, stubbornly refused to take part in supporting a constitution which, they said, "destroyed the sovereignty of Massachusetts." †

The measure was referred to a committee formed on the principle of selecting from each county one of its friends and one of its opponents; but as both of the two delegates from Dukes county were federalists, only one of them took a place in the committee. Thirteen of its members were federalists from the beginning. At the decision, the committee consisted of twenty-four members; one absented himself and one declined to vote; so that in the afternoon of Monday, the fourth of February, Bowdoin as chairman of the committee could report its approval of the constitution with the recommendation of amendments by a vote of fifteen to seven.

At this result opposition flared anew. Thomas Lusk of West Stockbridge revived complaints of the slave-trade, and of opening the door to popery and the inquisition by dispensing with a religious test. But Isaac Backus, the Baptist minister of Middleborough, one of the most exact of New England historians, replied: "In reason and the holy scriptures religion is ever a matter between God and individuals; the imposing of religious tests hath been the greatest engine of tyranny in the world." Rebuking the importation of slaves with earnestness, he trusted in the passing away of slavery itself, saying: "Slavery grows more and more odious to the world." ‡  "This constitution," said Fisher Ames, on the fifth

---

* Elliot, ii., 123–125. Let no one be misled by the words "conditional amendments" in the report of Mr. Adams's speech. He spoke not of amendments offered as the condition of the acceptance of the constitution by Massachusetts, but advised that Massachusetts should connect with its ratification a recommendation of amendments; the ratification to be valid whatever fate might await the amendments. This is exactly the proposition concerted between Parsons, Hancock, and himself. Rufus King to Knox, in Drake's Knox, 98.

† Elliot, ii., 133, 134.  ‡ Elliot, ii., 148–151.

day, "is comparatively perfect; no subsisting government, no government which I have ever heard of, will bear a comparison with it. The state government is a beautiful structure, situated, however, upon the naked beach; the union is the dike to fence out the flood." *

John Taylor of Worcester county objected that the amendments might never become a part of the system, and that there was no bill of rights. "No power," answered Parsons, "is given to congress to infringe on any one of the natural rights of the people; should they attempt it without constitutional authority, the act would be a nullity and could not be enforced." Gilbert Dench of Middlesex, coinciding with the wishes of the opposition in Virginia, and with a motion of Whitehill in the convention of Pennsylvania, proposed an adjournment of the convention to some future day. A long and warm contest ensued; but Samuel Adams skilfully resisted the motion, and of the three hundred and twenty-nine members who were present, it obtained but one hundred and fifteen votes.†

On the sixth the office of closing the debate was by common consent assigned to Samuel Stillman, a Baptist minister of Boston. Recapitulating and weighing the arguments of each side, he said, in the words of a statesman of Virginia: "Cling to the union as the rock of our salvation," and he summoned the state of Massachusetts "to urge Virginia to finish the salutary work which hath been begun." ‡

Before putting the question, Hancock spoke words that were remembered: "I give my assent to the constitution in full confidence that the amendments proposed will soon become a part of the system. The people of this commonwealth will quietly acquiesce in the voice of the majority, and, where they see a want of perfection in the proposed form of government, endeavor, in a constitutional way, to have it amended."

The question being taken, the counties of Dukes, Essex, Suffolk, and Plymouth, and, in Maine, of Cumberland and Lincoln, all counties that touched the sea, gave majorities in favor of the constitution; Middlesex and Bristol, the whole of Massachusetts to the west of them, and the county of York in

* Elliot, ii., 154–159. † Elliot, ii., 161, 162. ‡ Elliot, ii., 162, 170.

Maine, gave majorities against it. The majority of Maine for the constitution was in proportion greater than in Massachusetts.

The motion for ratifying the constitution was declared to be in the affirmative by one hundred and eighty-seven votes against one hundred and sixty-eight.* The bells and artillery announced the glad news to every part of the town.

With the declaration of the vote, every symptom of persistent opposition vanished. No person even wished for a protest. The convention, after dissolving itself, partook of a modest collation in the senate-chamber, where, merging party ideas in mutual congratulations, they all "smoked the calumet of love and union." "The Boston people," wrote Knox to Livingston, "have lost their senses with joy." † The Long Lane by the meeting-house, in which the convention held its sessions, took from that time the name of Federal street. The prevailing joy diffused itself through the commonwealth. In New York, at noon, men hoisted the pine-tree flag with an appropriate inscription. Six states had ratified, and six salutes, each of thirteen guns, were fired.

The example of Massachusetts was held worthy of imitation. "A conditional ratification or a second convention," so wrote Madison to Randolph in April, "appears to me utterly irreconcilable with the dictates of prudence and safety. Recommendatory alterations are the only ground for a coalition among the real federalists." ‡

Jefferson, while in congress as the successor of Madison, had led the way zealously toward rendering the American constitution more perfect. "The federal convention," so he wrote to one correspondent on hearing who were its members, "is really an assembly of demigods;" and to another: "It consists of the ablest men in America." He hoped from it a broader reformation, and saw with satisfaction "a general disposition through the states to adopt what it should propose." To Washington he soberly expressed the opinions from which during his long life he never departed: "To make our states one as to all foreign concerns, preserve them several as to all

---

\* Elliot, ii., 174–176, 181.
† Knox to Livingston, 13 February 1788.
‡ Madison's Works, i., 386, and compare 376–379.

merely domestic, to give to the federal head some peaceable mode of enforcing its just authority, to organize that head into legislative, executive, and judiciary departments, are great desiderata." *

Early in November Jefferson received a copy of the new constitution, and approved the great mass of its provisions.† But once he called it a kite set up to keep the hen-yard in order; ‡ and with three or four new articles he would have preserved the venerable fabric of the old confederation as a sacred relic.

To Madison # he explained himself in a long and deliberate letter. A house of representatives elected directly by the people he thought would be far inferior to one chosen by the state legislatures; but he accepted that mode of election from respect to the fundamental principle that the people are not to be taxed but by representatives chosen immediately by themselves. He was captivated by the compromise between the great and smaller states, and the method of voting in both branches of the legislature by persons instead of voting by states; but he utterly condemned the omission of a bill of rights, and the abandonment of the principle of rotation in the choice of the president. I own, he added of himself, "I am not a friend to a very energetic government;" for he held that it would be "always oppressive." He presumed that Virginia would reject the new constitution; ‖ for himself he said: "It is my principle that the will of the majority should prevail; if they approve, I shall cheerfully concur in the proposed constitution, in hopes they will amend it whenever they shall find that it works wrong." ᴀ In February 1788 he wrote to Madison ◊ and at least one more of his correspondents: "I wish with all my soul that the nine first conventions may accept the new constitution, to secure to us the good it contains; but I equally wish that the four latest, whichever they may be, may refuse to accede to it till a declaration of rights be annexed; but no objection to the new form must produce a schism in

---

\* Jefferson, i., 349, 260, 149, 264, 250, 251.
† Jefferson, i., 79, and ii., 586. ‖ Jefferson, ii., 325.
‡ Jefferson, ii., 319. ᴀ Jefferson, ii., 332.
# Jefferson, ii., 328–331. ◊ Jefferson to Madison, 6 February 1788.

our union." This was the last word from him which reached America in time to have any influence. But in May of that year, so soon as he heard of the method adopted by Massachusetts, he declared that it was far preferable to his own, and wished it to be followed by every state, especially by Virginia.* To Madison he wrote in July: "The constitution is a good canvas on which some strokes only want retouching." †  In 1789 to a friend in Philadelphia he wrote with perfect truth: "I am not of the party of federalists; but I am much further from that of the anti-federalists." ‡

The constitution was to John Adams more of a surprise than to Jefferson; but at once he formed his unchanging judgment, and in December 1787 he wrote of it officially to Jay: "The public mind cannot be occupied about a nobler object than the proposed plan of government. It appears to be admirably calculated to cement all America in affection and interest as one great nation. A result of compromise cannot perfectly coincide with every one's ideas of perfection; but, as all the great principles necessary to order, liberty, and safety are respected in it, and provision is made for amendments as they may be found necessary, I hope to hear of its adoption by all the states." #

* Jefferson, ii., 398, 399, 404.   † Jefferson, ii., 445.   ‡ Jefferson, ii., 585, 586.
# John Adams's Works, viii., 467; Diplomatic Correspondence, 1783–1789, v., 356.

## CHAPTER IV.

THE CONSTITUTION IN NEW HAMPSHIRE, MARYLAND, AND SOUTH CAROLINA.

FROM FEBRUARY TO 23 MAY 1788.

LANGDON, the outgoing chief magistrate of New Hampshire, and Sullivan, his successful competitor, vied with each other in zeal for federal measures; but when, in February 1788, the convention of the state came together there appeared to be a small majority against any change. In a seven days' debate, Joshua Atherton of Amherst; William Hooper, the minister of Marbury; Matthias Stone, deacon of the church in Claremont; Abiel Parker, from Jaffrey, reproduced the objections that had been urged in the neighboring state; while John Sullivan, John Langdon, Samuel Livermore, Josiah Bartlett, and John Pickering explained and defended it with conciliatory moderation. When zealots complained of the want of a religious test, Woodbury Langdon, lately president of Harvard college, but now a minister of the gospel at Hampton Falls, demonstrated that religion is a question between God and man in which no civil authority may interfere. Dow, from Weare, spoke against the twenty years' sufferance of the foreign slave-trade; and to the explanation of Langdon that under the confederation the power exists without limit, Atherton answered: "It is our full purpose to wash our hands clear of becoming its guarantees even for a term of years."

The friends of the constitution won converts enough to hold the balance; but these were fettered by instructions from their towns. To give them an opportunity to consult their constituents, the friends of the constitution proposed an adjournment till June, saying, with other reasons, that it would be very prudent for a small state like New Hampshire to wait and see what the other states would do. This was the argument which had the greatest weight.* The place of meeting was changed from Exeter, a stronghold of federalism, to Concord; and the adjournment was then carried by a slender majority.†

The assembly of Maryland, in November 1787, summoned its delegates to the federal convention to give them information of its proceedings; and Martin rehearsed to them and published to the world his three days' arraignment of that body for having exceeded its authority. He was answered by McHenry, who, by a concise analysis of the constitution, drew to himself the sympathy of his hearers. The legislature unanimously ordered a convention of the people of the state; it copied the example set by Virginia of leaving the door open for amendments; ‡ and by a majority of one the day for the choice and the day for the meeting of its convention were postponed till the next April.

The long delay gave opportunity for the cabalings of the anti-federalists of Virginia.# Richard Henry Lee was as zealous as ever; and Patrick Henry disseminated propositions for a southern confederacy; ‖ but Washington, who felt himself at home on the Maryland side of the Potomac, toiled fearlessly and faithfully, with Madison at his side, for the immediate and unconditioned ratification of the constitution by the South.

In the three months' interval before the election, the fields and forests and towns of Maryland were alive with thought; the merits of the constitution were scanned and sifted in every public meeting and at every hearth; and on the day in 1788 for choosing delegates, each voter, in designating the candidate of his preference, registered his own deliberate decision. In fifteen counties, and the cities of Baltimore and Annapolis, there was no diversity of sentiment. Two counties only re-

* Report in the Mass. Spy, copied into Ind. Gazetteer of 9 April 1788.
† Ind. Gazetteer, 17 March 1788.
‡ Madison to Jefferson, 9 December 1787; Madison, i., 363, 364.
# Letters to Washington, iv., 196.
‖ This is repeatedly told of Henry by Carrington. See also Madison, i., 365.

turned none but anti-federalists; Harford county elected three of that party and one trimmer.

The day before the convention was to assemble, Washington, guarding against the only danger that remained, addressed a well-considered letter to Thomas Johnson: "An adjournment of your convention will be tantamount to the rejection of the constitution. It cannot be too much deprecated and guarded against. Great use is made of the postponement in New Hampshire, although it has no reference to the convention of this state. An event similar to this in Maryland would have the worst tendency imaginable; for indecision there would certainly have considerable influence upon South Carolina, the only other state which is to precede Virginia; and it submits the question almost wholly to the determination of the latter. The pride of the state is already touched, and will be raised much higher if there is fresh cause." *

The advice, which was confirmed by similar letters from Madison, was communicated to several of the members; so that the healing influence of Virginia proved greater than its power to wound. But the men of Maryland of themselves knew their duty, and Washington's advice was but an encouragement for them to proceed in the way which they had chosen.

On Monday, the twenty-first of April, a quorum of the convention assembled at Annapolis. The settlement of representation in the two branches of the federal legislature was pleasing to all the representatives of fifteen counties, and the cities of Baltimore and Annapolis agreed with each other perfectly that the main question had already been decided by the people in their respective counties; and that the ratification of the constitution, the single transaction for which they were convened, ought to be speedily completed. Two days were given to the organization of the house and establishing rules for its government; on the third the constitution was read a first time, and the motion for its ratification was formally made. The plan of a confederacy of slave-holding states found not

---

* Washington to Thomas Johnson, 20 April 1788; T. Johnson to Washington, 10 October 1788. Compare Washington to James McHenry, 27 April 1788; to Daniel of St. Thomas Jenifer, 27 April 1788; to James Madison, 2 May 1788.

VOL. VI.—28

one supporter; not one suggested an adjournment for the purpose of consultation with Virginia. The malcontents could embarrass the convention only by proposing pernicious amendments.

On the morning of the twenty-fourth, Samuel Chase took his seat, and at the second reading of the constitution began from elaborate notes the fiercest opposition: The powers to be vested in the new government are deadly to the cause of liberty, and should be amended before adoption; five states can now force a concession of amendments which after the national government shall go into operation could be carried only by nine.* He spoke till he was exhausted, intending to resume his argument on the following day.

In the afternoon, William Paca of Harford county, a signer of the declaration of independence, appeared for the first time and sought to steer between the clashing opinions, saying: "I have a variety of objections; not as conditions, but to accompany the ratification as standing instructions to the representatives of Maryland in congress." To Johnson the request seemed candid; and on his motion the convention adjourned to the next morning.† The interval was employed in preparing a set of amendments to the constitution, which were adapted to injure the cause of federalism in Virginia. ‡

On Friday morning a member from each of eleven several counties and the two cities, one after the other, declared "that he and his colleagues were under an obligation to vote for the government;" and almost all declared further that they had no authority to propose amendments which their constituents had never considered, and of course could never have directed.# When Paca began to read his amendments, he was called to order by George Gale of Somerset county, the question before the house being still "on the ratification of the constitution." Chase once more "made a display of all his eloquence;" John F. Mercer discharged his whole "artillery of inflammable

---

* Notes of Chase on the constitution, MS.; and the historical address of Alex. C. Hanson, MS. † Hanson's MS. narrative.
‡ James McHenry to Washington, 18 May 1788.
# Alex. C. Hanson. MS. Elliot, ii., 548.

matter;" and Martin rioted in boisterous "vehemence;" "but no converts were made; no, not one."\*

The friends to the federal government "remained inflexibly silent." The malcontents having tired themselves out, between two and three o'clock on Saturday, the twenty-sixth, the constitution was ratified by sixty-three votes against eleven, Paca voting with the majority. Proud of its great majority of nearly six to one, the convention fixed Monday, at three o'clock, for the time when they would all set their names to the instrument of ratification.

Paca then brought forward his numerous amendments, saying that with them his constituents would receive the constitution, without them would oppose it even with arms.† After a short but perplexed debate he was indulged in the appointment of a committee of thirteen, of which he himself was the chairman; but they had power only to recommend amendments to the consideration of the people of Maryland. The majority of the committee readily acceded to thirteen resolutions, explaining the constitution according to the construction of its friends, and restraining congress from exercising power not expressly delegated. The minority demanded more; the committee fell into a wrangle; the convention on Monday sent a summons for them; and Paca, taking the side of the minority, would make no report. Thereupon the convention dissolved itself by a great majority.

The accession of Maryland to the new union by a vote of nearly six to one brought to the constitution the majority of the thirteen United States, and a great majority of their free inhabitants. The state which was cradled in religious liberty gained the undisputed victory over the first velleity of the slave-holding states to form a separate confederacy. "It is a thorn in the sides of the leaders of opposition in this state!" wrote Washington to Madison. ‡ "Seven affirmative without a negative would almost convert the unerring sister. The fiat of your convention will most assuredly raise the edifice," # were his words to Jenifer of Maryland.

---

\* Washington to Madison, 2 May 1788.  † Hanson. MS.
‡ Washington to Madison, 2 May 1788.
# Washington to Daniel of St. Thomas Jenifer, 27 April 1788.

In his hours of meditation he saw the movement of the divine power which gives unity to the universe, and order and connection to events: "It is impracticable for any one who has not been on the spot to realize the change in men's minds, and the progress toward rectitude in thinking and acting.

"The plot thickens fast. A few short weeks will determine the political fate of America for the present generation, and probably produce no small influence on the happiness of society through a long succession of ages to come. Should everything proceed with harmony and consent according to our actual wishes and expectations, it will be so much beyond anything we had a right to imagine or expect eighteen months ago that it will, as visibly as any possible event in the course of human affairs, demonstrate the finger of Providence." *

In South Carolina the new constitution awakened fears of oppressive navigation acts and of disturbance in the ownership of slaves. The inhabitants of the upper country, who suffered from the undue legislative power of the city of Charleston and the lower counties, foreboded new inequalities from a consolidation of the union. A part of the low country, still suffering from the war, had shared the rage for instalment laws, paper money, and payment of debts by appraised property; and to all these the new constitution made an end.

The opposition from Virginia † intrigued for a southern confederacy, while Madison, in entire unison with Washington, wrote to his friends in behalf of union. ‡ They both knew that there was to be resistance to the constitution, with Rawlins Lowndes for its spokesman; and as he could by no possibility be elected into the convention, the chief scene of the opposition could only be the legislature.#

In January 1788 the senate unanimously voted thanks to the members from their state in the federal convention for their faithfulness. On the sixteenth, in the committee of the whole house of representatives, Charles Pinckney gave a his-

---

* Washington to the Marquis de la Fayette, 28 May 1788.
† Jefferson to Shippen, 14 July 1788. "Mr. Henry disseminated propositions there for a southern confederacy."
‡ Madison to Washington, 10 April 1788. Works, i., 384, 385.
# Madison, i., 382; Elliot, iv., 274.

tory * of the formation and the character of "the federal republic;" which was to operate upon the people and not upon the states. At once Lowndes † objected that the interests of South Carolina were endangered by the clause in the constitution according to which a treaty to be made by two thirds of the senate, and a president who was not likely ever to be chosen from South Carolina or Georgia, would be the supreme law of the land. Cotesworth Pinckney condemned the reasoning as disingenuous. "Every treaty," said John Rutledge, "is law paramount and must operate," not less under the confederation than under the constitution. ‡ "If treaties are not superior to local laws," asked Ramsay, "who will trust them?" Lowndes proceeded, saying of the confederation: "We are now under a most excellent constitution—a blessing from heaven, that has stood the test of time, and given us liberty and independence; yet we are impatient to pull down that fabric which we raised at the expense of our blood." # Now, Rawlins Lowndes had pertinaciously resisted the declaration of independence; and when, in 1778, South Carolina had made him her governor, had in her reverses sought British protection. He proceeded: "When this new constitution shall be adopted, the sun of the southern states will set, never to rise again. What cause is there for jealousy of our importing negroes? Why confine us to twenty years? Why limit us at all? This trade can be justified on the principles of religion and humanity. They do not like our slaves because they have none themselves, and, therefore, want to exclude us from this great advantage." ‖

"Every state," interposed Pendleton, "has prohibited the importation of negroes except Georgia and the two Carolinas."

Lowndes continued: "Without negroes this state would degenerate into one of the most contemptible in the union. Negroes are our wealth, our only natural resource; yet our kind friends in the North are determined soon to tie up our hands and drain us of what we have."

"Against the restrictions that might be laid on the African trade after the year 1808," said Cotesworth Pinckney on the

* Elliot, iv., 253-263.     ‡ Elliot, iv., 267, 268.
† Elliot, iv., 265, 266.     # Elliot, iv., 270-272.
‖ Elliot, iv., 272.

seventeenth, " your delegates had to contend with the religious and political prejudices of the eastern and middle states, and with the interested and inconsistent opinion of Virginia. It was alleged that slaves increase the weakness of any state which admits them; that an invading enemy could easily turn them against ourselves and the neighboring states; and that, as we are allowed a representation for them, our influence in government would be increased in proportion as we were less able to defend ourselves. 'Show some period,' said the members from the eastern states, 'when it may be in our power to put a stop, if we please, to the importation of this weakness, and we will endeavor, for your convenience, to restrain the religious and political prejudices of our people on this subject.' The middle states and Virginia made us no such proposition; they were for an immediate and total prohibition. A committee of the states was appointed in order to accommodate this matter, and, after a great deal of difficulty, it was settled on the footing recited in the constitution.

" By this settlement we have secured an unlimited importation of negroes for twenty years. The general government can never emancipate them, for no such authority is granted, and it is admitted on all hands that the general government has no powers but what are expressly granted by the constitution. We have obtained a right to recover our slaves in whatever part of America they may take refuge, which is a right we had not before. In short, considering all circumstances, we have made the best terms in our power for the security of this species of property. We would have made better if we could; but, on the whole, I do not think them bad." *

" Six of the seven eastern states," continued Lowndes, " form a majority in the house of representatives. Their interest will so predominate as to divest us of any pretensions to the title of a republic. They draw their subsistence, in a great measure, from their shipping; the regulation of our commerce throws into their hands the carrying trade under payment of whatever freightage they think proper to impose. Why should the southern states allow this without the consent of

* Elliot, iv., 277–286.

nine states? If at any future period we should remonstrate, 'mind your business' will be the style of language held out toward the southern states." "The fears that the northern interests will prevail at all times," said Edward Rutledge, "are ill-founded. Carry your views into futurity. Several of the northern states are already full of people; the migrations to the South are immense; in a few years we shall rise high in our representation, while other states will keep their present position." *

The argument of Lowndes rested on the idea that the southern states are weak. "We are weak," answered Cotesworth Pinckney; "by ourselves we cannot form a union strong enough for the purpose of effectually protecting each other. Without union with the other states, South Carolina must soon fall. Is there any one among us so much a Quixote as to suppose that this state could long maintain her independence if she stood alone, or was only connected with the southern states? I scarcely believe there is. As, from the nature of our climate and the fewness of our inhabitants, we are undoubtedly weak, should we not endeavor to form a close union with the eastern states, who are strong? We certainly ought to endeavor to increase that species of strength which will render them of most service to us both in peace and war. I mean their navy. Justice to them and humanity, interest and policy, concur in prevailing upon us to submit the regulation of commerce to the general government.†

Lowndes renewed his eulogy on the old confederation. "The men who signed it were eminent for patriotism and virtue; and their wisdom and prudence particularly appear in their care sacredly to guarantee the sovereignty of each state. The treaty of peace expressly agreed to acknowledge us free, sovereign, and independent states; but this new constitution, being sovereign over all, sweeps those privileges away." ‡

Cotesworth Pinckney answered: "We were independent before the treaty, which does not grant, but acknowledges our independence. We ought to date that blessing from an older charter than the treaty of peace; from a charter which our

* Elliot, iv., 272, 274, 276, 277, 288.
† Elliot, iv., 283, 284.    ‡ Elliot, iv., 287.

babes should be taught to lisp in their cradles; which our youth should learn as a *carmen necessarium*, an indispensable lesson; which our young men should regard as their compact of freedom; and which our old should repeat with ejaculations of gratitude for the bounties it is about to bestow on their posterity. I mean the declaration of independence, made in congress the 4th of July 1776. This manifesto, which for importance of matter and elegance of composition stands unrivalled, confutes the doctrine of the individual sovereignty and independence of the several states. The separate independence and individual sovereignty of the several states were never thought of by the enlightened band of patriots who framed this declaration. The several states are not even mentioned by name in any part of it; as if to impress on America that our freedom and independence arose from our union, and that without it we could neither be free nor independent. Let us, then, consider all attempts to weaken this union by maintaining that each state is separately and individually independent, as a species of political heresy which can never benefit us, but may bring on us the most serious distresses." *

Lowndes sought to rally to his side the friends of paper money, and asked triumphantly: "What harm has paper money done?" "What harm?" retorted Cotesworth Pinckney. "Beyond losses by depreciation, paper money has corrupted the morals of the people; has diverted them from the paths of honest industry to the ways of ruinous speculation; has destroyed both public and private credit; and has brought total ruin on numberless widows and orphans." †

James Lincoln of Ninety-six pressed the objection that the constitution contained no bill of rights. Cotesworth Pinckney answered: "By delegating express powers, we certainly reserve to ourselves every power and right not mentioned in the constitution. Another reason weighed particularly with the members from this state. Bills of rights generally begin with declaring that all men are by nature born free. Now, we should make that declaration with a very bad grace when a large part of our property consists in men who are actually born slaves." ‡

* Elliot, iv., 301, 302.   † Elliot, iv., 306.   ‡ Elliot, iv., 315, 316.

Lowndes, following the lead of the opposition of Virginia, had recommended another convention in which every objection could be met on fair grounds, and adequate remedies applied.* The proposal found no acceptance; but he persevered in cavilling and objecting. At last John Rutledge impatiently expressed a hope that Lowndes would find a seat in the coming convention, and pledged himself there to prove that all those grounds on which he dwelt amounted to no more than mere declamation; that his boasted confederation was not worth a farthing; that if such instruments were piled up to his chin they would not shield him from one single national calamity; that the sun of this state, so far from being obscured by the new constitution, would, when united with twelve other suns, astonish the world by its lustre." †

The resolution for a convention to consider the constitution was unanimously adopted. In the rivalry between Charleston and Columbia as its place of meeting, Charleston carried the day by a majority of one vote. ‡

The purest spirit of patriotism and union and veneration for the men of the revolution pervaded South Carolina at the time of her choice of delegates. Foremost among them were the venerable Christopher Gadsden and John Rutledge, Moultrie and Motte, William Washington, Edward Rutledge, the three Pinckneys, Grimké, and Ramsay; the chancellor and the leading judges of the state; men chiefly of English, Scotch, Scotch-Irish, and Huguenot descent; a thorough representation of the best elements and culture of South Carolina.

The convention organized itself on the thirteenth of May, with Thomas Pinckney, then Governor of South Carolina, as president. The ablest man in the opposition was Edanus Burke; but the leader in support of the Virginia malcontents was Sumter. A week's quiet consideration of the constitution by paragraphs showed the disposition of the convention, when on the twenty-first Sumter, as a last effort of those who wished to act with Virginia, made a motion for an adjournment for five months, to give time for the further consideration of the federal convention. A few gave way to the hope of conciliating by moderation; but after debate the motion

* Elliot, iv., 290.   † Elliot, iv., 312.   ‡ Elliot, iv., 316, 317.

received only eighty-nine votes against one hundred and thirty-five. Three or four amendments were recommended; and then, at five o'clock in the evening of the twenty-third, the constitution was ratified by one hundred and forty-nine votes against seventy-three—more than two to one.* As the count was declared, the dense crowd in attendance, carried away by a wild transport of joy, shook the air with their cheers.

When order was restored, the aged Christopher Gadsden said: "I can have but little expectation of seeing the happy effects that will result to my country from the wise decisions of this day, but I shall say with good old Simeon: Lord, now lettest thou thy servant depart in peace, for mine eyes have seen the salvation of my country." †

The delegates of South Carolina to the federal convention received a vote of thanks. Those in the opposition promised as good citizens to accept the result. In 1765 South Carolina was one of the nine states to meet in convention for resistance to the stamp-act; and now she was the eighth state of the nine required for the adoption of the constitution.

When the astonishing tidings reached New Hampshire, her people grew restless to be the state yet needed to assure the new bond of union; but for that palm she must run a race with Virginia.

* Elliot, iv., 318, 338–340.  † Penn. Packet, 14 June 1788.

## CHAPTER V.

### THE CONSTITUTION IN VIRGINIA AND IN NEW HAMPSHIRE.

### FROM MAY 1785 TO 25 JUNE 1788.

FROM Virginia proceeded the southern opposition to the consolidation of the union. A strife in congress, in which the North was too much in the wrong to succeed, united the five southernmost states together in a struggle which endangered the constitution.

In May 1785, Diego Gardoqui arrived, charged with the affairs of Spain, and seemingly empowered to fix the respective limits and adjust other points * between two countries which bordered on each other from the Atlantic to the headspring of the Mississippi. On the twentieth of July 1785 congress invested Secretary Jay with full powers to negotiate with Gardoqui,† instructing him, however, previous to his making or agreeing to any proposition, to communicate it to congress. The commission was executed, and negotiations immediately began. Jay held the friendship of Spain most desirable as a neighbor; as a force that could protect the United States from the piracies of the Barbary powers and conciliate the good-will of Portugal and Italy; as a restraint on the influence of France and of Great Britain; and as the ruler of dominions of which the trade offered tempting advantages. He therefore proposed that the United States, as the price of a treaty of reciprocity in commerce, should forego the navigation of the Mississippi for twenty-five or thirty years.

On the third of August 1786, Jay appeared before congress

---

* Diplomatic Correspondence, vi., 81–97. Secret Journals, iii., 569, 570.
† Secret Journals, iii., 568–570.

and read an elaborate paper, in which he endeavored to prove that the experiment was worth trying.* The proposal sacrificed a vitally important right of one part of the union to a commercial interest of another; yet the instruction which made the right to the navigation of the Mississippi an ultimatum in any treaty with Spain was, after three weeks' reflection, repealed by a vote of seven northern states against Maryland and all south of it.

On the twenty-fifth of August, Secretary Jay was enjoined in his plan of a treaty with the king of Spain to stipulate the right of the United States to their territorial bounds, and the free navigation of the Mississippi from its source to the ocean as established in their treaties with Great Britain; and neither to conclude nor to sign any treaty with the Spanish agent until he should have communicated it to congress and received their approbation.†

The members of the southern states were profoundly alarmed. On the twenty-eighth Charles Pinckney, supported by Carrington, in their distrust of Jay, sought to transfer the negotiation to Madrid; but in vain. The delegates of Virginia, Grayson at their head, strove to separate the commercial questions from those on boundaries and navigation. "The surrender or proposed forbearance of the navigation of the Mississippi," they said, "is inadmissible upon the principle of the right, and upon the highest principles of national expedience. In the present state of the powers of congress, every wise statesman should pursue a system of conduct to gain the confidence of the several states in the federal council, and thereby an extension of its powers. This act is a dismemberment of the government. Can the United States then dismember the government by a treaty of commerce? But Jay, supported by the North, persisted. ‡

Monroe still loyally retained his desire that the regulation of commerce should be in the hands of the United States, and his opinion that without that power the union would infallibly tumble to pieces; but now he looked about him for means to strengthen the position of his own section of the country; and

---

\* Diplomatic Correspondence, vi., 177.     † Secret Journals, iii., 586.
‡ Secret Journals, iv., 87–110.

to Madison on the third of September he wrote: "I earnestly wish the admission of a few additional states into the confederacy in the southern scale." * "There is danger," reported Otto to Vergennes, † "that the discussion may become the germ of a separation of the southern states." Murmurs arose that plans were forming in New York for dismembering the confederacy and throwing New York and New England into one government, with the addition, if possible, of New Jersey and Pennsylvania. "Even should the measure triumph under the patronage of nine states or even the whole thirteen," wrote Madison in October, "it is not expedient because it is not just." ‡ The next legislature of Virginia unanimously resolved "that nature had given the Mississippi to the United States, that the sacrifice of it would violate justice, contravene the end of the federal government, and destroy confidence in the federal councils necessary to a proper enlargement of their authority."

The plan could not succeed, for it never had the consent of Spain; and if it should be formed into a treaty, the treaty could never obtain votes enough for its ratification. In the new congress, New Jersey left the North; Pennsylvania, of which a large part lay in the Mississippi valley, became equally divided; and Rhode Island began to doubt. But already many of Virginia's "most federal" statesmen were extremely disturbed; Patrick Henry, who had hitherto been the champion of the federal cause, refused to attend the federal convention that he might remain free to combat its result; and an uncontrollable spirit of distrust drove Kentucky to listen to Richard Henry Lee, and imperilled the new constitution.

The people of Virginia, whose undisputed territory had ample harbors convenient to the ocean, and no western limit but the Mississippi, had never aspired to form a separate republic. They had deliberately surrendered their claim to the north-west territory; and true to the idea that a state should not be too large for the convenience of home rule, they seconded the desire of Kentucky to become a commonwealth by itself. The opinion of Washington that the constitution would

* Monroe to Madison, 3 September 1786.
† Otto to Vergennes, 10 September 1786. ‡ Madison, i., 250.

be adopted by Virginia was not shaken.* Relieved from anxiety at home, he found time to watch the gathering clouds of revolution in Europe, and shaped in his own mind the foreign policy of the republic. His conclusions, which on New Year's day 1788 he confided to Jefferson, his future adviser on the foreign relations of the country, were in substance precisely as follows: The American revolution has spread through Europe a better knowledge of the rights of mankind, the privileges of the people, and the principles of liberty than has existed in any former period; a war in that quarter is likely to be kindled, especially between France and England; in the impending struggle an energetic general government must prevent the several states from involving themselves in the political disputes of the European powers. The situation of the United States is such as makes it not only unnecessary but extremely imprudent for them to take part in foreign quarrels. Let them wisely and properly improve the advantages which nature has given them, and conduct themselves with circumspection. By that policy, and by giving security to property and liberty, they will become the asylum of the peaceful, the industrious, and the wealthy from all parts of the civilized world.†

Nor did Washington cease his vigilant activity to confirm Virginia in federal opinions. Especially to Edmund Randolph, then governor of Virginia and in the height of his popularity, he addressed himself ‡ with convincing earnestness, and yet with a delicacy that seemed to leave the mind of Randolph to its own workings.

Madison, likewise, kept up with Randolph a most friendly and persuasive correspondence. As a natural consequence, the governor, who began to see the impossibility of obtaining amendments without endangering the success of the constitution, soon planted himself among its defenders; while Monroe, leaving his inconsistency unexplained, was drawn toward the adversaries of Madison.

* Washington to Lafayette, 10 January 1788.
† Washington to Jefferson, 1 January 1788. Compare Washington to Knox, 10 January 1788. MS.
‡ Washington to Edmund Randolph, 8 January 1788. Sparks, ix., 297.

The example of Massachusetts had great influence by its recommendation of amendments; and still more by the avowed determination of the defeated party honestly to support the decision of the majority. But while the more moderate of the malcontents "appeared to be preparing for a decent submission," and even Richard Henry Lee set bounds to his opposition,* the language of Henry was: "The other states cannot do without Virginia, and we can dictate to them what terms we please." "His plans extended contingently even to foreign alliances." †

The report from the federal convention agitated the people more than any subject since the first days of the revolution, and with a greater division of opinion. ‡ It was remarked that while in the seven northern states the principal officers of government and largest holders of property, the judges and lawyers, the clergy and men of letters, were almost without exception devoted to the constitution, in Virginia the bar and the men of the most culture and property were divided. In Virginia, too, where the mass of the people, though accustomed to be guided by their favorite statesmen on all new and intricate questions, now, on a question which surpassed all others in novelty and intricacy, broke away from their lead and followed a mysterious and prophetic influence which rose from the heart. The phenomenon was the more wonderful, as all the adversaries of the new constitution justified their opposition on the ground of danger to the liberties of the people.#
And over all discussions, in private or in public, there hovered the idea that Washington was to lead the country safely along the untrodden path.

In the time preceding the election the men of Kentucky were made to fear the surrender of the Mississippi by the federal government; and the Baptists, the reunion of church and state. ‖ The election of Madison to the convention was

* Compare Cyrus Griffin to Thomas Fitzsimons, 15 February 1788.
† Carrington to Madison, 18 January 1788.
‡ Monroe to Madison, 13 October 1787.
# Madison, i., 365, 366.
‖ James Madison, Sr., to his son, 30 January 1788; Semple's Baptists in Virginia, 76, 77.

held to be indispensable.* " He will be the main pillar of the constitution," thought Jefferson; "but though an immensely powerful one, it is questionable whether he can bear the weight of such a host." † But the plan for a southern confederacy was crushed by the fidelity of South Carolina; and Washington, who had foreseen the issue, cheered Madison on with good words: " Eight affirmatives without a negative carry weight of argument if not eloquence with it that would cause even 'the unerring sister' to hesitate." ‡

On the day appointed for the meeting of the convention a quorum was present in Richmond. It was auspicious that Edmund Pendleton, the chancellor, was unanimously chosen its president. The building which would hold the most listeners was made the place of meeting, but Henry was alarmed at the presence of short-hand reporters from the Philadelphia press, as he wished " to speak the language of his soul " # without the reserve of circumspection. During the period of the confederation, which had existed but little more than seven years, it had become known that slavery and its industrial results divided the South from the North; and this conviction exercised a subtle influence.

George Mason, following the advice of Richard Henry Lee, ‖ and the precedent of Massachusetts, proposed that no question relating to the constitution should be propounded until it should have been discussed clause by clause; and this was acquiesced in unanimously. The debates which ensued cannot be followed in the order of time, for Henry broke through every rule; but an outline must be given of those which foreshadowed the future.

Patrick Henry dashed instantly into the battle, saying: " The constitution is a severance of the confederacy. Its language, 'WE THE PEOPLE,' is the institution of one great consolidated national government of the people of all the states, instead of a government by compact with the states for its agents. The people gave the convention no power to use their name." △

* Washington in Rives, ii., 547.
† Jefferson, Randolph's ed., ii., 270; in Rives, ii., 558.
‡ Washington to Madison, 2 May 1788.  # Penn. Packet, 12 June 1788.
‖ R. H. Lee to G. Mason, 7 May 1788. Life of R. H. L., ii., 89.
△ Elliot, iii., 21–23.

"The question," said Randolph, "is now between union and no union, and I would sooner lop off my right arm than consent to a dissolution of the union." * "It is a national government," said George Mason, losing his self-control and becoming inconsistent. "It is ascertained by history that there never was one government over a very extensive country without destroying the liberties of the people. The power of laying direct taxes changes the confederation. The general government being paramount and more powerful, the state governments must give way to it; and a general consolidated government is one of the worst curses that can befall a nation." †

"There is no quarrel between government and liberty," said Pendleton; "the former is the shield and protector of the latter. The expression 'We the people' is a common one, and with me is a favorite. Who but the people can delegate powers, or have a right to form government? The question must be between this government and the confederation; the latter is no government at all. Common danger, union, and the spirit of America carried us through the war, and not the confederation of which the moment of peace showed the imbecility. Government, to be effectual, must have complete powers, a legislature, a judiciary, and executive. No gentleman in this committee would agree to vest these three powers in one body. The proposed government is not a consolidated government. It is on the whole complexion of it a government of laws and not of men." ‡

Madison explained at large that the constitution is in part a consolidated union, and in part rests so completely on the states that its very life is bound up in theirs. And on another day he added: "The powers vested in the proposed government are not so much an augmentation of powers in the general government as a change rendered necessary for the purpose of giving efficacy to those which were vested in it before." #

The opposition set no bounds to their eulogy of the British constitution as compared with the proposed one for America. "The wisdom of the English constitution," said Monroe, "has given a share of the legislation to each of the three branches,

---

\* Elliot, iii., 25–26.    † Elliot., iii., 29–33.    ‡ Elliot, iii., 35–41.
# Elliot, iii., 86–97, and 259.

which enables it to defend itself and to preserve the liberty of the people. In the plan for America I can see no real checks." *
"We have not materials in this country," said Grayson, "for such a government as the British monarchy; but I would have a president for life, choosing his successor at the same time; a senate for life, with the powers of the house of lords; and a triennial house of representatives, with the powers of the house of commons in England." † "How natural it is," said Henry, "when comparing deformities to beauty, to be struck with the superiority of the British government to the proposed system. In England self-love, self-interest stimulates the executive to advance the prosperity of the nation. Men cannot be depended on without self-love. Your president will not have the same motives of self-love to impel him to favor your interests. His political character is but transient. In the British government the sword and purse are not united in the same hands; in this system they are. Does not infinite security result from a separation?" ‡

Madison on the fourteenth replied: "There never was, there never will be, an efficient government in which both the sword and purse are not vested, though they may not be given to the same member of government. The sword is in the hands of the British king; the purse in the hands of the parliament. It is so in America, as far as any analogy can exist. When power is necessary and can be safely lodged, reason commands its cession. From the first moment that my mind was capable of contemplating political subjects I have had a uniform zeal for a well-regulated republican government. The establishment of it in America is my most ardent desire. If the bands of the government be relaxed, anarchy will produce despotism. Faction and confusion preceded the revolutions in Germany; faction and confusion produced the disorders and commotions of Holland. In this commonwealth, and in every state in the union, the relaxed operation of the government has been sufficient to alarm the friends of their country. The rapid increase of population strongly calls for a republican organization. There is more responsibility in the proposed government than in the English. Our representatives are chosen

* Elliot, iii., 218, 219.   † Elliot, iii., 279.   ‡ Elliot, iii., 387, 388.

for two years, in England for seven. Any citizen may be elected here; in Great Britain no one without an estate of the annual value of six hundred pounds sterling can represent a county; nor a corporation without half as much. If confidence be due to the government there, it is due tenfold here." *

Against the judiciary as constituted by the constitution Henry on the twentieth exceeded himself in vehemence, finding dangers to the state courts by the number of its tribunals, by appellate jurisdictions, controversies between a state and the citizens of another state; dangers to the trial by jury; dangers springing out of the clause against the impairment of the obligations of a contract.

On the same day Marshall, following able speakers on the same side, summed up the defence of the judiciary system: "Tribunals for the decisions of controversies, which were before either not at all or improperly provided for, are here appointed. Federal courts will determine causes with the same fairness and impartiality as the state courts. The federal judges are chosen with equal wisdom, and they are equally or more independent. The power of creating a number of courts is necessary to the perfection of this system. The jurisdiction of the judiciary has its limit. The United States court cannot extend to everything, since, if the United States were to make a law not warranted by any of the enumerated powers, the judges would consider it as an infringement of the constitution. The state courts are crowded with suits; if some of them should be carried to a federal court, the state courts will still have business enough. To the judiciary you must look for protection from an infringement on the constitution. No other body can afford it. The jurisdiction of the federal courts over disputes between a state and the citizens of another state has been decried with unusual vehemence. There is a difficulty in making a state defendant which does not prevent its being plaintiff. It is not rational to suppose that the sovereign power should be dragged before a court. The intent is to enable states to recover claims against individuals residing in other states. This construction is warranted by the words."

On the clause relating to impairing the obligation of con-

* Elliot, iii., 393-395.

tracts, Marshall said this: "A suit instituted in the federal courts by the citizens of one state against the citizens of another state will be instituted in the court where the defendant resides, and will be determined by the laws of the state where the contract was made. The laws which govern the contract at its formation govern it at its decision. Whether this man or that man succeeds is to the government all one thing. Congress is empowered to make exceptions to the appellate jurisdiction of the supreme court, both as to law and as to fact; and these exceptions certainly go as far as the legislature may think proper for the interest and liberty of the people." *

The planters of Virginia were indebted to British merchants to the amount of ten millions of dollars; and the Virginia legislature, under the influence of Henry, had withheld from these creditors the right to sue in the courts of Virginia until England should have fulfilled her part of the treaty of peace by surrendering the western posts and by making compensation for slaves that had been carried away; he now censured the federal constitution for granting in the case retrospective jurisdiction. Marshall replied: "There is a difference between a tribunal which shall give effect to an existing right, and creating a right that did not exist before. The debt or claim is created by the individual; a creation of a new court does not amount to a retrospective law." †

Questions as to the powers which it would be wise to grant to the general government, and as to the powers which had been granted, divided the convention. The decision of Maryland and South Carolina dashed the hope of proselyting Virginia to propose a separate southern confederacy; but Henry on the ninth still said: "Compared with the consolidation of one power to reign with a strong hand over so extensive a country as this is, small confederacies are little evils. Virginia and North Carolina could exist separated from the rest of America." ‡ But he limited himself to proposing that Virginia, "the greatest and most mighty state in the union," # followed by North Carolina and by New York, which state he announced as being in high opposition, ‖ should hold the con-

\* Elliot, iii., 551–560. † Elliot, iii., 539, 546, 561.
‡ Elliot, iii., 161. # Elliot, iii., 142. ‖ Elliot, iii., 157, 183.

stitution in suspense until they had compelled the other states to adopt the amendments on which she should insist. He cited Jefferson as advising "to reject the government till it should be amended." * Randolph interpreted the letter which Henry had cited, as the expression of a strong desire that the government might be adopted by nine states with Virginia for one of the nine; † and two days later Pendleton cited from the same letter the words that " a schism in our union would be an incurable evil." ‡

On the eleventh and the seventeenth Mason introduced a new theme, saying: "Under the royal government the importation of slaves was looked upon as a great oppression; but the African merchants prevented the many attempts at its prohibition. It was one of the great causes of our separation from Great Britain. Its exclusion has been a principal object of this state and most of the states in this union. The augmentation of slaves weakens the states. Such a trade is diabolical in itself and disgraceful to mankind; yet by this constitution it is continued for twenty years. Much as I value a union of all the states, I would not admit the southern states into the union unless they agree to its discontinuance. And there is no clause in this constitution to secure the property of that kind which we have acquired under our former laws, and of which the loss would bring ruin on a great many people; for such a tax may be laid as will amount to manumission." #

Madison equally abhorred the slave-trade; but on the seventeenth answered, after reflection and with reserve: "The gentlemen of South Carolina and Georgia argued, 'By hindering us from importing this species of property the slaves of Virginia will rise in value, and we shall be obliged to go to your markets.' I need not expatiate on this subject; great as the evil is, a dismemberment of the union would be worse. Under the articles of confederation the traffic might be continued forever; by this clause an end may be put to it after twenty years. From the mode of representation and taxation, congress cannot lay such a tax on slaves as will amount to manumission. At present, if any slave elopes to any of those states where

* Elliot, iii., 152.  
† Elliot, iii., 200.  
‡ Elliot, iii., 304.  
# Elliot, iii., 270, 452.

slaves are free, he becomes emancipated by their laws; in this constitution a clause was expressly inserted to enable owners of slaves to reclaim them."

Tyler supported Madison, speaking at large and with warmth: "This wicked traffic is impolitic, iniquitous, and disgraceful. It was one cause of the complaints against British tyranny; nothing can justify its revival. But for this temporary restriction, congress could have prohibited the African trade. My earnest desire is that it should be handed down to posterity, that I have opposed this wicked clause." *

On the twenty-fourth Henry raised a new cry on the danger of emancipation: "The great object of national government is national defence; the northern states may call forth every national resource; and congress may say, 'Every black man must fight.' In the last war acts of assembly set free every slave who would go into the army. Slavery is detested; we feel its fatal effects; we deplore it with all the pity of humanity. Let that urbanity which I trust will distinguish Americans, and the necessity of national defence, operate on their minds; they have the power, in clear, unequivocal terms, to pronounce all slaves free, and they will certainly exercise the power. Much as I deplore slavery, I see that the general government ought not to set the slaves free; for the majority of congress is to the North and the slaves are to the South." †

The governor of Virginia first showed that the constitution itself did not, even in the opinion of South Carolina, menace enfranchisement; and thus proceeded: "I hope that there is no one here who, considering the subject in the calm light of philosophy, will advance an objection dishonorable to Virginia; that, at the moment they are securing the rights of their citizens, there is a spark of hope that those unfortunate men now held in bondage may, by the operation of the general government, be made free." ‡

The representative from Augusta county, Zachariah Johnson, complained that the bill of rights which the convention was preparing as an amendment to the constitution did not acknowledge that all men are by nature equally free and inde-

* Elliot, iii., 453, 454, 455.    † Elliot, iii., 590.    ‡ Elliot, iii., 598.

pendent. "Gentlemen tell us," he said, "that they see a progressive danger of bringing about emancipation. The total abolition of slavery would do much good. The principle has begun since the revolution. Let us do what we may, it will come round."*

To the declamations of Henry that the adoption of the constitution would be the renunciation of the right to navigate the Mississippi, Madison, on the twelfth, after a candid relation of what had transpired in congress, and giving the information that New Jersey and Pennsylvania were now strenuous against even any temporary cession of the navigation of that river, made the further irrefragable reply: "The free navigation of the Mississippi is our right. The confederation is so weak that it has not formed, and cannot form, a treaty which will secure to us the actual enjoyment of it. Under an efficient government alone shall we be able to avail ourselves fully of our right. The new government will have more strength to enforce it." "Should the constitution be adopted," said Monroe on the thirteenth, "the northern states will not fail to relinquish the Mississippi in order to depress the western country and prevent the southern interest from preponderating." † "To preserve the balance of American power," continued Henry, "it is essentially necessary that the right of the Mississippi should be secured, or the South will ever be a contemptible minority." ‡

"This contest of the Mississippi," said Grayson on the fourteenth, "is a contest for empire, in which Virginia, Kentucky, the southern states are deeply interested. It involves this great national question, whether one part of the continent shall govern the other. From the extent of territory and fertility of soil, God and nature have intended that the weight of population should be on the southern side. At present, for various reasons, it is on the other. If the Mississippi be shut up, emigrations will be stopped entirely; no new states will be formed on the western waters; and this government will be a government of seven states." # To the last Grayson said: "The seven states, which are a majority, being actually in possession,

---

\* Elliot, iii., 648.   ‡ Elliot, iii., 352.
† Elliot, iii., 340.   # Elliot, iii., 365, 366.

will never admit any southern state into the union so as to lose that majority." *

The power of the government to establish a navigation act by a bare majority was bitterly complained of by George Mason; † by Grayson, who complained that the interests of the carrying states would govern the producing states; ‡ by Tyler, who mourned over his own act in having proposed to cede the regulation of commerce to the confederation, since it had led to the grant of powers too dangerous to be trusted to any set of men whatsoever.# Complaint was further made that treaties were to go into effect without regard to the opinion of the house of representatives; and especially that there was no bill of rights, and that there was no explicit reservation of powers not delegated to the general government. In some parts of the country the settlers were made to dread a resuscitation of old land companies through the federal judiciary.

The prohibition on the states to issue paper money weighed on the minds of the debtor class; but it was not much discussed, for on that point George Mason and Richard Henry Lee were the great leaders in favor of the suppression of paper money "as founded upon fraud and knavery." ‖ And Mason had forced the assembly of Virginia in their last session to adopt a series of resolutions declaring that paper currency created scarcity of real money, and substituted for the real standard of value a standard variable as the commodities themselves, ruining trade and commerce, weakening the morals of the people, destroying public and private credit and all faith between man and man, and aggravating the very evils which it was intended to remedy.^ And yet there were those in the convention whose votes were swayed by the consideration that, if the constitution should be established, there would be an end of inconvertible bills of credit forever. But that which affected the decision more than anything else was that the constitution would bring with it to British creditors a right to

* Elliot, iii., 585. † Elliot, iii., 604.
‡ Elliot, iii., 616. # Elliot, iii., 640, 641.
‖ George Mason to Washington, 6 November 1787, in Letters to G. W., iv., 190.
^ Independent Gazetteer, 17 November 1787.

recover through the federal courts claims on Virginia planters for about ten millions of dollars.

The discussions had been temperately conducted till just at the last, when for a moment pretending that the acceptance of the constitution would make an end of the trial by jury, Henry said, on the twentieth : " Old as I am, it is probable I may yet have the appellation of rebel. But my neighbors will protect me." * This daring drew out the reply that Virginia would be in arms to support the constitution ; and on the twenty-fifth James Innes of Williamsburg, quoting against him his own words, said : " I observe with regret a general spirit of jealousy with respect to our northern brethren. If we had had it in 1775 it would have prevented that unanimous resistance which triumphed over our enemies ; it was not a Virginian, a Carolinian, a Pennsylvanian, but the glorious name of an American, that extended from one end of the continent to the other." † But the feeling was soon pacified, and the last words of Henry himself were : " If I shall be in the minority, I shall yet be a peaceable citizen, my head, my hand, and my heart being at liberty to remove the defects of the system in a constitutional way." ‡ The last word was from the governor of Virginia : " The accession of eight states reduces our deliberations to the single question of union or no union." #

For more than three weeks the foes of the constitution had kept up the onset, and day after day they had been beaten back as cavalry that tries in vain to break the ranks of infantry. For more than three weeks Henry and Grayson and Mason renewed the onslaught, feebly supported by Monroe, and greatly aided by the weight of character of Benjamin Harrison and John Tyler ; day by day they were triumphantly encountered by Madison, on whom the defence of the constitution mainly rested ; by Pendleton, who, in spite of increased infirmities, was moved even more deeply than in the beginning of the revolution ; and by the popular eloquence of Randolph. These three champions were well seconded by

---

\* Elliot, iii., 546.  ‡ Elliot, iii., 652.
† Elliot, iii., 633.  # Ibid.

George Nicholas, John Marshall, James Innes, Henry Lee, and Francis Corbin.*

On the twenty-fifth, after debates for three weeks, the malcontents had no heart for further resistance. The convention was willing to recommend a bill of rights in twenty sections, with twenty other more questionable amendments. The first motion was: "Ought the declaration of rights and amendments of the constitution to be referred by this convention to the other states in the American confederacy for their consideration previous to the ratification of the new constitution of government?" It was lost, having only eighty voices against eighty-eight. Then the main question was put, that the constitution be ratified, referring all amendments to the first congress under the constitution. The decision would be momentous, not for America only, but the whole world. Without Virginia, this great country would have been shivered into fragmentary confederacies, or separate independent states.

The roll was called; and eighty-nine delegates, chiefly from the cities of Richmond and Williamsburg, from counties near the ocean, from the northern neck, from the north-western border counties, and from the counties between the Blue Ridge and the Alleghanies, voted for the constitution. Seventy-nine, mainly from other central and southern border counties, and from three fourths of the counties of Kentucky, cried No.

The committee for reporting the form of ratification were Randolph, Nicholas, Madison, Marshall, and Corbin—all from among the stanchest supporters of the constitution.

In the form which was adopted they connected with the ratification "a few declaratory truths not affecting the validity of the act;" † and shielded the rights of the states by the assertion "that every power not granted by the constitution remains for the people of the United States and at their will." ‡

After the vote was taken, the successful party were careful not to ruffle their opponents by exultation. Henry showed his genial nature, free from all malignity. He was like a billow of the ocean on the first bright day after the storm, dashing itself against the rocky cliff, and then, sparkling with light, re-

---

* Compare Rives, ii., 561.
† Madison to Washington, in Rives, ii., 608.  ‡ Elliot, iii., 656.

treating to its home. It was more difficult for Mason to calm the morbid sensibility of his nature and to heal his sorrow at having abandoned one of the highest places of honor among the fathers of the constitution which he had done so much to initiate, to form, and to improve. He was pacified by words from Harrison and from Tyler, who held it the duty of good citizens to accept the decision of the majority, and by precept and example to promote harmony and order and union among their fellow-citizens. But that which did most to soothe the minority was their trust in Washington. "For the president," said Mason, "there seldom or never can be a majority in favor of one, except one great name, who will be unanimously elected." * "Were it not for one great character in America," said Grayson, "so many men would not be for this government. We do not fear while he lives; but who beside him can concentrate the confidence and affections of all America?" † And Monroe reported to Jefferson: "Be assured, Washington's influence carried this government." ‡

Nor was that influence confined to Virginia alone. The country was an instrument with thirteen strings, and the only master who could bring out all their harmonious thought was Washington. Had he not attended the federal convention, its work would have met a colder reception and more strenuous opponents. Had the idea prevailed that he would not accept the presidency, it would still have proved fatal.#

Virginia lost the opportunity of being the ninth state to constitute the union. While the long winter of New Hampshire intercepted the labors of husbandry, the fireside of the freeholders in its hundreds of townships became the scene for discussing the merits of the federal constitution with the delegates of their choice and with one another. Their convention reassembled in June. Four days served them to discuss the constitution, to prepare and recommend twelve articles of amendment, and, by fifty-seven voices against forty-six, to ratify the constitution. They took care to insert in their record that their vote was taken on Saturday, the twenty-first

---

\* Elliot, iii., 493; and compare 134.      † Elliot, iii., 616.
‡ Monroe to Jefferson, 12 July 1788.
\# Life of Morris by Sparks, i., 289, 290.

of June, at one o'clock in the afternoon, that Virginia by a vote at a later hour of the same day might not dispute with them the honor of giving life to the constitution.*

By their decision, accompanied by that of Virginia, the United States of America came formally into existence. As the glad tidings flew through the land, the heart of its people thrilled with joy that at last the tree of union was firmly planted. Never may its trunk be riven by the lightning; nor its branches crash each other in the maddening storm; nor its beauty wither; nor its root decay.

* Tobias Lear to Washington, 22 June 1788. Letters to Washington, iv., 225.

# THE

# FORMATION OF THE CONSTITUTION

### OF THE

# UNITED STATES OF AMERICA.

*IN FIVE BOOKS.*

## BOOK FIFTH.
### THE FEDERAL GOVERNMENT.

JUNE, 1787.

# CHAPTER I.

### THE CONSTITUTION.

### 1787.

"THE American constitution is the most wonderful work ever struck off at a given time by the brain and purpose of man;" but it had its forerunners.

England had suffered the thirteen colonies, as free states, to make laws each for itself and never for one of the others; and had established their union in a tempered subordination to the British crown. Among the many guides of America, there had been Winthrop and Cotton, Hooker and Haynes, George Fox and William Penn, Roger Williams and John Clarke; scholars of Oxford and many more of Cambridge; Gustavus Adolphus and Oxenstiern; the merchants of the United Netherlands; Southampton and Baltimore, with the kindliest influences of the British aristocracy; Shaftesbury with Locke, for evil as well as for good; all the great slave-traders that sat on thrones or were fostered by parliament; and the philanthropist Oglethorpe, who founded a colony exclusively of the free on a territory twice as large as France, and though he had to mourn at the overthrow of his plans for liberty, lived to see his plantation independent.

There were other precursors of the federal government; but the men who framed it followed the lead of no theoretical writer of their own or preceding times. They harbored no desire of revolution, no craving after untried experiments. They wrought from the elements which were at hand, and shaped them to meet the new exigencies which had arisen. The least possible reference was made by them to abstract doctrines;

they moulded their design by a creative power of their own, but nothing was introduced that did not already exist, or was not a natural development of a well-known principle. The materials for building the American constitution were the gifts of the ages.

Of old, the family was the rudiment of the state. Of the Jews, the organization was by tribes. The citizens of the commonwealths of the Hellenes were of one blood. Among the barbarous tribes of the fourth continent, the governments and the confederacies all rested on consanguinity. Nations, as the word implied, were but large communities of men of one kin; and nationalities survive to this day, a source of strength in their unity, and yet of strife where two or more of them exist in their original separateness and are nevertheless held in subjection under one ruler. Rome first learned to cherish the human race by a common name and transform the vanquished into citizens.

The process of assimilation which Rome initiated by war received its perfect development in the land where the Dutch and the Swedes, and in the country north-west of the Ohio the French, competed in planting colonies; where the English, the Irish, the Scotch for the most part came over each for himself, never reproducing their original nationality; and where from the first fugitives from persecution of all nations found a safe asylum. Though subjects of the English king, all were present in America as individuals.

The English language maintained itself without a rival, not merely because those speaking it as their mother tongue very greatly outnumbered all others, and because all acknowledged English supremacy; but for the simplicity of its structure; its logical order in the presentment of thought; its suitableness for the purposes of every-day life; for the discussion of abstract truths and the apprehension of Anglo-Saxon political ideas; for the instrument of the common law; for science and observation; for the debates of public life; for every kind of poetry, from humor to pathos, from descriptions of nature to the action of the heart and mind.

But the distinctive character of the new people as a whole, their nationality, so to say, was the principle of individuality which prevailed among them as it had nowhere done before. This individuality was strengthened by the struggles with Nature in her wildness, by the remoteness from the abodes of ancient institutions, by the war against the traditions of absolute power and old superstitions, till it developed itself into the most perfect liberty in thought and action; so that the American came to be marked by the readiest versatility, the spirit of enterprise, and the faculty of invention. In the declaration of independence the representatives of the United States called themselves "the good people of these colonies." The statesmen who drew the law of citizenship in 1776 made no distinction of nationalities, or tribes, or ranks, or occupations, or faith, or wealth, and knew only inhabitants bearing allegiance to the governments of the several states in union.

Again, this character of the people appeared most clearly in the joint action of the United States in the federal convention, where the variant prejudices that still clung to separate states eliminated each other.

The constitution establishes nothing that interferes with equality and individuality. It knows nothing of differences by descent, or opinions, of favored classes, or legalized religion, or the political power of property. It leaves the individual alongside of the individual. No nationality of character could take form, except on the principle of individuality, so that the mind might be free, and every faculty have the unlimited opportunity for its development and culture. As the sea is made up of drops, American society is composed of separate, free, and constantly moving atoms, ever in reciprocal action, advancing, receding, crossing, struggling against each other and with each other; so that the institutions and laws of the country rise out of the masses of individual thought, which, like the waters of the ocean, are rolling evermore.

The rule of individuality was extended as never before. The synod of the Presbyterians of New York and Philadelphia, a denomination inflexibly devoted to its own creed, in their pastoral letter of May 1783, published their joy that "the rights of conscience are inalienably secured and interwoven with the very constitutions of the several states." Religion was become avowedly the attribute of man and not of a corporation. In the earliest states known to history, government and religion were one and indivisible. Each state had its special deity, and of these protectors one after another might be overthrown in battle, never to rise again. The Peloponnesian war grew out of a strife about an oracle. Rome, as it adopted into citizenship those whom it vanquished, sometimes introduced, and with good logic for that day, the worship of their gods. No one thought of vindicating liberty of religion for the conscience of the individual till a voice in Judea, breaking day for the greatest epoch in the life of humanity by establishing for all mankind a pure, spiritual, and universal religion, enjoined to render to Cæsar only that which is Cæsar's. The rule was upheld during the infancy of this gospel for all men. No sooner was the religion of freedom adopted by the chief of the Roman Empire, than it was shorn of its character of universality and enthralled by an unholy connection with the unholy state; and so it continued till the new nation—the least defiled with the barren scoffings of the eighteenth century, the most sincere believer in Christianity of any people of that age, the chief heir of the reformation in its purest form—when it came to establish a government for the United States, refused to treat faith as a matter to be regulated by a corporate body, or having a headship in a monarch or a state.

Vindicating the right of individuality even in religion, and in religion above all, the new nation dared to set the example of accepting in its relations to God the principle first divinely ordained in Judea. It left the management of temporal things to the temporal power; but the American constitution, in harmony with the people of the several states, withheld from the federal government the power to invade the home of reason, the citadel of conscience, the sanctuary of the soul; and not from indifference, but that the infinite spirit of eternal truth might move in its feedom and purity and power.

With this perfect individuality extending to conscience, freedom should have belonged to labor. What though slavery existed and still exists in the older states known to history, in Egypt, in China, coming down continuously from an unknown date; what though Aristotle knew no mode of instituting a republican household but with a slave; and Julius Cæsar, when Italy was perishing by the vastness of its slave estates, crowded them with new hordes of captives? What though the slave-trade was greedily continued under the passionate encouragement of the British parliament, and that in nearly all of the continent of Europe slavery in some of its forms prevailed? In America, freedom of labor was the moral principle of the majority of the people; was established, or moving toward immediate establishment, in a majority of the states; was by the old confederation, with the promptest and oft-repeated sanction of the new government, irrevocably ordained in all the territory for which the United States could at that time make the law. The federal convention could not interfere with the slave laws of the separate states; but it was careful to impose no new incapacitation on free persons of color; it maintained them in all the rights of equal citizenship; it granted those rights to the emancipated slave; and it kept to itself the authority to abolish the slave-trade instantly in any territory that might be annexed; in all other states and lands, at the earliest moment for which it had been able to obtain power.

The tripartite division of government into legislative, executive, and judicial, enforced in theory by the illustrious Montesquieu, and practiced in the home government of every one of the American states, became a part of the constitution of the United States, which derived their mode of instituting it from their own happy experience. It was established by the federal convention with a rigid consistency that went beyond the example of Britain, where one branch of the legislature was still a court of appeal. Each one of the three departments proceeded from the people, and each is endowed with all the authority needed for its just activity. The president may recommend or dissuade from enactments, and has a limited veto on them; but whatever becomes a law he must execute. The power of the legislature to enact is likewise uncontrolled except by the paramount law of the constitution. The judiciary passes upon every case that may be presented, and its decision on the case is definitive; but without further authority over the executive or the legislature, for the convention had wisely refused to make the judges a council to either of them.

Tripartite division takes place not only in the threefold powers of government; it is established as the mode of legislation. There, too, three powers, proceeding from the people, must concur, except in cases provided for, before an act of legislation can take place. This tripartite division in the power of legislation—so at the time wrote Madison, so thought all the great builders of the constitution, so asserted John Adams with vehemence and sound reasoning—is absolutely essential to the success of a federal republic; for if all legislative powers are vested in one man or in one assembly, there is despotism; if in two branches, there is a restless antagonism between the two; if they are distributed among three, it will be hard to unite two of them in a fatal strife with the third. But the executive, and each of the two chambers, must be so chosen as to have a character and strength and popular support of its own. The government of the United States is thoroughly a government of the people. By the English aristocratic revolution of 1688, made after the failure of the popular attempt at reform, the majority of the house of commons was in substance composed of nominees of the house of lords, so that no ministry could prevail in it except by the power of that house; and as the prime minister and cabinet depend on the majority in the house of commons, the house of lords directly controlled the government not only in its own branch but in the commons, and through the commons in the nomination of the ministry. All three branches of the government were in harmony, for in those days, before the house of commons had entered successfully upon its long struggle for reform of the mode of its election, all three branches represented the aristocracy. In the United States, on the other hand, all the branches of power —president, senators, and representatives—proceed directly or indirectly from the people. The government of the United States is a government by the people, for the people.

To perfect the system and forever prevent revolution, power is reserved to the people by amendments of their constitution to remove every imperfection which time may lay bare, and adapt it to unforeseen contingencies. But no change can be hastily made. An act of parliament can at any time alter the constitution of England; no similar power is delegated to the congress of the United States, which, like parliament, may be swayed by the shifting majorities of party. As to the initiation of amendments, it could not be intrusted to the president, lest it might lead him to initiate changes for his own advantage; still less to a judiciary holding office for life, for, such is human nature, a tribunal so constituted and deciding by a majority, by whatever political party its members may have been named, cannot safely be invested with so transcendent a power. The legislatures of the states or of the United States are alone allowed to open the "constitutional door to amendments;" and these can be made valid only through the combined intervention of the state legislatures and of congress, or a convention of all the states elected expressly for the purpose by the people of the several states. In this way no change of the constitution can be made in haste or by stealth, but only by the consent of three quarters of the states after a full and free and often-repeated discussion. There is no legal road to amendment of the constitution but through the consent of the people given in the form prescribed by law. America, being charged with the preservation of liberty, has the most conservative polity in the world, both in its government and in its people.

The new nation asserted itself as a continental republic. The discovery was made that the time had passed for little commonwealths of a single city and its environs. The great Frederick, who had scoffed at the idea of attempting to govern an imperial domain without a king, was hardly in his grave when a commonwealth of more than twenty degrees in each direction, containing from the first an area six or seven times as large as the whole of Great Britain and Ireland, fifty or sixty times as great as the Netherlands or Switzerland, able to include more than a thousand confederacies as large as the Achaian, and ready to admit adjoining lands to fellowship, rose up in the best part of the temperate zone on a soil that had been collecting fertility for untold centuries. The day of the Greek commonwealth had passed forever; and, after the establishment of the representative system, it was made known that a republican government thrives best in a vast territory. Monarchy had held itself a necessity for the formation of large states; but now it was found out that even in them monarchy can be dispensed with; and the world was summoned to gaze at the spectacle of a boundless society of republican states in union.

The United States of America are not only a republic, they are "a society of societies," "a federal republic." * Toward foreign powers the country has no seam in its garment; it exists in absolute unity as a nation, with full and undisputed national resources. At home it is "a union," or "one out of many;" within its own sphere supreme and self-supporting. For this end it has its own legislature to make enactments; its own functionaries to execute them; its own courts; its own treasury; and it alone may have an army and a navy. All-sufficient powers are so plainly given that there is no need of striving for more by straining the words in which they are granted beyond their natural import.

The constitution, the laws of the United States made in pursuance of it, and all treaties framed by their authority, are the supreme law of the land, binding the judges in every state even if need be in spite of the constitution and the laws of the state; and all executive, legislative, and judicial officers, both of the United States and of the several states, are to be sworn to its support. The constitution provides within itself for the redress of every wrong. The supreme court offers relief in a "case" of injustice or conflict with the constitution; the remedy for a bad law is to be sought through the freedom and frequency of elections; a fault in the constitution by its amendment.

Except for the powers granted to the federal government, each state is in all things supreme, not by grace, but of right. The United States may not interfere with any ordinance or law that begins and ends within a state. This supremacy of the states in the powers which have not been granted is as essentially a part of the system as the supremacy of the general government in its sphere. The states are at once the guardians of the domestic security and the happiness of the individual, and they are the parents, the protectors, and the stay of the union. The states are members of the United States

* Words used by Montesquieu, Esprit des Lois, livre ix., ch. i.

as one great whole; and the one is as needful as the other. The powers of government are not divided between them; they are distributed; so that there need be no collision in their exercise. The union without self-existent states is a harp without strings; the states without union are as chords that are unstrung. But for state rights the union would perish from the paralysis of its limbs. The states, as they gave life to the union, are necessary to the continuance of that life. Within their own limits they are the guardians of industry, of property, of personal rights, and of liberty. But state rights are to be defended inside of the union; not from an outside citadel from which the union may be struck at or defied. The states and the United States are not antagonists; the states in union form the federal republic; and the system can have life and health and strength and beauty only by their harmonious action. In short, the constitution knows nothing of United States alone, or states alone; it adjusts the parts harmoniously in an organized unity. Impair the relations or the vigor of any part, and disease enters into the veins of the whole. That there may be life in the whole, there must be healthy life in every part. The United States are the states in union; these are so inwrought into the constitution that the one cannot perish without the other.

Is it asked who is the sovereign of the United States? The words "sovereign" and "subjects" are unknown to the constitution. There is no place for princes with unlimited power, or conquering cities, or feudal chiefs, or privileged aristocracies, ruling absolutely with their correlative vassals or subjects.

The people of the United States have declared in their constitution that the law alone is supreme; and have defined that supreme law. Is it asked who are the people of the United States that instituted the "general government"? The federal convention and the constitution answer, that it is the concurring people of the several states. The constitution is constantly on its guard against permitting the action of the aggregate mass as a unit, lest the whole people, once accustomed to acting together as an individual, might forget the existence of the states, and the states now in union succumb to centralization and absolutism. The people of the states demanded a federal convention to form the constitution; the congress of the confederation, voting by states, authorized that federal convention; the federal convention, voting likewise by states, made the constitution; at the advice of the federal convention the federal congress referred that constitution severally to the people of each state; and by their united voice taken severally it was made the binding form of government. The constitution, as it owes its life to the concurrent act of the people of the several states, permits no method of amending itself except by the several consent of the people of the states; and within the constitution itself the president, the only officer who has an equal relation to every state in the union, is elected not by the aggregate people of all the states, but by the separate action of the people of the several states according to the number of votes allotted to each of them.

Finally, there is one more great and happy feature in the constitution. Rome, in annexing the cities around itself, had not given them equal influence with itself in proportion to their wealth and numbers, and consequently there remained a cause of dissatisfaction never healed. America has provided for admission of new states upon equal terms, and only upon equal terms, with the old ones.

For Europe there remained the sad necessity of revolution. For America the gates of revolution are shut and barred and bolted down, never again to be thrown open; for it has found a legal and a peaceful way to introduce every amelioration. Peace and intercitizenship and perfect domestic free-trade are to know no end. The constitution is to the American people a possession for all ages; it creates an indissoluble union of imperishable states.

The federal republic will carry tranquillity, and freedom, and order throughout its vast domain. Will it, within less than a century, extend its limits to the capes of Florida, to the mouth of the Mississippi, to the region beyond the Mississippi, to California, to Oregon, to San Juan? Will it show all the Spanish colonies how to transform themselves into independent republics stretching along the Pacific till they turn Cape Horn? Will it be an example to France, teaching its great benefactor how to gain free institutions? In the country from which it broke away will it assist the liberal statesmen to bring parliament more nearly to a representation of the people? Will it help the birthplace of the reformation to gather together its scattered members and become once more an empire, with a government so entirely the child of the nation that it shall have but one hereditary functionary, with a federal council or senate representing the several states, and a house elected directly by universal suffrage? Will it teach England herself how to give peace to her groups of colonies, her greatest achievement, by establishing for them a federal republican dominion, in one continent at least if not in more? And will America send manumitted dark men home to their native continent, to introduce there an independent republic and missions that may help to civilize the races of Africa?

The philosophy of the people of the United States was neither that of optimism nor of despair. Believing in the justice of "the Great Governor of the world," and conscious of their own honest zeal in the cause of freedom and mankind, they looked with astonishment at their present success and at the future with unclouded hope.

## CHAPTER II.

### THE LINGERING STATES.

### 1787 TO 2 AUGUST 1788.

WHEN the constitution was referred to the states Hamilton revived a long-cherished plan, and, obtaining the aid of Jay and Madison, issued papers which he called The Federalist, to prepare all the states and the people for accepting the determinations of the federal convention. Of its eighty-five numbers, Jay wrote five, Madison twenty-nine, and Hamilton fifty-one.* They form a work of enduring interest, because they are

* Mr. Madison's list of the authors of The Federalist:
Number 1 by A. H.   No. 2, J. J.   No. 3, J. J.   No. 4, J. J.   No. 5, J. J.
No. 6, A. H.   No. 7, A. H.   No. 8, A. H.   No. 9, A. H.   No. 10, J. M.   No. 11, A. H.
No. 12, A. H.   No. 13, A. H.   No. 14, J. M.   No. 15, A. H.   No. 16, A. H.   No. 17, A. H.
No. 18, J. M.   No. 19, J. M.   No. 20, J. M.   No. 21, A. H.   No. 22, A. H.   No. 23, A. H.
No. 24, A. H.   No. 25, A. H.   No. 26, A. H.   No. 27, A. H.   No. 28, A. H.   No. 29, A. H.
No. 30, A. H.   No. 31, A. H.   No. 32, A. H.   No. 33, A. H.   No. 34, A. H.   No. 35, A. H.
No. 36, A. H.   No. 37, J. M.   No. 38, J. M.   No. 39, J. M.   No. 40, J. M.   No. 41, J. M.
No. 42, J. M.   No. 43, J. M.   No. 44, J. M.   No. 45, J. M.   No. 46, J. M.   No. 47, J. M.
No. 48, J. M.   No. 49, J. M.   No. 50, J. M.   No. 51, J. M.   No. 52, J. M.   No. 53, J. M.
No. 54, J. M.   No. 55, J. M.   No. 56, J. M.   No. 57, J. M.   No. 58, J. M.   No. 59, A. H.
No. 60, A. H.   No. 61, A. H.   No. 62, J. M.   No. 63, J. M.   No. 64, J. J.   No. 65, A. H.
No. 66, A. H.   No. 67, A. H.   No. 68, A. H.   No. 69, A. H.   No. 70, A. H.   No. 71, A. H.
No. 72, A. H.   No. 73, A. H.   No. 74, A. H.   No. 75, A. H.   No. 76, A. H.   No. 77, A. H.
No. 78, A. H.   No. 79, A. H.   No. 80, A. H., and to the end.

*Note in Mr. Madison's own hand.*

"No. 18 is attributed to Mr. Hamilton and Mr. Madison jointly. A. H. had drawn up something on the subjects of this (No. 18) and the two next Nos. (19 and 20). On finding that J. M. was engaged in them with larger materials, and with a view to a more precise delineation, he put what he had written into the hands of J. M. It is possible, though not recollected, that something in the draught may have been incorporated into the numbers as printed. But it was certainly not of a nature or amount to affect the impression left on the mind of the earliest commentary on the new experiment of mankind in establishing a republican government for a country of boundless dimensions; and were written by Madison, who was the chief author of the constitution, and Hamilton, who took part in its inception and progress.

Hamilton dwelt on the defects of the confederation; the praiseworthy energy of the new federal government; its relations to the public defence; to the functions of the executive; to the judicial department, to the treasury; and to commerce. Himself a friend to the protection of manufactures, he condemned "exorbitant duties on imported articles," because they "beget smuggling," are "always prejudicial to the fair trader, and eventually to the revenue itself;" tend to render "other classes of the community tributary in an improper degree to the manufacturing classes," and to "give them a premature monopoly of the markets;" to "force industry out of its most natural channels," and to "oppress the merchant." *

Madison commented with severe wisdom on its plan; its conformity to republican principles; its powers; its relation to slavery and the slave-trade; its mediating office between the union and the states; its tripartite separation of the depart-

---

J. M., from whose pen the papers went to the press, that they were of the class written by him. As the historical materials of A. H., as far as they went, were doubtless similar, or the same with those provided by J. M., and as a like application of them probably occurred to both, an impression might be left on the mind of A. H. that the Nos. in question were written jointly. These remarks are made as well to account for a statement to that effect, if made by A. H., as in justice to J. M., who, always regarding them in a different light, had so stated them to an inquiring friend, long before it was known or supposed that a different impression existed anywhere. (Signed) J. M."

There exists no list of the authors of The Federalist by the hand of Hamilton. There exists no authentic copy of any list that may have been made by Hamilton. It is a great wrong to Hamilton's memory to insist that he claimed the authorship of papers which were written for him at his request by another, and which the completest evidence proves that he could not have written. The list of the authors of the several papers given above rests on the written authority of Madison. From this list Madison has never been known to vary in the slightest degree. The correctness of his statement is substantiated beyond room for a cavil by various evidence. Meeting an assertion that Madison in some paper in the department of state had changed one figure in his list, I requested a former secretary of state to order a search to be made for it. A search was made, and no such paper was found. * The Federalist, xxxv.

ments; and its mode of constructing the house of representatives. Hamilton began the work by saying that a wrong decision would not only be "the dismemberment of the union," but "the general misfortune of mankind;"* he closed with the words: "A nation without a national government is an awful spectacle. The establishment of a constitution, in time of profound peace, by the voluntary consent of a whole people, is a prodigy, to the completion of which I look forward with trembling anxiety." † During the time in which the constitution was in jeopardy Hamilton and Madison cherished for each other intimate and affectionate relations, differing in temperament, but one in purpose and in action. To the day of their death they both were loyally devoted to the cause of union.

New York, having the most convenient harbor for worldwide commerce, rivers flowing directly to the sea, to Delaware bay, to the Chesapeake, to the Mississippi, and to the watercourse of the St. Lawrence, and having the easiest line of communication from the ocean to the great West, needed, more than any other state, an efficient general government; and yet of the thirteen it was the most stubborn in opposition. More than half the goods consumed in Connecticut, in New Jersey, in Vermont, and the western parts of Massachusetts, were bought within its limits and paid an impost for its use. ‡ During the war it agreed to give congress power to collect a five per-cent impost; as soon as it regained possession of the city it preferred to appropriate the revenue to its own purposes; and, as a consequence, the constitution called forth in New York the fiercest resistance that selfish interests could organize.

To meet the influence of The Federalist, the republicans published inflammatory tracts, and circulated large editions of the Letters from the Federal Farmer by Richard Henry Lee. They named themselves federal republicans. Their electioneering centre was the New York custom-house, then an institution of the state with John Lamb as collector. After the fashion of the days of danger they formed a committee of correspondence and sought connections throughout the land.

* The Federalist, i.     † The Federalist, lxxxv.
‡ Williamson to Iredell, 7 July 1788. McRee's Iredell, ii., 227, 228.

They sent their own emissaries to attend the proceedings of the Massachusetts convention, and, if possible, to frustrate its acceptance of the union. Their letters received answers from Lowndes, from Henry and Grayson, from Atherton of New Hampshire, and from Richard Henry Lee, of whom the last wrote that "the constitution was an elective despotism."

At the regular meeting of the legislature in January 1788, Clinton recommended the encouragement of commerce and of manufactures, but sent in the proceedings of the federal convention without remark.* All others remaining silent for twenty days, Egbert Benson, on the last day of January, proposed a state convention in the precise mode recommended by congress. Schoonmaker offered a preamble, condemning the federal convention for having exceeded its powers. Benson conducted the debate with rare ability, and the amended preamble gained but twenty-five votes against twenty-seven. In the senate the motion to postpone the question mustered but nine votes against ten. The convention was ordered; but in its choice the constitutional qualifications of electors were thrust aside, and every free male citizen of twenty-one years of age, though he had been a resident but for a day, might be a voter and be voted for.

According to the wish of the Virginia opposition, the time for the meeting of the convention was delayed till the seventeenth of June. Of its sixty-five members, more than two thirds were enemies to the constitution.† But it was found that the state was divided geographically. The seat of opposition was in Ulster county, the home of Governor Clinton, and it extended to the counties above it. The southern counties on the Hudson river and on Long Island, and the city of New York, were so unanimously for union as to encourage the rumor that they would at all events adhere to it. Clinton himself began to think it absolutely necessary that the state should in some form secure a representation under the new constitution.

The greater number of his friends were, like him, averse to its total rejection; but, while some were willing to be content with recommendatory amendments, and others with explanatory ones to settle doubtful constructions, the majority

* Ind. Gazetteer, 19 January 1788. † Hamilton, i., 454.

seemed unwilling to be reconciled with less than previous amendments. All the while the people of the state were drifting toward union.*

On the seventeenth of June, fifteen days after the organization of the Virginia convention, that of New York met at Poughkeepsie and unanimously elected Clinton as its president. Among the delegates of the city of New York were Jay, Chief-Justice Morris, Hobart, Livingston, then chancellor of the state, Duane, and Hamilton. On the other side the foremost men were George Clinton, the governor; Yates and Lansing, who had deserted the federal convention under the pretence that it was exceeding its power; Samuel Jones, a member of the New York bar, who excelled in clearness of intellect, moderation, and simplicity of character; and Melancthon Smith, a man of a religious cast of mind, familiar with metaphysical discussions, of undaunted courage, and gifted with the power of moderation.†

On the nineteenth the chancellor opened the debate, showing the superiority of a republic to a confederacy. Without a strong federal government and union New York was incapable of self-defence, and the British posts within the limits of the state would continue to form connections with hostile tribes of Indians, and be held in defiance of the most solemn treaties.

In the course of the discussion every objection that had been made to the constitution either in Massachusetts or in Virginia was strongly stated; and replied to. Lansing, adhering to the system of the confederation, loved union; but professed to love liberty more. ‡ Melancthon Smith declared himself most strongly impressed with the necessity of union, and refused to say that the federal constitution was at war with public liberty. Hamilton, speaking in the spirit of gentleness and wisdom, contrasted the method of requisitions to be enforced by coercion of the states, with general laws operating directly on individuals; and he showed how greatly the new system excelled in simplicity, in efficiency, in respect for personal rights, in the protection of the public liberty, and, above all, in humanity.

On the twenty-fourth swift riders, dispatched by Langdon,

* Compare Jay's Jay, i., 268.
† Thompson's Long Island, ii., 504, 505, 495.   ‡ Elliot, ii., 208–216, 219

brought to Hamilton the tidings that New Hampshire as the ninth state had assented to the constitution; yet the vote did not decide New York. " Our chance of success depends upon you," wrote Hamilton to Madison. " Symptoms of relaxation in some of the leaders authorize a gleam of hope if you do well, but certainly I think not otherwise." *

Clinton claimed that he and his own partisans were " the friends to the rights of mankind;" their opponents "the advocates of despotism;" "the most that had been said by the new government men had been but a second edition of The Federalist well delivered. One of the New York delegates," meaning Hamilton, " had in substance, though not explicitly, thrown off the mask, his arguments tending to show the necessity of a consolidated continental government to the exclusion of any state government."

On the twenty-seventh Hamilton replied by a full declaration of his opinions. " The establishment of a republican government on a safe and solid basis is the wish of every honest man in the United States, and is an object, of all others, the nearest and most dear to my own heart. This great purpose requires strength and stability in the organization of the government, and vigor in its operations. The state governments are essentially necessary to the form and spirit of the general system.† With the representative system a very extensive country may be governed by a confederacy of states in which the supreme legislature has only general powers, and the civil and domestic concerns of the people are regulated by the laws of the several states. State governments must form a leading principle. They can never lose their powers till the whole people of America are robbed of their liberties." ‡

In answer to Hamilton on this and two other occasions, Clinton carefully set forth the principles on which he reposed. During the war he had wished for a strong federal government; he still wished a federal republic for the mutual protection of the states and the security of their equal rights. In

---

* Hamilton's Works, i., 462.

† Elliot, ii., 301, 304. For Hamilton's brief of his speeches in June [not of those in July], see Hamilton, ii., 463-466.

‡ Elliot, ii., 352-355.

such a confederacy there should be a perfect representation; but of that representation "the states are the creative principle," and, having equal rights, ought for their protection to be equally represented. The delegates and the senators of a state should be subject to its instructions and liable to be recalled at its pleasure, for the representation should be an exact and continuous representation of its reflection and judgment and will. Moreover, the senators should vote in their place not as individuals, but collectively, as the representation of the state. He would further have the members of congress depend on the states for support. Above all, he abhorred the idea of reducing the states to the degraded situation of petty corporations and rendering them liable to suits. "The sovereignty of the states he considered the only stable security for the liberties of the people against the encroachments of power."*

On the third of July, while the convention was still engaged in considering the constitution, and noting the propositions of amendments, the decisive news of the unconditional ratification of the constitution by Virginia broke on its members; and from that moment it was certain that they would not venture to stand alone against the judgment of every state in New England except Rhode Island, and every other state except North Carolina. The question at first became whether the constitution should be accepted with or without previous amendments. On the tenth Lansing offered a bill of rights, to which no one objected; and numerous amendments,† of which the class relating to a standing army in time of peace, direct taxes, the militia, and elections to congress were made conditions of the ratification. After they were read, the convention, on the proposal of Lansing, adjourned, leaving an informal committee of equal numbers of both parties to bring the business by compromise to a quick and friendly decision. In the committee Jay declared that the word "conditional" must be erased before any discussion of the merits of the amendments. As this point was refused, the committee was dissolved; but

---

* This summary of three speeches made by Clinton, one in June, two in July after Virginia had been heard from, is compiled from the manuscripts of Clinton preserved in the state library at Albany.

† Penn. Packet, 18 July 1788; Ind. Gazetteer, 18 July 1788.

already Melancthon Smith and Samuel Jones showed signs of relenting.

On the eleventh Jay, taking the lead, moved the ratification of the constitution and the recommendation of amendments. After a long debate, Melancthon Smith interposed with a resolution which meant in substance that New York would join the union, reserving the right to recede from it if the desired amendments should not be accepted. Against this motion Hamilton, after vainly proposing a form of ratification * nearly similar to that of Virginia, spoke on Saturday, the nineteenth, with such prevailing force that Smith confessed himself persuaded to relinquish it. At this Lansing revived the proposition to enter the union, but only with a reserved right to withdraw from it; and on the following Monday the question might be taken.† Madison having resumed his place in congress, Hamilton wrote in all haste for his advice. On Sunday, Madison speeded an answer to Poughkeepsie, and on the morning of Monday, the twenty-first, Hamilton read to the convention its words, which were as follows:

"My opinion is, that a reservation of a right to withdraw, if amendments be not decided on under the form of the constitution within a certain time, is a *conditional* ratification; that it does not make New York a member of the new union, and, consequently, that she could not be received on that plan. The constitution requires an adoption *in toto* and *forever*. It has been so adopted by the other states. An adoption for a limited time would be as defective as an adoption of some of the articles only. In short, any *condition* whatever must vitiate the ratification. The idea of reserving a right to withdraw was started at Richmond, and considered as a conditional ratification, which was itself abandoned as worse than a rejection." ‡

The voice of Virginia, heard through Madison, was effective. Following the example of Massachusetts, and appropriating the words of its governor, on the twenty-third Samuel

---

* Hamilton, ii., 467–471.

† For the latter part of the convention there is need to resort to the Penn Packet and the Independent Gazetteer for July 1788, where details are given.

‡ Hamilton's Works, i., 465.

Jones, supported by Melancthon Smith, proposed, like Hancock, to make no "condition" and to ratify the constitution "in full confidence" of the adoption of all needed amendments. Lansing's motion for conditions was negatived in committee by a vote of thirty-one to twenty-eight, and on Friday, the twenty-fifth, the convention agreed to the report of its committee of the whole in favor of the form of Samuel Jones and Melancthon Smith by thirty yeas to twenty-five nays, the largest vote on any close division during the whole session. This vote was purchased at the price of consenting to the unanimous resolution, that a circular letter be prepared to be laid before the different legislatures of the United States recommending a general convention to act upon the proposed amendments of the different legislatures of the United States. On Saturday, the twenty-sixth, the form of ratification of the constitution was agreed to by a vote of thirty against twenty-seven. More persons were absent from the vote than would have been necessary to change it. On the following Monday New York invited the governors of the several states in the union to take immediate and effectual measures for calling a second federal convention to amend the constitution. "We are unanimous," said Clinton, "in thinking this measure very conducive to national harmony and good government." Madison, as he read the letter, called the proposal a pestilent one, and Washington was touched with sorrow at the thought that just as the constitution was about to anchor in harbor it might be driven back to sea.

But the city of New York set no bounds to its gladness at the acceptance of the constitution; the citizens paraded in a procession unrivalled in splendor. The miniature ship which was drawn through the streets bore the name of Hamilton. For him this was his happiest moment of unclouded triumph.

North Carolina held its convention before the result in New York was known. The state wanted geographical unity. A part of its territory west of the mountains had an irregular separate organization under the name of Frankland. Of the rest there was no natural centre from which a general opinion could emanate; besides, toward the general government the state was delinquent, and it had not yet shaken from itself the bewildering influence of paper money.

"In this crisis," wrote Washington, "the wisest way for North Carolina will be to adjourn until the people in some parts of the state can consider the magnitude of the question and the consequences involved in it, more coolly and deliberately." * The convention, which consisted of two hundred and eighty-four members, assembling on the twenty-first of July, elected as its president Johnston, then governor of the state, organized itself with tranquillity and dignity, and proceeded to discuss the constitution in committee, clause by clause. The convention employed eight days in its able debates, of which very full and fair accounts have been preserved.

First among the federalists,† and the master mind of the convention, was James Iredell, who, before he was forty years old, was placed by Washington on the supreme bench of the United States. He was supported by William Richardson Davie, who had gained honor in the war and at the bar, and afterward held high places in North Carolina and in the union; by Samuel Johnston, Archibald Maclaine, and Richard Dobbs Spaight.

The other side was led by Willie Jones of Halifax, noted for wealth and aristocratic habits and tastes, yet by nature a steadfast supporter of the principles of democracy. ‡ He was sustained by Samuel Spencer of Anson, a man of candor and moderation, and as a debater far superior to his associates; by David Caldwell from Guilford, a Presbyterian divine, fertile in theories and tenacious of them; and by Timothy Bloodworth, a former member of congress, who as a preacher abounded in offices of charity, as a politician dreaded the subjection of southern to northern interests.

The friends of the constitution had the advantage of spreading their arguments before the people; on the other side Willie Jones, who held in his hand the majority of the convention, citing the wish of Jefferson that nine states might

---

\* Sparks, ix., 390, 391.
† McRee's Iredell, ii., 180–183; for instruction an invaluable work.
‡ McRee's Iredell, ii., 232; Moore's N. C., i., 384.

ratify the constitution, and the rest hold aloof for amendments, answered in this wise: "We do not determine on the constitution; we neither reject nor adopt it; we leave ourselves at liberty; there is no doubt we shall obtain our amendments and come into the union."

At his word the convention on the first of August deferred the ratification of the constitution, and proposed amendments by one hundred and eighty-four votes against eighty-four. But harmony between the state and the new federal government was pre-established by a rule adopted on the next day, that any impost which congress might ordain for the union should be collected in North Carolina by the state "for the use of congress."

The scales were ready to drop from the eyes of Rhode Island. That state, although it had taken no part in the federal convention and for a year and more had neglected to attend in congress, watched without disapprobation the great revolution that was taking place. Neither of the two states which lingered behind remonstrated against the establishment of a new government before their consent; nor did they ask the United States to wait for them. The worst that can be said of them is, that they were late in arriving.

## CHAPTER III.

### THE FEDERAL GOVERNMENT OF THE UNITED STATES.

#### 1788 TO 5 MAY 1789.

It was time for America to be known abroad as a nation. The statesmen of France reproached her unsparingly for failing in her pecuniary engagements. Boatmen who bore the flag of the United States on the father of rivers were fearlessly arrested by Spain, while Don Gardoqui, its agent, in private conversation tempted the men of Kentucky " to declare themselves independent" by the assurance that he was authorized to treat with them as a separate power respecting commerce and the navigation of the Mississippi.*

The colonists in Nova Scotia were already absorbing a part of south-eastern Maine, and inventing false excuses for doing so. Great Britain declined to meet her own obligations with regard to the slaves whom she had carried away, and who finally formed the seed of a British colony at Sierra Leone. She did not give up her negotiations with the men of Vermont. She withheld the interior posts, belonging to the United States; in the commission for the government of Upper Canada she kept out of sight the line of boundary, in order that the commanding officer might not scruple to crowd the Americans away from access to their inland water-line, and thus debar them from their rightful share in the fur-trade. She was all the while encouraging the Indian tribes within the bounds of New York and to the south of the western lakes to assert their independence. Hearing of the discontent of the Kentuckians and the men of west North Carolina, she sought to foment the

* Letters to Washington, iv., 248.

passions which might hurry them out of the union, as far as it could be done without promising them protection.

In England John Adams had, in 1786, vainly explained the expectation of congress that a British plenipotentiary minister should be sent to the United States.* The bills regulating Newfoundland and intercourse with America were under the leadership of the same Jenkinson who had prepared the stamp act; and, with the acquiescence of Pitt, the men and the principles which had governed British policy toward America for most of the last twenty years still prevailed.† In February 1788 the son of George Grenville, speaking for the ministry in the house of commons, said: "Great Britain, ever since the peace, has condescended to favor the United States." ‡ Moreover, the British government would take no notice of American remonstrances against the violations of the treaty of peace. Self-respect and patriotic pride forbade John Adams to remain.

Adams and Jefferson had exchanged with each other their portraits, as lasting memorials of friendship; and Adams, on leaving Europe, had but two regrets: one, the opportunity of research in books; the other, that immediate correspondence with Jefferson which he cherished as one of the most agreeable events in his life. "A seven months' intimacy with him here and as many weeks in London have given me opportunities of studying him closely," wrote Jefferson to Madison. "He is vain, irritable, and a bad calculator of the force and probable effect of the motives which govern men. This is all the ill which can possibly be said of him. He is disinterested, profound in his views, and accurate in his judgment, except where knowledge of the world is necessary to form a judgment. He is so amiable that you will love him, if ever you become acquainted with him." #

In America the new constitution was rapidly conciliating the affections of the people. Union had been held dear ever since it was formed; and now that the constitution was its

---

* Adams to Carmarthen, 6 February 1786.
† Adams to Jay, 27 February 1786.
‡ Speech of Grenville, 11 February 1788. Almon's Parliamentary Register, 23, p. 179.
# Jefferson, ii., 107.

surest guarantee, no party could succeed which did not inscribe union, and with union the constitution, on its banner. In September 1788 the dissidents of Pennsylvania held a conference at Harrisburg. With the delegates from beyond the mountains came Albert Gallatin, a native of Geneva, and educated there in a republic of a purely federal form. Their proceedings bear the marks of his mind. They resolved for themselves and recommended to all others to acquiesce in the organization of the government under "the federal constitution, of which the ratification had formed a new era in the American world;" they asked, however, for its speedy revision by a general convention. All their actions were kept within the bounds of legality.*

In Virginia there had been a great vibration of opinion. Its assembly, which met on the twentieth of October 1788, was the first to take into consideration the proposal for another federal convention. The enemies to the government formed a decided majority of the legislature.† No one of its members was able to encounter Patrick Henry in debate, and his edicts were registered without opposition. ‡ He had only to say, "Let this be law," and it became law. Taking care to set forth that so far as it depended on Virginia the new plan of government would be carried into immediate operation, the assembly, on the thirtieth, proposed a second federal convention, and invited the concurrence of every other state.# Madison was the fittest man in the union to be of the senate of the United States: Henry, on the eighth of November, after pouring forth a declamation against his federal principles, ‖ nominated Richard Henry Lee and Grayson for the two senators from Virginia, and they were chosen at his bidding. He divided the state into districts, cunningly restricting each of them to its own inhabitants in the choice of its representative, and taking care to compose the district in which Madison would be a candidate out of counties which were thought to be unfriendly

---

* Life of Gallatin by Henry Adams, 77; Elliot, ii., 544.
† Madison, i., 436, 437.
‡ Washington to Madison, 17 November 1788. Tobias Lear to Langdon, 31 January 1789.
# Rives's Madison, ii., 646. ‖ Madison, i., 443, 444.

to federalism. Assured by these iniquitous preparations, Monroe, without scruple, took the field against Madison.

In Connecticut, in October, the circular letter of New York had a reading among other public communications, but "no anti-federalist had hardiness enough to call it up for consideration or to speak one word of its subject." *

The legislature of Massachusetts concurred with Hancock, the governor, that an immediate second federal convention might endanger the union.† The legislature of Pennsylvania put the question at rest by saying : " The house do not perceive this constitution wanting in any of those fundamental principles which are calculated to ensure the liberties of their country. The happiness of America and the harmony of the union depend upon suffering it to proceed undisturbed in its operation by premature amendments. The house cannot, consistently with their duty to the good people of this state or with their affection to the citizens of the United States at large, concur with Virginia in their application to congress for a convention of the states." This vote Mifflin, the governor, early in March 1789, communicated to the governor of Virginia, ‡ and the subject was heard of no more.

Congress, as early as the second of July 1788, was notified that the constitution had received the approval of nine states ; but they wasted two months in wrangling about the permanent seat of the federal government, and at last could agree only on New York as its resting-place. Not till the thirteenth of September was the first Wednesday of the following January appointed for the choice of electors of president in the several states ; and the first Wednesday in March, which in that year was the fourth, for commencing proceedings under the constitution. The states, each for itself, appointed the times and places for electing senators and representatives.

The interest of the elections centred in New York, Virginia, and South Carolina. In four districts out of the six into which New York was divided the federalists elected their

---

* Trumbull to Washington, 28 October 1788. Letters to Washington, iv., 238.

† New York Daily Gazette of 17 February 1789.

‡ Pennsylvania Archives, xi., 557, 558.

candidates. Having in the state legislature but a bare majority in the senate, while their opponents outnumbered them in the house, each branch made a nomination of senators; but the senate refused to go into a joint ballot. For this there was the excuse that the time for a new election was close at hand. But the senate further refused to meet the house for the choice of electors of president, and this was an act of faction.

The star of Hamilton was then in the ascendant, and he controlled the federalists; but only to make his singular incapacity to conduct a party as apparent as his swiftness and power of thought. He excluded the family of the Livingstons from influence. To defeat Clinton's re-election as governor, he stepped into the camp of his opponents, and with Aaron Burr and other anti-federalists selected for their candidate Robert Yates, who had deserted his post in the federal convention, but had since avowed the opinion which was held by every one in the state that the new constitution should be supported. New York at the moment was thoroughly federal, yet Clinton escaped defeat through the attachment of his own county of Ulster and the insignificance of his opponent, while the federalists were left without any state organization. In the new legislature both branches were federal, and, at the behest of Hamilton, against the remonstrances of Morgan Lewis and others, Rufus King, on his transfer of residence from Massachusetts to New York, received the unexampled welcome of an immediate election with Schuyler to the senate.

In Virginia, Madison went into the counties that were relied on to defeat him, reasoned with the voters face to face, and easily won the day. Of the ten delegates from the state, seven were federalists, of whom one was from Kentucky. South Carolina elected avowed anti-federalists, except Butler, of the senate, who had conceded many points to bring about the union, and yet very soon took the alarm that "the southern interest was imperilled." *

Under the constitution the house of representatives formed a quorum on the first of April 1789. The senate on the sixth chose John Langdon of New Hampshire its president. The

* Pierce Butler to Iredell, in Life of Iredell, ii., 264, 265.

house of representatives was immediately summoned, and in the presence of the two branches he opened and counted the votes. Every one of the sixty-nine, cast by the ten states which took part in the election, was for Washington. John Adams had thirty-four votes; and as no other obtained more than nine, he was declared to be the vice-president. The house devolved upon the senate the office of communicating the result to those who had been chosen; and proceeded to business.

"I foresee contentions," wrote Madison, "first between federal and anti-federal parties, and then between northern and southern parties, which give additional disagreeableness to the prospect." * The events of the next seventy years cast their shadows before. Madison revived the bill which he had presented to congress on the eighteenth of March 1783, for duties on imports, adding to it a discriminating duty on tonnage. For an immediate public revenue, Lawrence of New York proposed a general duty *ad valorem*. England herself, by restraining and even prohibiting the domestic industry of the Americans so long as they remained in the condition of colonial dependence, had trained them to consider the establishment of home manufactures as an act of patriotic resistance to tyranny. Fitzsimons of Pennsylvania disapproved a uniform *ad valorem* duty on all imports. He said: "I have in contemplation to encourage domestic manufactures by protecting duties." Tucker of South Carolina enforced the necessity of great deliberation by calling attention to the antagonistic interests of the eastern, middle, and southern states in the article of tonnage. Boudinot of New Jersey wished glass to be taxed, for there were already several manufactures of it in the country. "We are able," said Hartley of Pennsylvania, "to furnish some domestic manufactures in sufficient quantity to answer the consumption of the whole union, and to work up our stock of materials even for exportation. In these cases I take it to be the policy of free, enlightened nations to give their manufactures that encouragement necessary to perfect them without oppressing the other parts of the community."

"We must consider the general interests of the union," said Madison, "as much as the local or state interest. My

* Madison, i., 450, 451.

general principle is that commerce ought to be free, and labor and industry left at large to find their proper object." But he admitted that "the interests of the states which are ripe for manufactures ought to have attention, as the power of protecting and cherishing them has by the present constitution been taken from the states and its exercise thrown into other hands. Regulations in some of the states have produced establishments which ought not to be allowed to perish from the alteration which has taken place, while some manufactures being once formed can advance toward perfection without any adventitious aid. Some of the propositions may be productive of revenue and some may protect our domestic manufactures, though the latter subject ought not to be too confusedly blended with the former." "I," said Tucker, "am opposed to high duties because they will introduce and establish a system of smuggling, and because they tend to the oppression of citizens and states to promote the benefit of other states and other classes of citizens." *

The election to the presidency found Washington prepared with a federal policy, which was the result of long meditation. He was resolved to preserve freedom; never to transcend the powers delegated by the constitution; even at the cost of life to uphold the union, a sentiment which in him had a tinge of anxiety from his thorough acquaintance with what Grayson called "the southern genius of America;" to restore the public finances; to establish in the foreign relations of the country a thoroughly American system; and to preserve neutrality in the impending conflicts between nations in Europe.

Across the Atlantic Alfieri cried out to him: "Happy are you, who have for the sublime and permanent basis of your glory the love of country demonstrated by deeds."

On the fourteenth of April he received the official announcement of his recall to the public service, and was at ten o'clock on the morning of the sixteenth on his way. Though reluctant "in the evening of life to exchange a peaceful abode for an ocean of difficulties," he bravely said: "Be the voyage long or short, although I may be deserted by all men, integrity and firmness shall never forsake me."

* Annals of Congress, i., 291.

But for him the country could not have achieved its independence; but for him it could not have formed its union; and but for him it could not have set the federal government in successful motion. His journey to New York was one continued march of triumph. All the way he was met with addresses from the citizens of various towns, from societies, universities, and churches.

His neighbors of Alexandria crowded round him with the strongest personal affection, saying: "Farewell, and make a grateful people happy; and may the Being who maketh and unmaketh at his will, restore to us again the best of men and the most beloved fellow-citizen."\*

To the citizens of Baltimore, Washington said: "I hold it of little moment if the close of my life shall be embittered, provided I shall have been instrumental in securing the liberties and promoting the happiness of the American people." †

He assured the society for promoting domestic manufactures in Delaware that "the promotion of domestic manufactures may naturally be expected to flow from an energetic government;" and he promised to give "a decided preference to the produce and fabrics of America." ‡

At Philadelphia, "almost overwhelmed with a sense of the divine munificence," he spoke words of hope: "The most gracious Being, who has hitherto watched over the interests and averted the perils of the United States, will never suffer so fair an inheritance to become a prey to anarchy or despotism." #

At Trenton he was met by a party of matrons and their daughters, dressed in white, strewing flowers before him, and singing an ode of welcome to "the mighty chief" who had rescued them from a "mercenary foe."

Embarking at Elizabeth Point in a new barge, manned by pilots dressed in white, he cleaved his course swiftly across the bay, between gayly decorated boats, filled with gazers who cheered him with instrumental music, or broke out in songs. As he touched the soil of New York he was welcomed by the two houses of congress, by the governor of the state, by the

---

\* Sparks, xii., 139, note.  ‡ Sparks, xii., 141.
† Sparks, xii., 140, 141.  # Sparks, xii., 145.

magistrates of the city, by its people; and so attended he proceeded on foot to the modest mansion lately occupied by the presiding officer of the confederate congress. On that day he dined with Clinton; in the evening the city was illuminated. The senate, under the influence of John Adams and the persistency of Richard Henry Lee, would have given him the title of "Highness;" but the house, supported by the true republican simplicity of the man whom they both wished to honor, insisted on the simple words of the constitution, and prevailed.

On the thirtieth, the day appointed for the inauguration, Washington, being fifty-seven years, two months, and eight days old, was ceremoniously received by the two houses in the hall of the senate. Stepping out to the middle compartment of a balcony, which had been raised in front of it, he found before him a dense throng extending to Broad street, and filling Wall street to Broadway. All were hushed as Livingston, the chancellor of the state, administered the oath of office; but when he cried, "Long live George Washington, President of the United States!" the air was rent with huzzas, which were repeated as Washington bowed to the multitude.

Then returning to the senate-chamber, with an aspect grave almost to sadness and a voice deep and tremulous, he addressed the two houses, confessing his distrust of his own endowments and his inexperience in civil administration. The magnitude and difficulty of the duties to which his country had called him weighed upon him so heavily that he shook as he proceeded: "It would be peculiarly improper to omit, in this first official act, my fervent supplications to that Almighty Being who presides in the councils of nations, that his benediction may consecrate to the liberties and happiness of the people of the United States a government instituted by themselves. No people can be bound to acknowledge the invisible hand which conducts the affairs of men more than the people of the United States. Every step by which they have advanced to the character of an independent nation seems to have been distinguished by some token of providential agency. There exists in the economy of nature an indissoluble union between an honest and magnanimous policy and public prosperity. Heaven can never smile on a nation that disregards the eternal rules of order and right. The preservation of liberty, and the destiny of the republican model of government, are justly considered as deeply, perhaps as finally, staked on the experiment intrusted to the American people."

At the close of the ceremony the president and both branches of congress were escorted to the church of St. Paul, where the chaplain of the senate read prayers suited to the occasion, after which they all attended the president to his mansion.

"Every one without exception," so reports the French minister to his government,* " appeared penetrated with veneration for the illustrious chief of the republic. The humblest was proud of the virtues of the man who was to govern him. Tears of joy were seen to flow in the hall of the senate, at church, and even in the streets, and no sovereign ever reigned more completely in the hearts of his subjects than Washington in the hearts of his fellow-citizens. Nature, which had given him the talent to govern, distinguished him from all others by his appearance. He had at once the soul, the look, and the figure of a hero. He never appeared embarrassed at homage rendered him, and in his manners he had the advantage of joining dignity to great simplicity."

To the president's inaugural speech one branch of the legislature thus responded : " The senate will at all times cheerfully co-operate in every measure which may strengthen the union and perpetuate the liberties of this great confederated republic."

The representatives of the American people likewise addressed him : "With you we adore the invisible hand which has led the American people through so many difficulties; and we cherish a conscious responsibility for the destiny of republican liberty. We join in your fervent supplication for our country; and we add our own for the choicest blessings of heaven on the most beloved of her citizens."

In the same moments of the fifth day of May 1789, when these words were reported, the ground was trembling beneath the arbitrary governments of Europe as Louis XVI. proceeded to open the states-general of France. The day of

* Moustier's report on the inauguration of the president of the United States.

wrath, against which Leibnitz had warned the monarchs of Europe, was beginning to break, and its judgments were to be the more terrible for the long delay of its coming. The great Frederick, who alone of them all had lived and toiled for the good of his land, described the degeneracy and insignificance of his fellow-rulers with cynical scorn. Not one of them had a surmise that the only sufficient reason for the existence of a king lies in his usefulness to the people. Nor did they spare one another. The law of morality was never suffered to restrain the passion for conquest. Austria preyed upon Italy until Alfieri could only say, in his despair, that despotic power had left him no country to serve; nor did the invader permit the thought that an Italian could have a right to a country. The heir in the only line of protestant kings on the continent of Europe, too blind to see that he would one day be stripped of the chief part of his own share in the spoils, joined with two other robbers to divide the country of Kosciuszko. In Holland dynastic interests were betraying the welfare of the republic. All faith was dying out; and self, in its eagerness for pleasure or advantage, stifled the voice of justice. The atheism of the great, who lived without God in the world, concealed itself under superstitious observances which were enforced by an inquisition that sought to rend beliefs from the soul, and to suppress inquiry by torments which surpassed the worst cruelties that savages could invent. Even in Great Britain all the branches of government were controlled by the aristocracy, of which the more liberal party could in that generation have no hope of being summoned by the king to frame a cabinet. The land, of which every member of a clan had had some share of ownership, had been for the most part usurped by the nobility; and the people were starving in the midst of the liberality which their own hands extorted from nature. The monarchs, whose imbecility or excesses had brought the doom of death on arbitrary power, were not only unfit to rule, but, while their own unlimited sovereignty was stricken with death, they knew not how to raise up statesmen to take their places. Well-intentioned friends of mankind burned with indignation, and even the wise and prudent were incensed by the conscious endurance of wrong;

while the lowly classes, clouded by despair, were driven sometimes to admit the terrible thought that religion, which is the poor man's consolation and defence, might be but an instrument of government in the hands of their oppressors. There was no relief for the nations but through revolution, and their masters had poisoned the weapons which revolution must use.

In America a new people had risen up without king, or princes, or nobles, knowing nothing of tithes and little of landlords, the plough being for the most part in the hands of free holders of the soil. They were more sincerely religious, better educated, of serener minds, and of purer morals than the men of any former republic. By calm meditation and friendly councils they had prepared a constitution which, in the union of freedom with strength and order, excelled every one known before; and which secured itself against violence and revolution by providing a peaceful method for every needed reform. In the happy morning of their existence as one of the powers of the world, they had chosen justice for their guide; and while they proceeded on their way with well-founded confidence and joy, all the friends of mankind invoked success on the unexampled endeavor to govern states and territories of imperial extent as one federal republic.

# THE CONSTITUTION

OF THE

# UNITED STATES OF AMERICA,

*WITH THE AMENDMENTS.*

COMPARED WITH THE ORIGINAL IN THE DEPARTMENT OF STATE, SEPTEMBER 17, 1872, AND FOUND TO BE CORRECT.

# CONSTITUTION

OF THE

# UNITED STATES OF AMERICA.

---

WE THE PEOPLE of the United States, in Order to form a more perfect Union, establish Justice, insure domestic Tranquility, provide for the common defence, promote the general Welfare, and secure the Blessings of Liberty to ourselves and our Posterity, do ordain and establish this CONSTITUTION for the United States of America.

## ARTICLE. I.

SECTION. 1. All legislative Powers herein granted shall be vested in a Congress of the United States, which shall consist of a Senate and House of Representatives.

SECTION. 2. The House of Representatives shall be composed of Members chosen every second Year by the People of the several States, and the Electors in each State shall have the Qualifications requisite for Electors of the most numerous Branch of the State Legislature.

No Person shall be a Representative who shall not have attained to the Age of twenty-five Years, and been seven Years a Citizen of the United States, and who shall not, when elected, be an Inhabitant of that State in which he shall be chosen.

Representatives and direct Taxes shall be apportioned among the several States which may be included within this Union, according to their respective Numbers, which shall be determined by adding to the whole Number of free Persons, including those bound to Service for a Term of Years, and excluding Indians not taxed, three fifths of all other Persons. The actual Enumeration shall be made within three Years after the first Meeting of the Congress of the United States, and within every subsequent Term of ten Years, in such Manner as they shall by Law direct. The Number of Representatives shall not exceed one for every thirty Thousand, but each State shall have at Least one Representative; and until such enumeration shall be made, the State of New Hampshire shall be entitled to chuse three, Massachusetts eight, Rhode-Island and Providence Plantations one, Connecticut five, New York six, New Jersey four, Pennsylvania eight, Delaware one, Maryland six, Virginia ten, North Carolina five, South Carolina five, and Georgia three.

When vacancies happen in the Representation from any State, the Executive Authority thereof shall issue Writs of Election to fill such Vacancies.

The House of Representatives shall chuse their Speaker and other Officers; and shall have the sole Power of Impeachment.

SECTION. 3. The Senate of the United States shall be composed of two Senators from each State, chosen by the Legislature thereof, for six Years; and each Senator shall have one Vote.

Immediately after they shall be assembled in Consequence of the first Election, they shall be divided as equally as may be into three Classes. The Seats of the Senators of the first Class shall be vacated at the Expiration of the second Year, of the second Class at the Expiration of the fourth Year, and of the third Class at the Expiration of the sixth Year, so that one third may be chosen every second Year; and if Vacancies happen by Resignation, or otherwise, during the Recess of the Legislature of any State, the Executive thereof may make temporary Appointments until the next Meeting of the Legislature, which shall then fill such Vacancies.

No Person shall be a Senator who shall not have attained to the Age of thirty Years, and been nine Years a Citizen of the United States, and who shall not, when elected, be an Inhabitant of that State for which he shall be chosen.

The Vice President of the United States shall be President of the Senate, but shall have no Vote, unless they be equally divided.

The Senate shall chuse their other Officers, and also a President pro tempore, in the Absence of the Vice President, or when he shall exercise the Office of President of the United States.

The Senate shall have the sole Power to try all Impeachments. When sitting for that Purpose, they shall be on Oath or Affirmation. When the President of the United States is tried, the Chief Justice shall preside : And no Person shall be convicted without the Concurrence of two thirds of the Members present.

Judgment in Cases of Impeachment shall not extend further than to removal from Office, and disqualification to hold and enjoy any Office of honor, Trust or Profit under the United States : but the Party convicted shall nevertheless be liable and subject to Indictment, Trial, Judgment and Punishment, according to Law.

SECTION. 4. The Times, Places and Manner of holding Elections for Senators and Representatives, shall be prescribed in each State by the Legislature thereof ; but the Congress may at any time by Law make or alter such Regulations, except as to the Places of chusing Senators.

The Congress shall assemble at least once in every Year, and such Meeting shall be on the first Monday in December, unless they shall by Law appoint a different Day.

SECTION. 5. Each House shall be the Judge of the Elections, Returns and Qualifications of its own Members, and a Majority of each shall constitute a Quorum to do Business ; but a smaller Number may adjourn from day to day, and may be authorized to compel the Attendance of absent Members, in such Manner, and under such Penalties as each House may provide.

Each House may determine the Rules of its Proceedings, punish its Members for disorderly Behaviour, and, with the Concurrence of two thirds, expel a Member.

Each House shall keep a Journal of its Proceedings, and from time to time publish the same, excepting such Parts as may in their Judgment require Secrecy ; and the Yeas and Nays of the Members of either House on any question shall, at the Desire of one fifth of those Present, be entered on the Journal.

Neither House, during the Session of Congress, shall, without the Consent of the other, adjourn for more than three days, nor to any other Place than that in which the two Houses shall be sitting.

SECTION. 6. The Senators and Representatives shall receive a Compensation for their Services, to be ascertained by Law, and paid out of the Treasury of the United States. They shall in all Cases, except Treason, Felony and Breach of the Peace, be privileged from Arrest during their Attendance at the Session of their respective Houses, and in going to and returning from the same; and for any Speech or Debate in either House, they shall not be questioned in any other Place.

No Senator or Representative shall, during the Time for which he was elected, be appointed to any civil Office under the Authority of the United States, which shall have been created, or the Emoluments whereof shall have been encreased during such time; and no Person holding any Office under the United States, shall be a Member of either House during his Continuance in Office.

SECTION. 7. All Bills for raising Revenue shall originate in the House of Representatives; but the Senate may propose or concur with Amendments as on other Bills.

Every Bill which shall have passed the House of Representatives and the Senate, shall, before it become a Law, be presented to the President of the United States; If he approve he shall sign it, but if not he shall return it, with his Objections to that House in which it shall have originated, who shall enter the Objections at large on their Journal, and proceed to reconsider it. If after such Reconsideration two thirds of that House shall agree to pass the Bill, it shall be sent, together with the Objections, to the other House, by which it shall likewise be reconsidered, and if approved by two thirds of that House, it shall become a Law. But in all such Cases the Votes of both Houses shall be determined by yeas and Nays, and the Names of the Persons voting for and against the Bill shall be entered on the Journal of each House respectively. If any Bill shall not be returned by the President within ten Days (Sundays excepted) after it shall have been presented to him, the Same shall be a Law, in like Manner as if he had signed it, unless the Congress by their Adjournment prevent its Return, in which Case it shall not be a Law.

Every Order, Resolution, or Vote to which the Concurrence of the Senate and House of Representatives may be necessary (except on a question of Adjournment) shall be presented to the President of the United States; and before the Same shall take Effect, shall be approved by him, or being disapproved by him, shall be repassed by two thirds of the Senate and House of Representatives, according to the Rules and Limitations prescribed in the Case of a Bill.

SECTION. 8. The Congress shall have Power To lay and collect Taxes, Duties, Imposts and Excises, to pay the Debts and provide for the common Defence and general Welfare of the United States; but all Duties, Imposts and Excises shall be uniform throughout the United States;

To borrow Money on the credit of the United States;

To regulate Commerce with foreign Nations, and among the several States, and with the Indian Tribes;

To establish an uniform Rule of Naturalization, and uniform Laws on the subject of Bankruptcies throughout the United States;

To coin Money, regulate the Value thereof, and of foreign Coin, and fix the Standard of Weights and Measures;

To provide for the Punishment of counterfeiting the Securities and current Coin of the United States;

To establish Post Offices and post Roads;

To promote the Progress of Science and useful Arts, by securing for limited Times to Authors and Inventors the exclusive Right to their respective Writings and Discoveries;

To constitute Tribunals inferior to the supreme Court;

To define and punish Piracies and Felonies committed on the high Seas, and Offences against the Law of Nations;

To declare War, grant Letters of Marque and Reprisal, and make Rules concerning Captures on Land and Water;

To raise and support Armies, but no Appropriation of Money to that Use shall be for a longer Term than two Years;

To provide and maintain a Navy;

To make Rules for the Government and Regulation of the land and naval Forces;

To provide for calling forth the Militia to execute the Laws of the Union, suppress Insurrections and repel Invasions;

To provide for organizing, arming, and disciplining, the Militia, and for governing such Part of them as may be employed in the Service of the United States, reserving to the States respectively, the Appointment of the Officers, and the Authority of training the Militia according to the discipline prescribed by Congress;

To exercise exclusive Legislation in all Cases whatsoever, over such District (not exceeding ten Miles square) as may, by Cession of particular States, and the Acceptance of Congress, become the Seat of the Government of the United States, and to exercise like Authority over all Places purchased by the Consent of the Legislature of the State in which the Same shall be, for the Erection of Forts, Magazines, Arsenals, dock-Yards, and other needful Buildings ;—And

To make all Laws which shall be necessary and proper for carrying into Execution the foregoing Powers, and all other Powers vested by this Constitution in the Government of the United States, or in any Department or Officer thereof.

Section. 9. The Migration or Importation of such Persons as any of the States now existing shall think proper to admit, shall not be prohibited by the Congress prior to the Year one thousand eight hundred and eight, but a Tax or duty may be imposed on such Importation, not exceeding ten dollars for each Person.

The Privilege of the Writ of Habeas Corpus shall not be suspended, unless when in Cases of Rebellion or Invasion the public Safety may require it.

No Bill of Attainder or ex post facto Law shall be passed.

No Capitation, or other direct, Tax shall be laid, unless in Proportion to the Census or Enumeration herein before directed to be taken.

No Tax or Duty shall be laid on Articles exported from any State.

No Preference shall be given by any Regulation of Commerce or Revenue to the Ports of one State over those of another : nor shall Vessels bound to, or from, one State, be obliged to enter, clear, or pay Duties in another.

No Money shall be drawn from the Treasury, but in Consequence of Appropriations made by Law ; and a regular Statement and Account of the Receipts and Expenditures of all public Money shall be published from time to time.

No Title of Nobility shall be granted by the United States : And no Person holding any Office of Profit or Trust under them, shall, without the Consent of the Congress, accept of any present, Emolument, Office, or Title, of any kind whatever, from any King, Prince, or foreign State.

Section. 10. No State shall enter into any Treaty, Alliance, or Confederation ; grant Letters of Marque and Reprisal ; coin Money ; emit Bills of Credit ; make any Thing but gold and silver Coin a Tender in Payment of Debts ; pass any Bill of Attainder, ex post facto Law, or Law impairing the Obligation of Contracts, or grant any Title of Nobility.

No State shall, without the Consent of the Congress, lay any Imposts or Duties on Imports or Exports, except what may be absolutely necessary for executing it's inspection Laws : and the net Produce of all Duties and Imposts, laid by any State on Imports or Exports, shall be for the Use of the Treasury of the United States ; and all such Laws shall be subject to the Revision and Controul of the Congress.

No State shall, without the Consent of Congress, lay any Duty of Tonnage, keep Troops, or Ships of War in time of Peace, enter into any Agreement or Compact with another State, or with a foreign Power, or engage in War, unless actually invaded, or in such imminent Danger as will not admit of delay.

## ARTICLE. II.

Section. 1. The executive Power shall be vested in a President of the United States of America. He shall hold his Office during the Term of four Years, and, together with the Vice President, chosen for the same Term, be elected, as follows

Each State shall appoint, in such Manner as the Legislature thereof may direct, a Number of Electors, equal to the whole Number of Senators and Representatives to which the State may be entitled in the Congress : but no Senator or Representative, or Person holding an Office of Trust or Profit under the United States, shall be appointed an Elector.

The Electors shall meet in their respective States, and vote by Ballot for two Persons, of whom one at least shall not be an Inhabitant of the same State with themselves. And they shall make a List of all the Persons voted for, and of the Number of Votes for each ; which List they shall sign and certify, and transmit sealed to the Seat of the Government of the United States, directed to the President of the Senate. The President of the Senate shall, in the Presence of the Senate and House of Representatives, open all the Certificates, and the Votes shall then be counted. The Person having the greatest Number of

Votes shall be the President, if such Number be a Majority of the whole Number of Electors appointed ; and if there be more than one who have such Majority, and have an equal Number of Votes, then the House of Representatives shall immediately chuse by Ballot one of them for President ; and if no Person have a Majority, then from the five highest on the List the said House shall in like Manner chuse the President. But in chusing the President, the Votes shall be taken by States, the Representation from each State having one Vote ; A quorum for this Purpose shall consist of a Member or Members from two thirds of the States, and a Majority of all the States shall be necessary to a Choice. In every Case, after the Choice of the President, the Person having the greatest Number of Votes of the Electors shall be the Vice President. But if there should remain two or more who have equal Votes, the Senate shall chuse from them by Ballot the Vice President.

The Congress may determine the Time of chusing the Electors, and the Day on which they shall give their Votes ; which Day shall be the same throughout the United States.

No Person except a natural born Citizen, or a Citizen of the United States, at the time of the Adoption of this Constitution, shall be eligible to the Office of President ; neither shall any Person be eligible to that Office who shall not have attained to the Age of thirty five Years, and been fourteen Years a Resident within the United States.

In Case of the Removal of the President from Office, or of his Death, Resignation, or Inability to discharge the Powers and Duties of the said Office, the Same shall devolve on the Vice President, and the Congress may by Law provide for the Case of Removal, Death, Resignation or Inability, both of the President and Vice President, declaring what Officer shall then act as President, and such Officer shall act accordingly, until the Disability be removed, or a President shall be elected.

The President shall, at stated Times, receive for his Services, a Compensation, which shall neither be encreased nor diminished during the Period for which he shall have been elected, and he shall not receive within that Period any other Emolument from the United States, or any of them.

Before he enter on the Execution of his Office, he shall take the following Oath or Affirmation :—" I do solemnly swear (or affirm) that I will faithfully execute the Office of President of the United States, and will to the best of my Ability, preserve, protect and defend the Constitution of the United States."

Section. 2. The President shall be Commander in Chief of the Army and Navy of the United States, and of the Militia of the several States, when called into the actual Service of the United States; he may require the Opinion, in writing, of the principal Officer in each of the executive Departments, upon any Subject relating to the Duties of their respective Offices, and he shall have Power to grant Reprieves and Pardons for Offences against the United States, except in Cases of Impeachment.

He shall have Power, by and with the Advice and Consent of the Senate, to make Treaties, provided two thirds of the Senators present concur; and he shall nominate, and by and with the Advice and Consent of the Senate, shall appoint Ambassadors, other public Ministers and Consuls, Judges of the supreme Court, and all other Officers of the United States, whose Appointments are not herein otherwise provided for, and which shall be established by Law: but the Congress may by Law vest the Appointment of such inferior Officers, as they think proper, in the President alone, in the Courts of Law, or in the Heads of Departments.

The President shall have Power to fill up all Vacancies that may happen during the Recess of the Senate, by granting Commissions which shall expire at the End of their next Session.

Section. 3. He shall from time to time give to the Congress Information of the State of the Union, and recommend to their Consideration such Measures as he shall judge necessary and expedient; he may, on extraordinary Occasions, convene both Houses, or either of them, and in Case of Disagreement between them, with Respect to the Time of Adjournment, he may adjourn them to such Time as he shall think proper; he shall receive Ambassadors and other public Ministers; he shall take Care that the Laws be faithfully executed, and shall Commission all the Officers of the United States.

Section. 4. The President, Vice President and all civil Officers of the United States, shall be removed from Office on Impeachment for, and Conviction of, Treason, Bribery, or other high Crimes and Misdemeanors.

## ARTICLE III.

SECTION. 1. The judicial Power of the United States, shall be vested in one supreme Court, and in such inferior Courts as the Congress may from time to time ordain and establish. The Judges, both of the supreme and inferior Courts, shall hold their Offices during good Behaviour, and shall, at stated Times, receive for their Services, a Compensation, which shall not be diminished during their Continuance in Office.

SECTION. 2. The judicial Power shall extend to all Cases, in Law and Equity, arising under this Constitution, the Laws of the United States, and Treaties made, or which shall be made, under their Authority;—to all Cases affecting Ambassadors, other public Ministers and Consuls;—to all Cases of admiralty and maritime Jurisdiction;—to Controversies to which the United States shall be a Party;—to Controversies between two or more States;—between a State and Citizens of another State; —between Citizens of different States,—between Citizens of the same State claiming Lands under Grants of different States, and between a State, or the Citizens thereof, and foreign States, Citizens or Subjects.

In all Cases affecting Ambassadors, other public Ministers and Consuls, and those in which a State shall be Party, the supreme Court shall have original Jurisdiction. In all the other Cases before mentioned, the supreme Court shall have appellate Jurisdiction, both as to Law and Fact, with such Exceptions, and under such Regulations as the Congress shall make.

The Trial of all Crimes, except in Cases of Impeachment, shall be by Jury; and such Trial shall be held in the State where the said Crimes shall have been committed; but when not committed within any State, the Trial shall be at such Place or Places as the Congress may by Law have directed.

SECTION. 3. Treason against the United States, shall consist only in levying War against them, or in adhering to their Enemies, giving them Aid and Comfort. No Person shall be convicted of Treason unless on the Testimony of two Witnesses to the same overt Act, or on Confession in open Court.

The Congress shall have Power to declare the Punishment of

Treason, but no Attainder of Treason shall work Corruption of Blood, or Forfeiture except during the Life of the Person attainted.

## ARTICLE. IV.

SECTION. 1. Full Faith and Credit shall be given in each State to the public Acts, Records, and judicial Proceedings of every other State. And the Congress may by general Laws prescribe the Manner in which such Acts, Records and Proceedings shall be proved, and the Effect thereof.

SECTION. 2. The Citizens of each State shall be entitled to all Privileges and Immunities of Citizens in the several States.

A Person charged in any State with Treason, Felony, or other Crime, who shall flee from Justice, and be found in another State, shall on Demand of the executive Authority of the State from which he fled, be delivered up, to be removed to the State having Jurisdiction of the Crime.

No Person held to Service or Labour in one State, under the Laws thereof, escaping into another, shall, in Consequence of any Law or Regulation therein, be discharged from such Service or Labour, but shall be delivered up on Claim of the Party to whom such Service or Labour may be due.

SECTION. 3. New States may be admitted by the Congress into this Union; but no new State shall be formed or erected within the Jurisdiction of any other State; nor any State be formed by the Junction of two or more States, or Parts of States, without the Consent of the Legislatures of the States concerned as well as of the Congress.

The Congress shall have Power to dispose of and make all needful Rules and Regulations respecting the Territory or other Property belonging to the United States; and nothing in this Constitution shall be so construed as to Prejudice any Claims of the United States, or of any particular State.

SECTION. 4. The United States shall guarantee to every State in this Union a Republican Form of Government, and shall protect each of them against Invasion; and on Application of the Legislature, or of the Executive (when the Legislature cannot be convened) against domestic Violence.

## ARTICLE. V.

The Congress, whenever two thirds of both Houses shall deem it necessary, shall propose Amendments to this Constitution, or, on the Application of the Legislatures of two thirds of the several States, shall call a Convention for proposing Amendments, which, in either Case, shall be valid to all Intents and Purposes, as part of this Constitution, when ratified by the Legislatures of three fourths of the several States, or by Conventions in three fourths thereof, as the one or the other Mode of Ratification may be proposed by the Congress; Provided that no Amendment which may be made prior to the Year One thousand eight hundred and eight shall in any Manner affect the first and fourth Clauses in the Ninth Section of the first Article; and that no State, without its Consent, shall be deprived of its equal Suffrage in the Senate.

## ARTICLE. VI.

All Debts contracted and Engagements entered into, before the Adoption of this Constitution, shall be as valid against the United States under this Constitution, as under the Confederation.

This Constitution, and the Laws of the United States which shall be made in Pursuance thereof; and all Treaties made, or which shall be made, under the Authority of the United States, shall be the supreme Law of the Land; and the Judges in every State shall be bound thereby, any Thing in the Constitution or Laws of any State to the Contrary notwithstanding.

The Senators and Representatives before mentioned, and the Members of the several State Legislatures, and all executive and judicial Officers, both of the United States and of the several States, shall be bound by Oath or Affirmation, to support this Constitution; but no religious Test shall ever be required as a Qualification to any Office or public Trust under the United States.

## ARTICLE. VII.

The Ratification of the Conventions of nine States, shall be sufficient for the Establishment of this Constitution between the States so ratifying the Same.

DONE in Convention by the Unanimous Consent of the States present the Seventeenth Day of September in the Year of our Lord one thousand seven hundred and Eighty seven and of the Independence of the United States of America the Twelfth **In Witness** whereof We have hereunto subscribed our Names,

G°: WASHINGTON—
*Presidt. and deputy from Virginia*

| | |
|---|---|
| *New Hampshire* ....... | { JOHN LANGDON<br>NICHOLAS GILMAN } |
| *Massachusetts*.......... | { NATHANIEL GORHAM<br>RUFUS KING |
| *Connecticut*............ | { WM. SAML. JOHNSON<br>ROGER SHERMAN |
| *New York* .............. | ALEXANDER HAMILTON |
| *New Jersey* ............ | { WIL: LIVINGSTON<br>DAVID BREARLEY.<br>WM. PATERSON.<br>JONA: DAYTON |
| *Pensylvania* ........... | { B FRANKLIN<br>THOMAS MIFFLIN<br>ROBT. MORRIS.<br>GEO. CLYMER<br>THOS. FITZSIMONS<br>JARED INGERSOLL<br>JAMES WILSON<br>GOUV MORRIS |
| *Delaware*.............. | { GEO: READ<br>GUNNING BEDFORD Jun<br>JOHN DICKINSON<br>RICHARD BASSETT<br>JACO: BROOM |
| *Maryland*............. | { JAMES MCHENRY<br>DAN OF ST THOS. JENIFER<br>DANL. CARROLL |
| *Virginia*............... | { JOHN BLAIR—<br>JAMES MADISON Jr. |
| *North Carolina*........ | { WM. BLOUNT<br>RICHD. DOBBS SPAIGHT<br>HU WILLIAMSON |

*South Carolina* ........ { J. RUTLEDGE
CHARLES COTESWORTH PINCKNEY
CHARLES PINCKNEY
PIERCE BUTLER.

*Georgia*.............. { WILLIAM FEW
ABR BALDWIN

Attest            WILLIAM JACKSON *Secretary*

The Word, "the", being interlined between the seventh and eighth Lines of the first Page, The Word "Thirty" being partly written on an Erazure in the fifteenth Line of the first Page, The Words "is tried" being interlined between the thirty second and thirty third Lines of the first Page and the Word "the" being interlined between the forty third and forty fourth Lines of the second Page.

[NOTE BY THE DEPARTMENT OF STATE.—The foregoing explanation in the original instrument is placed on the left of the paragraph beginning with the words, "Done in Convention," and therefore precedes the signatures. The interlined and rewritten words, mentioned in it, are in this edition printed in their proper places in the text.]

# ARTICLES

### IN ADDITION TO, AND AMENDMENT OF

## THE CONSTITUTION OF THE UNITED STATES OF AMERICA,

#### PROPOSED BY CONGRESS,

AND RATIFIED BY THE LEGISLATURES OF THE SEVERAL STATES, PURSUANT TO THE FIFTH ARTICLE OF THE ORIGINAL CONSTITUTION.

---

### [ARTICLE I.]

Congress shall make no law respecting an establishment of religion, or prohibiting the free exercise thereof; or abridging the freedom of speech, or of the press; or the right of the people peaceably to assemble, and to petition the Government for a redress of grievances.

### [ARTICLE II.]

A well regulated Militia, being necessary to the security of a free State, the right of the people to keep and bear Arms, shall not be infringed.

### [ARTICLE III.]

No Soldier shall, in time of peace be quartered in any house, without the consent of the Owner, nor in time of war, but in a manner to be prescribed by law.

### [ARTICLE IV.]

The right of the people to be secure in their persons, houses, papers, and effects, against unreasonable searches and seizures, shall not be violated, and no Warrants shall issue, but upon probable cause, supported by Oath or affirmation, and particularly describing the place to be searched, and the persons or things to be seized.

[ARTICLE V.]

No person shall be held to answer for a capital, or otherwise infamous crime, unless on a presentment or indictment of a Grand Jury, except in cases arising in the land or naval forces, or in the Militia, when in actual service in time of War or public danger ; nor shall any person be subject for the same offence to be twice put in jeopardy of life or limb ; nor shall be compelled in any Criminal Case to be a witness against himself, nor be deprived of life, liberty, or property, without due process of law ; nor shall private property be taken for public use, without just compensation.

[ARTICLE VI.]

In all criminal prosecutions, the accused shall enjoy the right to a speedy and public trial, by an impartial jury of the State and district wherein the crime shall have been committed, which district shall have been previously ascertained by law, and to be informed of the nature and cause of the accusation ; to be confronted with the witnesses against him ; to have compulsory process for obtaining Witnesses in his favor, and to have the Assistance of Counsel for his defence.

[ARTICLE VII.]

In suits at common law, where the value in controversy shall exceed twenty dollars, the right of trial by jury shall be preserved, and no fact tried by a jury shall be otherwise re-examined in any Court of the United States, than according to the rules of the common law.

[ARTICLE VIII.]

Excessive bail shall not be required, nor excessive fines imposed, nor cruel and unusual punishments inflicted.

[ARTICLE IX.]

The enumeration in the Constitution, of certain rights, shall not be construed to deny or disparage others retained by the people.

[ARTICLE X.]

The powers not delegated to the United States by the Constitution, nor prohibited by it to the States, are reserved to the States respectively, or to the people.

[ARTICLE XI.]

The Judicial power of the United States shall not be construed to extend to any suit in law or equity, commenced or prosecuted against one of the United States by Citizens of another State, or by Citizens or Subjects of any Foreign State.

[ARTICLE XII.]

The Electors shall meet in their respective states, and vote by ballot for President and Vice-President, one of whom, at least, shall not be an inhabitant of the same state with themselves; they shall name in their ballots the person voted for as President, and in distinct ballots the person voted for as Vice-President, and they shall make distinct lists of all persons voted for as President, and of all persons voted for as Vice-President, and of the number of votes for each, which lists they shall sign and certify, and transmit sealed to the seat of the government of the United States, directed to the President of the Senate;—The President of the Senate shall, in the presence of the Senate and House of Representatives, open all the certificates and the votes shall then be counted;—The person having the greatest number of votes for President, shall be the President, if such number be a majority of the whole number of Electors appointed; and if no person have such majority, then from the persons having the highest numbers not exceeding three on the list of those voted for as President, the House of Representatives shall choose immediately, by ballot, the President. But in choosing the President, the votes shall be taken by states, the representation from each state having one vote; a quorum for this purpose shall consist of a member or members from two-thirds of the states, and a majority of all the states shall be necessary to a choice. And if the House of Representatives shall not choose a President whenever the right of choice shall devolve upon them, before the fourth day of March next following, then the Vice-President shall act as President, as in the case of the death or other constitutional disability of the President. The person having the greatest number of votes as Vice-President, shall be the Vice-President, if such number be a majority of the whole number of Electors appointed, and if no person have a majority, then from the two highest numbers on the list, the Senate shall choose the Vice-President; a quorum for the purpose shall consist of two-thirds of the whole number of Senators, and a majority of the whole number shall be necessary to a choice. But no person constitutionally ineligible to the office of President shall be eligible to that of Vice-President of the United States.

## ARTICLE XIII.

SECTION 1. Neither slavery nor involuntary servitude, except as a punishment for crime whereof the party shall have been duly convicted, shall exist within the United States, or any place subject to their jurisdiction.

SECTION 2. Congress shall have power to enforce this article by appropriate legislation.

## ARTICLE XIV.

SECTION 1. All persons born or naturalized in the United States, and subject to the jurisdiction thereof, are citizens of the United States and of the State wherein they reside. No State shall make or enforce any law which shall abridge the privileges or immunities of citizens of the United States; nor shall any State deprive any person of life, liberty, or property, without due process of law; nor deny to any person within its jurisdiction the equal protection of the laws.

SECTION 2. Representatives shall be apportioned among the several States according to their respective numbers, counting the whole number of persons in each State, excluding Indians not taxed. But when the right to vote at any election for the choice of electors for President and Vice President of the United States, Representatives in Congress, the Executive and Judicial officers of a State, or the members of the Legislature thereof, is denied to any of the male inhabitants of such State, being twenty-one years of age, and citizens of the United States, or in any way abridged, except for participation in rebellion, or other crime, the basis of representation therein shall be reduced in the proportion which the number of such male citizens shall bear to the whole number of male citizens twenty-one years of age in such State.

SECTION 3. No person shall be a Senator or Representative in Congress, or elector of President and Vice President, or hold any office, civil or military, under the United States, or under any State, who, having previously taken an oath, as a member of Congress, or as an officer of the United States, or as a member of any State legislature, or as an executive or judicial officer of any State, to support the Constitution of the United States, shall have engaged in insurrection or rebellion against the same, or given aid or comfort to the enemies thereof. But Congress may by a vote of two-thirds of each House, remove such disability.

SECTION 4. The validity of the public debt of the United States, authorized by law, including debts incurred for payment of pensions and bounties for services in suppressing insurrection or rebellion, shall not be questioned. But neither the United States nor any State shall assume or pay any debt or obligation incurred in aid of insurrection or rebellion against the United States, or any claim for the loss or emancipation of any slave; but all such debts, obligations and claims shall be held illegal and void.

SECTION 5. The Congress shall have power to enforce, by appropriate legislation, the provisions of this article.

## ARTICLE XV.

SECTION 1. The right of citizens of the United States to vote shall not be denied or abridged by the United States or by any State on account of race, color, or previous condition of servitude.

SECTION 2. The Congress shall have power to enforce this article by appropriate legislation.

# D. APPLETON AND COMPANY'S PUBLICATIONS.

## NEW EDITION, REVISED TO MAY 1, 1898.

*A* HISTORY OF THE UNITED STATES NAVY, from *1775* to *1898*. By EDGAR STANTON MACLAY, A. M. With Technical Revision by Lieutenant Roy C. Smith, U. S. N. New edition, revised and enlarged, with new chapters and several new illustrations. In two volumes. 8vo. Per vol., cloth, $3.50.

" When this work first appeared it was hailed with delight. . . There are now important additions. The splendid material which Mr. Maclay has collected has been treated in admirable tone and temper. This history of the navy is a standard work."—*Boston Herald.*

" The new edition of this valuable book has rendered the general reader a service."—*New York Sun.*

" It will rank as a standard, and it will deserve the commendation it has had to the public."—*Chicago Tribune.*

" Few books of the kind have met with as cordial a reception as ' The History of the United States Navy,' by Edgar S. Maclay. . . . Since then the book has increased steadily in popularity, purely on its merits. The History shows how the navy was built up and its traditions kept alive as active forces through evil and good days. It shows how it has become possible for men to make a navy almost without ships. It shows more than that—the important fact that the United States to-day owes, if not its liberty, the full measure of its greatness to the navy primarily. . . . Maclay's ' History of the United States Navy ' is the history of the importance of sea power to this nation."—*New York Press.*

" The author writes as one who has digged deep before he began to write at all. He thus appears as a master of his material. This book inspires immediate confidence as well as interest."—*New York Times.*

" Mr. Maclay is specially qualified for the work he has undertaken. Nine years has he devoted to the task. The result of his labors possesses not only readableness but authority. . . . Mr. Maclay's story may be truthfully characterized as a thrilling romance, which will interest every mind that is fed by tales of heroism, and will be read with patriotic pride by every true American."—*Chicago Evening Post.*

" It fills a place which has almost escaped the attention of historians. Mr. Maclay's work shows on every page the minute care with which he worked up his theme. His style is precise and clear, and without any pretense of rhetorical embellishment."—*New York Tribune.*

" It has been accepted as a standard authority, and its adoption as a text-book at Annapolis is a sufficient testimony of its technical merit."—*Philadelphia Press.*

" The author's clearness and compactness, and, where the action is important or animated, his spirited but never diffuse descriptive power, make the reading of his History a pleasure as well as a means of information on a subject of the highest interest to all Americans."—*Baltimore Sun.*

" The very best history of the United States navy in existence."—*Boston Journal.*

" The best history of the United States navy is that of Edgar S. Maclay."—*Philadelphia Inquirer.*

" Taken as a whole, this history of the navy is the best in print."—*New York Nation.*

" Every page thrills and gives fresh impetus to that yet unshaken faith that there is something in the republic that fashions her sons into invincible defenders of her flag and freedom."—*Boston Globe.*

---

### D. APPLETON AND COMPANY, NEW YORK.

## D. APPLETON & CO.'S PUBLICATIONS.

HISTORY OF THE PEOPLE OF THE UNITED STATES, from the Revolution to the Civil War. By JOHN BACH MCMASTER. To be completed in six volumes. Vols. I, II, III, and IV now ready. 8vo. Cloth, gilt top, $2.50 each.

JOHN BACH MCMASTER.

" . . . Prof. McMaster has told us what no other historians have told. . . . The skill, the animation, the brightness, the force, and the charm with which he arrays the facts before us are such that we can hardly conceive of more interesting reading for an American citizen who cares to know the nature of those causes which have made not only him but his environment and the opportunities life has given him what they are."—*N. Y. Times.*

"Those who can read between the lines may discover in these pages constant evidences of care and skill and faithful labor, of which the old-time superficial essayists, compiling library notes on dates and striking events, had no conception; but to the general reader the fluent narrative gives no hint of the conscientious labors, far-reaching, world-wide, vast and yet microscopically minute, that give the strength and value which are felt rather than seen. This is due to the art of presentation. The author's position as a scientific workman we may accept on the abundant testimony of the experts who know the solid worth of his work; his skill as a literary artist we can all appreciate, the charm of his style being self-evident."—*Philadelphia Telegraph.*

"The third volume contains the brilliantly written and fascinating story of the progress and doings of the people of this country from the era of the Louisiana purchase to the opening scenes of the second war with Great Britain—say a period of ten years. In every page of the book the reader finds that fascinating flow of narrative, that clear and lucid style, and that penetrating power of thought and judgment which distinguished the previous volumes."—*Columbus State Journal.*

"Prof. McMaster has more than fulfilled the promises made in his first volumes, and his work is constantly growing better and more valuable as he brings it nearer to our own time. His style is clear, simple, and idiomatic, and there is just enough of the critical spirit in the narrative to guide the reader."—*Boston Herald.*

"Take it all in all, the History promises to be the ideal American history. Not so much given to dates and battles and great events as in the fact that it is like a great panorama of the people, revealing their inner life and action. It contains, with all its sober facts, the spice of personalities and incidents, which relieves every page from dullness."—*Chicago Inter-Ocean.*

"History written in this picturesque style will tempt the most heedless to read. Prof. McMaster is more than a stylist; he is a student, and his History abounds in evidences of research in quarters not before discovered by the historian."—*Chicago Tribune.*

"A History *sui generis* which has made and will keep its own place in our literature."—*New York Evening Post.*

New York: D. APPLETON & CO., 72 Fifth Avenue.